FREUD AT WORK

The History of Psychoanalysis Series

Professor Brett Kahr and Professor Peter L. Rudnytsky (Series Editors)

Other titles in the Series

Ferenczi and His World: Rekindling the Spirit of the Budapest School
edited by Judit Szekacs-Weisz and Tom Keve

Freud in Zion: Psychoanalysis and the Making of Modern Jewish Identity
by Eran J. Rolnik

Ferenczi for Our Time: Theory and Practice
edited by Judit Szekacs-Weisz and Tom Keve

The Clinic and the Context: Historical Essays
by Elisabeth Young-Bruehl

Sandor Ferenczi–Ernest Jones: Letters 1911–1933
edited by Ferenc Eros, Judit Szekacs-Weisz, and Ken Robinson

The Milan Seminar: Clinical Applications of Attachment Theory
by John Bowlby, edited by Marco Bacciagaluppi

Ferenczi and Beyond: Exile of the Budapest School and Solidarity in the Psychoanalytic Movement during the Nazi Years
by Judit Mészáros

Looking Through Freud's Photos
by Michael Molnar

Psychoanalytic Filiations: Mapping the Psychoanalytic Movement
by Ernst Falzeder

The Abandonment Neurosis
by Germaine Guex (translated by Peter Douglas)

The Life and Times of Franz Alexander: From Budapest to California
by Ilonka Venier Alexander

Freud and the Dora Case: A Promise Betrayed
by Cesare Romano

The Freudian Orient: Early Psychoanalysis, Anti-Semitic Challenge, and the Vicissitudes of Orientalist Discourse
by Frank F. Scherer

Karl Abraham: Life and Work, a Biography
by Anna Bentinck van Schoonheten

The Skin-Ego
by Didier Anzieu, translated by Naomi Segal

A Forgotten Freudian: The Passion of Karl Stern
by Daniel Burston

Corresponding Lives: Mabel Dodge Luhan, A. A. Brill, and the Psychoanalytic Adventure in America
by Patricia R. Everett

What is this Professor Freud Like? A Diary of an Analysis with Historical Comments
edited by Anna Koellreuter

FREUD AT WORK
On the History of Psychoanalytic Theory and Practice, with an Analysis of Freud's Patient Record Books

Ulrike May

Translated from the German by Daniela Haller, Bettina Mathes, Michael Molnar, Philip Slotkin, and Deirdre Winter

Routledge
Taylor & Francis Group
LONDON AND NEW YORK

First published 2018
by Routledge
2 Park Square, Milton Park, Abingdon, Oxon OX14 4RN

and by Routledge
711 Third Avenue, New York, NY 10017

Routledge is an imprint of the Taylor & Francis Group, an informa business

Originally published in German in 2015
Ulrike May: *Freud bei der Arbeit. Zur Entstehungsgeschichte der psychoanalytischen Theorie und Praxis, mit einer Auswertung von Freuds Patientenkalender* Gießen (Psychosozial-Verlag)

British Library Cataloguing-in-Publication Data
A catalogue record for this book is available from the British Library

Library of Congress Cataloging-in-Publication Data
A catalog record has been requested for this book

ISBN: 9781782205012 (pbk)

Typeset in Palatino
by Medlar Publishing Solutions Pvt Ltd, India

CONTENTS

ACKNOWLEDGEMENTS

In all those years of studying the history of psychoanalysis, what sustained me the most were the acquaintance, friendship, and exchanges with colleagues who shared similar interests, primarily Michael Schröter. Our ongoing conversation about the history of psychoanalysis was and is the most stable and stimulating determinant of my productivity. In 1996 Michael and I founded a study and work group that we later named the *Alpenländisches Forum zur Geschichte der Psychoanalyse* (Alpine Forum for the History of Psychoanalysis). Wolfgang von Ungern-Sternberg, Herbert Will, and Anton Uhl were part of the group from the very beginning. Soon thereafter Elke Mühlleitner joined us, followed by Thomas Aichhorn und Friedl Früh as well as Inge Weber und Manfred Klemann. They were the first to read most of my papers. Their interest, curiosity, and warmth kept my thoughts company; their questions and objections supported me every step of the way. I thank them wholeheartedly. Without their support none of the papers collected in this volume would have been written. My special thanks go to Ernst Falzeder who for some time was also a member of the group. He generously provided me with his transcripts and copies of unpublished archival material.

The *Berliner Forum für die Geschichte der Psychoanalyse* (Berlin Forum for the History of Psychoanalysis) and its spiritus rector Ludger Hermanns was another source of collegial support; and so was the relatively new circle of younger Berlin-based colleagues who have taken an interest in Freud's theory: Andrea Huppke, Margarete Meador, Vera Müller, Monika Schwab, Laszlo Kruppa, Carsten Pilzecker, Ernst-Wolfgang Wäschle, and, lately, Robin Verner. To them, too, I owe the opportunity to discuss my work in a friendly and collegial way. The same is true for the colleagues who were part of the periodic workshop *Freudianische Liebhabereien* (Freud for Pleasure, 2008, 2011, 2015). The weeks spent together thinking through the history of psychoanalysis and its theory was a deeply gratifying experience. I thank all participants for their interest and lively contributions, especially Werner Lampl.

A big thank you goes to Magdalena Frank for her support in editing the manuscript and to Angelika Schönfeld und Vera Dobberkau who have helped me compile the bibliography. During the many months that it took to prepare this English language translation Angelika Schönfeld's patience, and her precise and reliable work, have been indispensable.

I thank my translators Daniela Haller, Bettina Mathes, Michael Molnar, Philip Slotkin, and Deirdre Winter. In exchanges with them I was able to clarify many a thought; at times the translation seems clearer and expresses my ideas better than the German original. In the course of the often-difficult process of adapting this book for an English language version Robin Verner has taken on a host of technical and translation related tasks that she executed in a selfless, efficient way, and with a sense of humour. Thanks Robin! Lastly, the opportunity to discuss some editorial and translation problems with Richard Skues was of great help to me.

Finally, yet importantly, I thank Brett Kahr of Karnac Books who has actively supported the English language edition.

Translated by Bettina Mathes

ABOUT THE AUTHOR

Ulrike May, PhD, is a practising psychoanalyst in Berlin and a member of the Karl-Abraham-Institute Berlin, the German Psychoanalytic Association, and the International Psychoanalytic Association. She has published two books—*Freuds frühe klinische Theorie (1894–1896). Wiederentdeckung und Rekonstruktion* (1996) and (with Elke Mühlleitner) *Edith Jacobson. Sie selbst und die Welt ihrer Objekte. Leben, Werk, Erinnerungen* (2005)—as well as numerous papers on the history of psychoanalytic theory and practice. Together with Michael Schröter, in 2015 she presented a critical edition of Freud's *Beyond the Pleasure Principle* (1920), including the first version of 1919.

ABBREVIATIONS

F/A	Freud & Abraham (2002)
F/Bi	Freud & Binswanger (2003)
F/Bl	Freud & Bleuler (2012)
F/E	Freud & Eitingon (2004)
F/Fl	Freud & Fließ (= Freud, 1985c)
F/Fer	Freud & Ferenczi (1993–2000)
F/G	Freud & Groddeck (2008)
F/Jo	Freud & Jones (1993)
F/Ju	Freud & Jung (1974)
F/L	Freud & Kata Lévy (= Freud, 2012)
F/P	Freud & Pfister (2014)
F/AF	Freud & Anna Freud (2006)
F/W	Freud & Weiss (1970a)
Korr	Korrespondenzblatt der Internationalen Psychoanalytischen Vereinigung
LoC/SFP	Library of Congress (Washington), Sigmund Freud Papers
Min	Minutes of the Vienna Psychoanalytic Society (= Nunberg & Federn, 1962–1975)

RB	Rundbriefe des Geheimen Komitees (= Wittenberger & Tögel, 1999–2006)
WSLA	Wiener Stadt- und Landesarchiv

SERIES EDITOR'S FOREWORD

In the wake of the publication of Professor Frederick Crews's (2017) flagrantly denigratory biography of Sigmund Freud, I happened to mention to a colleague that, in due course, we would have the pleasure of publishing a much more important and far more accurate text on Freud, namely, Dr. Ulrike May's wonderful volume of essays. My colleague raised his eyebrows sceptically and asked, "But surely, Freud's life has been raked over with a fine-tooth comb. I very much doubt that there is anything new to learn!"

Although I would agree that the vast majority of books on Freud often reveal nothing startlingly new to those of us already steeped in the historical literature, it delights me that Ulrike May's engaging tome, *Freud at Work: On the History of Psychoanalytic Theory and Practice, with an Analysis of Freud's Patient Record Books*, contains so much new data about Freud as both a theoretician and as a practitioner that one cannot help but be impressed by the depth of her scholarship and by the freshness with which she has approached her subject.

Across nine carefully scripted chapters, Dr. May guides us on a journey through some of Sigmund Freud's most important theoretical concepts ranging from narcissism to the death drive; moreover, she explores many little known aspects of his exhaustive clinical practice, treating us to a detailed exploration of the minutiae of his daily work in the consulting room. A consummate clinical psychoanalyst as well as an historian, May has drawn upon these parallel skills and capacities to examine not only Freud's published writings but, also, a plethora of rare archival materials. Just as the psychoanalyst often embraces the marginalised aspects of the patient's discourse, so, too, does Dr. May engage with not only the broad sweeps of Freud's contributions but, also, with the seemingly insignificant details. In having done so, she has created a truly rich and resonant portrait of Freud as a writer, as a practitioner, and as a colleague within the psychoanalytical community to which he gave birth.

Dr. May not only treats us to new insights into the life and work of Sigmund Freud, but she also provides us with fresh observations about the publications of many of his closest colleagues, not only the well-known ones such as Karl Abraham and Ernest Jones but, also, those whom historians have neglected, such as Isidor Sadger and August Stärcke, among others. As May has documented, Sadger contributed hugely to the development of the theory of narcissism, while Stärcke anticipated much of the work of both Karl Abraham and, in particular, Melanie Klein, by having underscored the sadistic aspects of infancy and the early roots of the Oedipus complex. Ulrike May has now filled in these historiographical gaps and, consequently, the reader enjoys an infinitely greater appreciation of the dynamics of the early psychoanalytical meetings in Vienna and about the ways in which Freud drew upon the clinical observations of some of the earliest generation of practitioners in order to elaborate theories of his own.

As a commentator on Freud's technical work with his psychoanalytical patients, Dr. May presents an unparalleled feast, full of rich documentary material. Having studied Freud's rare patient record books with great care, May has reconstructed Freud's clinical timetable with great care, and we now have a much fuller understanding of how many times per week Freud worked with his patients, and how long each one stayed in treatment. Her engrossing reconstruction of the life of the Hungarian aristocrat, Viktor von Dirsztay, one of Freud's longest-serving patients—yet one almost completely neglected hitherto—alone justifies the purchase of this riveting book.

Although May approaches the early psychoanalysts with great respect and passion, she does not idealise them. Indeed, she writes bluntly, not only about the genius of Freud but, also, about his shadow side, describing his work as both "moving" and, also, as "jarring", noting that while he often treated his patients lovingly, he could also speak of them "disrespectfully" to fellow psychoanalysts. In similar vein, May has expressed great appreciation of the valuable publications of men such as Isidor Sadger while also recognising the regrettable way in which he engaged quite confrontationally and judgementally with his analysands.

In recent decades, the study of the history of psychoanalysis has developed in creative ways across the planet. But in spite of some of the great contributions from colleagues in Austria, in France, in Great Britain, in Italy, in the United States of America, and elsewhere, May has had the particular privilege of honing her historical acumen in Germany, where the discipline of psychoanalytical historiography flourishes in the most admirable fashion. Scholars from other parts of the world will hunger for the strong community of German psychoanalytical historians who have helped to shape and nurture May's work in this arena, from the fellow members of the Aplenländisches Forum zur Geschichte der Psychoanalyse which she founded with Dr. Michael Schröter, to the annual symposia on the history of psychoanalysis, held originally in Kassel, then in Tübingen, and now, in Berlin. The organisation of psychoanalytical historiography in Germany, and the work of May and her colleagues, serves as an inspiration to those of us practising in other parts of the world.

Ulrike May has made numerous important contributions to the history of psychoanalysis, providing us with ample evidence that, in spite of nearly 100 years of Freud studies, we still have much to learn about that great man and about the legacy that he has bequeathed to generations of practitioners ever since. Dr. May (2017) has continued to produce new and important work, including a study of the correspondence between Sigmund Freud and the Dutch psychoanalyst August Stärcke and, also, quite significantly, an examination of a little-known version of Freud's famous text *Jenseits des Lustprinzips*, better known to English speakers as *Beyond the Pleasure Principle*. May's unique investigation has appeared both in German (May, 2013) and, more recently, in English (May, 2015).

We thank Ulrike May for this wonderful book, which will help English-speaking researchers appreciate her work more fully than ever before, and we await her future studies in this field with much anticipation.

Professor Brett Kahr
Series Co-Editor, "History of Psychoanalysis Series"
London

References

Crews, Frederick (2017). *Freud: The Making of an Illusion*. New York: Metropolitan Books/Henry Holt and Company/Macmillan Publishing Group.

May, Ulrike (2013). Der dritte Schritt in der Trieblehre: Zur Entstehungsgeschichte von *Jenseits des Lustprinzips. Luzifer-Amor, 26,* Number *51,* 92–169.

May, Ulrike (2015). The Third Step in Drive Theory: On the Genesis of *Beyond the Pleasure Principle. Psychoanalysis and History, 17,* 205–272.

May, Ulrike (2017). "Lieben heißt Sterbenwollen. Das steht felsenfest in mir": Der Todestrieb im Briefwechsel zwischen Freud und August Stärcke. *Luzifer-Amor, 30,* Number *59,* 112–142.

INTRODUCTION

Why history?

My interest in the history of psychoanalysis dates back to the 1960s when, as a psychology student at Munich University, I became acquainted with the writings of North American psychoanalysts, among them Robert R. Holt, George S. Klein, Roy Schafer, and Merton M. Gill. They seemed to engage with Freud, whose work we had studied in seminars and lectures, in a new and critical way, further developing his theories and thinking beyond them at the same time. Only later did I realise that they had been students of David Rapaport. After their teacher's death in 1960, they carried on with his project of building a new conceptual framework of psychoanalysis. Rapaport, who had systematised Freud's theory in a new and unique way, proposed primary and secondary models of action, cognition, and affect, all of which revolved around the crying, the hungry, and the eventually satiated baby (Rapaport, 1951, 1967). Rapaport and Gill made metapsychology more stringent and more compatible with the new emphases of Hartmann's "American" ego-psychology that he formulated while still in Vienna (Rapaport & Gill, 1959). In an effort to demonstrate that psychoanalysis was treading on theoretically firm ground and could be integrated into the corpus of psychology, Rapaport, in a veritable *tour de force,* combined the theories of Freud and of some of his successors with state-of-the-art empirical-experimental psychology.

But things were to change after Rapaport's death. Where Rapaport was concerned with substantiating psychoanalysis as a legitimate science, his students, little by little, began to question Freud's theory. They criticised Freud's biologism, and discovered that metapsychology was anchored in the philosophical and scientific traditions of his time (e.g., Holt, 1965, 1967). Meanwhile in Germany, Habermas (1968) coined the term "scientific self-misunderstanding" of psychoanalysis. Over time Rapaport's students, each in his own way, took an increasingly distant and critical attitude towards psychoanalytic theory, and, eventually, towards psychoanalytic practice and technique (e.g., Gill, 1976, 1982). I was fascinated by two aspects of their work: the thorough, exact, and careful reading of Freud and their attention to the historical situatedness of his theory to which they alerted us. As aspirations they have shaped my own writing as well.

Against this backdrop, and after graduating with a degree in psychology, I decided to train as a psychoanalyst. It took a long time until I found my own voice in the discourse of psychoanalytic theory. I still remember the day on which I began the studies that would lead to the writing of the articles collected in this volume: it was precisely the day after I completed my psychoanalytic training. All those years—it began to dawn on me—I had surrendered to the spell of self-censorship whose scope and depth I had not been aware of. I broke the spell, but not completely; repeatedly obstacles had to be overcome. What I am saying is that the work on and with psychoanalysis involves a psychic process that is shaped by unconscious dynamics. They may further and push the work along or they may interfere with and even prevent it. Theory is not all grey, not just words written on a page. Engaging with it produces strong, to some degree unconscious, resistances.

Another incentive driving my interest in the history of psychoanalysis goes back to my training experience. Throughout I felt a certain discomfort with the way we practise. I sensed it in seminars and in supervision with colleagues who saw themselves as Freudians; here and there it would come up with colleagues who belonged to other theoretical schools as well. In turning to the study of the history of psychoanalysis I was hoping to find explanations for my discomfort. Was it related to specific theories or aspects of them, or did it apply across theoretical schools? Was it to do with explicitly stated theories, or did it refer to implicit assumptions and the ways in which each analyst uses the theory? Was my discomfort triggered by some attributes of current psychoanalytic technique or by the ways in which analysts practised in the past, or both? My work addresses these questions; and while the papers included in this volume touch upon them, they do not answer them in any systematic way.

Instrumental in nourishing my reawakened post-training interest in the history of psychoanalysis was the annual *Symposium on the History of Psychoanalysis* co-founded in 1978 by Helmut Junker and Gerhard Wittenberger. The meetings were first held in Kassel, then in Tübingen under the direction of Gerhard Fichtner und Albrecht Hirschmüller. Since 2010 Michael Schröter and Thomas Aichhorn have been hosting the yearly gatherings in Berlin. I have appreciated the friendly and collegial atmosphere of these meetings, an important part of which, it seems to me, is the fact that they are not organised by one institute and are open to participants from all schools and disciplines, be they academic or non-academic. In this, the gatherings are a kind of return to the psychoanalysis before 1920 when everybody who could prove his interest in psychoanalysis could become a member of a psychoanalytic society regardless of whether he had undergone an analysis.

Why history? For me the answer is obvious: engaging with history opens our eyes to the present as a process, a becoming, and it allows us to explore whether we want to keep this present the way it has become. In its core, historical research is critical research. Norms, theories, and definitions become fluid. As the specific conditions of their installation become apparent, they prove to be less self-evident than they appear; and change can become a possibility. There is something deeply moving and gladdening about this work, which has to do with the animation of the inanimate. From behind the concepts authors begin to emerge as individuals who held specific ideas and convictions that they developed in response to other ideas and other authors. As we discover the origins of certain concepts—their provenance, if you will—as we place them in the history of psychoanalytic research, new, fresh meanings come to the fore. Psychoanalytic texts begin to appear as part of a continuous process of research and collegial conversations; and this is true for both Freud's work and that of his disciples and colleagues.

On the articles

The nine articles I have chosen for this volume date from 1991 to 2012 and they exclusively deal with the early and middle Freud, that is, with works completed by the beginning of the 1920s.

Part I focuses on the relations between Freud and his disciples and begins with a reconstruction of how Freud arrived at the concept of narcissism (Chapter One). In the course of my research I came across an important aspect of Freud's theorising, which concerned the ways in which he engaged with the ideas of his students and colleagues, specifically with the work of Isidor Sadger. I found that Freud was remarkably ready to revise his own "world of thought" if it seemed necessary to him. In the case of narcissism the first theoretical modifications date back to a meeting of the Vienna Psychoanalytic Society in November 1909 and were made in response to a paper by Sadger, leading Freud to introduce a narcissistic stage of psychic development and a narcissistic type of object choice.

Chapter Two, on Karl Abraham's discovery of the "bad mother", restates the early beginnings of a psychoanalytic theory of depression. I show that at that point in time (1911) the young Abraham was ahead of Freud, pursuing his own theoretical approach whose most important feature was to introduce the notion of the "bad mother" into psychoanalytic theory (Abraham, 1911). Over time Abraham elaborated his concept into a comprehensive theory with its own unique flavour, very much distinct from Freud's world of images and thoughts. Here, too, it is instructive to see how Freud responded to his disciple. Sadger's communications, as we have seen, he took up, appropriated, and in that process fundamentally changed them. With Abraham Freud was much more reluctant. For a long time he could not or perhaps did not want to assimilate his student's approach into his own theory.

Differences between Freud and Abraham—noted already in my very first publication on the history of psychoanalytic theory (May [-Tolzmann], 1990)—are also the focus of Chapter Three. "From anger to reflection" discusses an early paper of Abraham's (1907a) that became known for the introduction of the term "traumatophilia". At that time Abraham was still at the beginning of working his way towards understanding Freud's theory, which explains some of the peculiarities in his paper, especially his tendency to perceive infantile and adult psychic life in harsh and rigid terms, as opposed to Freud's calm equanimity which invited reflection and deliberation. With hindsight I would say that this inclination to judge, so striking in this early paper, is also present in Abraham's later works, as is his highly-charged interest in questions of guilt and guilty feelings which one does not encounter in Freud's work in the same way.

Chapters Four to Seven address the conceptualisation of anal and oral erotism by Abraham and other disciples of Freud's, especially August Stärcke and Ernest Jones. The papers are part of an ongoing study in which I hope to find an answer to the question as to how I position myself towards Freud's theory as a whole, specifically towards his "vision" (a term I borrowed from Toulmin, 1978) of the primacy of the sexual that permeates Freud's entire oeuvre (May[-Tolzmann], 1996). As a starting point I chose *Three Essays on the Theory of Sexuality* (Freud, 1905d). I set out to reconstruct whether and in what ways Freud over time changed his ideas about anal and oral erotism and how colleagues and disciples engaged with his conceptualisations. The years around 1920 lent themselves as a preliminary endpoint of my research project. This is the time when Freud in *Beyond the Pleasure Principle* (1920g) made the theoretical turn towards the death drive and Abraham wrote his main work, "A Short Study of the Development of the Libido" (1924). Guided by the maxim "how to eat an elephant?—bit by bit" I began with a reconstruction of the history of oral erotism followed by that of anal erotism.

With the exception of Freud's work, the most important contributions to oral erotism came from Abraham. Diving deep into his work, especially into "The First Pregenital Stage of the Libido", the founding paper of oral aggression (Abraham, 1916–1917), I once more had the impression that his view differed from Freud's even though the latter had in 1915 introduced the "oral or, as it might be called cannibalistic" stage (Freud, 1905d, p. 198). And once again it became a question of the atmosphere each of them created in their texts, the flavour they added when speaking about the two core "objects" of psychoanalysis: the baby and the analysand. The term "revolution"—used in the title of Chapter Four to describe the impact of Abraham's writing on psychoanalytic theory—may feel too strong to some readers. I chose it because it seemed to me that the implied possibility for primary oral aggression introduced in "The First Pregenital Stage of the Libido" was at the origin of the debates that were to become the controversial discussions of the British School, which remain virulent to this day. What is most controversial is the role and place of aggression in psychoanalytic theory and in the practice of interpretation. Finally but importantly, there is the surprising insight gleaned from studying Abraham's "The First Pregenital Stage of the Libido" that without being aware of it we have become accustomed to reading Freud through Abraham's eyes. This is, for instance, true for Laplanche and Pontalis's *The Vocabulary of Psychoanalysis* (1967), a book in other respects rightly regarded as a reliable and precise account of Freudian theory. In the course of the canonisation of the theory, Abraham's approach, it seems to me, became amalgamated with our idea of Freudian theory, which means that it is necessary to excavate Freud's own conceptualisations of oral erotism and infantile development.

There is one other work, besides Abraham's innovative "The First Pregenital Stage of the Libido", in which Freud's notion of oral erotism is developed further: it is a study by the Dutch psychiatrist and psychoanalyst August Stärcke (1921a) whose paper I discuss in Chapter Five. As I see it, Stärcke, who is rarely mentioned in accounts of the history of psychoanalytic theory, is the most important among the first generation of pioneers of psychoanalytic theory. His work opened up a new perspective on psychic development and the earliest years of life, and has been adopted by many colleagues since the mid-1920s. Stärcke is the first to explicitly liken the baby at the mother's breast to a predatory animal, a beast of prey as it were. The image of the predatory baby was not just a simple comparison; in its emphasis on aggression it became part of psychoanalytic theory. As Stärcke saw it, the sucking baby sadistically attacked the mother and felt attacked by her as she "withdrew the nipple" at the end of each feed. The baby experienced the withdrawing of the nipple as "primary castration" and his attacks on the mother triggered guilty feelings stemming from his sadistic phantasies of devouring mother. Stärcke was most likely the first author who suggested moving the oedipus complex forward to the oral stage. Here I sense an affinity to Abraham's world of thoughts and images, as it is implied in "The First Pregenital Stage of the Libido" of 1916–1917 and elevated to the level of theory and further developed in "A Short Study of the Development of the Libido" (1924). In Chapter Five I show that Stärcke's and Abraham's views of the psychic processes in the oral stage are not congruent with Freud's notions, at least not until the early 1920s. It is possible that Freud's introduction of the phallic stage (1923e) as well as his increasing emphasis on the centrality of the oedipus complex—both of which fall into the same time period—are a response to Stärcke and Abraham's notion of "pregenital primacy" (Simmel, 1933).

Unlike oral erotism, anal erotism was a field in which Freud's disciples and colleagues contributed numerous works that advanced the concept in innovative ways, Karl Abraham being the most important among them. In Chapter Six, entitled "On the early history of anal erotism", I therefore focus on authors who were close to Karl Abraham—Ernest Jones, Jan van Ophuijsen, and, again, August Stärcke. Jones (1913) was one of the very first analysts to attempt a modification of Freud's description of anal erotism. In several papers, Abraham (1920, 1923, 1924) drew on Jones' work. The main difference was that Freud conceived of anal erotism and sadism as two distinct groups of drives that simultaneously governed the psychic life of the child in the sadistic-anal stage, whereas Jones—followed by Abraham, Stärcke (1919), and Ophuijsen (1920)—understood sadism as an intrinsic component of anal erotism. Abraham's "anal-sadistic" stage (1924) reflects this new conceptualisation of anal erotism and must therefore be distinguished from Freud's "sadistic-anal" stage (1913i). Jones and Abraham, Stärcke and Ophuijsen, it seems to me, had a tendency to make the libidinal impulses more aggressive, thereby tipping the balance of forces from libidinal to aggressive impulses. In the 1920s this modification met with a warm response almost immediately, while Freud for the time being, and in accordance with his vision, continued to hold on to the primacy of the sexual drives.

Moreover, between 1910 and 1920 the conceptualisation of the "object" and of the component drives was undergoing a modification that has remained in place to this day. For Freud the component drives were relegated to the sidelines, waiting to be put into the service of the oedipus complex. For Jones and Abraham, however, they became motivating forces pursuing aims of their own. As shown in my review of Freud's notion of "omnipotence of thoughts" (1909d, 1912–1913) this modification of the theory also affected the dichotomy of ego and drive. Abraham and Jones attributed "omnipotence of thoughts" to anality and sadism, whereas Freud understood it as a feature of the ego, that is, as a characteristic of the psychic processes occurring at a specific stage of ego development. Envisaged this way, between 1910 and 1920 some of Freud's disciples ascribed ego-states and ego functions (as well as the concept of the object) to drive processes, while Freud continued to hold on to the difference between ego and drive, which is to say that drive impulses are not the only psychic processes that a psychoanalytic understanding of the life of the psyche ought to concern itself with: other psychic processes, that is, ego processes, are of interest as well.

Finally, researching the history of oral and anal erotism I was able to show that between 1910 and 1920 differing models of psychic development were being formulated in Freud's circle of disciples and colleagues. Freud understood psychic development as a "love" story, a story of allo- and autoerotic sexual impulses, and one that ended with the capacity to choose a "foreign" object as love object. For Abraham, and those close to him, psychic development was predominantly a development *away* from aggressive impulses and *towards* the overcoming of ambivalence, along with the ability to feel concern for the object. In their view, development moved the psyche from a predominantly object-hostile towards a more object-friendly attitude, one that "goes easy" on the object (Abraham, 1924). This aspect, which is essentially a question of morality, did not play a *leading* role in Freud's theory of psychic development. That different approaches implied differing uses of the goals and contents of interpretation is understood.

Despite my emphasis on the differences between Freud and his disciples, it is of course inevitable, or so it seems to me, that students should fashion new theories with novel emphases. A theory such as psychoanalysis cannot simply be "adopted". It has to pass through the subject's internal world made up of convictions, both conscious and unconscious, presumptions, prejudices, guiding principles, and visions. This is the topic of Chapter Seven. In it I try to approach the controversial *Beyond the Pleasure Principle* (1920g), the paper that marks the beginning of Freud's late work. One of the most important determinants of Freud's process of theorisation is his convictions or visions, which are conscious and yet stem from earlier, predominantly unconscious experiences. Charged with strong affect they can hardly be changed, let alone given up in adult life. Freud's principal vision, I should like to suggest, consists of the notion of the primacy of the sexual that he formulated as early as 1893 (Freud, 1985c, p. 45) prior to any—in the real sense of the word—psychoanalytic experience. As my studies on oral and anal erotism have shown, Freud tried to uphold his vision, and defended it from modifications or objections made by his disciples and colleagues. In addition to the "visions" there are the "projects" by which I mean the specific tasks Freud set for himself in the course of the evolution of his (adult) scientific and therapeutic interests. These projects are an aetiological theory of the neuroses and psychoses, a comprehensive and overarching metapsychology, and, as an ambitious side project, the "conquest" of the biological sciences. Chapter Seven shows in what ways *Beyond the Pleasure Principle* both reflects this principal vision and can be read as a contribution to his projects, which acted as a kind of filter for Freud's hyper-vivid imagination.

* * *

Part II of this volume begins with Chapter Eight, which serves as a transition from theory to practice and from disciples to patients. My research led me to Baron Victor von Dirsztay, a Hungarian writer, author of the 1923 novel *Der Unentrinnbare* [The Inescapable One], and an analysand of Freud's. I argue that almost 1,500 hours of analysis with Dirsztay provided Freud with material that led him to acknowledge the psychic reality of two egos, an account of which he published in his paper "The 'Uncanny'" (1919h). The two egos were soon to become the ego and the super-ego of the so-called structural model (1923b). I wonder what it means when one encounters the very "real" trigger that gave way to the formulation of a theory (see Falzeder, 1994, on the analysis of Elfriede Hirschfeld). If nothing else, definitions and theories become more concrete and convincing. And it might well be that the uncovering of their empirical grounding will help to demystify the process by which theories come into being.

Victor von Dirsztay's analysis is one of the thirty-six analyses described in Chapter Nine. Using the surviving volumes of Freud's patient record books (1910–1920) as a new resource, I extracted the course of these analyses, their duration, and their frequency. Among his analysands were writers like Dirsztay, an actor (Claire von Wallentin-Metternich), a visual artist (Rudolf Kriser), a member of the diplomatic service (George M. Young), Sergej Pankejeff (alias "the Wolf Man"), and analysts such as Sándor Ferenczi, René Spitz, Helene Deutsch, and John Rickman. Most analysands suffered from neurotic symptoms, some of them chronic; a few analysands had psychotic episodes, and more than a few exhibited symptoms of full-blown addiction. I describe each analysis, mark its beginning and end, and summarise additional information that I obtained mostly from Freud's correspondence.

My historical survey revealed a transformation in analytic practice from Freud's times to our own, and it raises the question as to why our way of working with patients has undergone such profound changes. How do we feel about these changes? Can we still call ourselves "Freudians"? The changes pertain to the duration of an analysis as well as to the frequency of sessions. The majority of the thirty-six analyses were short but with frequent sessions, not just three or four hours per week but at least six or more. Few analysands received long, comprehensive analyses of a thousand hours or more, also conducted at high frequency. In many cases Freud changed the frequency several times during the course of the treatment. Two analysands, Erszébét Révész and Helene Deutsch, who mainly went to see Freud for training purposes, did not receive six hours per week but three. What a surprise that the "training analyses" of all things were conducted at a relatively low frequency, something Freud had suggested for less severe cases (1913c).

In Freud's practice pure open-ended analysis, given so much attention in psychoanalytic discourse, was the rare exception. Only three of the thirty-six analyses included in my survey were not bound by time constraints: those of Elfriede Hirschfeld, Viktor von Dirsztay, and Sergej Pankejeff. All three of them were independently wealthy at the time of the analysis, free from professional obligations and able to reside in Vienna for extended periods. Each of these analyses led Freud to new insights, which he went on to publish (1913i, 1918b, 1919h etc.), but did not lead to a cure in the stricter sense, as Freud himself admitted about Hirschfeld, and as we have come to know about Pankejeff and Dirsztay. After years of analysis with Freud all three went on to seek analytic treatment with other analysts. Freud described it as a variant of psychoanalysis that in some cases may be necessary: lifelong analytic treatment, broken up into segments. This is evidence of Freud's broad understanding of "analysis" which comprised what we today call analysis proper, but also various forms of psychotherapy.

Finally I want to briefly mention that I found the ways in which Freud behaved towards his analysands to be both moving and jarring. Moving because of the space that he allowed them and the love he sometimes showed for those who never even in the end accepted that psychoanalysis was in any way useful or helpful. I was impressed with the extent to which he often accommodated his patients, meeting them where they needed him to be. At other times, though, he would draw strict boundaries, and speak of them disrespectfully to his colleagues. All in all I have found much that I deem desirable, most of all the equanimity with which he accepted our idiosyncrasies and weaknesses as human beings.

With respect to psychoanalytic theory, my studies have taught me that from the very beginning its history was steeped in differences and differentiations most of which were smoothed over and made to disappear in the process of canonisation, leaving us with the false impression that once upon a time there was just one theory, all of a piece—Freud's theory—and that the way Freud worked was comparable to how we practice today. Looking into the history of psychoanalysis, we are compelled to reconsider our assumptions.

This English language edition sometimes refers to sources that have not yet been made available in English, such as, for instance, some of Freud's correspondence, the *Jahrbuch für psychoanalytische und psychopathologische Forschungen*, and the *Internationale Zeitschrift für Psychoanalyse* with its *Korrespondenzblatt*. Moreover, since my book is concerned with the early and middle Freud, addressing the history of psychoanalysis before and up to 1920, the chapters necessarily focus on figures like Karl Abraham, Paul Federn, Karl Landauer, Isidor Sadger, August Stärcke, and other analysts whose writings have often only been published in German. I do hope, though, that the ties and connections between Freud's theoretical process (i.e., the ways in which he arrived at his theory) and the contributions of his colleagues and students that I have tried to illuminate in this book, will make sense to my English-speaking colleagues, too.

Berlin, 27 December 2016
Ulrike May

Translated by Bettina Mathes

PART I

FREUD AND HIS STUDENTS

CHAPTER ONE

How the concept of narcissism came into being: from Ellis and Näcke to Sadger and Freud

When Freud made his first statements about narcissism in 1909 and 1910 he was referring to studies and communications by Isidor Sadger (Min 2, p. 312; Freud, 1910c, p. 99, fn. 1). He also cited Sadger after 1910 when he gave his reasons for introducing the concept of narcissism (1911c, p. 60, fn. 1; 1914c, p. 73). The question thus arises as to what Sadger contributed to Freud's understanding of narcissism.

Before continuing I should point out that Freud's first remarks on narcissism concerned only *one* aspect of the concept, that is, love of one's own person (or, to use Freud's term, one's own "ego") and of love objects that are similar to it. This component was initially the "strongest of the reasons" for introducing narcissism (Freud, 1914c, p. 88). Later this aspect was no longer as prominent. Today we find it in a refined and expanded form in Kohut's descriptions of the narcissistic transferences, especially in the alter ego or twinship transferences, in which the need for essential alikeness plays a central role (Kohut, 1984). Thus in this article I shall be attempting to lay bare the early roots of some contemporary ideas about narcissism.

Questions

Freud's earliest statement about narcissism is to be found in the *Minutes of the Vienna Psychoanalytic Society* dated 10 November 1909 (Min 2, pp. 312–313). On this evening Sadger had presented a case report and according to the *Minutes* he had, among other things, expressed the opinion that "autoerotism in the form of narcissism" played an important role in homosexuality and that the love objects of male homosexuals had characteristics that were the same as their own (Min 2, p. 307).[1] In the discussion Freud picked up on this detail of Sadger's presentation. His remarks are recorded in the *Minutes* as follows:

> PROF. FREUD: [...] Sadger's comment with regard to narcissism seems new and valuable. This is not an isolated phenomenon but a necessary developmental stage in the transition from autoerotism to object love. Being enamoured of oneself (of one's genitals) is an indispensable stage of development. From there one passes to similar objects. In general, man has two primary sexual objects, and his future existence depends on which of these objects he remains fixated on. These two sexual objects are for every man the woman (the mother, nurse, etc.) and his own person; and it follows from this that [the question] is to become free from both and not to linger on too long with either. Usually, one's own person is replaced by the father—who, however, soon moves into a hostile position. It is at this point that homosexuality branches off. Man does not set himself free of himself so soon, as this case very beautifully demonstrates. (Min 2, pp. 312–313)

There can be no doubt that it was here, on 10 November 1909, that Freud introduced the concept of narcissism into the terminology of psychoanalysis and that he was referring to Sadger. In the two essays in which his ideas on narcissism were first published he also referred

---

[1] This and all the following quotations refer to male narcissism and male homosexuality. See Rank (1910, 1911b) for the first papers on female narcissism.

to "investigations" and "material" by Sadger (1905d/1910, p. 135, fn. 1; 1910c, p. 99, fn. 1).[2]

Two questions arise. First, what was Sadger's contribution to the concept of narcissism, and which ideas are attributable to him and which to Freud? And second, to what "investigations" and "communications" of Sadger's was Freud referring?

In the remark made by Sadger quoted above and in the places where Freud's first published statements on narcissism appeared, narcissism seems to be a phenomenon that is tied to homosexuality. As we can see from the above quotation Freud already detached it from this specific context in his first statement (1909) and put forward the hypothesis that love of oneself is not tied to homosexuality, but a necessary stage in normal development. Freud presented this idea with great assurance. In fact, all of his first statements about narcissism give the impression of being so well rounded and definitive that we must assume that they were the product of an extended process of exploration and reflection. But if we look for explicit references in Freud's publications we do not find anything about his "half-way stations". Perhaps there were precursors of the concept of narcissism, perhaps Freud observed and described manifestations of narcissism before 1909, but under a different name?

In this article I look for answers to these questions in Freud's work published in the years between 1905 and 1910, that is, in the period between the first and second editions of the *Three Essays on the Theory of Sexuality*. In the first edition (1905) we do not yet find any mention of narcissism, while the second edition (1910) contains the above-mentioned footnote on narcissism. Apart from Freud and Sadger's publications, my main source is the *Minutes of the Vienna Psychoanalytic Society* (Nunberg & Federn, 1962–1975).[3] To date these sources have only infrequently been drawn upon and they were not yet systematically

[2] On the first page of the second edition of the *Three Essays on the Theory of Sexuality* (1905d) we can read in a footnote: "The data obtained from the psycho-analytic investigation of inverts are based upon material supplied to me by I. Sadger and upon my own findings" (1905d/1910, p. 135). The footnote in the study on Leonardo is: "I refer in particular to the investigations of I. Sadger, which I can in the main confirm from my own experience" (1910c, p. 99). In order to distinguish between the different editions of the *Three Essays* I give the year of publication for the edition to which I am referring after the year of the essay's first publication.

[3] In what follows the *Minutes of the Vienna Psychoanalytical Society* are abbreviated as "Min", followed by the number of the volume (1 to 4).

taken into account by the English and German editors of Freud's works and letters.[4]

Isidor Sadger

Isidor Sadger (1867–1942) was admitted to the Psychological Wednesday Evening Society on 21 November 1906. The members of this group (which from 1908 onwards called itself the Vienna Psychoanalytical Society) in the period between 1905 and 1910 who are well known today were Alfred Adler, Paul Federn, Wilhelm Stekel, Otto Rank, Eduard Hitschmann, Fritz Wittels, and Max Graf, the father of "Little Hans". Freud was present every Wednesday evening to take part in the discussions of the lectures given by the members of the group and guests. Sometimes he would present drafts of his own publications. Sadger also participated regularly and actively in the weekly meetings during that period. Between November 1906 and December 1910 he gave twelve lectures to the group and thus spoke on more evenings than any of the other members. Ten of the twelve lectures were published. They account for only a small proportion of Sadger's total publications during that time.[5]

Today Sadger's papers and books are little known. They do not rank anywhere near those of Abraham, Ferenczi, Adler, and Jung. Their intellectual level is inferior to that of Rank's writings, and there is no comparison to the work of Stekel in regard to the art of interpretation. Today we associate Sadger's name with the early days of research on homosexuality and perversion. He is considered to be a pioneer in that field. The first insights into the aetiology of homosexuality and the first publications on the subject are generally ascribed to him *and* Freud.[6] In the "Bericht über die Fortschritte der Psychoanalyse in den Jahren 1909 bis 1913 [Report on the Progress of Psychoanalysis in the years 1909 to 1913]", which contains fourteen reviews, it was Sadger who provided an overview of research on perversion (1914a). The term "urethral

---

[4] James Strachey, the editor of the *Standard Edition of the Complete Psychological Works of Sigmund Freud* informs us that he was "unfortunately precluded from quoting" the *Minutes* (1957a, p. 60).

[5] See Sadger, 1908a, 1908c, 1909a, 1909b, 1910b, 1910d, 1910e, 1910g, 1911a, 1911b, 1912. Sadger's lectures were held on fifteen evenings; Stekel and Adler ranked second and third in regard to the number of evenings spoken on between 1906 and 1910.

[6] See, for example, Hitschmann, 1911, p. 42. Ferenczi's essays on homosexuality followed from 1911 onwards (Ferenczi, 1911, 1914b).

eroticism" that he introduced became broadly accepted, while others such as "Gesässerotik [buttock eroticism]", "Haut-, Schleimhaut- und Muskelerotik [skin, mucosa and muscle eroticism]" as well as "Assoziationswiderwille [unwillingness to associate]" did not.

To date no biographies of Sadger or collections of his work have been published. Very little is known about his life. He was born in Galicia in 1867, studied medicine in Vienna, graduated in 1891, and became interested in Freud's work at the end of the 1890s. He was known to Freud at the latest by 1899 and reported that he began to carry out psychoanalyses in 1898.[7] He started to publish even before graduating; according to Graf-Nold these were "popular articles on subjects in the areas of overlap between medicine, psychology, and literary science" (1988, p. 35).

From 1906 onwards he was a member of the group that had gathered around Freud and left it in 1933 for unknown reasons (Handlbauer, 1990, p. 47). The editors of the *Minutes* state that he had increasingly isolated himself as the years passed (Min 1, p. XXXVI). Angela Graf-Nold (1988) writes that he was the analyst and close friend of Hermine Hug-Hellmuth.[8] Karl Fallend (1988, pp. 29, 50, 42) reports that he taught at the Vienna training institute in the 1920s, gave courses in the "Seminar for Sexuology", and was the first analyst of Wilhelm Reich. At that time Sadger belonged to the group of older analysts whom the younger analysts called "libido hunters"—a label that suits him well (Sterba, 1982, p. 34). His tragic death is all that is known about his life during the time after he left the Vienna Psychoanalytic Society. He was deported to the concentration camp Theresienstadt in 1942 and died there.

---

[7] In his analysis of the dream of the "norekdal style" Freud mentions a colleague from whom he had received an essay that he considered to have been written "in too emotional a manner" (Freud, 1900a, p. 296). Freud understood the sentence in his dream "It is written in a positively norekdal style" as an allusion to the impression that the essay had made on him. He thought that "norekdal" was a combination of "Nora" and "Ekdal", two characters in plays by Ibsen. He added that on the day before he had the dream he had read a colleague's essay on Ibsen. Fritz Wittels, a nephew of Sadger's, believes that Sadger was the colleague to whom Freud was referring and that the essay was Sadger's "Das Wunder vom denkenden Eiweiß [The Miracle of the Thinking Protein]" (1897), in which Sadger drew attention to the papers of Paul Flechsig (who was the Flechsig in the case report on Schreber) (Wittels, 1924, p. 76).

[8] The tragic story of Hug-Hellmuth's murder by her nephew Rudolf Hug, whose guardian Sadger was, is recounted in detail by Graf-Nold (1988), whose book contains a large amount of information about Sadger.

In the biographies of Freud by Jones, Clark, Gay, and Sulloway, Freud's correspondence with Abraham, Jung, and Pfister and the smaller autobiographies and memoirs of Wittels, Sterba, Sachs, Stekel, Reik, Jones, Helene Deutsch, and Andreas-Salomé, Sadger is either not mentioned at all or only in passing, and almost always in an unfavourable light. The picture painted of him in the *Minutes* is similarly uncongenial. The editors remark that he "made himself disliked" (Min 1, p. 258, fn. 3).[9] Freud also does not seem to have liked him.

Apart from his awkward and tactless behaviour the main reason for the rejection that Sadger provoked lay in his obsession with sexuality. That this should have shocked a group of analysts may be surprising, but it becomes understandable if we consider that in Sadger's case the interest in sexuality had nothing to do with a tolerance and acceptance of drive impulses ("Triebfreundlichkeit"), but with a covert and unadmitted moral indignation. Sadger questioned his patients in a penetrating, inquisitorial way about the details of their sexual experiences and practices and publicised the results of these extended sexual histories in over-long case reports, describing unsavoury particulars in minute detail. Freud drew his attention to the fact that this led to "aversion" and that Sadger did not take into account his audience's and readers' normal defences (Min 2, p. 379). At another point Freud reproached him with a "lack of tolerance" which "manifests itself in a moralistic pathos" (ibid., pp. 224–225). This was referring to the fact that Sadger's detailed descriptions of his patients' sexual lives were permeated by a tone of moral judgement. His patients had to "admit" sexual wishes for which they were then condemned. Sadger thus failed to respect both his patients' defences and those of his audience. He may have denied feelings of shame and disgust of his own. At one point Freud remarked that Sadger neglected the "whole superstructure" of the mind (Min 4, p. 16).[10] He went on to say that Sadger neglected to describe his patients' resistances, which led to the impression that the "psychosexual factors which are at the deepest roots were the solutions that offered themselves

---

[9] For criticism of Sadger see Min 1, pp. 255–258; Min 2, pp. 220–226, pp. 376–381; Min 3, p. 13; Min 4, pp. 16–17.

[10] Andreas-Salomé wrote: "But there is something about Sadger giving one the impression that it is not so much ability that he lacks as the desire to elevate the material through intellectual penetration from the unattractiveness of its crude content—as if in fact the demands of analysis disturbed his blissful contemplation. He presumably enjoys his analysands more than he helps them or learns anything from them" (1957, p. 41).

at the start" (ibid.). Moreover, Freud felt that Sadger did not make any effort to develop a theoretical understanding of the material he had gleaned from his patients.

One can see Sadger as a representative of a mode of psychoanalytic conduct and thinking that is tied neither to that time, nor to personal idiosyncrasies or to his person. This mode is characterised by an overriding interest in primitive drive impulses, a tendency to condemn those very impulses, a lack of interest in psychoanalytic theory, a relatively rigid, dogmatic way of perceiving clinical material, a tendency to get lost in patients' histories, little appreciation of complexity or overdetermination, and a technique in which patience plays a minor role, while confrontation is central.

The questions we have asked focus our interest on the years between 1905 and 1910. During this period Sadger published no fewer than forty-two essays.[11] Twenty-two of these dealt with the application of hydriatics (treatment by means of water) in various organic and mental diseases. Five articles were written for German daily and weekly newspapers and are, for example, about the German poet Christian Friedrich Daniel Schubart (1905a), Ibsen (1905b), the psychology of taste (1905c), disturbances of child development (1910f), and transvestism (1910c). The remaining fifteen papers, all of which were published after 1907, can be considered psychoanalytic in the narrower sense, that is, pathographies on C. F. Meyer (1908c), Lenau (1909a), and Kleist (1910e), three clinical papers (1908a, 1909b, 1910d), and nine papers of a more general nature on psychoanalysis (1907, 1908b, 1908d, 1909c, 1909d, 1910a, 1910b, 1910g, 1910h). The following are of particular importance for our investigation: "Psychiatrisch-Neurologisches in psychoanalitischer Beleuchtung [A Psychoanalytic View of Some Psychiatric and Neurological Disorders]" (1908d), "Fragment der Psychoanalyse eines Homosexuellen [A Fragment of the Psychoanalysis of a Homosexual]" (1908a), "Ist die konträre Sexualempfindung heilbar? [Is Contrary Sexual Feeling Curable?]" (1908b), "Zur Ätiologie der konträren Sexualempfindung [On the Aetiology of Contrary Sexual Feeling]" (1909c), and

[11] My enquiry drew on the following sources: *Bibliographie der deutschen Zeitschriftenliteratur, Neurologisches Centralblatt, The Index of Psychoanalytic Writings* (Grinstein, 1956–1975), Abraham (1909), Hitschmann (1911), and the "Bericht über die Fortschritte der Psychoanalyse in den Jahren 1909–1913 [Report on the Progress of Psychoanalysis in the Years 1909–1913]" (1914).

"Ein Fall von multipler Perversion mit hysterischen Absenzen [A Case of Multiple Perversion with Hysterical Absences]" 1910d).[12]

In "A Psychoanalytic View of Some Psychiatric and Neurological Phenomena", published in April 1908, Sadger announced the discussion of two problems that "have not yet or hardly been clarified to date, that is, narcissism and the phenomenon of the *Doppelgänger*" (1908d, p. 53).[13] In view of the date on which Freud made his first statements on narcissism it seems surprising that Sadger should speak of narcissism quite matter-of-factly—one year before Freud did. Thus it needs to be clarified when the term "narcissism" was first used in everyday parlance and in medical terminology, and what was understood by it.

Ellis and Näcke: The concept of narcissism in sexology

It is well known that Havelock Ellis (1859–1939) drew attention to a "Narcissus-like tendency" in his essay "Auto-erotism: a Psychological Study" (1898a, p. 280). Paul Näcke, a German physician and sexologist, translated "Narcissus-like tendency" as "Narzißmus" (1899b, p. 375), thus coining the term that Freud was later to adopt.[14] As regards the term "autoerotism" it is known that Freud adopted it from Ellis, but gave it a different meaning: according to Freud a sexual activity is autoerotic when it "is not directed towards other people, but obtains satisfaction from the subject's own body" (1905d, p. 181). Neither "narcissism" nor "autoerotism" had been part of English or German vocabulary before 1899, just as many other terms for what was considered to be deviant sexual behaviour have only been used since about 1880, that is, only surprisingly recently.[15]

When Näcke translated Ellis' "narcissus-like tendency" as "Narzißmus", he not only created a new word, but also interpreted it differently from Ellis. It is worth looking more closely at this process, since

[12] "Contrary sexual feeling" was an expression used to mean a homosexual orientation.

[13] The subject of the *Doppelgänger*, which is closely related to that of narcissism and includes both the yearning for a twin-like partner and the threat arising from such a partner, is not discussed here: see Rank, 1914; Freud, 1919h.

[14] See also Näcke, 1899a, pp. 128, 131, 146.

[15] Ellis drew attention to the fact that before the word "narcissism" was coined there had already been isolated presentations of clinical pictures which described what was later to be called "narcissism" (1927, p. 134). Sulloway refers to a paper by Binet that compared fetishists to the fable of Narcissus before the turn of the century (1979, p. 278, fn. 1).

ultimately it sheds new light on the relationship between psychoanalysis and sexology.[16]

Ellis's paper entitled "Auto-erotism" is thirty-nine pages long and focuses on masturbation. Ellis went through the reports, observations, and surveys available at the time and presented the various masturbation practices and their frequencies in relation to age, sex, cultural affiliation, and so on. He classified the sexual arousal induced by masturbation in a group of sexual phenomena that he called "autoerotic". He understood autoerotism to mean, "the phenomena of spontaneous sexual emotion generated in the absence of an external stimulus proceeding, directly or indirectly, from another person" (1898a, p. 260). For instance, sexual arousal is autoerotic when it occurs during sleep or as a result of daydreams, masturbation, religious fervour, or ecstasy, or alternatively of self-love. Ellis saw it as his mission in life to describe normal sexuality, or sexuality as it occurs, in all its manifestations and to exercise reserve in regard to moral judgement. He always pleaded in favour of tolerance *vis à vis* different expressions of sexuality, including, for example, homosexuality. He took the same attitude towards autoerotism. It was important to him to remove the fear that masturbation and other autoerotic phenomena would lead to mental illness or do some other harm. In his view, all autoerotic phenomena are normal, which does not exclude the possibility that they can be practised to a pathological degree. Ellis considered a self-love pervaded by sexual arousal to be a rare phenomenon, a "curiosity", and wrote only a few lines about it, including the remark that love of the ego or self-admiration is "narcissus-like":

> To complete this summary of the main phenomena of autoerotism, I may briefly mention that tendency which is sometimes found, more especially perhaps in women, for the sexual emotions to be absorbed, and often entirely lost in self-admiration. This Narcissus-like tendency, of which the normal germ in women is symbolized by the mirror, is found in minor degree in some feminine-minded men, but appears to be very rarely found in men, apart from sexual attraction for other persons, to which attraction it is, of course,

---

[16] In the eighth chapter of his book on Freud, Sulloway (1979) gives a detailed description of the relationships between psychoanalysis and sexology.

> normally subservient. But occasionally in women, it appears to exist by itself to the exclusion of any attraction for other persons. (Ellis, 1898a, p. 280)

Ellis presents as an example the case of a young woman who was "active and healthy and intelligent" and found her body extraordinarily beautiful (ibid.). The pleasure afforded her by her own body was the most intense feeling she knew. This case concluded Ellis' remarks on narcissus-like tendencies. At the time nothing about those few lines gave reason to suspect that they were to become the reference point for a central psychoanalytic concept.

One year after Ellis' essay on autoerotism the German term "Narzißmus" first appeared in print, in Näcke's "Die sexuellen Perversitäten in der Irrenanstalt [The Sexual Perversities in the Mental Asylum]" (1899a). At that time Paul Näcke (1851–1913) was a senior physician at the Hubertusburg mental hospital. His publications were later discussed by the Vienna Society and mentioned by Freud in the second edition of *The Interpretation of Dreams* (Min 1, pp. 365, 398; Min 2, p. 39; Freud, 1900a, p. 396).[17] Näcke had collected data on sexual abnormalities in patients and wanted to investigate whether perversions—he referred to them as vices, bad habits, excesses—occur more frequently in psychiatric patients than in the general population, whether individual perversions occur more often in certain disorders, and whether masturbation causes mental illness and aggravates its symptoms—a theory that was currently under discussion. Näcke's findings can be roughly summarised as follows: with the exception of masturbation, perversions are rarely observed in mental illnesses. Masturbation can be ruled out as the cause of mental disorders and the dangers of masturbation are over-exaggerated.

The variants of sexual behaviour to which Näcke referred as perversions are interesting. He listed masturbation, exhibitionism, fetishism, smearing faeces, drinking urine, renifleurism, narcissism, mutual masturbation, and pederasty. Näcke does not explain in this essay what led him to coin the term "narcissism". However, we do discover something about why and under what conditions he assigned narcissism to the perversions. In the description of his results Näcke reports that of his

---

[17] Gröger (1990) published two of Freud's letters to Näcke from which it can be inferred that serious differences arose between the two of them in about 1907. Gröger reports that Näcke's attitude towards psychoanalysis was "definitely negative" (p. 144).

1,500 mentally ill subjects only four men and one woman had shown "Narcismus". The narcissistic men had obtained pleasure from regarding their reflections in the mirror, while the woman would kiss her arms and hands and look "completely in love" with herself (Näcke, 1899a, pp. 128, 131).[18] In none of these cases had there been there any "signs of voluptuousness", therefore it was only "pseudo-narcissism". Näcke continued: "Cases of genuine narcissism are no doubt very rare and a class of aberration on their own. I would like to call them the most serious form of 'auto-erotism' (H. Ellis)" (ibid., p. 146). Thus Näcke distinguished between pseudo-narcissism and genuine narcissism; in his view only narcissism that was associated with orgasm was "genuine".

In "Kritisches zum Kapitel der normalen und pathologischen Sexualität [Critical Remarks on Normal and Pathological Sexuality]" (1899b), a review of recent publications on sexology, Näcke referred to Ellis's essay on autoerotism. He then gave the source of his concept of narcissism, that is, Ellis' description of an erotically stimulating self-love, and commented on it as follows:

> At all events *narcisissm (Narcismus)*, self-love, is much rarer than day-dreaming. We must distinguish between narcissism and mere vanity. Only where contemplation of one's own body or its parts is accompanied by clear signs of orgasm can we justifiably speak of narcissism. That would then be a classical case of "autoerotism" as defined by *H. Ellis*, according to whom narcissism is to be found especially in women, perhaps because the normal basis of it "is symbolized by the mirror". Here, too, there is still much to investigate, but it in particular there is a need for suitable subjects. (Näcke, 1899b, p. 375)

Here again Näcke distinguishes between simple, common, normal vanity and pathological self-love, accepting only the latter as genuine

---

[18] Of the male patients Näcke wrote: "Three of them stand in front of the mirror very frequently, take pleasure in their own reflections in it and are, apart from one of them, very vain in regard to their own bodies, which they make every effort to smarten up. One of them pulls out every grey hair or has somebody do it for him. A fourth one often speaks of his beautiful body, although he has absolutely no reason to do so" (1899a, p. 128). About the female patient he wrote, "*Narcissism* was only observed in one woman with periodically high arousal. When she is in a storm she kisses her own arms and hands and looks completely lovestruck" (ibid., p. 131).

narcissism, and introduces orgasm as the criterion on which to base the differential diagnosis. This was not what Ellis had meant, and Ellis later complained that Näcke had not quoted him correctly (1927, p. 136). Ellis considered autoerotism in general and the specific case of narcissistic self-love to be *normal* phenomena that may take on pathological forms, whereas Näcke reduced narcissism to a *pathological* perversion and was only interested in it as such. Moreover, Näcke defined narcissism as sexual behaviour in the narrowest sense, considering it to be present only when it leads to orgasm. In this way Näcke and other sexologists tied the concept of narcissism strictly to sexual behaviour and "sexualised" it in a way that one would not expect of a non-psychoanalytic discipline.[19]

On the other hand Näcke's approach is also understandable. His frame of reference was medicine and sexual pathology. The latter discipline had become established as an area of research within medicine in the 1870s and 1880s (Wettley & Leibbrand, 1959). The most important contribution had been made by Richard v. Krafft-Ebing, the first edition of whose main work *Psychopathia Sexualis* was published in 1886. Näcke's reinterpretation of the concept of narcissism must be seen within the context of this medical sexology, which was oriented towards pathology, while Ellis' approach belonged more to the kind of sexology interested in normal sexual behaviour and its sociocultural bases and had developed at the beginning of the 20th century. Ellis himself is seen as one of its founders.

Ellis had made a name for himself with publications on sexology, for example, *Sexual Inversion* (Ellis & Symonds, 1897), which dealt with homosexuality. He had been considered an authority in this field since the turn of the century (Grosskurth, 1980).[20] Each of the seven volumes of his *Studies in the Psychology of Sex* was promptly translated into German

---

[19] Some years later Rohleder (1907) defined "automonosexualism" similarly to Näcke. In a paper subtitled "A Form of the Human Sexual Drive not Hitherto Observed" Rohleder distinguished automonosexualism in particular from Ellis' "narcissus-like tendencies", which Rohleder considered too broad. According to his definition a case could only be considered to be automonosexualism if sexual arousal and satisfaction were obtained through the person's own body, "that is, through it alone". As soon as phantasies were involved in the production of sexual arousal it could no longer be diagnosed as automonosexualism. Rohleder presented two cases of this perversion, which he believed to be very rare, and discussed similar cases described by Moll and Krafft-Ebing.

[20] The facts given in what follows have been taken from Grosskurth's (1980) informative biography of Ellis and from Ellis' autobiography *My Life* (1940). Grosskurth's biography includes an impressive picture of the strained relationship between Ellis and Freud.

and several editions were published in both English and German. Ellis was three years younger than Freud and had concluded his medical training in London in 1889, but had never worked as a doctor. He was not affiliated to any university institution and lived in England as a writer and private scholar. All the leading sexologists of the times, including Freud and his followers, discussed his views. In 1910 he had already published six of the seven volumes of the *Studies in the Psychology of Sex* and was, as Grosskurth remarks, better known than Freud in the circles of English-speaking sexologists. He had recognised Freud's importance very early on. As early as 1898 he had reported on Freud and Breuer's papers in detail in a publication on the connection between hysteria and sexuality, expressing the view that they were the only contributions of real significance since those of Charcot (Ellis, 1898b, p. 608). Freud was very pleased by this (F/Fl, p. 338),[21] while Ellis was proud to be among the first academics to have recognised Freud's genius and drawn the attention of English-speaking readers to his work. Ellis and Freud remained in touch with other throughout their lives. Although they never met, they kept up a correspondence and cited each other frequently. Particularly in the period between 1900 and 1910, in *The Interpretation of Dreams* and the *Three Essays on the Theory of Sexuality*, Freud often made reference to Ellis, while Ellis reviewed Freud's publications in English-language journals.

Phyllis Grosskurth reports that Ellis became increasingly sceptical about psychoanalysis over the years. Other sexologists shared this scepticism. To capture the direction of his criticism we must jump forward a little in history. In 1927 Ellis published an article entitled "The Conception of Narcissism" in which he described how the concept of narcissism had developed. On the one hand he acknowledged Freud's transformation of the concept as a brilliant accomplishment:

> In his hands the conception of Narcissism took on a new significance and became of immense importance. Everything that Freud has touched—that indeed is always the mark of genius—takes on a new significance and becomes of importance. For my own part,

---

[21] At the end of 1900 Freud read Ellis' *The Evolution of Modesty* (1899; F/Fl, p. 428). The chapter on "Auto-erotism" contains an expanded and revised version of his earlier essays on autoerotism and hysteria (1898a, 1898b). Ellis dedicated eight pages to Freud and Breuer's work (1899, pp. 216–224).

> I regard this transformation as a legitimate application of the original observation from which Narcissism started. (Ellis, 1927, p. 142)

However, he also had objections, the most important of which concerned the psychoanalytic postulate that the narcissistic phase was part of normal development. Ellis considered this "somewhat speculative" (ibid.). He pointed out that he was not alone in this and that many of the "most able and cautious of the older representatives of sexual psychology outside psychoanalysis" had come to the same conclusion as himself (ibid., p. 143). In his view, narcissism was a normal but rare form of autoerotism and he did not have the impression that narcissism—that is, vanity and self-love—was necessarily part of normal development, as psychoanalysis claimed.

Ellis' arguments are worthy of attention. Some of his objections had also been raised against psychoanalysis by other sexologists, for example, Leopold Löwenfeld and Magnus Hirschfeld. In 1914, Löwenfeld, who worked as a neurologist in Munich, was the editor of an important publication series entitled *Grenzfragen des Nerven- und Seelenlebens* [Between Neurology and Psychology] and had published some of Freud's papers at the beginning of the century, added a brief appendix on narcissism to the chapter entitled "The anomalies of the sex drive" in the fifth edition of *Sexualleben und Nervenleiden* [Sexual Life and Nervous Disorders] (Löwenfeld, 1914, pp. 392–393). He conceded that vanity could be considered to be a "variant of narcissism", but added that vanity or gaining "excessive pleasure from one's own person and over-valuation of one's own physical qualities" were particularly widespread in women (ibid., p. 392) and such so-to-speak normal narcissism could not be considered to be a perversion. In his view, narcissism was only a perversion when

> regarding one's own body either in the flesh or in the mirror triggers sexual arousal that can go as far as orgasm and there is a lack of interest in sexual intercourse. However, the observations to date show that such cases are extremely rare occurrences in persons who are mentally healthy. (Löwenfeld, 1914, p. 392)

Here Löwenfeld's thinking is similar to that of Näcke. He limits the scope of narcissism to that of a perversion, which he defines as a "sign of lust" (sexual arousal, orgasm). He also gives an exact definition of the behaviour that provokes it (regarding one's own body). Thus defined, narcissism could not be a characteristic of a phase of normal development.

Hirschfeld was a doctor in Berlin, editor of the *Jahrbuch für sexuelle Zwischenstufen* [Yearbook of Sexual Intermediate Stages], founder of the homosexual movement, and for some years also a member of the Berlin Psychoanalytic Society. In his main work *Die Homosexualität* [Homosexuality] (1914) he addressed the psychoanalytic theory that narcissism played a role in homosexuality. His objection was that only some adolescent homosexuals were "in love with their mirror images or photographs of themselves as youths" (1914, p. 344). The psychoanalytic rejoinder to this was that narcissism does not necessarily have to be associated with being in love with one's own reflection in the mirror. At this point the discussion between sexologists and psychoanalysts became difficult, if not impossible. The sexologists were searching for testable hypotheses and unambiguous definitions oriented towards observable behaviour. The psychoanalysts paid no attention to these requirements and refused to equate narcissism, self-love, and sexuality with observable behaviours. Moreover, they took into account the multifarious ways in which unconscious impulses can appear in disguise. This made it difficult to pursue a discussion with researchers from other disciplines.

Sadger's first paper on narcissism (1908)

We have now clarified how Sadger came to speak of narcissism with such assurance in "A Psychoanalytic View of Some Psychiatric and Neurological Disorders" (1908d). He was referring to the medical and sexological concept of narcissism that had been established in 1899. In his paper Sadger reports on two patients, a twenty-nine-year-old woman with hysteria and one eighteen-year-old boy, both of whom had a tendency to caress and kiss their own bodies and to obtain pleasure from them. Thus in these cases "narcissism" was present and Sadger subjected this narcissism to an analytical investigation. The paper was published in April 1908 and is the first attempt at a psychoanalytic elucidation of narcissism known to date.

The results of his analytic exploration of the female patient were: first, what is concealed behind a narcissistic relationship with one's own body is a homosexual relationship to the mother. When a person caresses or admires their own body, it is actually the mother's body that is meant; and second, the narcissistic relationship to the person's own body involves "identification" with the mother. In caressing and admiring their own body a person takes over the "role" of the mother and repeats the admiration and erotically stimulating touch that they received from their mother as a child. There may be a displacement on to parts of the body that are less indecent. Sadger summarises the results of his brief analytical treatment of his hysterical patient as follows:

> As the analysis [...] lasted only for a few weeks I was not able to follow the phenomenon of narcissism right to its ultimate roots. Nonetheless it would appear to me that I was able to throw some new light on our understanding. Here again we are initially concerned with sexual wishes that go back to early childhood, especially homosexual phantasies. There was a displacement from less respectable to more respectable parts of the body, [...] and finally our patient united both mother and child in her own body by kissing, as mother, her arms as those of the child. (Sadger, 1908d, p. 54)

In the case of the male patient Sadger came to a similar conclusion. He stated that the patient was actually maintaining a sexually stimulating relationship to his mother through his narcissistic admiration of himself. Moreover, that in his self-admiration he was identifying with the mother who had admired him in the past. Finally, he considered that self-love also fulfilled oedipal wishes. Sadger did not use the word "oedipal", but made reference to the oedipal constellation. He postulated that the young man saw his father in himself and admired himself as the father who was loved sexually by his mother. At the end of this second vignette, Sadger put forward the following hypothesis as to the aetiology of the symptom of narcissism:

> Here again we find as the basis of narcissism admiration of the child by its mother and identification with her arising from love of her, as in children's play. Similarly to the first patient, the patient then admires himself as a child, acting as the mother. (Sadger, 1908d, p. 54)

Thus far Sadger's initial attempt to analyse narcissism is not easy to assess. Parts of it appear to be surprisingly modern, while other parts seem confused. In his explanations of narcissism we easily lose sight of who is identifying with whom.[22] We must, however, take into account that the meaning of the word "identification" as Sadger uses it is superficial. He was not talking about a profound, persisting internal change, but the mental activity of role-play.

His conceptualisation is similar to the theory of hysterical identification that Freud had introduced in *The Interpretation of Dreams* (1900a). It would seem that Sadger frequently drew attention to the identification with the mother in the *Minutes*, more frequently than his colleagues in the Vienna Group. In these references he emphasised the mother's functions that are associated with bodily hygiene and her role as a teacher.

At first sight Sadger's approach appears to have been in line with the generally accepted understanding of the time insofar as he looked for manifestations of infantile sexuality in the symptom—in this case the erotic relationship to the person's own body. While Sadger's focus was on both the autoerotic and allo-erotic aspects of infantile sexuality, it was to the latter that he accorded most attention in his presentations. The symptom formation processes that he uncovered—in this case displacement—were simple and swiftly dealt with. It is likely that this was a reflection not only of the state of knowledge at the time, but also of an idiosyncrasy of Sadger's. As a rule he saw in the symptom only the element of repetition, that is, the fixation to real or wished for infantile gratifications. More complex derivations such as those of Freud from this period, as in the case of Little Hans (1909b), were not his line. Finally, Sadger assumed that the symptom of narcissism stemmed from admiration by the mother. He retained this hypothesis, which is reminiscent of contemporary theories of the "gleam in the mother's eye", in a modified form and placed importance on it, whereas in Freud's understanding of narcissism it played no role.[23] In Freud's view both narcissism and autoerotism were part of a child's *basic mental equipment* and not brought about by the admiration of the parents. Freud had made up his mind about this very early on. As early as 1906, when the term narcissism had not yet been integrated into psychoanalytic theory, in the discussion of a lecture entitled "On the Megalomania of the

---

[22] Freud was presumably referring to this idiosyncrasy of Sadger's when he once spoke of his "logical inaccuracy, throwing subject and object together" (Andreas-Salomé, 1957, p. 91).

[23] See Min 4, p. 190; Sadger (1914a, p. 311). Freud was familiar with Sadger's "A Psychoanalytic View" (Min 1, p. 401, with fn. 3), but never made explicit mention of it.

Normal Person", he said that (normal) megalomania "takes powerful nourishment from that portion of autoerotism which everyone has preserved to a greater or lesser extent" (Min 1, p. 56). Freud stayed with the idea of a normal infantile megalomania and justified it against Adler, in particular.[24] Whereas Adler assumed that feelings of inferiority are primary and compensated for by wishes for greatness, Freud assumed the opposite and claimed that children are generally initially convinced of their own grandiosity.

Sadger's formulations were still oriented towards the definition of narcissism as a symptom of sexual perversion and in no way anticipated Freud's introduction of the concept of narcissism. Despite these limitations, he can still be given the credit for having been the first to address the issue of narcissism and attempt to elucidate it analytically. The significance of Freud's approach as compared to Sadger's first attempt will become all the clearer.

After the first mention in "A Psychoanalytic View of Some Psychiatric and Neurological Disorders" the term and the phenomenon of narcissism appeared once more in Sadger's publications, in 1910, in the published version of the lecture that he gave in November 1909, in the discussion of which Freud made his first statement about narcissism.

Before we take a closer look at this historic evening we must familiarise ourselves with the history of the psychoanalytic theory on homosexuality since the remark of Sadger's that Freud considered to be "new and valuable" referred to the narcissism of (male) homosexuals. We are no longer accustomed to the close connection that was made between narcissism and homosexuality, whereas at the time it was quite familiar to the analysts who participated in the development of psychoanalytic theory. Thus, for example, Eduard Hitschmann who, like Sadger, was a member of the Vienna Psychoanalytic Society, wrote in his review of the progress of drive theory, "The first detailed observations of narcissism were made in the analysis of homosexuals" (1914, p. 288). Rank, who was keeper of the *Minutes* of the Vienna Group, also drew attention to the fact that it was especially experiences with homosexual patients that had thrown light on narcissism (Rank, 1911b, p. 401).

---

[24] See Min 2, pp. 537–541; Freud, 1909d, p. 234; Andreas-Salomé, 1957, p. 37.

The formula of the aetiology of male homosexuality proposed in 1910

Homosexuality, which was also referred to as "inversion", "contrary sexual feeling", and "uranism", was an important issue in research on sexuality at the turn of the century.[25] According to Sulloway (1979, p. 283) more than a thousand papers were published on the subject of homosexuality between 1898 and 1908. Among the authors whom Freud mentions in the *Three Essays on the Theory of Sexuality* we find Ellis, Näcke, Löwenfeld and Hirschfeld; also Krafft-Ebing, Moll, Moebius, von Schrenck-Notzing, Eulenberg, and Bloch. The impression we gain from an initial glance at the literature is that of a lively and differentiated discussion between the researchers. The problems that were considered central in their circle included questions as to whether homosexuality is congenital or acquired, whether it is pathological or not, and how it is related to bisexuality. Freud accordingly discussed these issues in detail in the *Three Essays*.

Around 1900, homosexuality was also a matter of public interest. Oscar Wilde was sent to prison in 1895 because of his homosexual tendencies. In 1896, Ellis had to publish *Sexual Inversion* in Germany (Ellis & Symonds, 1896) because he had failed to find a publisher in England; in 1897 the English edition was withdrawn for censorship reasons. In the same year the *Wissenschaftlich-Humanitäres Komitee* [Scientific Humanitarian Committee] was founded in Berlin and campaigned for the abolition of the criminal prosecution of homosexuals. It continued to exist until 1933, under the leadership of Magnus Hirschfeld. The Committee's journal was the *Jahrbuch für sexuelle Zwischenstufen unter besonderer Berücksichtigung der Homosexualität* [Yearbook of Sexual Intermediate Stages with special consideration of homosexuality].[26] The journals *Sexualprobleme* [Sexual Problems] and *Mutterschutz* [Maternity Protection] published by Max Marcuse in Berlin supported similar

---

[25] The terms "contrary sexual feeling" and "inversion" were not, as claimed by Socarides (1968, p. 22) coined by Freud. According to Wettley & Leibbrand (1959) "contrary sexual feeling" originated with Westphal in 1870, and "inversion" by Charcot and Magnan in 1882.

[26] The *Jahrbuch für sexuelle Zwischenstufen* was founded by Hirschfeld in 1899. In the period between 1909 and 1912 it was published under the name of *Vierteljahresberichte des Wissenschaftlich-Humanitären Komitees* [Quarterly Reports of the Scientific Humanitarian Committee], then again under its original name. The *Zeitschrift für Sexualwissenschaft* [Journal of Sexology], also published by Hirschfeld, only existed for one year (1908).

approaches to sexual reform. Freud published three papers in these journals (1908a, 1908c, 1908d).[27] Hirschfeld, especially, was among those to whom the psychoanalytic theory of homosexuality was addressed. His thinking was close to that of psychoanalysis for some years and he was, as mentioned above, from 1908 to 1911 a member of the Berlin group led by Abraham. As a representative of the homosexual movement he developed a wide range of activities and appeared as an expert witness at one of the Harden trials causing a sensation at the time.[28]

Following this rough background sketch we now return to the question of Sadger's role in the history of the insights into the aetiology of homosexuality. The reconstruction of the research process between 1905 and 1910 presented below is based mainly on the *Minutes of the Vienna Psychoanalytic Society* and on Sadger's publications.[29] The goal of the reconstruction is not to give a broad description of the beginnings of research on homosexuality, but rather to investigate *Sadger's contribution* to the formula of the aetiology of homosexuality of 1910, since it was in the course of the development of this formula that the concept of narcissism was introduced. The second edition of the *Three Essays* (1905d/1910) contains a first short version of the aetiological formula:

> In all the cases we have examined, we have established the fact that the future inverts, in the earliest years of their childhood, pass through a phase of very intense but short-lived fixation to a woman (usually their mother), and that, after leaving this behind, they identify themselves with a woman and take themselves as their sexual object. That is to say, they proceed from a narcissistic basis, and look for a young man who resembles *themselves* and whom they may love as their mother loved *them*. (Freud, 1905d/1910, p. 145, fn. 1)

---

[27] Regarding Freud's reservations about the *Jahrbuch für sexuelle Zwischenstufen* as official journal of the *Scientific Humanitarian Committee*, see his letter to Jung (F/Ju, pp. 125–126).

[28] Several cases were brought against Maximilian Harden because he had hinted in his journal *Die Zukunft* [The Future] that there were homosexual men among Kaiser Wilhelm's advisors. According to McGuire, Harden was sentenced to four months in prison at the beginning of 1908 (F/Ju, p. 126).

[29] The most important passages in the Minutes are: Min 1, pp. 19, 236, 405; Min 2, pp. 57–258, 303–314, 338–352, 433–434.

Here, as well as where it first appeared in the Leonardo study (1910c), three aspects of the aetiology are mentioned: an intense libidinous relationship to the mother, identification with her, and a narcissistic object choice. From whom did these theories originate, from Sadger or from Freud?

Before proceeding with the reconstruction let us jump ahead and take a look at a brief summary of its results.

- In the *first* edition of the *Three Essays* (1905d) Freud established the main points of his understanding of sexuality and perversion. At that time there were as yet no specifically psychoanalytic insights into the aetiology of homosexuality. A remark of Freud's that referred to the object choice of homosexuals was an exception. He postulated that homosexuals are looking for a compromise between a male body and a female one in their love objects and insist on the "condition that the object's body (i.e. genitals) shall be masculine" (ibid., p. 144).
- In the course of 1908 the *first component of the aetiological formula*, that is, the intense libidinous attachment of the subsequent homosexual to his mother, was put forward. This discovery was attributed to Sadger; he published it in three papers in 1908 and at the beginning of 1909 (Sadger, 1908a, 1908b, 1909c).
- Freud addressed the aetiology of male homosexuality in two essays that were published at the end of 1908 and the beginning of 1909, in "On the Sexual Theories of Children" (1908c) and "Analysis of a Phobia in a Five-Year-Old Boy" (1909b). He recognised the narcissistic character of the object choice of homosexuals, but did not yet use the adjective "narcissistic".
- The *second component of the aetiological formula* of 1910, the female identification of the male homosexual (with his mother) was probably "discovered" by Freud. The first evidence of it is to be found in the *Minutes* of the Vienna Society of May 1909 (Min 2, p. 257–258).
- The *third aspect of the aetiological formula*, the narcissistic object choice, was first mentioned in November and December of 1909, in the *Minutes* of the Vienna Society (Min 2, pp. 307, 343). This finding is more likely to be attributable to Freud than to Sadger. However, it was first *published* by Sadger (1910d). His paper appeared in February 1910, shortly before Freud disclosed his new insights in the second edition of the *Three Essays* (1905d/1910) and definitely before his Leonardo study (1910c), which came out at the end of May 1910.

In what follows, the gradual development of the aetiological formula will be described in more detail. Perhaps I have presented it as being clearer than it actually was, since Sadger's texts were often confused, "rubbish", and needed to go "to the barber's", as Freud once wrote (F/Ju, p. 283).

Sadger's contribution to the aetiological formula

Sadger became interested in the issue of homosexuality early on. Shortly after he was accepted as a member of Freud's circle, his first psychoanalytic paper, "The Importance of the Psychological Method According to Freud" (1907) was published. By his own account, at that time Sadger had already been working on Freud's writings for nine years and had carried out several analyses. As a result of his analytic work he put forward a hypothesis that emphasised the importance of homosexual impulses.[30] He argued that all hysterical and obsessional-compulsive symptoms were attributable to repressed hetero- and homosexual wishes, that is, that they were of bisexual origin:

> Behind all symptoms [there are] not simply a number of heterosexual roots and wishes, but also, in addition, as I know from my analyses, at least just as many and more important homosexual roots and wishes, which likewise go back to earliest childhood. (Sadger, 1907, p. 47)

By heterosexual wishes Sadger meant wishes that were directed at the parent of the opposite sex and by homosexual wishes those that were directed at the parent of the same sex. Freud referred to Sadger's paper in his essay "Hysterical Phantasies and Their Relation to Bisexuality" (1908a, p. 165). He conceded that Sadger had found the bisexual determination of symptoms independently from him, but rejected his hypothesis, expressing the view that bisexual determination "applies neither to all symptoms of a given case nor to all cases" (ibid., p. 165). Sadger nonetheless upheld his theory and soon afterwards applied it to homosexuality itself. In "Fragment der Psychoanalyse eines Homosexuellen

[30] In his case reports and pathographies Sadger frequently emphasised the homosexual components; see Sadger, 1909b, 1910e; Min 1, pp. 65, 154, 233, 243, 252; Min 2, pp. 14, 141, 156.

[A Fragment of the Psychoanalysis of a Homosexual]" (1908a), an essay that was published in the summer of 1908, he asserted that (male) homosexuals had in fact experienced heterosexual impulses in their childhood, that is, their sex drive had been directed towards their mothers and other female caregivers. These heterosexual impulses had then been suppressed and repressed.[31] In Sadger's words:

> In that context another thought came to me. If all human beings have a basic predisposition to bisexuality, then the heterosexual predisposition should never be lacking also in homosexuals and it should at least be possible to arouse it by psychoanalysis. (Sadger, 1908a, p. 345)

Sadger did *not* present his theory of the original heterosexuality of homosexuals as having resulted from the treatment that he had presented in his paper. In that thirteen-session analysis he had pursued another idea, namely that as a child the patient must have experienced sexual feelings when he was together with his father and other men. The relationship to the mother and other female figures was not yet central; it was only briefly discussed in *one* session (1908a, p. 382). The patient reported that he had loved his mother "with great ardour" but denied that sexual wishes had been involved. Sadger interpreted this as a resistance to admitting homosexual wishes in the transference, but did not further discuss whether or to what extent the patients' statements were indicative of the oedipal relationship to the mother that he (Sadger) assumed.

The detailed, eighty-page case report is nonetheless interesting. It is based on session protocols and gives us some insight into Sadger's theoretical and technical understanding of psychoanalysis. He saw analysis as a kind of sexual confession or sexual history, the goal of which was to get the patient to admit sexual "cravings" in childhood and in the transference. Accordingly only *one* form of relationship between children and their parents was relevant, the "directly sensual" or overt

[31] Sadger uses "suppression" and "repression" synonymously. The concept of repression had not yet been clearly defined in 1908. Sadger had probably voiced the above-mentioned theory at the first psychoanalytic meeting in Salzburg in April 1908, where he gave a lecture on the aetiology of homosexuality, the manuscript of which is not available. See Sadger on the "Salzburg Conference" (1910d, p. 78) and Rank's congress report (1911a, p. 127).

sexual relationship. Sadger had, as Freud once phrased it, no tolerance for aim-inhibited sexual wishes (Min 3, p. 13). Sadger's focus on sexuality may have been the reason why in his pathographies and case reports from the period between 1905 and 1910 he only relatively rarely mentioned oedipal parricide wishes and limited himself to exposing sexual wishes.[32] These he understood literally as a physical sensation of lust in the penis, as an impulse to penetrate the mother with the penis, to take the father's penis into the mouth, to be penetrated anally by the father, and so on.

If we compare this to the above synopsis of the state of sexology at that time we can see that Sadger's view of sexuality was similarly narrow. To put it explicitly, for him sexuality was synonymous with sexual intercourse; manifestations of sexuality that were symbolic or were distorted in some other way were irrelevant. He either overlooked them or considered them to be a form of annoying resistance.[33] Admittedly, unlike the sexologists, he took not only overt behaviour, but also sexual wishes and phantasies into account. He did not, however, have access to Freud's much broader view of sexuality, at least not in the period under investigation here. Freud's and Sadger's views of sexuality differed in that Freud assumed that human beings had sexual wishes and asked himself how the patient's current symptoms could have developed from unconscious sexual wishes. Freud may have had a tolerance for sexual wishes as the basis for his work, while Sadger's capacity for practical and theoretical work was more limited by his fascination for and aversion to sexuality.

In a shorter paper entitled "Zur Ätiologie der konträren Sexualempfindung [On the Aetiology of Contrary Sexual Feeling]" (1909c) Sadger was able to support his claim that male homosexuals had desired their mothers particularly intensely in childhood with material from an analysis that lasted six months. His homosexual patient stated that he had "already as an infant, and even more so in early childhood, had an erotic desire for his mother" (ibid., p. 56). He had wanted to get into

---

[32] See Sadger, 1908c, 1909a, 1909b, 1910d, 1910e, 1911a, etc. It would be interesting to to compare Sadger's mode of interpretation with those of his colleagues (Adler, Stekel, Rank, Abraham, and Ferenczi). Initial impressions indicate that in the early days of psychoanalysis, when the theory and technique appear to us to be so under-developed, there were in fact different modes of procedure, the fundamentals of some of which have survived down to the present day.

[33] Characteristically, in Sadger's case reports from these years we find hardly any dream interpretations or deciphering of associations or symptoms.

bed and the bath with her and touch her breasts, and so on. As an adolescent he had had "all kinds of coitus phantasies about her", and also with his nanny. For Sadger, this meant that "the first love was, as in all such cases, his own mother" (ibid., p. 54). In "Is Contrary Sexual Feeling Curable?" (1908b) Sadger for the first time gave another, possibly better substantiated, piece of evidence in favour of an infantile sexual relationship to the mother and other female caregivers. He reported the observation that homosexuals' "sexual ideal", that is, the type of man with whom they fell in love, always had characteristics of their mothers or other women:

> Freud has taught us a new procedure for combating hysteria and obsessive-compulsive neurosis, the psychoanalytic method [...]. When I recently employed this method once again in the case of a man with contrary sexual feeling it proved that behind the apparently highly male ideals of the invert there are always female ones, originating in the earliest childhood, which had only been suppressed. (Sadger, 1908b, p. 714)

Sadger believed that homosexuals love the mother in men and what a homosexual once "loved and desired in the woman, he still loves and desires today in men" (1909c, p. 55). This was the core of his finding regarding the aetiology of homosexuality. Today it no longer seems controversial, whereas in the past its validity was doubted, even in the circle of the Vienna Psychoanalytic Society. Thus, for example, in the *Minutes* we find the following remark made by Federn in May 1909: "The connection between homosexuality and being in love with one's mother exists only in Sadger's head" (Min 2, p. 222). Freud, however, considered Sadger's thesis to be correct. He mentioned it in the *Three Essays* and in the Leonardo study, despite the fact that there were other assumptions regarding the aetiology of homosexuality under discussion in the Vienna group,[34] which did not gain acceptance.

[34] In the *Minutes* taken in 1906 and 1908 there are entries according to which homosexual affection is a reversal and a defence against infantile oedipal hate (e.g., Min 1, pp. 19, 405). It has not been established who was the originator of the hypothesis. It was only later published by Freud (1922b). On the sidelines another assumption was put forward by Stekel, who asserted that homosexuality was a "flight from incest" (Min 1, p. 393; Stekel, 1908, p. 311; Stekel, 1909, p. 34). The following footnote from Freud's Leonardo study may have been a reference to this: "I am also aware that Wilhelm Stekel of Vienna and Sandor Ferenczi of Budapest have arrived at the same results" (1910c, p. 99).

We have just outlined the hypothesis of an oedipal relationship with the mother in male homosexuality as Sadger's discovery. That is correct, but we also need to add that Freud had made the same assertion in the Vienna Group at the end of 1907 and the beginning of 1908, when he said that three analyses of male homosexuals had shown that homosexuality was preceded by a "period of very intense affection for a woman" (Min 1, p. 283). That Sadger has gone down in history as the originator of this theory is probably because he was the first to *publish* it and support it with case material.

The question of who was first to publish this hypothesis once more became complicated at another point in the *Minutes*. The *Minutes* dated 27 May 1908 contain the following passage:

> Finally Prof. Freud reports [fragments] from the analysis of a latent homosexual. This case confirms a statement made by Sadger, and also found in Stekel's book, namely, that homosexuality sets in only after a certain period and that the libido is then transferred from the woman onto the man. (Min 1, p. 405)

But it is also true that Stekel only briefly mentioned this hypothesis and that he couldn't therefore claim to have been the first. Here, Sadger is cited as the originator of the hypothesis and Freud also repeatedly confirmed that he (Sadger) had been the first to mention it, for example, in May 1909 in the discussion of his Leonardo study by the Vienna Group (Min 2, p. 342).[35]

If homosexuals had loved their mothers particularly passionately as children, why did they then turn away from them? And why did they reject women as love objects? These questions remained open. According to the theory developed in the *Three Essays* the suppression and repression of infantile sexuality in the latency period is "organically determined and fixed by heredity, and it can occasionally occur without any help at all by education" (1905d, p. 177). Child-rearing is just "following the lines which have already been laid down organically" and "impressing them somewhat more clearly and deeply" (ibid., p. 178).

---

[35] In the *Minutes* a remark made by Freud was recorded as follows: "Thus we are inclined to suppose that, in Leonardo's case, an enormous mother fixation took place at an early age; that is (as Sadger has shown in reference to homosexuals) he adored his mother and in repression of this love became a homosexual" (Min 2, pp. 341–342).

Freud believed that the incestuous wishes should be revived in puberty and then repudiated with the aid of the incest barrier, which would have developed by then. The actual object choice could then be made after separation from the parents. At that time there were no more exact ideas about what was later to be called the "dissolution of the oedipus complex". Repression of the love for the mother was considered to be a normal phenomenon that is both organically determined and influenced by culture and child-rearing practices. Homosexuals' rejection of women as love objects, which goes beyond that, demanded more explanation. Sadger's response was that the reasons for the "elimination" of the mother and of all women lay in serious rejections, "disappointed love, betrayed hope and distortion of an admired ideal" (Sadger, 1909c, p. 55). In the case of the patient mentioned above, the decisive disappointments had taken place when he was four years old. His mother had rejected her son's advances, had become pregnant, and had thus "thrown him roughly out of all heavens, causing him to turn away not only from her, but from all women" (ibid.). Sadger considered disappointment by the mother to be the most important reason for homosexuals' disgust for women. He believed that the marked disgust could only have resulted from an especially passionate love and was an inversion of the original love. This laid the foundations for Sadger's paper on the derivation of male homosexuality: an intense libidinous relationship with the mother—disappointment by the mother—repression and abandonment of the relationship to the mother and all women.

With these insights Sadger thought that the way to finding a cure for homosexuality was clear. He was the first analyst to speak up on this question and his answer to the question "Is Contrary Sexual Feeling Curable?" was an unequivocal "yes" (Sadger, 1908b, p. 718). His therapeutic optimism stood in contrast to the views of various sexologists including, for example, Havelock Ellis.[36] Sadger thought that homosexuality was a disorder that could be treated and should be treated. He believed that if it were possible in analysis to render the suppressed and repressed memory of the beloved mother conscious and to show the patient that behind his wish for a man was a latent wish for his mother, his desire for the same sex would disappear. He reported that

[36] Despite their divergent opinions, Ellis referred to Sadger in a review as "perhaps the ablest and the most enthusiastic of Freud's pupils" (Ellis, 1908, p. 754).

such a development had taken place after six months in a case that he had presented (Sadger, 1909c).

In 1910 Freud mentioned the libidinous attachment to the mother, but not Sadger's disappointment hypothesis. He presumably thought that there was not sufficient evidence to support it. He had a different explanation for the homosexual's turning away from the mother. It built on the above-mentioned initial theoretical formulations that he had put forward in the *Three Essays* (1905d), in which he had described the homosexual object choice as an insistence on the condition that the body is male. In 1908 he was able to give a reason for this. In the case report on Little Hans (1909b) and in "On the Sexual Theories of Children" (1908c), two papers that he wrote in the summer of 1908, he advanced the hypothesis that in male homosexuality there was a fixation on the infantile over-estimation of the penis, and that all boys believed that their mothers had a penis (1908c, p. 215; 1909b, p. 109).[37] If the boy remained unable to revise this theory, women would become unacceptable as love objects because they lacked this "essential sexual attraction" (1908c, p. 216). Freud added that homosexuals' aversion to women also had something to do with the penis or its lack: women's lack of a penis would remind the boy of his castration anxiety, the main motive for turning away from women.[38] Thus Freud was not referring to disappointed love in the sense that Sadger meant it, but to castration anxiety.

In 1910 Freud did not address the insights he had gained from the discovery of the infantile sexual theories to his sexologist colleagues in general, but to the homosexual movement. He considered their humanitarian cause worthy of support, but rejected the theory of Hirschfeld, their leading representative. Hirschfeld's "theory of intermediate stages" postulates a continuum from pronounced heterosexuality to pronounced homosexuality, with bisexuality between the two. According to this theory, homosexuality is a non-pathological congenital sexual

---

[37] "On the Sexual Theories of Children" was published in December 1908, "Little Hans" at the beginning of 1909.

[38] In "Leonardo da Vinci" (1910c) Freud emphasises not only disappointment, but also *too much affection* on the part of the mother. His mother's unrequited need for love had been Leonardo's ruin: "After being kissed by her into precocious sexual maturity" he had been "robbed [...] of a part of his masculinity" (ibid., pp. 131, 117). He had unconsciously been fixated on his mother and as a homosexual he had remained true to her (ibid., pp. 100, 117).

variant, a kind of "third sex". Freud refers to this in his writings.[39] It is not possible to explore the background to Freud's sharp comments in the Leonardo paper (1910c) here. What is certain is that from about 1910 onwards, tensions arose between psychoanalysis and the homosexual movement. Whereas in 1908 Hirschfeld had published Sadger's "Fragment" and "Is Contrary Sexual Feeling Curable?" in his journals and prefaced them with some friendly remarks, after 1910 vehement attacks were levelled at the psychoanalytic theory of homosexuality in the *Jahrbuch für sexuelle Zwischenstufen*. Hirschfeld himself discussed the work of Sadger and Freud in 1914, rejected the psychological aetiology of homosexuality, and considered the assumption of an erotic fixation on the mother, in particular, to be incorrect.[40]

Although Freud wrote only a few lines on the fixation on the small boy's high regard for the penis and castration anxiety as factors involved in the aetiology of male homosexuality, they are of interest for several reasons. Despite the significance of their content they remained unheeded for many years. Sadger only mentioned the small boy's high regard for the penis in 1915 (Sadger, 1915, p. 23) and castration anxiety even as late as 1921 (1921, p. 137). He can hardly be reproached for this. Freud himself only returned to his above-mentioned insights into the aetiology of homosexuality in 1920, since it was only then that the ubiquitous and far-reaching significance of the castration complex was fully recognised (Freud, 1922b, p. 231). The remarks that Freud made in 1908 are relevant to our discussion mainly because they announce the imminent introduction of the concept of narcissism. Immediately after the above-mentioned lines on the fixation of the infantile high regard for the penis Freud wrote: "In the course of their development from auto-erotism to object-love, they [= the homosexuals] have remained at a point between the two" (1909b, p. 109).[41]

Here Freud states that due to the fixation on the concordance with the person himself or the person's own genitalia he does not consider the homosexual object choice to be the fully developed form of object love. On the other hand the homosexual object choice is also not pure

---

[39] Freud, 1910c, p. 98; see also the note on p. 99 that was added in 1919 and the footnote added in 1920 to the *Three Essays* (1905d/1920, p. 147).

[40] See Sadger, 1914b, 1915, 1921; Hirschfeld, 1914, pp. 244, 397–402, 493–495; Praetorius, 1910, 1911.

[41] Strachey's translation is not accurate. Freud did not think that the fixation occurred at any point, but at one that was "closer to autoerotism" (1909b, German edition: p. 95).

autoerotism, since "another" object is loved. Freud therefore postulated an intermediate stage, thus creating space for that quality of the object choice or its developmental stage between infantile autoerotism and object love that was soon to be called narcissistic.[42] The period that was closer to autoerotism did not yet have a name in 1908. However, it was already discernible what phenomena would be assigned to it—that is, those that Freud had noted in his studies on infantile sexual theories (in boys) and male homosexuality: first the egocentric (later: narcissistic) conviction that all human beings have the same sexual organs as oneself and second the also egocentric (later: narcissistic) preference for that sexual organ that is the same as one's own. Thus we can note that Freud's concept of narcissism was firmly established in his investigations on the infantile sexual theories (1908c).

The next step in the history of the theory of homosexuality can be briefly dealt with. In the *Minutes of the Vienna Psychoanalytic Society* dated May 1909 a remark by Freud was reported as follows:

> In some cases Freud came to know of the transition to homosexuality in a different way. A young boy, who, until well in pre-puberty, had been strongly attached to his mother and had no friends, suddenly felt hatred and jealousy toward other boys, because the beloved mother once praised another boy in his presence. In puberty the mother is repressed into the unconscious, which is accomplished by means of identification with her: from then on he too likes boys. (Min 2, pp. 257–258)

Here we have the second element of the aetiological formula of 1910, the identification with the mother, for the first time in the *Minutes*. The idea of attributing the turn to the love object of the same sex to identification with the female probably came from Freud himself.[43] Up to this point Sadger had not made any reference to identification with the

---

[42] Hints can already be found in November 1907: "It [= the homosexual component] lies on a deeper level, and therefore is closer to autoerotism than is heterosexuality" (Min 1, p. 245).

[43] The editors of the *Minutes* were of the opinion that Sadger was elaborating on Freud's remark in "Zur Aetiologie der konträren Sexualempfindung" (Sadger, 1909c; Min 2, p. 258, fn. 1). That was probably not the case, since Sadger's paper was already published in January 1909, whereas Freud's remark was recorded in May 1909. Moreover, there is no reference to identification with the female in "Zur Ätiologie der konträren Sexualempfindung".

mother as a woman. He had mentioned a role-play-like identification with the mother, but restricted this to her bodily care and teaching activities.[44] In the above quotation Freud presents a more complex concept of identification. The female identification includes a lasting internal change in sexual identity, and explains the homosexual's tendency towards men in a plausible way. Sadger adopted this thesis from Freud (Min 2, p. 305).

We can break off our reconstruction of the beginnings of the theory of homosexuality at this point. We have established to which studies and communications Freud was referring when he spoke of new insights into homosexuality in 1910. We have clarified which thoughts on the aetiology of male homosexuality are attributable to Sadger and which to Freud. We have also found precursors of the concept of narcissism in Freud's perception of children's sexual theories (in boys) and the dynamics of male homosexuality: the fixation to the high esteem for the penis, the homosexual's fixation to the similarity with his own body and own genitalia and the specific quality of the relationship to the love object which he located between autoerotism and object love. Only *one* element of the aetiological formula is still missing, namely the explicit recognition of the narcissistic quality of the homosexual object choice.

10 November 1909

We will now have no difficulty in assessing the events of 10 November 1909, that evening when Freud spoke *explicitly* of narcissism in the Vienna Psychoanalytic Society for the first time. Sadger presented the second of three parts of a case report that he published in 1910 under the title "A Case of Multiple Perversion with Hysterical Absences" (1910d).[45] The publication was seventy-four pages long and presents the case of a thirty-two-year-old man cured of his absences after five months of analysis. According to Sadger, his homosexual tendencies had also undergone considerable transformation. In contrast to his presentation in the "Fragment" (1908a), this time Sadger did not describe the course of the analysis, reporting only the "results", that is, the story

[44] Freud later mentioned Leonardo's motherly relationships towards his students (1910c, p. 102); he may have owed this perception to Sadger.

[45] He held the two other lectures on 3 November 1909 and 5 January 1910. The thirty-two-year-old Swedish baron presented in the lecture became a thirty-two-year-old Danish count in the publication.

of the patient's various sexual interests. They did not cause the patient any suffering and he played them out relatively without hindrance. In the discussion Freud permitted himself the remark that "this patient is an absolute swine, a case of infantile and homologously inflated sexuality" (Min 2, p. 379), a statement that is included in Sadger's published text (1910d, p. 114). Sadger included "narcissism" in his enumeration of the patients' sexual "perversions" and described, for example, the classical narcissistic symptom of masturbation in front of the mirror (ibid., p. 102).

Freud's remark begins with an acknowledgement of Sadger's contribution: "Sadger's comment with regard to narcissism seems new and valuable. This is not an isolated phenomenon but a necessary developmental stage" and so on (Min 2, p. 312). The "comment" that Freud was referring to was a passage in which Sadger summarised his insights into male homosexuality, repeating the aspects that were already known: disappointment in the beloved mother, the turn to men who introduce the young man to love, as he had previously wanted his mother to do, the identification with the mother, and the formation of specific sexual ideals (Min 2, pp. 306–307). Sadger's comments on the formation of the ideal are recorded in the *Minutes* of 10 November as follows:

> In the types of people that the person loves one can recognize, in addition to the characteristics of the individuals who are loved homosexually or heterosexually, traits also of the person himself. Another of Sadger's patients still loves the type that evolved in him at the time when he came to do without the love for his mother. At the bottom of this kind of narcissism, there seems to be a flight from the mother who is no longer [toward him] the mother who once admired and loved him. (Min 2, p. 307)

Here we have Sadger's observation to which Freud was referring. It was that the sexual ideals of homosexuals did not merely, as Sadger had already reported in 1908, show characteristics of earlier love objects, including the mother, alone, but also *similarities with themselves*. As a result it was himself that the homosexual loved in his love object, that is, narcissism was involved. Sadger understood narcissistic love of oneself as a "flight" to the mother who had once been loving. But what exactly was "new and valuable"? I believe that this new and valuable aspect only became visible after Freud had revised Sadger's comments and transformed them into an insight of major significance.

Sadger's achievement lay in the fact that he had seen narcissism at a point where it had not yet been discovered, in the sexual ideal or in the relationship to the love object that is loved because of the similarity to oneself. Without being aware of it, he understood narcissism on the one hand as the actual observable act of sexual gratification (for example, masturbation in front of the mirror), but on the other hand as a covert, unconscious gratification that occurred in the relationship to the love object who was experienced as similar. Sadger himself believed that his statement was a contribution to the theory of homosexuality. In his view, he had noted the similarity between the sexual ideal of the homosexual and the homosexual himself and thus discovered his narcissism. In itself, this finding—that male homosexuals love themselves in their love objects—was not yet significant and would probably have been forgotten, had not Freud singled it out among many other statements of Sadger's and modified it in a way that was decisive.

Freud's modifications on 10 November 1909 were first, that he did not consider narcissism to be a perversion, but a *normal* and even central phenomenon of psychic development; second, that he did not see it as a symptom that concealed something else—in Sadger's conceptualisation the relationship to the mother. For Freud narcissism was, similarly to autoerotism, on the contrary, an irreducible, *primary given* that was just as important as the love of the primary caregiver, the mother. To the love of the mother Freud now added the love of oneself; and to the mother as a primary sexual object he added the person himself (or, as Freud preferred to say, his "ego"). To the developmental task of separating from the mother he added the task of moving on from loving oneself and one's products. To the idea that object choice is guided by similarity to the love objects of infancy he added the idea that we seek and choose objects that are similar to ourselves.[46] To the stages of autoerotism and object-love he added the stage of narcissism.

On 10 November 1909 Freud only informed the participants of the Vienna Group of the "introduction" of narcissism. In the two papers published 1910 in which he spoke of narcissism for the first time (1910c,

[46] The terms "narcissistic object choice" and "anaclitic object choice" were published in "On Narcissism: An Introduction" (1914c, p. 87). However, the distinction is already contained in the *Minutes* of the meeting on 10 November 1909.

1905d/1910), he was still presenting it as a phenomenon associated with *male homosexuality,* and only two years after the first oral communication did he publish the notion of narcissism as a *normal* phenomenon and a phase of normal psychic development in the Schreber case (Freud, 1911c, p. 60).[47] Neither in the *Minutes* of Sadger's lecture nor in Sadger's paper (1910d) do we find any indication that Sadger had any thoughts about how his observations and impressions were related to psychoanalytic theory. Sadger could, for example, have seen that the similarity between the sexual ideal and the self that he had observed stood in contradiction to the theory of object choice.

The quotation on the sexual ideal of homosexuals above was taken from the *Minutes*. The corresponding passage in Sadger's paper is followed by a paragraph that is puzzling:

> Here we are addressing a quite new point which I consider decisive for the genesis of inversion: *the road to homosexuality always leads via narcissism, that is, self-love*. I have been able to demonstrate this in all of my cases and Freud has also confirmed it in response to my question about his homosexual patients. Narcissism is not simply an isolated phenomenon, but a necessary developmental stage in the transition from autoerotism to later object love. Love of one's own ego, behind which is the love of one's own genitalia, is a developmental stage that is never missing. Only after traversing it do we proceed to objects which are similar to our own ego. In general human beings have two primary, original sexual objects and how their lives continue depends on whether and on which of these they finally remain fixated. For men these two objects are the mother [...] and themselves [...]. Homosexuality then branches off and the sexual object is chosen in accordance with the person's own ideal, both the real one and the idealised one. (Sadger, 1910d, pp. 111–112)

If we compare this passage with Freud's first remark on narcissism that he made on 10 November 1909 we see that Sadger quoted Freud's remarks from the *Minutes* in his publication, with small modifications and without giving the source. The statements in the above quotation,

---

[47] Freud left the question as to when this stage occurs open until 1914 (see Min 4, p. 148). In Rank's 1911 essay on narcissism it is given as being at the beginning of puberty (1911b, p. 401), also in a review by Sadger that was published in 1914 (1914a, p. 311).

which were actually made by *Freud*, begin "Narcissism is not simply [...]" and go on for several lines after the quotation.

We need not necessarily see the passage in Sadger's publication as plagiarism. Having agreed to practise a kind of "intellectual communism" the members of the Vienna group, including Freud, placed their ideas at each other's disposal (Min 1, p. 302). Sadger's behaviour would, however, still seem somewhat audacious. His paper was, after all, published in February 1910, *before* Freud's Leonardo study and roughly at the same time as the second edition of the *Three Essays*.[48] If we did not know about the discussions in the Vienna group we might believe that Sadger's statements on narcissism were his own. However, once again, Sadger's contribution consisted merely in the observation that the sexual ideals of homosexuals are similar to themselves and they thus love themselves in their partners, that is, exhibit the symptom of narcissism. It was Freud who was responsible for this observation becoming part of the theory of the aetiology of homosexuality of 1910. At the time when he made his first remark on narcissism he was working on his essay on Leonardo da Vinci (1910c) and presented a draft of this study to the Vienna Group three weeks after Sadger had given his lecture (Min 2, pp. 338–346). In it he stated that the aspects of the aetiology of homosexuality that had already been established also applied in the case of Leonardo.[49] He reiterated his agreement with Sadger's finding of an erotic fixation on the mother, recapitulated the mechanism of identification with the mother and added the mechanism of the (narcissistic) object choice that he had just discovered. With that the understanding of the aetiology of male homosexuality had reached the stage of development that it had in 1910, as published in "Leonardo da Vinci and a Memory of his Childhood" and in the second edition of the *Three Essays*. We have thus arrived at the starting point of our investigation.

We have been able to reconstruct part of the background to Freud's first published mentions of narcissism and also to clarify what was Sadger's and what was Freud's contribution. Freud mentioned narcissism in the Leonardo study and in the *Three Essays*, together with the initial results of the research on homosexuality, because the (narcissistic)

---

[48] Regarding the dates of publication see Strachey's editorial remarks (1957a, p. 60) and F/A, p. 101; F/Ju, pp. 296, 301.

[49] They possibly also applied to a patient whom Freud was treating at the time and whom he described as Leonardo's "image and likeness" (F/Ju, p. 255).

object choice that was guided by similarity to the love object had been observed in male homosexuals for the first time—by Sadger. And thus it was Sadger who took the first step towards the psychoanalytic concept of narcissism. The actual introduction of the concept of narcissism was then carried out by Freud.

The remark that Freud made on 10 November 1909 gives the impression of being so definite, condensed, and well thought through that it is hard to believe that it only came into being on that evening. As mentioned above, in mid-1908 Freud had already spoken about a stage between autoerotism and object love which he considered to be characterised by special regard for the child's own genitalia. He had noted the phenomenon in his studies on infantile sexual theories and homosexuality. On 10 November he built on these impressions. He had also come across the phenomenon of high regard for the self and for one's own mental processes in the analysis of the rat man where he discovered a belief in the "omnipotence of thoughts". Additionally, in his investigations on the psychoses he had gained the impression that the psychoses could be distinguished from the neuroses by a regression to autoerotism or a return to the over-valuation of the self, to the "old megalomania of infancy" (1909d, p. 234).[50] Sadger's findings fitted into this train of thought well. It also referred to self-love and high regard for the self and provided an explanation for the introduction of a phase of development that Freud had been thinking about for some time. In this respect Sadger's remark was "valuable".

For Freud narcissism was the central characteristic of a stage of psychological development that followed autoerotism. It was still very close to autoerotism and was distinguished from it by the fact that the sexual drives were now directed towards an "object", the ego, whereas autoerotism was seen as being objectless. A further difference between autoerotism and narcissism was that the former has to do with the *erotic enjoyment* of the infant's own body. The prototypes are sensual sucking, anal and genital masturbation. In contrast, narcissism refers *to the value* attached to the subject's own body, its products and person. Thus one could contrast the erotic, sensual pleasurable enjoyment that is associated with the erotogenic zones with the equally important feeling of uniqueness, value, and high regard. From this perspective, Freud

---

[50] Freud, 1955a, pp. 260, 279, 299; Min 1, pp. 55–56, 109; see also F/A, p. 2, Freud's manuscript on paranoia dated April 1907 (F/Ju, pp. 38–40) and the article published by Abraham (1908) that was inspired by Freud's suggestions.

radically transformed the concepts of narcissism developed by Näcke and Ellis. Freud's narcissism would then no longer be a form of self-arousal (Ellis), a technique of masturbation, or a perversion (Näcke), but a stage of normal development, characterised by the distinctive feature that the subject adopts the position of the love-object.

The sexologists were astonished by Freud's redefinition. This is understandable because "narcissism" had a different, fixed meaning in that discipline. It was seen as a mode of sexual gratification: orgasm at the sight of or on imagining the person's own body. From the sexological viewpoint there was no reason why this specific form of sexual arousal should be the main characteristic of a developmental phase. What the sexologists overlooked or failed to consider was that Freud's definition of narcissism was much broader and not restricted to manifest sexual behaviour.

Sadger would not have been able to introduce the concept of narcissism. He lacked the genius and authority of Freud, and also a more profane willingness to reconsider his observations. He simply reported them without making the effort to define more precisely their "position [...] within the system", as Freud put it (Min 2, p. 256). The work of assessing the weight of observations and examining how they related to the current state of knowledge was often neglected, not only by Sadger. When we read the early psychoanalytic essays or the *Minutes of the Vienna Psychoanalytic Society*, it is perplexing to see how many thoughts and observations were brought up and immediately disappeared again, only gaining importance again many years or decades later. In some cases this was because their implications for the theory were not thought through. Sadger's observation would presumably also have suffered the same fate and been forgotten had Freud not selected it from among the dozens of "observations" and impressions of Sadger's and assigned it a place in the theory.

On the other hand, the history of psychoanalytic theory is anything but a linear sequence of brilliant theoretical ideas of Freud's. As we have shown here, for a very small segment of it, the development of the theory followed a very serpentine course and was influenced both by the state of the art in the field of medicine and other adjoining disciplines as well as the issues that concerned the public and society at the time, and not least by the exchanges between Freud and his followers. In this sense Sadger did, despite his shortcomings, play a role in shaping the history of psychoanalytic theory.

Translated by Deirdre Winter

CHAPTER TWO

Abraham's discovery of the "bad mother": a contribution to the history of the theory of depression

The theory of depression has a history of its own, the beginnings of which will be described in this chapter. I start with a consideration of the efforts at theorisation dating from the period before 1911. These include both Freud's essays from the 1890s and the publications of his pupils in the period after 1900, as well as the 1910 discussion of student suicide in the Vienna Psychoanalytic Society. I then turn to the next important step in the history of the theory, Abraham's study of Giovanni Segantini published in 1911. A central facet of this paper is the idea of the "bad mother", or of repressed hate for the mother, as a pathogenic factor in the aetiology of depression. Abraham's view of the mother-son relationship is compared with that of Freud and also placed in the context of the contemporary debate within the Vienna Group. Next I consider the fate of Abraham's conceptualisation of the mother-son relationship up to 1924. The inner worlds of Freud and Abraham, or, as we might say, the aspects of their inner worlds imparted to us in their publications, are here seen to differ fundamentally.

Contributions to the theory of depression in the period to 1911

Freud's somatic theory of depression (1893–1900)

The fact that Freud quite often saw depressive patients is evident from his "neurasthenia project", planned at the beginning of 1893 (Schröter, 1988). The intention was to compare 100 patients suffering from anxiety neurosis, an equal number of neurasthenic patients, and subjects with "the much rarer periodic mild depression" with each other and with non-neurotic people (F/Fl, p. 44; see May[-Tolzmann], 1996, p. 104). A few depressive patients are mentioned in Freud's publications from this time and in the letters to Fließ: five patients with *predominantly* depressive symptomatology (Freud & Breuer, 1895d, p. 163; F/Fl, pp. 68, 93, 226, 341) and three others who exhibited both depressive and other symptoms (F/Fl, pp. 90, 92, 239; Freud & Breuer, 1895d, p. 106).

We know that during the 1890s Freud was using the theses of contemporary psychiatry and neuropathology as the basis for an etiological theory of the neuroses and psychoses in which depression was also to have a place (F/Fl, pp. 43, 44). An example is the fairly long theoretical Draft G of 1895 which Freud sent to Fließ (ibid., pp. 98–105). In it, depressive mood disturbances are included not among the neuroses of psychic origin but essentially among those with *sexual-somatic* causation (ibid., pp. 37, 43, 80, 216; see also 1892–1893, p. 117). These neuroses were attributed to inappropriate discharge of somatic sexual excitation. Their nature—that is, the somatic mechanisms that lead to depression and its subsidiary forms—is comprehensively discussed in Draft G. For example, the production of sexual excitation is stated to come entirely to a halt in severe depression, whereas the depression associated with anxiety neurosis is ascribed to a conversion of sexual excitation into depressive affect; the neurasthenic form of depression, for its part, is attributed to a diminution of sexual excitability due to excessive masturbation. Freud did not publish this theory, no doubt because he was not entirely satisfied with it. Nor, however, did he think it wrong, for he communicated it to the circle then forming around him. Around 1910, it was still being propounded by Hitschmann and Federn (cf., Min 2, pp. 298, 505; Min 3, p. 90); similarly, in 1914 it still plays an important part in a paper by Ferenczi on the aetiology of depression (Ferenczi, 1914a).

The sources dating from the 1890s include no more than a few lines in which Freud deems melancholia to be *partly due to psychic factors*.

The relevant passages are contained in the famous oedipus manuscript of May 1897 (F/Fl, pp. 250–252). Here he states in essence that melancholia arises when death wishes (due to oedipal rivalry) directed towards the parent of the same sex are repressed. However, this psychological approach did not then occupy a prominent position, and it must therefore be accepted that in the 1890s Freud was concerned mainly with developing a somatic theory of depression (further isolated psychogenic indications from the period around 1900 may be found in F/Fl, pp. 239, 341; see also 1896b, p. 171; 1905e, p. 54, fn. 1).

It is an open question why Freud did not propose a distinctively psychological means of access to depression from the outset, as he had for hysteria, obsessional neurosis, and the schizophrenic psychoses, previously describing their specifically psychic mechanisms (conversion, substitution, projection, etc.) in work published in the 1890s. I do not wish to speculate here on whether and to what extent the history of the mapping of the unconscious has anything to do with the structure of Freud's personality. Instead, I should like to draw attention to Freud's own statements on the matter. For example, he took the view that the periodicity of depression was indicative of a somatic causation (F/Fl, pp. 99, 226): if depressions came and went with autonomous regularity, psychic causes could not play an important part. Another reason for the preference given to somatic theories might lie in Freud's experiences during the 1880s. At that time, cocaine had helped him to combat depressive mood disturbances and other neurasthenic complaints such as dyspepsia and headaches (Hirschmüller, 1996, p. 33), possibly suggesting to him that depressive moods were caused and cured by substances.

I regard Freud's relationship with Flieβ as another reason. In the second half of the 1890s, Flieβ was working on a theory to the effect that neurotic symptoms, including mood swings, as well as creative work, pregnancy, birth and death, were due to the periodic production of hypothetical sexual substances. Freud supported Flieβ in his investigations, which fitted in well with his own theory of the neuroses of sexual-somatic origin. Freud sent him records of the dates of his own "critical" days—that is, those on which he himself suffered from ill humour or migraine and depression (cf., F/Fl, pp. 373, 378). In this connection he informed Fließ on several occasions that he considered it likely that his mood disturbances were periodic in character and occurred without psychic causation (ibid., pp. 378, 386, 389). Fließ will have been open to such confirmations and may well have encouraged Freud in his inclination to attribute his bad moods to non-psychic (somatic/sexual/periodic) causes.

We now find this confusing because we associate the aspect of *psychic* aetiology with Freud's name and tend to deem "good" those theoretical approaches that stress the psychogenic rather than the somatogenic character of symptoms (Rosenberg, 1962). This prejudice underlies, for example, Kris's remark that "Freud naturally soon found this attempt [contained in Draft G] to derive 'melancholia' from a reaction to sexual excitation insufficient" (1950a, p. 101). Strachey's statement that the "purely neurological" conception of Draft G "was soon replaced by a psychological approach to the subject" [of melancholia] (1957b, p. 239) also lacks a convincing foundation of evidence. At any rate, twenty years were to pass before Freud found a psychic mechanism for depression and published his account in "Mourning and Melancholia" (1917e).

Freud's treatment of J. v. T. (1907–1909)

Freud had little to say about the genesis of depression during the period around the turn of the twentieth century. Apart from the position he took in the discussion of student suicide (1910, see below), there is only one source for his view of depression at the time—namely, the correspondence with Ludwig Binswanger. Here Freud several times mentions J. v. T., a young homosexual man suffering from manic-depressive mood swings.

This patient had been in treatment with Freud from the beginning of 1907 until early 1909 and was admitted to Binswanger's Bellevue Sanatorium in January 1909 (and on a further two occasions in subsequent years) owing to the risk of suicide (F/Bi, p. 19, fn. 1). Freud's reports to Binswanger indicate that he assumed J. v. T.'s mood swings to have hereditary causes (see, for example, p. 7) and that they were reinforced or triggered only secondarily by psychic factors, by the struggle against masturbation, for example (ibid., pp. 7, 31, 34). Freud alluded only cursorily and in a small number of passages to a psychic aetiology (ibid., pp. 7–8, 26).

Publications by Freud's pupils and colleagues (up to 1911)

Not only Freud but also his pupils were seeking to understand depression. Their work can be understood only in the context of the particularities of contemporary nosology. For example, there are contributions by Gross (1907) and Ferenczi (1908) that promise a psychoanalytic view of "manic-depressive" pathology. Closer examination shows that the diagnoses used in these studies are based on Kraepelin's systematisation. However, according to Kraepelin, hallucinations, delusions of persecution and megalomania belonged to the picture of manic-depressive insanity. This means that the cases presented by Gross and Ferenczi involved pathologies that we would now classify among the schizophrenias and not the depressions. The same applies to Jones's paper "Psycho-analytic Notes on a Case of Hypomania" (1909): this too was not mania as we understand it today (on the debate about the diagnoses, see Bleuler & Jung, 1908, p. 225; Maeder, 1911; Jones, 1911; Ferenczi, 1908).

Maeder's paper (1910) is different. His case was diagnosed in accordance with Bleuler's nosology and would be seen even today as a depression. He describes a cure within four analytic sessions, but fails to give a theoretical account of the process and to formulate hypotheses about the aetiology of depression, so that his contribution after all remains insubstantial. Another paper dating from this time is mentioned here only for the sake of completeness: it is Brill's (1911) study of a depression "of psychogenic origin". As Abraham remarks in his review paper (1914, p. 354), it is diagnostically too confused.

In the period up to 1911, it was probably Stekel who came closest to a psychological theory of depression. In his book *Nervöse Angstzustände* (1908), he reported on the analytic treatment of two patients who would even today be regarded as depressives (pp. 249–261). On the one hand, his theoretical derivation was in line with Freud's early notions of the 1890s, as he observed an underlying anxiety neurosis in one case and an "actual neurosis" in the other. On the other hand, he asserted in relation to the psychic aetiology that unresolved conflicts concerning "motives of love" were responsible for the depression (1908, p. 259). The hypostatisation of psychic conflicts was the distinguishing feature of Stekel's theoretical standpoint. Whereas Freud considered psychic conflict to be the cause of *some* neuroses and symptoms, Stekel tended to ascribe *all* neuroses and psychoses to conflict. In the discussion about Stekel's treatment of depression, one of Freud's criticisms was that Stekel had "neglected to investigate the psychic mechanism" of depression (Min 1, p. 280; see also Min 2, p. 182). By this he meant that Stekel was unable to specify *why and by what psychic pathway (or defensive process)* the psychic conflict led to depressive rather than, say, hysterical or obsessional symptoms. This, in my view, is the main reason why his contribution could not be acknowledged as innovative.

The discussions about student suicide (1910)

In view of the foregoing, it is virtually self-evident that the discussion of the problem of student suicide that occupied the Vienna Group for two evenings in April 1910 could not lead to new discoveries (Min 2, pp. 479–506; Diskussionen, 1910), but produced only isolated insights. For example, Freud considered that identification with a loved person who had also committed suicide played a part in such cases; other motives might be self-reproach and anxiety at unconscious incestuous wishes (Min 2, p. 493). Sadger saw unrequited love—especially the student's homosexual love for his teacher/father—as an important reason (1909c, p. 492). One of the grounds for suicide adduced by Stekel was guilt feelings due to death wishes: "No one kills himself who did not wish to kill another, or at least wish for another's death" (Diskussionen, 1910, p. 33). All these theories were not "wrong", but so to speak too short, for they each comprised only a single proposition and were unable to answer the decisive question of why unrequited love or guilt feelings due to death wishes should lead to a depression and not to other symptoms—in other words, as Freud put it, what was lacking was insight into the "mechanism". Freud was not afraid to admit that nothing could yet be said about suicide. This was because no theory of depression was so far available: "at the moment nothing is known about its nature; its mechanism, especially, has not yet been studied at all" (Min 2, p. 505; see Freud, 1910g, p. 232). This statement dates from April 1910 and may be assumed to reflect correctly the status of the psychoanalytic exploration of depression at the time.

Abraham's Segantini (1911)

After these fruitless efforts, Abraham's "Giovanni Segantini. A Psychoanalytical Study" (1911) comes as a relief. The Segantini study has hitherto been assigned to the field of *applied* psychoanalysis (Jones, 1926a, p. 32; Cremerius, 1969, p. 32). However, I contend that it contains a new, differentiated, and surprising approach to a theory of depression, making it the earliest published psychoanalytic contribution on the subject.

This would mean that the theory of depression was—perhaps uniquely—first developed not by Freud but by one of his pupils, Abraham.

Dating of the Segantini paper

Abraham first mentions his interest in the personality and work of the painter Giovanni Segantini in a letter of 14 February 1909 (F/A, p. 81). About two years elapsed before the Segantini study was completed in February 1911—"an unusually long interval" according to his daughter, Hilda Abraham (1974, p. 41). What took so long may have been the necessary internal psychic work. This is consistent with Abraham's sending the manuscript to Freud "with a request for your criticism", which, he added, was "particularly necessary to me this time, as it is a piece of work with some personal complexes behind it" (F/A, p. 126). In May 1911, the study appeared as Monograph 11 of the *Schriften zur angewandten Seelenkunde* [Writings on Applied Psychology].

In September 1911 Abraham spoke at the Third International Psychoanalytic Congress on "The Psychosexual Foundation of States of Depression and Exaltation". The revised paper was published in May 1912 (1912b). This publication is generally regarded as Abraham's *first* contribution on the theory and therapy of depression (Jones, 1926a, p. 24; Cremerius, 1969, pp. 24–25). However, it must yield this priority to the Segantini paper, which was composed and published before it.

Segantini's mother pictures

Giovanni Segantini (1858–1899) was one of the best-known painters at the turn of the twentieth century. He was an Alpine painter with a preference for rural and rustic subjects. Many of his pictures show mothers—"good", loving, and tender ones as well as "bad" ones (see Quinsac, 1982, p. 442)—who are depicted with their small children and babies, and sometimes also with their dead children or at a child's grave. Segantini himself tells us (1909) how enormously important the maternal was for him. He contrasts the "good" mother with the vain, lustful woman and the wicked, bad mother.

Between 1891 and 1897 he painted six pictures on the theme of the "bad mother", which are grouped together as the Nirvana cycle (Quinsac, 1982, p. 476). We know from Abraham's daughter Hilda that her father rated Segantini very highly and gave his wife prints of the master's pictures—of *Ave Maria a trasbordo* and of *The Fruit of Love*, which shows a mother with her baby (H. Abraham, 1974, p. 43).

Abraham accompanied the study of Segantini with two pictures, *The Two Mothers (Zwei Mütter/Le due madri*, 1889, Galleria d'Arte Moderna, Milan) and *The Wicked Mothers (Die bösen Mütter/Le cattive madri*, 1894, Kunsthistorisches Museum, Vienna). *The Two Mothers* shows a woman, illuminated by the light of a lamp in a cowshed with a sleeping baby on her lap, and beside her a cow with a little calf—in its atmosphere most certainly a depiction of two "good" mothers (Abraham, 1911, p. 234). In the picture *The Wicked Mothers*, included only in the German and not in the English edition, a woman has become caught in a tree by her hair and is suspended above the ground (see Illustration 1). In her arms she holds a baby who is drinking at her bare breast. A distant procession of veiled figures can be seen in the background (Abraham, 1971, p. 304).

Illustration 1. Giovanni Segantini: The wicked mothers (1894). Österreichische Galerie, Wien.

Segantini's biographer Servaes writes of this picture:

> The whole curve of the body is one of weeping lamentation; the outstretched arms convey a feeling of helpless despair; the streaming hair entangled in the tree suggests the suffering of a suicide; and the deathly pale face, the twisted mouth, the sunken eyes are

> eloquent of the torments of remorse. The sight of the head of the little abandoned child, vainly seeking sustenance at the naked breast of the mother, cold and dried up in lovelessness, is most moving. (1907, quoted from Abraham, 1911, p. 239)

Problems with the English edition of Abraham's Segantini study

After its first appearance in the *Psychoanalytic Quarterly* (1937), the English translation of the Segantini study was published in *Clinical Papers and Essays on Psycho-Analysis* (Abraham, 1955). It includes the same good-mother picture as the German edition, but a *different* bad-mother example, *The Hell of the Voluptuaries* (ibid., p. 238). That is the title printed under the picture. The correct title, *Punishment of Luxury (II castigo delle lussuriose*; see Quinsac, 1982, p. 477) is given elsewhere (Abraham, 1955, p. 8); this is the title by which the picture is known at its home in the Walker Art Gallery, Liverpool. It shows two recumbent female figures floating above the earth (without a baby). The background landscape, an empty wilderness with withered trees, is similar in both pictures. The choice of *Punishment of Luxury* was justified as far as it belongs to the same series of Nirvana pictures as the one in the German edition. However, from today's standpoint and in terms of the history of theory, the choice of this picture has the disadvantage that, in both title and subject matter, it does not constitute as clear a counterpart to *The Two Mothers* as the German edition's *The Wicked Mothers (Die bösen Mütter).*

A similar blurring of content is evident in the text of the study. Abraham refers consistently to the "*schlechte Mutter*" (literally, the "bad mother") or the "*böse Mutter*" (literally, the wicked, evil or angry mother)—in describing little Giovanni's experiences of his mother; in relation to the mothers in Segantini's pictures; and also, of course, in the names of the relevant pictures (Abraham, 1971, p. 302, twice on p. 303, three times on pp. 304, 305, 310, 311, 326, and twice on p. 327). A German reader versed in psychoanalysis is bound to associate the adjectives *böse* and *schlecht*, where applied to the mother, with the "good" and "bad" mothers of later theories. In the English edition, on the other hand, the reference is usually to the "wicked mother" (1955, p. 239, twice on pp. 241, 242, 260), and only twice to the "bad mother" (p. 240). The picture title *Le cattive madri* has also been rendered as *The Wicked Mothers* (twice on pp. 239, 245, 246, 260). It seems to me that the association with the "good mother" and the "bad mother" is thus rendered less insistent, although, as I shall show below, it is very apt.

For readers of Abraham's text who may be puzzled by contradictions in the picture titles given, I can explain that it was an idiosyncrasy of Segantini to give a picture not just one title but several. For example, the bad-mother picture contained in the German edition, for which the designation *Die bösen Mütter* has come to be accepted in German-language art history, is also known by four other titles, including *Die schlechten Mütter*. This title is also used several times by Abraham. The bad-mother picture in the English edition has three titles (Quinsac, 1982, pp. 47, 482). Even more confusingly, Segantini used the same title for a number of pictures, so that, for instance, several other pictures are also entitled *The Two Mothers*. Again, according to Quinsac, "lussuria" was wrongly rendered as "luxury" in the translation of the title of the Liverpool bad-mother picture (p. 477).[1] However, none of this affects the only salient point here, namely that the title *Die bösen Mütter* appears under the picture reproduced in the German edition, whereas that in the English edition is entitled *The Hell of the Voluptuaries or Punishment of Luxury*.

Notes on Segantini's life

Abraham based his interpretation of the life and work of Segantini on the biography by Franz Servaes (1907) and on a posthumously published collection of the painter's letters and texts (Segantini, 1909). We have known since the appearance of Quinsac's publications (1982, 1985) that both sources contain a number of inaccuracies, originally put about by Segantini himself. Ultimately, however, this is irrelevant for our purposes. Even if the picture of the artist formed by Abraham was wrong in some respects, in his exploration of the material available to him he nevertheless developed ideas that have remained of interest to this day. From the material on Segantini's life, I shall now select a small number of details—those important to Abraham's interpretation of the painter's depressive and manic mood disturbances. In so doing, I shall not distinguish between correct and false information.

---

[1] Translator's note: The word actually means "voluptuousness" or "lust", which is an archaic sense of "luxury" in English. "Lussuriose" literally means "female voluptuaries".

Giovanni Segantini was born near Trento, Italy, in 1858 and lost his mother when he was five years old. He believed that she had been physically harmed by his birth and had later died of this injury. An earlier son of Segantini's parents had died in a fire before Giovanni was born. After the death of Segantini's mother, his father left the village and entrusted little Giovanni to relations. Left alone for long periods, he ran away several times and was sent to a reformatory, but was apprenticed to a painter and eventually became known as a painter himself. He suffered all his life from mood swings—now melancholy, now the enthusiastic joy of creation. From the valley he moved successively higher and higher up into the mountains, finally settling in the Upper Engadine, where he died relatively unexpectedly at the age of only 41 while working on a picture of the high Alps in 1899.

Abraham inferred from Segantini's autobiography that the painter cherished the memory of his mother with great love. She "became idealised into a goddess" (1911, p. 214). He had spoken of her like a "lover speaking of his lost beloved" (p. 215). At the same time he had felt guilty about her death. This was suggested not only by his own account of his birth but also by a description of the origins of his artistic career included in his autobiography. Here Segantini (1909) wrote that, as a boy, he had once been asked to draw the dead child of a young mother:

> The beautiful tear-filled eyes of the young mother turned towards me. She said nothing, but went to her room, and I followed her. In a cradle lay the body of a tiny girl, who could not have been much more than a year old. The mother handed me paper and pencil, and I began. I worked for several hours, as the mother wished me to draw the child as if she were still alive. I do not know whether my picture was an artistic success, but I remember that for a moment the poor woman looked so happy that she seemed to forget her grief. (Quoted in Abraham, 1911, p. 219)

According to Segantini himself, this experience might have induced him to become an artist.

Abraham's interpretation of the depressive mood disturbances

From Abraham's long and highly complex text, I shall single out the strand of reflections that relate to the analytic examination of

Segantini's depressive mood swings and that associate them with the repression of the image of the bad mother. All other aspects will have to be disregarded.

Abraham attributed the depressive and manic mood swings to the "mother complex" (1911, p. 234). By this he meant—in exactly the same sense as Freud—the erotic and tender oedipal wishes directed by boys towards their mothers. Badly disappointed in this respect, Segantini had conceived wishes for revenge on his mother and for her death. As evidence for this contention Abraham adduces the story of his first drawing, as reproduced above: "In the scene just described, the sadistic impulse finds satisfaction in the contemplation of the child's dead body, and of the mother's grief" (ibid., p. 220). In Abraham's view, little Giovanni had observed his mother's mourning over his dead brother, had hated her in consequence and had felt sadistic satisfaction at the perception of her pain (ibid., p. 246). In addition, she had abandoned him through her death—another reason for the feeling of not having been loved by her. A further source of the infantile hate, according to Abraham, was the presumed (oedipal) rivalry with the father: the boy had the feeling that the mother loved the father more than she did him (ibid., p. 241). In addition, following Freud (1909d, p. 237), Abraham assumed that the intense infantile hatred also had its origins in constitutionally powerful sadism (1911, p. 240).

Abraham considered, too, that the impulses of hate—as described by Freud (1905d)—were repressed at the end of childhood together with the libidinal wishes and could recur in adulthood upon a loosening of the repression. This process underlay the picture *Die bösen Mütter*. As Segantini himself stated, he wanted to punish "the bad mothers [...] and the vain and barren voluptuaries" by means of such pictures (1909, p. 42). Abraham writes:

> Now he depicted cruel punishment in the hereafter! And it was for mothers that such punishment was reserved! Here we see the early hostile impulses, the child's death wishes against his own mother, returning from repression [...] Behind his wish to punish bad mothers in general now appears *the unconscious desire to punish his own mother and to take revenge upon her*. (1911, p. 240; italics and exclamation marks only in the German edition)

Segantini was avenging himself on the mother by banishing her, in the picture, to the desolate snowfields.

Before continuing, I should like to point out that the English translation omits throughout the entire text the emphases marked by Abraham, as well as the exclamation marks after "hereafter" and "reserved". This editorial measure obliterates Abraham's intentional stressing of certain statements and a certain excitement. The highly animated and involved style that is in my view characteristic of the Segantini text is thereby lost; this is particularly regrettable because we find such excitement in Abraham surprising and out of keeping with the image we have formed of him.

Let us now return to Abraham. He wrote that the repressed hate could be replaced by its opposite, excessive goodness, resulting in Segantini's "cult of motherhood" and the pictures that portrayed an excessively good mother (1911, p. 218). The depressive guilt feelings inferred by Abraham from the painter's comment that he had caused his mother's death were due to the infantile hate. This could be turned against the subject's own person (ibid., p. 232). However, it might also have the consequence of impulses for "*Gutmachen*" (reparation; rendered in the English translation as "to make amends"). Segantini's artistic creation was an attempt at reparation for the harm he had done to his mother through his phantasies:

> *For the sake of a mother he becomes an artist* [...] he tries to make amends to a strange mother for the wrong he has done to his own mother by his death wishes [...] Segantini states that the reason for staying for hours beside the corpse *was to represent the dead child as living* [...] So there was an art by which one could, as it were, summon the dead back to life [...] Therein lay, as we can now understand, an act of atonement which the adult imposed upon himself for the sins of his childhood. (1911, p. 220, italics only in the German edition)

The innovative aspect of Abraham's interpretation

Abraham's basic conception of psychic development (the infantile oedipus complex, repression, and return in neurosis) stems, of course, from Freud. The mechanisms of "reversal into the opposite (reaction formation)" and "turning against the subject's own person" were also not new. The former had been introduced by Freud (1905d, p. 178, 238; 1909d, p. 238), while the latter had been used before, for example by Adler (Min 1, p. 402). The process of "*Gutmachen*" is a borderline case. On the one hand, it appears, to my knowledge, in Abraham's paper on

Segantini for the first time in the psychoanalytic literature in the sense of reparation by artistic activity for harm done to the object in phantasy. It may perhaps be seen as a precursor of the subsequent Kleinian "reparation" (in German: "*Wiedergutmachung*"; see Klein, 1929a), although the verbal similarity is not so conspicuous in the English version, where the word "reparation" is used only once ("attempts at making reparation", Abraham, 1911, p. 218); on the other occasion the phrase used is "he tries to make amends" (p. 220). On the other hand, Abraham ascribes the process of "*Gutmachen*" not to depression but to the obsessional-neurotic traits of Segantini's personality. Furthermore, he is *not* to my mind yet using the term in a technical sense.

However, what was certainly new was Abraham's thesis that the childhood revenge and death wishes directed towards the heterosexual love object constitute a central infantile factor in the causation of depression (in men). From Freud, Abraham took only the concept of the "struggle between love and hate" (later: ambivalence), which is discussed in the case history of the "Rat Man" (Freud, 1909d). Unlike Freud, though, he saw ambivalence, or the boy's infantile hate impulses, not primarily in relation to the father but *in the relationship with the mother*. Hate for the father is also mentioned by Abraham but is assigned only an insignificant part in the causation of depressive mood swings.

In a word, therefore, we have two innovations in the Segantini paper: a new approach to the understanding of depression—the son's infantile hate for the mother and its various vicissitudes are stated to be partly responsible for depressive mood swings—and a new affective dimension of the son's relationship with the mother: hate and wishes for revenge and death. This dimension is tellingly brought out by Abraham with the repeated evocation of the "bad mother". The novelty is thus situated in the domain of the drive impulses and affects, or, if you will, of object relations, whereas Freud's demand that Abraham discover a specific *psychic mechanism* in the Segantini paper could not yet be satisfied (apart from allusions; see, e.g., 1911, p. 241).

Abraham's and Freud's views of the mother-son relationship (up to 1911)

Abraham's idea that the son hates the mother *at a deep level* nowadays seems to us hardly worth mentioning. At the time, however, it was new. After all, Freud's account in 1900 of the simple, positive oedipus complex stated that the son's wishes towards the mother were primarily of a libidinal, tender, erotic, and sexual nature. Intense negative feelings, hostility, anxiety, guilt, and death wishes were supposed to apply only to the father and siblings (Freud, 1900a, pp. 250, 254). This primal form of the oedipus complex still held sway in 1911 and was only later replaced by the constellation of the complete oedipus complex.

The question therefore arises as to the origins of Abraham's novel view, which does not coincide with the positive oedipus complex. Would Freud have come to the same conclusion as Abraham if he had studied Segantini rather than Little Hans, Leonardo or the Rat Man? Or did the two men's differing positions have more to do with their respective inner propensities to perceive particular kinds of relationships?

The point to which I now wish to draw attention—Freud's tendency to see the boy's relationship with the mother as primarily libidinal and to regard the aggressive element as secondary—has already been made by other authors, and I shall therefore be brief.

The depiction of normal development in the account of Little Hans (1909b) includes both erotic-sexual and "sadistic–tender" impulses and desires on the part of the boy (see, for example, ibid., pp. 83, 129, 139). The sadistic impulses are closely integrated within the context of the libidinal relationship. As Freud writes in a well known passage, they represent the "familiar components of the sexual libido" (ibid., p. 141). Hence the little boy's sadistic impulses are actually libidinal in nature. Frankiel comes to the same conclusion in his examination of Little Hans: "At this point in the development of his thinking, Freud seems unable to consider destructiveness directed at the mother" (Frankiel, 1991, p. 182). Similarly, there is no mention in the study of *Leonardo da Vinci* (1910c) of hate and death wishes towards the mother, although Leonardo was given away by his mother as a little boy, so that he might well have felt disappointed by his mother and hated her. What Freud discusses at length in his Leonardo contribution and in his account of the development of male homosexuality is and remains the mutual, erotic-tender relationship between mother and son (see Collins, 1997; Schmidbauer, 1992). Again, the question why male homosexuals turn away from women is answered by Freud not in terms of disappointment and hate but based on the mother's lack of a penis and the associated castration anxiety (1908c, p. 217; 1909d, p. 238). The unconscious pattern of experience here postulated by Freud introduced an element of contempt and horror (1910c, p. 96), but not of hate, into the mother-son relationship.

Interestingly enough, Freud's pupil Isidor Sadger, in precisely the same context, had advanced the thesis that the little boy turned away from women if he had been massively disappointed by the mother and "unceremoniously expelled from a state of heavenly bliss" (Sadger, 1909c, p. 56). Freud did not accept this explanation, which, like Abraham's in the Segantini paper, elevated the disappointment in love caused by the mother to the status of a pathogenic factor. This was perhaps partly because Freud often preferred explanations that did not imply a dependence on *individual* experience (see Freud, 1918b, p. 119). In other words, a disappointment in love in relation to the mother may or may not be experienced, whereas the perception of her lack of a penis and the resulting anxiety are unavoidable and relatively independent of the subject's individual life history.

A further variant of the mother-son relationship can be found in "A Special Type of Choice of Object Made by Men" (1910h). In essence, it runs as follows: when the son discovers (in prepuberty) that the mother entertains a sexual relationship with the father, he is seized with jealousy and "takes revenge" by imputing infidelity to the mother and imagining her engaging in activities about which he develops sexually stimulating phantasies (see also Freud, 1912d). Love in the adult man then becomes conditional on the woman concerned being "of bad repute sexually" and attached to another man (1910h, p. 166). In this case, too, Freud postulates an (unconscious) fixation on the libidinal relationship with the mother. The "revenge" consists in the moral condemnation of the mother/woman as a whore—an attribution that at the same time makes her attractive. In this variant, the mother is disparaged and devalued, but not hated as described by Abraham for Segantini.

In the case of Rat Man, the relationship with the mother appears only marginally—it is literally consigned to a footnote (Freud, 1909d, pp. 206–208, fn.). It did not feature in the treatment at all. This is not so with the "lady" and other women from the Rat Man's adult life and childhood. Hostile and ambivalent impulses are certainly directed against them. However, *nowhere* in the published text does Freud attribute these attitudes to the relationship with the mother. Zetzel (1966) has pointed out that, while Freud's posthumously published case notes (1955a) refer in a few places to disturbing affects between son and mother, these passages are not included in the published version of the case history. For example, Freud notes a "hostile current" against the mother (ibid., p. 297), disgust (p. 296), contempt and rejection

(p. 297), and the phantasy that she is a "whore" (pp. 301, 312)—yet these tendencies were *not* incorporated in the *theory* of the aetiology of obsessional neurosis. Freud manifestly took the view that there was no essential correlation between them and the symptoms (and transference). The situation is more extreme in the case of Schreber (Freud, 1911c), where the son's relationship with the mother is not mentioned at all (see Gay, 1988, p. 505). Freud sees the pathology as centring on the "father complex" with its passive-homosexual wishful phantasies and anxieties directed towards the father, the regression to the narcissistic and homoerotic phase of development and the paranoia-specific mechanism of projection, whereas the relationship with the mother appears as pathogenetically irrelevant.

Overall, in Freud's *theory* either the relationship between son and mother is not present or it is highly cathected with libido. In the latter case the mother is fundamentally the oedipally desired and beguiling object, which sometimes also arouses anxiety, and the threat emanating from her is limited. Only marginally—in shorter contributions such as the dream of the *Three Fates* (1900a, p. 204), with the associated phantasy of the woman as the "goddess of death", which recurs in "The Theme of the Three Caskets" (1913f)—did Freud suggest a different image of the mother as an all-powerful object associated with death; however, he did not include these aspects in the explicit theory used in the major clinical studies.

The idealisation of the son's relationship with the mother and the neglect of the early mother relationship have now been noted by a number of authors and attributed to Freud's own early development and traumas (Atwood & Stolorow, 1993; Bonomi, 1996; Barron et al., 1991; Grubrich-Simitis, 1991; Hardin, 1987, 1988; Holt, 1992). Perhaps the mother featuring in my essay, who is on the one hand desired and on the other not present (or is "dead"), could be connected with a split in the relationship. This would be consistent with the results of Hardin's carefully nuanced study, according to which Freud's relationship with his mother was characterised by emotional coolness and distance and at the same time sexualised.

Nevertheless, the above summary to my mind clearly shows that Freud's view of the mother-son relationship was determined less by the difference between clinical pictures than by a pattern to which he was clinging. The analysis of homosexual and obsessional-neurotic patients—and also, as shown above, that of depressives—constituted (up to 1911) just as little occasion for him to undertake a revision of the basic pattern as did the study of a case of schizophrenic psychosis (Schreber). He clung to the pattern either because his own life history compelled him to do so or because, quite apart from that history, he felt that his theory of the oedipus complex proved heuristically fruitful when applied to a wide variety of clinical pictures and entitled him to assert its universal validity.

The "bad mother" in the Vienna group (up to 1911)

A glance at the *Minutes of the Vienna Psychoanalytic Society* shows just how delicate was the question of the bad mother. Abraham had sent his Segantini paper to Freud in February 1911. At precisely this time, in February, March, and April 1911, the Vienna Group spent three evenings discussing how the son's aggression towards the mother was to be understood, so that we can once again verify Freud's position at this time (Min 3, pp. 150, 190–193, 219–222).

At the beginning of February 1911, Adler presented one of the papers that led to his resignation and exclusion from the Vienna Group in the summer of the same year (Min 3, pp. 140–145). In the discussion, Stekel, who at this time shared Adler's views on aggression, made the differences explicit. According to the *Minutes*:

> With regard to the conception that incest is the central problem of neurosis, Stekel, too, has come to change his opinion somewhat. Behind the sexual element stands a second instinct, which Adler calls "aggression" and he himself calls "criminality". The primary factor to him is no longer love, but hate; excess of love is nothing but overcompensation for primary hatred. This hatred breaks through alongside love—as, for instance, in impulses to kill one's mother, which we had previously conceived of symbolically (knife, dagger, weapon, etc.). (Min 3, p. 150)

In other words, the son's death wishes towards the mother had previously been understood symbolically as a disguise for the wish to have sexual intercourse with her; but now Adler and Stekel saw the matter differently—that is, differently from Freud—assuming a primary aggression on the part of the son towards the mother.

About a month later, Dattner presented a paper in which he discussed the reasons for Raskolnikov's murder of the mother in Dostoevsky's

Crime and Punishment (Min 3, pp. 189–190). Hitschmann, who had just been elected Freud's deputy and was described by Freud at this time as "quite orthodox" (F/Ju, p. 400), adopted precisely his position: "Most likely, here, too, the oedipus complex played a major role, so that we may assume that originally there existed a father-murder complex, from which emerged only secondarily the complex of mother hate" (Min 3, pp. 191–192). Tausk and Grüner also saw the murder (of the mother) as equivalent to coitus, thereby indicating that they shared Freud's view that hate for the mother was ultimately attributable to libidinal wishes (ibid., pp. 191, 193).

Four weeks later, Freud addressed the issue spontaneously (Min 3, p. 219). He showed based on a vignette from the treatment of a *female* patient that the wish for the mother's death lay concealed behind her dream of the death of her father. I believe that Freud presented this vignette because he felt it necessary to make clear his position on the question of the primacy of libidinal wishes in the oedipal relationship (whether of the boy or the girl) to the parent of the opposite sex. We do not, of course, know whether he was thinking of Abraham in this connection, but it is hardly conceivable that he could have overlooked the problems inherent in Abraham's approach, considering that, as described above, he had discussed them many times with his pupils.

In conclusion, let us turn to Jung's *Symbols of Transformation* (1911–1912), the book that heralded its author's separation from Freud. The mythologem of the "Terrible Mother" makes a number of appearances in this volume (e.g., pp. 175, 236, 316). To that extent, Abraham was not alone with Segantini and the "bad mother". Unlike Jung and Adler, however, he remained within the framework of Freudian theory. For all the ardour of his depiction of the son's hate for the mother, he abided by Freud's views, agreeing with him that sadism/hate was a "component of the libido" (see Freud, 1909d, p. 240) rather than accepting Adler's notion (1908) that it was an aggressive instinct independent of sexuality. Abraham may perhaps be said to have been *basically* in harmony with Freud, even though he diverged from him considerably on certain points within the common framework. When Freud wrote to him in March 1911: "Adler's behaviour was no longer reconcilable with our psa. interests, he denies the role of the libido, and traces everything back to aggression" (F/A, p. 131), Abraham was able to agree unstintingly: "I do not think, however, that I do him [Adler] an injustice if I find the 'aggressive drive' very one-sided. The giving up of the libido [...] appear[s] to me as a retrograde step" (F/A, p. 132). Even so, Abraham too was eventually to find himself unable to reach agreement with Freud on the significance of aggression as an etiological factor in depression. A second difference arose only during the course of the ensuing years. It concerned the importance of the mother—as compared with that of the father—in the development of boys.

The subsequent fate of Abraham's theory of depression (1912–1925)

After his paper on Segantini, Abraham produced three more contributions on depression (1912b, 1916–1917, 1924). I shall examine them with a view to determining whether and to what extent Abraham's position on hate for the mother changed. I cannot go into contributions on depression by other pupils of Freud *after* the Segantini paper. Freud's own studies on the subject (1917e, 1921c, 1923b), too, can only be touched upon.

Holding fast to the significance of sadism (1912)

The reaction of Freud and some of his pupils to Abraham's analysis of depression was, on the whole, unfavourable. This was not the case with the Segantini paper, which was as yet spared the full weight of criticism, probably because it was regarded as applied psychoanalysis. After all, Abraham had not yet claimed in his Segantini paper to have depicted a *typical* course of development. This he was to do only in "Notes on the Psycho-analytical Investigation and Treatment of Manic-depressive Insanity and Allied Conditions" (1912b). He based this contribution on the analytic treatment of six patients (ibid., p. 138) and asserted that he was presenting a clinically valid theoretical approach.

He persisted in the view that depression was attributable essentially to the repression of an "attitude of the libido in which hatred predominates" (1912b, p. 144), or of an "insatiable sadism" (ibid., p. 146). The formula for depression was: "I cannot love people; I have to hate them" (ibid., p. 145). Abraham believed that he could name a specific mechanism of depression, namely projection (ibid., p. 144). He reported *inter alia* on the analysis of a male patient who, like Segantini—or, at least, Segantini as Abraham saw him—had felt as a child that he was not loved as much by his parents as his siblings were. In Abraham's view, the patient was repressing his hostility towards the parents and projecting it on to other people. I cannot here reproduce Abraham's justifications for this view, which he based on the material at his disposal. The only important point for our purposes is that, in contrast to the view put forward in the Segantini paper, Abraham then considered that it was the *parents* and not only the *mother* who disappointed the child. We do not know whether this important change was made because the clinical material so demanded or whether other considerations also played a part—for example, allowance for the basic outline of Freud's theory.

At any rate, Freud rapped Abraham over the knuckles in June 1912—that is, *after* the publication of the "Notes". Referring not to the "Notes' but to a manuscript about Amenhotep (1912a) and a statement on the relative importance of the father and the mother, Freud wrote:

> you claim that when the mother is particularly important, the conflict with the father takes milder forms. I for my part have no evidence of this, and must assume that you have had special experiences in this respect. As the matter is not clear to me, I ask you to revise this passage. (F/A, p. 154)

Abraham replied that he would examine the matter based on his analytic material: "There is some truth in my statement, but it is untenable in the general form in which I put it forward" (F/A, p. 155). Shortly afterwards, Freud commented that he liked Amenhotep "in its revised form very much better" (ibid., p. 164).

This exchange had a minor precursor in April and May 1909—the period when Abraham was beginning to take an interest in Segantini. After reading Jung's essay "The Significance of the Father in the Destiny of the Individual" (Jung, 1909), Abraham asked Freud whether he agreed with Jung "that the *father* is so predominant" (F/A, p. 87, italics only in the German edition). In some of his (Abraham's) analyses, it was "definitely the mother; in others one cannot decide whether it is the f.[ather] or the m.[other] who is of greater importance. It seems to me to depend very much on the individual circumstances" (ibid.). Freud replied that in his view the same-sex parent was the more important. However, he could "also adapt to greater individual variations" (ibid., p. 89). Jung later stated that his opinion on the significance of the father had changed while he was working on *Symbols of Transformation* (1911–12), when it had become clear to him that the mother was just as important as the father (reported by Hurwitz, 1979, p. 55).

In a discussion on Abraham's "Notes" in the Vienna Group in May 1912, Federn rejected the linchpin of Abraham's theoretical approach: sadism (Min 4, p. 99). In his opinion, the case presented by Abraham was inappropriate for proving the author's thesis: "when Abraham [...] draws upon the sadistic instincts as the pathogenic ones, the objection must be made that his case gives no indication thereof" (ibid.). Marcinowski took a similar view in a short contribution in the *Internationale Zeitschrift für Psychoanalyse*:

> *Abraham* refers again and again to the attitude of hate as something primary. According to my observations, this is not true for these cases. In *Abraham's* observations, hate should surely also be understood as having grown out of *disappointment in love* [...] Not *'repressed sadism'* [...] but profoundly repressed hunger for love was the formative determinant of this neurosis. (Marcinowski, 1912, p. 542, italics in the German edition)

Marcinowski addresses the crucial problem: is (repressed) sadism the primary, profound factor that must be made conscious—or, as Freud's position would have been, did the wish to be loved by the mother lie even "deeper"?

Freud himself encouraged Abraham to continue his investigations after the publication of the "Notes", but at the same time rejected Abraham's "formula":

> In cyclothymic cases you should just go on digging; one can see more the next time. [...] I have also got the impression from your paper, which I value so highly, that the formula is not assured and the elements not yet convincingly linked. (F/A, p. 154)

Abraham's reaction to "Mourning and Melancholia" and his continued emphasis on sadism (1916)

Abraham did not allow himself to be put off. When, at the beginning of 1915, Freud sent him a draft of "Mourning and Melancholia"—the first contribution of Freud's own specifically devoted to depression—Abraham waited a while before reacting to the manuscript. He wanted, he wrote, to avoid the danger of "too subjective" a judgement on a subject with which he himself had been occupied for a long time (F/A, p. 303). In an unusually long letter dating from the end of March 1915, he then defended his view of the aetiology of depression: "I [...] accept all the essentials in your work. I do think, however, that *one* element from my earlier work should be more heavily stressed than it is in yours" (ibid., p. 303; italics in the German edition). This element is sadism. Abraham had strongly stressed it in his Segantini paper (1911) as well as in "Notes on the Psycho-analytical Investigation" (1912b). In his letter to Freud he went on:

> I must still hold to this view. Too much violence and criminality was uncovered in the analyses of my melancholic patients. The self-reproaches do indicate repressed hostile feelings. The complete motor inhibition leads one also to assume that strong motor impulses have had to be made harmless. The same tendency is manifest in the way the melancholic torments those around him. Added to this is the reappearance of the most open sadism in the manic phase. These are only *a few* of the reasons why I still rate this factor as highly as ever. (F/A, p. 304)

In the same letter Abraham reported on observations suggesting that orality played an important part in depression. A few months before, in October 1914, in the third edition of the *Three Essays*, Freud had introduced the oral or cannibalistic phase with the sexual aim of incorporation (1905d/1915, p. 198), describing incorporation as the "prototype" of identification (as he had already written in 1912–1913, pp. 82, 142). Freud had sent the new text of the *Three Essays* to Abraham at the end of December 1914 (F/A, p. 294). In now forwarding further evidence for a correlation between orality and depression to Abraham, he agreed with him, but, even on this occasion, was not prepared to follow him completely with regard to sadism (ibid., p. 309). He also pointed out that Abraham had not taken appropriate account of his (Freud's) remarks on the depressive mechanism. One of his charges was that Abraham, in concentrating on sadism, was overlooking "the real explanation". This could "be derived only from its mechanism [...] I know that soon you will agree with me" (ibid.). This was the familiar admonition that all Freud's pupils were bound to receive at some stage. Earlier I mentioned Stekel;

now it was Abraham; and at the same time Freud was reprimanding Tausk—who had presented a paper on melancholia to the Vienna Group in December 1914 (Min 4, pp. 272–274)—on this point.

Since the publication of the Ferenczi correspondence, we have become acquainted with the draft of "Mourning and Melancholia" (F/Fer 2, p. 47), that Freud also sent to Abraham, and have known that Freud had alluded to the mechanism of narcissistic identification in his communication with Abraham. This, for Freud, was the key to the understanding of depression; it was an insight that, incidentally, was published not by Freud himself but—with an explicit reference to Freud's "special permission"—by Tausk (Tausk, 1916, p. 398; see Eissler, 1971, p. 214). A narcissistic identification was supposed to lie at the root of the depressive's self-reproaches: when a depressive criticised and accused himself, the attack was really directed not to the ego but to the object with which it was identified. In other words, instead of attacking the disappointing object, the depressive regressed, with the consequence of a narcissistic identification with the object, so that all hostility was now directed towards the ego. As Abraham frankly admitted to Freud, he was unable to follow this idea (F/A, p. 304). Many years later he was to justify his lack of understanding by the fact that he himself was inclined towards narcissistic identification after object losses (Abraham, 1924, p. 437).

The exchange on the draft of "Mourning and Melancholia" tends to bear out the above supposition that it was not only the clinical material that was responsible when Abraham and Freud differed in their "observations" and theoretical approaches. Although Freud emphasised in "Mourning and Melancholia" that his empirical material did not suffice to justify the theory he was presenting (1917e, p. 250), he had had depressive patients in treatment in the period before he set down the draft (Min 4, pp. 108–110; 275–276). Immediately after completing the manuscript, he informed Abraham that his "solution of melancholia" had now been confirmed by a case (F/A, p. 302; this may perhaps have been Karl Mayreder, who began treatment with Freud on 21 January 1915; see Mayreder, 1988, p. 151). Will this and other patients have been very different from the depressive patients seen by Abraham? Were the differences really due to the patients? If so, why did Freud never see a patient to whom Abraham's observations applied? In a word, I think it very likely that the differences in emphasis between Freud and Abraham—object loss, regression and narcissistic identification on the one hand and a sadistic, profoundly ambivalent attitude to the love object on the other—have less to do with the patients seen by the two men than with their differing pre-observational views of depression (see May[-Tolzmann], 1990, p. 701). Freud saw mainly the narcissistic identification, the assimilation of the ego to the object, the alteration of the ego and the conflict in the ego. In addition, in "Mourning and Melancholia" he discussed at length the ambivalence and sadism of the depressive. Yet this factor never assumed the central position it occupied with Abraham.

In "The First Pregenital Stage of the Libido" (1916–1917), a paper written *after* "Mourning and Melancholia" but published before it,[2] Abraham again laid stress on sadism as an etiological factor in depression and now specifically assigned it to the oral phase. Depression, in his view, involved a regression to this phase. The depressive had a wish "to devour and demolish his object" (ibid., p. 276). His guilt feelings and self-accusations had to do with precisely these cannibalistic wishes (ibid., p. 277). In Abraham's view, the depressive incorporation of the object was primarily a (destructive) drive wish, whereas the aspect of alteration of the ego and assimilation to the object, or of narcissistic identification, as emphasised by Freud, remained alien to him. As for the figure of the mother, she is no more directly present in "The First Pregenital Stage" than in "Mourning and Melancholia". Abraham uses the neutral term "object" and refers to oral, cannibalistic wishes, although it can, after all, only have been the mother to whom these wishes applied.

The return of the bad mother (1924)

In "A Short Study on the Development of the Libido" (1924), Abraham presented a highly differentiated etiological theory of depression. He was now able to name a complex configuration of infantile etiological conditions (ibid., pp. 457–460) and to give a comprehensive account of the significance of the mechanism of narcissistic identification, or, as he preferred to say, of introjection. Furthermore, his investigations of

---

[2] Abraham's "The First Pregenital Stage of the Libido" (1916–17) appeared in issue 2 of vol. 4 (1916–1917) of the *Internationale Zeitschrift*. Freud's "Mourning and Melancholia" appeared in issue 6 of the same journal. Issue 2 actually came out in 1916, but issue 6 not until 1918 (see F/A, p. 375).

depression had led him to subdivide the oral and anal phases, so that he was able to determine the fixation points more precisely. As before, sadistic (now oral-sadistic and anal-sadistic) drive impulses were stated to be central to depression. Just as Abraham remained faithful to his basic idea, notwithstanding all the fine distinctions that cannot be gone into here, so too did Freud hold fast to the fundamentals of *his* theory. In *Group Psychology and the Analysis of the Ego* (1921c), he again referred to the importance of narcissistic identification and drew attention to the conflict, specific to depression, between the ego ideal and the ego.

Surprisingly, the mother returns to Abraham's theory in his 1924 paper. Abraham is substantially certain that it is the *mother* who puts pre-oedipal disappointments in love in the way of the boy, and against whom, consequently, the boy directs his oral-sadistic hate (1924, p. 460). Abraham portrays the hate of the boy and of the depressive in drastic words: he "wants to revenge himself on his mother [...] by castrating her in his turn, either taking away her breasts or her imaginary penis"—and, moreover, to do so by biting (ibid., p. 463). The depressive, in his view, longs for a (positive) incorporation of the mother, while at the same time wanting "her castration or death" (ibid., p. 463). Abraham does not mention the study of Segantini, but its atmosphere is present when he refers to the disappointed boy's thirst for vengeance. Abraham uses the phrase "bad mother" three times, placing it twice in quotation marks (pp. 446, 447, 462). However, it has not yet become a technical term in its own right.

In some places Abraham alternates between the mother thesis and the other view, to the effect that love disappointments in relation to *both* parents form part of the infantile background to depression (cf., 1924, p. 459). At one point he mentions this problem explicitly:

> In this connection we may consider a characteristic of melancholia which would seem to put it in a place apart from the other neuroses. My analyses showed that the ambivalent attitude of the male patients, with its hostile, cannibalistic impulses, was mainly directed against the *mother*, whereas we know that in other neurotic conditions the father is pre-eminently the object of the patient's hostile tendencies. (Abraham, 1924, p. 460; italics only in the German edition)

Abraham is here openly stating that his analyses have led him to conclusions that conflict with Freud's theory of the neuroses. It seems to me that he did not find it easy to tolerate the difference from Freud, because he goes on immediately after the passage quoted above, in which he had given priority to rage against the mother, to state that the child experiences disappointment from *both* parents, but follows this by the contrary remark that nevertheless "the whole psychological process centres *in the main* round the mother" (1924, p. 461). His position on Freud's comparison of mania to the totem meal varies in a similar way. Abraham first points out that "the criminal phantasies of the manic patient are for the most part directed against his mother" (ibid., p. 474), but qualifies this observation in the next sentence, stating that the impulses directed against the mother are "of a secondary kind"; it is the father who is, after all, their primary object.

In his "Epilogue" (1925a) to the second edition of the Segantini paper, composed in 1924 and published in 1925, Abraham then unequivocally espoused the "mother" aetiology of depression (in men). He proudly noted in the "Preface" to the second edition (1925c) that he did not need to change any of the views he had set down in 1911 (ibid., p. 210). It had since been found that psychic losses experienced during childhood—especially disappointments—were a crucial factor in later depressions: "Our experience is that in the case of the man it is always the mother who is the cause of such disappointment in the earliest phase of childhood" (1925a, p. 259). That Abraham saw Segantini as an exemplary case of depression is clear from, for instance, his comment that depressive patients "often reveal to us trains of thought very similar to those we have met with in Segantini" (ibid., p. 260). A depressive patient had recently reported to him a dream which reminded him "in a surprising way of Segantini's paintings of *The Wicked Mothers* (ibid., "böse Mütter" in the German text). As with Segantini, the longing "for the earliest satisfaction at the mother's breast" (ibid., p. 260) lay beneath the hate in depressive patients. This longing was evident in Segantini's love for nature and the mountains, which became fused with the love for the mother. Abraham ended his epilogue with the following sentence: "It thus becomes even clearer than before that the longing for his mother, originally gratified, but later disappointed, lay at the root of Segantini's alternating moods; by this longing he lived and through it he died" (ibid., p. 261).

Abraham's bad mother—a new inner world

In the Segantini study, one has the impression that Abraham is emotionally very involved when he refers to the "languid peace", "sweet melancholy", or "grave tranquillity" of the painter's pictures (1911, pp. 230, 231). Although these qualities of feeling may be detected in the pictures, they indicate a particular sensitivity on Abraham's part to precisely these qualities. A similarly high degree of inner commitment is discernible in the description of the death and revenge wishes of the little boy and the depressive. Abraham evidently possessed a particular capacity to perceive dark and disruptive impulses of agitation, hate, revenge, retribution and guilt on the one hand and loving, tranquil, blissful, fusional, affection on the other—or, put more cautiously, to take account of these in a theory of psychic life. To qualify this characterisation, Abraham's particular sensitivity may be said to have extended to the relationship with the mother and, to qualify it further, to the relationship of the *son* with the mother. This applies not only to the Segantini paper (1911) but also to "A Short Study of the Development of the Libido" (1924). Here the passages on the aetiology of depression are based mainly on analyses of male patients (ibid., p. 421) and are drafted in a similar dark, sombre, and heavy tone to comparable passages in the Segantini paper. I would rather leave open the aspects of Abraham's life history that play a part in these preferences, including that for the painter Segantini, and refer the reader to the work of other authors (Jones, 1926a; H. Abraham, 1974, p. 41; Cremerius, 1997; Decke, 1997; Mächtlinger, 1997; Petersdorff, 1997; Jaeger, 2000).

The states of mind plumbed by Abraham in the Segantini paper do not play a prominent part in Freud's view of the mother-son relationship (up to 1911), just as it is scarcely imaginable that the "languid peace" of a picture might have appealed to Freud. Freud's sensibility was directed elsewhere. For this reason I should like to assert that the "good/bad mother" dimension in Abraham's Segantini paper went beyond the status of Freud's theory at the time and was innovative in character, on both the *theoretical* and *atmospheric* levels. Although I would not claim that the innovation lay in Abraham's addressing the domain of pre-oedipality, on which Freud himself had not yet focused (he was not to do so explicitly until 1913), there is no doubt that Abraham was describing a different internal world from Freud's.

As to the *theoretical* innovation, our examination of the Segantini paper has shown that Abraham ascribed great importance to the mother and the hate directed by the boy against her in laying the foundations for subsequent depressive tendencies, and that he temporarily (1912b, 1916–1917) replaced this conception by one that was more easily reconcilable with Freud's theory, in which the hate was directed at both parents. In subsequent publications (1924, 1925a), Abraham basically returned to the original notions found in the Segantini paper. He was aware of the differences between his views and Freud's and defended his approach against Freud for many years—until the end of his life in the case of the theory of depression. Abraham, in my opinion, was not as much of a "rebel" as Good (1995) assumes. It seems to me rather that he could not but express in words those aspects of the internal world that were accessible to him. Perhaps he did not feel the pressure of the *need* to distinguish himself from Freud to the same degree as some of Freud's other pupils did, so that open conflict never arose. Abraham instead remained tenaciously faithful to Freud, as he did to his own ideas, even when he found himself partly at odds with his mentor.

Little attention has hitherto been devoted to the theoretical differences between Freud and Abraham, although they were addressed early on in Jones's major obituary of Abraham. Jones wrote:

> On studying his original contributions one is struck by the preponderance of themes dealing with the pregenital stages of development, including auto-erotism and the component instincts, and with the element of repressed hate, especially in regard to the mother. The latter theme recurs again and again in his works and far outweighs in extent his contributions in the sphere of love, transference, and akin problems. (1926a, p. 35)

Jones is alluding in these lines to the particular features of Abraham's theorisation without clearly and explicitly stating that they were at variance with Freud's ideas. Jones is, to my knowledge, the only author to have seen that the Segantini study was about the "bad mother". However, he overlooks the fact that the concept was developed in this study *for the first time*. On the Segantini paper, Jones writes: "he [Abraham] was able to trace in detail the ambivalent attitude of love and hate the painter bore to her; once more we have a study of the 'evil mother'" (1926a, p. 33). This sounds as if Abraham's Segantini paper were a further contribution to the theme of the bad mother—whereas the publications to which Jones refers, and which he discussed in earlier passages of the obituary, appeared long *after* the study of Segantini.

It is no coincidence that Jones's attention was attracted by precisely this aspect of Abraham's creation, for he himself saw the relationship of the son (or of the pre-oedipal child) with the mother in similar terms to Abraham. In 1913 Jones produced a paper—written *after* the Segantini study—containing the thesis that cleanliness training as a rule aroused intense feelings of hate towards the mother in the child (Jones, 1913). Jones, too, was concerned with the localization of hate in the relationship with the mother, and his thesis was unwelcome to Freud at the time. This is clear from a remark that has come down to us in the *Minutes*: "PROF. FREUD knows nothing about an origin of hate in thwarted anal erotism, as assumed by Jones" (Min 4, p. 213).

Jones's comments about Abraham, quoted above, which date from 1926, can be seen as foreshadowing events to come. It was after all Jones who invited Melanie Klein to London after Abraham's death, and whose invitation she took up. I have now explicitly mentioned the name that occurred to me repeatedly in reading Abraham's Segantini paper. As we know, Klein was in analysis with Abraham in 1924–1925 and was valued and supported by him (see Frank, 1999, p. 63). Abraham saw her observations as confirmation of his views even before 1924. We are familiar with his report to Freud in October 1923 that Klein had succeeded in observing, in the analysis of a three-year-old child, the "Ur-Verstimmung" postulated by him—the infantile depression he regarded as the indispensable precondition for a subsequent depression (F/A, p. 471).

As I read the Segantini paper, the idea that Klein had a great affinity with Abraham's internal world imposed itself at times to such an extent that I felt the study to be in effect a primary source book of the Kleinian school. Even if this view is exaggerated, it nevertheless seems to me that, in Abraham, Klein found a colleague and analyst whose inner world, in its darkness and gravity, was similar to her own, or to the aspects of it manifested in her publications. Perhaps, as stated above, something of the kinship between the two theories or worlds has been lost in the English translation. However, it is surely not only the translation that is responsible. Could it be that historians of theory have concentrated excessively on the content of concepts at the expense of their non-linguistic emotional climate?

Klein herself mentions Abraham not infrequently in her published works, especially in connection with her view of oral and anal sadism and the possibility of early, pre-oedipal guilt feelings (see references in Klein, 1932, 1935). She also draws attention to differences between her theory and Abraham's, for example in the studies of the psychogenesis of depression (Klein, 1935, 1940). She dedicated her first book, *The Psycho-Analysis of Children* (1932), to Abraham, thanking him explicitly in her preface for the trust he had placed in her. She noted that her "theoretical conclusions are a natural development of his own discoveries" (ibid., p. xi). Elsewhere she describes Abraham as "the link between my own work and F[reud]'s" (Grosskurth, 1986, p. 109). However, I have not so far come across a single passage in which she refers to Abraham's early, innovative view of the "bad mother" or to his study of Segantini.[3] Nor have I discovered any such indications in Hinshelwood (1989), Petot (1990–1991), Laplanche & Pontalis (1967), Spillius (1988), or Taylor (1996), although Petot and Taylor deal at length with the question of the relationship between Klein's and Abraham's theories. Rather, the authors unanimously take the view that the concept of the good/bad mother was introduced by Klein (1932, 1935) (cf., Laplanche & Pontalis, 1967, pp. 187–189). While this is surely correct on the purely conceptual and theoretical level, I think it justifiable in this connection to mention Abraham, who, in his Segantini paper, was the first to deal at length with infantile disappointment and the resulting hate for the mother, experienced as "bad" and longed for as "good", and who was thereby beginning to describe an internal world that differed from Freud's and was, in its atmosphere, a precursor of the internal world that Klein was later to explore and to put into words in her theory.

Translated by Philip Slotkin

---

[3] In this connection Klein refers to Radó (1927) and his thesis that the mother imago, by virtue of oral frustration, is split into a "good" and a "bad" mother (Klein, 1929b, p. 198, fn.). Radó was an analysand of Abraham (1922–1924). The work of Radó is also mentioned by Jacobson (1930, p. 233, fn.), in whose subsequent ego-psychological theory the good/bad object and the good/bad self play a central part. It seems to have been Radó who saw the split into a good and a bad object as a process of paramount importance and explicitly elevated it to a theoretical level, whereas Abraham considered the same process from the point of view of drive impulses and had therefore stressed ambivalence.

CHAPTER THREE

From anger to reflection: remarks on Freud's commentary on an early paper by Karl Abraham (1907)

In June 1907, Karl Abraham contacted Freud from Zurich sending him an offprint, fresh from the press, of his very first psychoanalytic paper ("On the Significance of Sexual Trauma in Childhood for the Symptomatology of Dementia Praecox"; Abraham, 1907b). From Freud's response letter, dated June 25, we gather that Abraham announced further "communications" which he indeed must have sent, as Freud refers to them in his next letter to Abraham dated July 7, 1907 (F/A, p. 1). We can assume that Abraham's "communications" are in fact the manuscript or perhaps a draft of his paper "The Experiencing of Sexual Traumas as a Form of Sexual Activity" (Abraham, 1907a).[1] Except for Good's (1995) in-depth discussion not much has been written about this paper even though it deserves more attention for it demonstrates some of the difficulties in approaching Freud's theories, then and now. Abraham's paper gains additional significance when read together with Freud's detailed commentary of 7 July 1907 (F/A, pp. 1–4), a masterpiece regarding Freud's handling of this young colleague who had just

[1] The original German title is slightly different: "Das Erleiden sexueller Traumen als Form *infantiler* Sexualbetätigung" (The suffering of sexual traumas as a form of *infantile* sexual activity).

begun to find his way into the new etiological theories of the neuroses and psychoses.

In October 1907, Abraham likely delivered "The Experiencing of Sexual Trauma" at the second or third meeting of the Freud Group at Burghölzli (F/Ju, p. 93; F/A, p. 10). On 15 November, the paper appeared in the *Zentralblatt für Nervenheilkunde und Psychiatrie* as a contribution "from the psychiatric clinic of Zurich University" identifying the author as one "K. Abraham, MD, former first resident physician" (1907a, p. 854). It seems that by the time Abraham submitted his manuscript he had already left his position at Burghölzli. We know that at the end of October 1907 he moved to Berlin, where he began his private practice as a "specialist for nervous and mental diseases" (F/A, p. 8). Freud, who had first responded to "The Experiencing" in July, wrote a second, much briefer comment after its publication in November (ibid., p. 13).

Abraham's paper (1907a) and Freud's comprehensive letter of July 7 form the basis of this chapter. I have tried to sketch the affinities and differences as they unfolded between the two men in 1907. As the title of this chapter indicates, I have found Abraham's paper and Freud's letter to be imbued with two distinct and opposing affective tonalities, that is, anger (an attitude of acrimony) and thoughtfulness. Both terms are taken from a short paper Freud wrote in 1913, entitled "Two Lies Told by Children" (1913g). Freud opened this paper with the cautionary remark that children's lies "should cause those in charge of them to reflect rather than be angry" (1913g, p. 305). Anger and reflection express divergent psychic responses: on the one hand the tendency to condemn the other person, often prematurely; on the other hand the capacity for a certain kind of deliberation or mindfulness that operates at a slower pace, doesn't rush to arrive at a "verdict", and takes its time to investigate what might have happened all the while presuming the innocence of the "accused". In the psychoanalytic setting, "anger" points to the analyst's impulsive countertransference reactions whereas "mindfulness", "thoughtfulness", or "reflection" mean the working-through and containing of the analyst's aggressive impulses. Both are important, and both have their time and place in psychoanalytic work.

Karl Abraham: "The Experiencing of Sexual Traumas as a Form of Sexual Activity" (1907)

In his introductory paper to the 1926 issues of the *Internationale Zeitschrift für Psychoanalyse* and *The International Journal of Psychoanalysis* dedicated to the memory of Karl Abraham, Ernest Jones offered a both brilliant and subtle account of Abraham's work (1926a).[2] He divided Abraham's contributions into four groups: "pioneering", classical, "original", and "shorter" papers (ibid., pp. 17–18). Among the papers that make up the first group of pioneering works, Jones put, among others, Abraham's Salzburg paper (1908) on the differences between neurosis and psychosis. "The Experiencing" was assigned to the group that comprises "shorter papers always containing data that illustrated, confirmed or expanded our knowledge of psycho-analytical theory and practice" (ibid., p. 18). In Jones' view the significance of "The Experiencing" seems to have been secondary.

The manuscript of "The Experiencing" that Freud refers to in his letter from July 1907 has not survived. We will have to infer its content from Freud's reactions and from the published final version which, however, does not seem to differ greatly from the draft. For the most part, Freud's commentary from July applies to the final version as well.

In contrast to Abraham's first paper (1907b), which concerned itself with psychiatric disorders, "The Experiencing" was conceptualised as a contribution to the aetiology of neurotic *and* psychotic disorders. Abraham may have written the paper with his departure from institutional psychiatry in mind. What follows is a summary of the paper.

> Abraham begins with a (not always accurate) summary of Freud's theory. Since "My Views on the Part Played by Sexuality in the Aetiology of the Neuroses" (1906a) Freud, says Abraham, no longer believed in infantile sexual trauma as the decisive factor in the aetiology of hysteria. In Abraham's reading of Freud, Freud had replaced trauma with an "abnormal psychosexual constitution" (1907a, p. 47), and had realised that children with an abnormal constitution reacted abnormally to sexual trauma and later became neurotic. Abraham claimed to have found that later in life those children became either neurotic or even psychotic.
>
> If this was true the question was why so many neurotic and psychotic persons experienced a sexual trauma in their childhood. In his paper Abraham set out to offer an answer by showing that "in a great number of cases the trauma was desired by the child unconsciously" (ibid., p. 48), cases which, in Abraham's

[2]Jones' paper (1926a) served as "Introductory Memoir" to the *Selected Papers of Karl Abraham* edited by him (1927).

view, pointed to an abnormal sexual constitution. Children with this abnormal disposition were easily seduced and took pleasure in seducing others. Therefore, those children were predisposed to provoke trauma. Unlike normal children they did not "actively and in earnest" resist the trauma but submit and surrender to violence (ibid., p. 49). In every single case that Abraham had published in "On the Significance of Sexual Trauma" (1907b) the children could have "called for help, run away, or offered resistance", which was also true for other cases he had examined (1907a, p. 50).

Children with an abnormal disposition did not tell their parents about the traumatic experience: they kept silent and repressed the trauma (ibid.)—something that Freud and Breuer (1895d) had observed as well. The children supposedly kept silent about the trauma because they felt guilty for having felt masochistic pleasure. It was therefore safe to assume that the experiencing of sexual traumata in childhood was "a masochistic expression of the sexual impulse" (ibid., p. 54). The experiencing of the trauma was a form of "infantile sexual activity" (ibid.).

As he had already assumed in "On the Significance" this abnormal constitution was characterised by precocious sexual development, quantitatively abnormal sexuality as well as an abnormal inclination to engage in sexual phantasies: "children belonging to this category show an abnormal desire for obtaining sexual pleasure, and in consequence of this undergo sexual traumas" (ibid., p. 54). A desire that could be found "in the early history of the neurotic or mentally afflicted individuals" whose adult life was characterised by "numerous sexual abnormalities" (ibid.).

Abraham claimed that his findings showed that individuals who had suffered a sexual trauma, "of which they were partly guilty through their compliant behaviour and which at the same time afforded them pleasure", experienced further sexual trauma (ibid., p. 57). One might thus speak of a "traumatophilic diathesis", a "tendency to expose themselves to further occurrences of the same nature" (ibid.). The trauma was unconsciously sought out because the individual's unconscious wished "to keep the traumatic symptom complex alive" (ibid., p. 62). The unconscious was "untiring in its efforts to give expression to a complex. It takes care that the affective value of the trauma suffered shall not be lost" (ibid.). Using vignettes Abraham claimed to have shown that accidents occurring later in life might be caused by unconscious wishes, just as Freud had argued in *The Psychopathology of Everyday Life* (1901b).

Abraham's later commentary (1920)

In the introduction of his *Klinische Beiträge aus den Jahren 1907–1920* [Clinical Papers from 1907–1920] (1921) Abraham commented on his early works. He states that "every work has to be understood in the context of the time it was written" and he reminds us, as if to apologise, how little Freud had published when he, Abraham, first began to familiarise himself with psychoanalysis (Abraham 1921).[3] At the end of "The Experiencing" he adds a passage entitled "Postscript (1920)":

> This paper, which was written in 1907, contains certain errors in its rendering of Freud's views. At the time of writing I had only recently begun to interest myself in the psycho-analytic method of thought. I consider it better to point out this fact in a general way than to make the necessary corrections in each place in the text, particularly since those errors do not invalidate the results of my investigations. (Abraham, 1927, p. 63)

Clearly, Abraham gave us permission to search for those "errors"—and we find them easily. Essentially there are two: one has to do with the significance of psychic reality; the other refers to the nature of infantile sexuality.

Psychic reality: a new aetiological factor

In 1907 Abraham had not yet understood how complex of a process Freud's letting go of his so called "seduction theory", conceptualised between 1896 and 1898, was. In contrast to what some authors have later tried to suggest (e.g., Masson, 1984), Freud was far from replacing one simplistic theory with another equally simplistic theory.[4] At no point did he assume infantile-sexual trauma as the only pathogenic factor in the aetiology of the neuroses and psychoses, not even during

---

[3] The preface was not included in the English edition.

[4] Grubrich-Simitis (1987, 1991) offers an in-depth discussion of trauma theory and its history; see also Eissler's (2001) posthumously published book on the seduction theory.

the period when he was still holding on to the seduction theory. Similarly, Freud did not give up his conviction that real sexual seduction was of great significance when he relinquished the seduction theory in 1898. Even after 1898 he maintained that even though he had overestimated the frequency with which sexual seductions occurred the "unique significance of sexual experiences [...] remains to this day one of the corner stones of my theory" (1906a, p. 273). It was merely the weight attributed to that factor that Freud decreased in favour of the sexual constitution, that is, the given, hereditarily fixed disposition. At the same time, Freud introduced a new aetiological factor: the phantasies. A move that, as was often the case when he modified his theories, increased the level of complexity of his theory as the new version now emphasised two opposing dimensions: the biological-constitutional-hereditary dimension (sexual constitution) *and* the psychic, experience-based dimension (phantasies). In other words, Freud's theory became at once more biological and more psychological. This specific quality is not only true for the modifications made in 1906 but is a common feature of his theorising in general (see May[-Tolzmann], 1996). More often than not, however, our intellect resists such challenging complexity. This is one of the reasons why Freud's theories continue to be interpreted in different ways—depending on what period of his theorising one refers to and how sensitive one is to registering subtle shifts of emphasis. To grasp Freud's theory as a whole, to comprehend it in its ever-shifting structure, seems to be almost impossible.

It is thus understandable that Abraham in 1907 did not consider that the sexual traumata he believed to have found in his cases—and which he traced back to an abnormal sexual constitution—might not have been "real" but created by phantasies. Freud's introduction of the notion of phantasy and of the importance of psychic reality was a revolutionary idea, one that quite literally introduced a new level of reality into scientific thinking. A move that even his best disciples struggled to comprehend.

Jung, too, found the notion of psychic reality impossible to accept. In a letter written in May 1907, in which he turns to Freud for advice, he reports the case of a six-year-old girl who was brought to him "for excessive masturbation and lying after alleged seduction by her foster father" (F/Ju, p. 45). Jung was unsure how to handle this case, because it seemed "as if the trauma were a fake" but then "where does the child get all those sexual stories from?" (ibid.). "In your six-year-old girl," Freud responded, "you must surely have discovered in the meantime that the attack is a phantasy that has become conscious, something which is regularly disclosed in analysis and which misled me into assuming the existence of generalised traumas in childhood" (ibid., p. 48). Freud encourages Jung to find out the concrete sources from which the child may have obtained her detailed sexual knowledge, which is to say that by 1907, Jung, just like Abraham, could not think beyond the alternatives "true/false" and "truth/lie". He could not yet grasp that something that in fact did not happen may nonetheless be experienced as true, and that not telling the "objective" truth doesn't necessarily make one a liar.

Even though his young disciples lagged behind in keeping up with his theories, Freud treated their lack of understanding with empathy and consideration. Instead of admonishing Jung, he flattered and accommodated him: Surely Jung must have noticed by now that the seduction was really a phantasy. In the same way he responded to Abraham: you are right, he told him, and you have overlooked the most important aspect. He wooed Abraham, praised him for his "acute" and "conclusive" arguments; "whole large parts" of his communications made a "fascinating, even convincing impression" (F/A, pp. 1, 4). Freud encouraged Abraham to continue his work, emphasised the commonalities in their thinking—while casually pointing out all the details Abraham had overlooked. What Freud communicated in his letter to Abraham, he could have picked up in Freud's "My Views" (1906a): for instance the insight that seductions may be phantasies assuming a defensive function. In his letter Freud wrote:

> There is one consideration that I must not withhold from you that is certainly valid in the case of hysteria—I do not know whether it also applies to dementia praecox. The hysteric [...] phantasizes his need of objects back into his childhood and clothes his auto-erotic childhood in phantasies of love and seduction. [...] i.e. a part of the sexual traumas reported by patients are or may be phantasies; distinguishing them from the very frequent genuine ones is not easy, and the complication of these circumstances and the relationship of sexual traumas to forgetting and remembering is one of the chief reasons why I cannot persuade myself to a definitive presentation. (F/A, p. 2)

Gently, and with great tact, Freud suggested to his young colleague that the sexual seductions which Abraham had eagerly reported—even in the final version of his paper, that is, after he had received Freud's epistolary corrections—may be phantasies. Hilda Abraham, Karl's daughter, however, overlooked Freud's response to Abraham. Perhaps because of the great care and overly diplomatic manner in which he conveyed his views to the young follower (H. Abraham, 1974, p. 33). At the beginning of his letter Freud wrote, "You have, of course, been spared the mistake, through which I had to pass, of considering sexual traumas to be the specific aetiology of neurosis" (F/A, p. 2). What Hilda Abraham misunderstood was the fact that here Freud simply stated that Abraham—not unlike Freud himself had suggested in "My Views"—regarded the abnormal constitution rather than the trauma itself as the key aetiological factor. Similarly, Freud's unassuming remark that distinguishing between "genuine" and phantasied trauma was "not easy" (F/A, p. 2) may refer to Abraham's manuscript (1907a) as well as to a passage in his previous paper (1907b), where Abraham, with the self-confidence of the psychiatrist he was, stated: "Moreover, in cases of dementia praecox we can *easily* distinguish between delusional and factual reports" (ibid., p. 20; italics U.M.). This passage shines a strange light on Freud's "My Views", in which he admitted his errors. Almost as though Freud, somehow, did not know his own art.

In a long article dedicated to Abraham's "The Experiencing", Good (1995) put forward far-reaching and at times surprising arguments. For example, Good compared Abraham's paper with Ferenczi's work on the confusion of tongues (1933) concluding that Abraham "rather abruptly" dropped his interest in the importance of real trauma (1995, p. 1138). Good argues that unlike Ferenczi Abraham did not want to risk a falling out with Freud—"a price Abraham evidently did not wish to pay" (ibid., p. 1151). In Good's opinion the views that Abraham expounded in "The Experiencing" made him "the first psychoanalytic rebel, albeit an ambivalent and tentative one" (ibid., p. 1159). As Good sees it, much seems to support his thesis that Abraham's take on the trauma issue was being suppressed: for example, Abraham's lecture on the importance of real incest delivered on 10 November 1910 was apparently lost and never published (ibid., p. 1144).[5] For Good, the question

[5] Here Good refers to the lecture "Incest and Incest Phantasies in Neurotic Families. Clinical contributions concerning actual sexual relations within neurotic families and symptoms of illness based on incest phantasies" delivered on 12 November 1910 in the Berlin Group and never published.

then is: "Would publishing it have gone too far at the time"—and: "might there even have been an attempt to suppress it" (ibid.)? Good, moreover, speculates whether the premature deaths of both Abraham and Ferenczi reinforced the tendency to turn real seductions, real incest and Freud's seduction theory into a kind of taboo among psychoanalysts (ibid., p. 1161).[6]

I can accept Good's argument, which he himself qualifies as "hypothetical" (ibid., p. 1162) only with regard to Ferenczi. As far as Abraham is concerned a look at his bibliography shows that numerous lectures, dealing with a wide range of topics were never published neither in his lifetime nor posthumously (Abraham, 1927, pp. 503–510). In 1910, for instance, Abraham delivered five lectures that remained unpublished, among them the one mentioned by Good. In general, Abraham's significance for psychoanalysis is not associated with the seduction theory and the importance of real trauma but—and in my view rightfully so—for questions relating to "traumatophilia", that is, the unconscious, constitutionally predisposed tendency to seek out and experience trauma—a concept which other psychoanalysts, following Abraham, took up and engaged with.[7] It is of course possible that some of the aspects mentioned by Good have not received the attention they deserve. Even so, I do not see where Abraham—in 1907, writing his first papers—"went too far" and was ahead of his time. My impression is that Abraham lagged behind, that he had only partially caught up with Freud's evolving theory. What I observe in Abraham's papers is a lack of awareness. He did not consider that patients' communications regarding their history contain more than "facts"; he didn't understand that patients may also communicate screen memories and experiences that have been transformed by phantasy without the analyst having the "tools" to distinguish one from the other.

Discussing Freud's remark on the function of seduction phantasies in more depth would take us too far away from our topic. In the interest of putting things into their historical perspective suffice it to mention that Hilda Abraham's view that in his July letter Freud reminded her father "in some detail of the fate of object cathexis in the childhood memories

[6] In Good's view Abraham's 1921 postscript suggests that the trauma issue had not been resolved between Abraham and Freud: "That it took thirteen years to write this ambivalently worded concession, which remains entirely vague on the specifics of his mistakes, is noteworthy" (Good, 1995, p. 1144).

[7] See Ferenczi, 1916–1917; Lowenfeld, 1941; Fenichel, 1945, pp. 543–546.

and in the adult phantasies of hysterics" (H. Abraham, 1974, p. 33) is misleading. Here Hilda creates the impression that Freud's remarks on the hysteric's specific object relatedness and her/his capacity for transference had been common knowledge. That, however, was not the case. Even though Freud had entertained this idea for quite some time, he had not yet published it.[8] Clearly, Freud did not *remind* Abraham but shared his thoughts with him. A few months later Abraham presented those thoughts at the Salzburg congress and fleshed them out in a subsequent publication (Abraham, 1908).

In regard to the defensive function of phantasies mentioned in the same letter, we can say that at this point in his thinking it was important to Freud to emphasise that phantasies that contained libidinous relationships to primary objects may cover over another "truth": masturbation, that is, "the primary addiction".[9] Freud shared his thoughts with his disciples, who, it seems to me, wanted to hear nothing of it. Some even maintained that Freud was too hesitant when it came to admitting that from the very beginning (of psychic life) drives were directed at objects.[10] Given how difficult it was for his disciples to comprehend the level of complexity in Freud's thinking, Good's accusation seems an overstatement. It seems to me that Freud's disciples were rather averse to the pains of careful interpretation; they preferred a shorter, easier path, conflating manifest content and unconscious wish. In his comment on the defensive aspects of phantasies Freud did note the difference between manifest content and unconscious wish. Envisaged in this way Freud at all times sought to keep a distance from both the communications received by his patients as well as to his own insights. Both may falsely give the appearance of truth. In November 1906, at a meeting of the Vienna Group, Freud, referring to his own ideas, said that all of us tended to believe that whatever crossed our minds was true: "every man believes himself" (Min 1, p. 61).

---

[8] See F/Fl, p. 390; Min 1, pp. 59, 108–109.

[9] see F/Fl, p. 287; Freud, 1906a, p. 274; 1909d, pp. 206–207; 1914d, p. 18; 1916–1917, p. 370.

[10] Jones writes about Freud: "It seems a curious thing to say of the very man who explored the child's mind to an extent that had never before been possible, that he should nevertheless have retained some inhibitions about coming too close quarters with it. [...] We remarked earlier on the slowness with which Freud was willing to admit the existence of infantile sexuality, particularly its allo-erotic aspects, and to the end of his life he displayed certain reservations about the limit of what it was possible to accomplish in child analysis and the exploration of the more remote and hidden regions of the earliest mental processes" (1953–1957, vol. 2, p. 261).

In his letter to Abraham Freud does not tire of reminding his young colleague not to forget how complicated things really are. He draws Abraham's attention to the fact that aside from constitution and unconscious intent "later life events so often become the decisive factor" (F/A, p. 3). In another passage Freud asks Abraham to consider that in some milieus the circumstances for the experiencing of sexual trauma are "very favourable, while in another they are meagre" (ibid., p. 2). Freud's reservations demonstrate that "a *number* of aetiological factors are required which support one another and must therefore not be regarded as being in mutual opposition" (1906a, p. 279). This commitment to careful assessment combined with tolerating not-knowing and uncertainty is part of Freud's approach to the theory and practice of psychoanalysis. In his July letter Freud repeatedly stresses how difficult it was to find adequate theoretical formulations for his observations: "everything becomes more indistinct" he wrote, leaving him uncertain about many aspects, making it clear to him that "a thorough examination of the whole question is still necessary" (F/A, p. 3).

The normality of infantile sexuality

Abraham's second error refers to infantile sexuality. It was the discovery of infantile sexuality, hidden behind the screen of seduction phantasies, that prompted Freud—as he himself stated—to revise his seduction theory (Freud, 1914d, p. 17). In *Three Essays on the Theory of Sexuality* (1905d) Freud gave an account of infantile sexual life. Abraham obviously was familiar with this work; and yet he, understandably, struggled to accept Freud's idea that the infantile-sexual constitution and its polymorphously perverse character were "normal".

My summary of Abraham's paper has perhaps not adequately conveyed the full extent to which it relies on a strict distinction between normality and abnormality—even though there are passages in which Abraham states the opposite, perhaps in reaction to Freud's letter (ibid., p. 55). In what can only be described as one-sided reasoning, Abraham equates abnormalities with the "sexual perversions" of neurotics and psychotics whose sexual life was characterised by "numerous abnormalities" (ibid., p. 54). Abraham's notion of traumatophilia rests on the idea of abnormality: only children with an abnormal constitution frequently experience sexual trauma; only abnormal children don't resist sexual violence, and only abnormal children keep the trauma a secret.

In his July 1907 letter Freud counters: "But why do some children talk all the same? It is hard to ascribe an abnormal organization to the others, because this abnormal constitution is the general infantile constitution. Perhaps here we are once again faced with a more-or-less rather than with a sharp dividing line" (F/A, p. 3). And a few lines below he reminds Abraham that the sexual constitution was "peculiar to all children, and the same infantile perversities, anal erotism, and so on, can be found in the mentally healthy" (ibid., p. 3).

In 1990, researching a paper on the responses of Freud's colleagues to the theory of narcissism, I noticed that Freud had repeatedly mentioned this thought to Abraham (May[-Tolzmann], 1990, p. 703, fn. 14).[11] In contrast to some of his disciples, Freud was convinced that infantile sexuality could *not* fully explain psychological disorders. Over and over again he emphasised the fact that all human beings pass through libidinous phases, and—as he would soon add—experience oedipal conflict. The mere evidence of those factors in an individual's life did therefore not lend itself to accounting for the aetiology of a psychological disorder. It was the "mechanism", that is, the ways in which development occurred and conflicts were processed internally that Freud deemed most important in understanding of the aetiology of disorders—both before and after the seduction theory. What mattered was the reaction to one's own experiences and whether or not the experiences had been repressed and to what extent (Freud, 1906a, p. 276). In his short letter from November 1907 Freud once again reminded Abraham that the strong "tendency to repression" must be accounted for, "otherwise we should get not neurotics, but scoundrels" (F/A, p. 13).

Apart from the fact that Abraham, who was just at the beginning of his development as a psychoanalyst, and therefore had a much more simplistic understanding of Freud's theories—how could he not?—his insistence on abnormality feels almost inappropriate. We miss Freud's tolerance. Freud, of course, did observe abnormalities and he regarded them as an indispensable factor in the aetiology of neuroses and psychoses—which is why he supported Abraham's operationalisation of abnormality (quantitatively increased libido, sexual precociousness, strong imaginative activity, F/A, p. 13). But when Freud speaks about abnormality, his tone is different. In his July letter he writes: "However, in hysteria in particular the perverse talents can be assumed to be greater than in the basically healthy" (ibid., p. 3). Isn't there a world of

[11] F/A, pp. 308, 311, 458.

difference between a "perverse talent" and a "pathological disposition", and whether neurotic patients are described as thoroughly abnormal, driven by abnormal wishes, or whether one emphasises their particularly strong tendency towards repression?

Sexuality as common ground

Even though Freud saw the weaknesses in Abraham's communications, and named them in his letter, he felt a great fondness for this young man. Right from the very beginning, after reading Abraham's 1907 dementia praecox paper, Freud "particularly" liked that, as he wrote in his letter from 25 June 1907, Abraham "tackled the sexual side of the problem, the side that hardly anybody is willing to approach" (F/A, p. 1). Soon thereafter he wrote to Jung: "I was predisposed in Abraham's favour by the fact that he attacks the sexual problem head on; consequently I was glad to provide him with what material I had" (F/Ju, p. 79). Jung, in letters and publications, would soon indicate that he did not agree with Freud's views on this matter;[12] Abraham seems to have shared Freud's conviction on the significance of sexuality both for the aetiology of psychic disturbances and psychic development (May [-Tolzmann], 1996, p. 129). And this may have made it easier for him to adopt Freud's views and to a certain extent make them his own.[13] Jung was much less able to accommodate Freud. But like Freud, he too was working towards a comprehensive theory of psychic life and thus had a better understanding of where Freud was going. And for a while Jung became for Freud a congenial interlocutor. In the end, though, the preference for preconceived convictions proved to be the stronger bond; it united Freud and Abraham, and separated Jung from Freud.

Guilt and guilt feelings as specific to Abraham's theorising

Even though Abraham wrote "The Experiencing" early on in his life as an analyst, in its focus on guilt and guilt feelings the paper already contains traces of the theoretician Abraham was to become. The question of

[12] See Jung's preface to *Psychology of Dementia Praecox* (1907).

[13] Abraham's adaptability contributed to the eruption of the rivalries between Jung and Abraham at the Salzburg Congress (1908). See Jones 1953–1957, vol. 2. pp. 46–51; Kerr, 1993; Cremerius. 1997; Kuhn, 2000; Falzeder, 2002.

guilt, of who is to blame for the sexual seduction is a, perhaps *the* major preoccupation of Abraham's paper. Is it not the abnormal, seducible, and seductive child who feels guilty, and rightfully so? Freud partially agreed with Abraham but as a close reading reveals, that part is tiny. "We" too, Freud writes—referring to himself and the Vienna Group—have found that children do not report the seduction "when they have experienced a pleasure gain", and that he too believed the pleasure to be of a masochistic quality (F/A, p. 2). However, in contrast to his disciple, Freud was not consumed with the question of guilt. In December 1907 Abraham arrived in Vienna and for the first time attended a session of the group in which "his topic" was discussed—certainly in honour of him. As recorded in the minutes, Freud remarked that Abraham's work represents "an advance" because in it he showed "that children themselves seek out their traumata" (Min 1, p. 273). But according to the minutes, neither Freud nor other attendants of the group mention unconscious wishes for the repetition of the trauma or of guilt and of guilty feelings. In "On the History of the Psycho-analytic Movement" (1914d) Freud proceeds in a similar way. He praises Abraham profusely without endorsing his views: "The last word on the subject of traumatic aetiology was spoken later by Abraham (1907), when he pointed out that the sexual constitution which is peculiar to children is precisely calculated to provoke sexual experiences of a particular kind—namely traumas" (ibid., p. 18). We need to read the passage closely. Freud does not mention unconscious motivation, unconscious wishes, or an intention to seek out trauma. Given his keen intellect we can assume that Freud regarded that part of Abraham's paper as unfounded. Freud only mentioned those aspects of Abraham's argument that he could support: the relation between trauma and sexual constitution—a notion he himself had introduced in "My Views" (1906a).

Putting the blame on the children did not sit well with Freud. In the July letter his tone becomes harsh only once, namely when he comments on Abraham's claim that children unconsciously sought out traumatic situations. Freud writes: "As for the unconscious purpose [...] this should be modified to the extent that the dividing line between consciousness and unconsciousness has not yet been established in early childhood" (F/A, p. 3). "The child reacts," Freud continues "as if compulsively to sexual impulses, as if unconsciously in fact, but without an inner conflict" which in most children only developed after the fact (ibid.), even though *some* children might experience a conflict. In this context Freud reminds Abraham of the concepts of "deferred action" and sexual latency. Concepts Freud had developed to account for his observation that sexual trauma was *not* immediately conflictual. Freud was considering the possibility that the capacity for repression developed only gradually and that the sexual inhibitions—shame, disgust, moral ideals (what would later be called the super-ego)—were put up over time. In short, as Freud saw it there was a fundamental difference between the psychic apparatus of an infant and that of an adult. Abraham, on the other hand, writes about children as if they were adults, claiming that the differences between child and adult were negligible (1907a, p. 50).[14] In a way this controversy between Freud and Abraham was a harbinger of later disagreements on the question of guilt feelings. Since *Totem and Taboo* (1912–1913) Freud saw feelings of guilt as firmly anchored in the oedipal conflict whereas Abraham prepared the ground for assigning them to earlier stages of development.

In a footnote in his *Psychopathology of Everyday Life* (1901b) Freud included a little episode from *Don Quijote*. Abraham retells the story in his "The Experiencing"—albeit with a slip (1907a, p. 50):

> A woman brought a man before the judge and accused him of having raped her. The judge (Sancho) takes away the man's money and indemnifies the woman with it. The woman leaves, and the judge asks the man to follow her and take back the money from her. Both come back "struggling with each other"; the woman boasts that the villain had been unable to seize the purse from her. Thereupon Sancho said: "If you had defended your honour with half the determination with which you have defended this purse, the man could not have robbed you of it." (Freud, 1901b, p. 181, fn. 1)

In Abraham's opinion the story tells us that we should have expected the woman to defend herself against the sexual assault, which is to say she was rightfully pronounced guilty. Freud, however, had drawn a very different conclusion. Here's what Freud wrote: "the ingenious judgement delivered by Sancho Panza [...] is psychologically *unjust*" (ibid.; my italics). Freud finds the sentence unjust because "a portion

---

[14] Thus Abraham assumes that the child may experience both fore-pleasure and end-pleasure (Abraham, 1907a, p. 53), whereas Freud maintained that children only experience fore-pleasure (1905d, pp. 210–211).

of [the woman's] unconscious impulses meets the attack with encouragement" (ibid.). For Freud this is a reason to *not* declare the woman fully "guilty". Abraham finds the woman guilty because she has sexual wishes while Freud for the same reason pleads for the woman's psychological innocence. Abraham judges the woman for her sexual desire while Freud sympathises with her wishes and, for a moment, takes her side. To put it more sharply: for Abraham analysis becomes a trial presided by a strict judge whereas Freud's judge is kinder, more flexible, willing to put himself in the defendant's shoes, temporarily siding with the woman's legitimate interests.

Abraham's "unconscious traumatophilia" and Freud's "repetition compulsion"

Abraham believed to have observed that his hysteric patients had a "tendency to experience sexual traumas repeatedly" (1907a, p. 57). He held the same to be true for all patients who had experienced multiple traumata. They too were motivated by an unconscious wish "to keep the traumatic symptom complex alive" (ibid., p. 61). Does that mean that Abraham was ahead of his time? That he was anticipating Freud's notion of the death drive? And should Freud have mentioned Abraham's contribution in his later conceptualisation of repetition compulsion and the death drive—as Good suggests (1995, p. 1148)? Is this a case of intentional or unintentional forgetting, as Shengold (1972) claims with regard to Amenhotep?

In one of his vignettes Abraham describes the case of a nineteen-year-old woman who suffered from the symptoms of a traumatic neurosis caused by an accident. Abraham found that as a child she was very unhappy. In recent years unfavourable circumstances had aggravated her depressive mood and she lost all desire to live. When a person prefers death to life, Abraham wrote, "and when that person meets with an accident under circumstances which suggest that it might have been avoided, then I consider that we are justified in assuming that there is an unconscious intention of suicide" (Abraham, 1907a, p. 59). According to Abraham, Freud had reported similar cases in his *Psychopathology of Everyday Life* (1901b).

Freud, indeed, spoke of "half-intentional self-injury"—and he apologised for using such a "clumsy expression" (1901b, p. 180). Further down on the same page he offered a more precise description: "there is such a thing as half-intentional self-destruction (self-destruction with an unconscious intention)" (ibid.). Conceptualising it this way, Freud, it seems to me, takes note of two processes: a preconscious wish (for suicide) and an unconscious intention. In passing, he calls this "trend to self-destruction" "an instinct" ("Trieb") (ibid., p. 181), contradicting his then current theoretical model which only stipulated libidinal wishes.[15] Already in 1901 we see Freud wrestling with a problem he began to tackle more systematically in 1920.

When Freud introduced repetition compulsion and the death drive in 1920, he might have quoted himself. He chose not to, and made no mention of Abraham either. Why? Because in 1901, Freud did not yet know how to integrate the tendency to repeat a trauma into his theory. Abraham, of course, did not know either. He came as close as saying that there is an unconscious wish that wants to "keep the traumatic symptom complex alive" (1907a, pp. 61–62). He did not state that his concept of traumatophilia was "beyond" the pleasure principle, and that it was thus necessary to propose processes that were not seeking libidinal satisfaction. Therefore Freud saw no reason to mention Abraham—which is not to say that he "was ordinarily scrupulous about crediting others and assigning priorities," as Good (1995, p. 1149) suggests. There were in fact colleagues—among them Spielrein, Stekel, and Adler—who had introduced the idea of a death drive or an aggressive instinctual drive before Freud. The way Freud handled referencing sources definitely deserves its own study.

There are two vignettes in "The Experience", in which Abraham concerns himself with suicide and "unconscious" suicidal wishes. I first noticed Abraham's special interest in this topic in his study on the painter Segantini (Abraham, 1911; see Chapter Two). This seems to be in line with his fascination with the clinical picture of depression, which is why, years before Freud, he was able to make a substantial contribution to the aetiology of depression. Mächtlinger (1997) noticed the interest in depression and self-destruction as well. She even argued that Abraham might have been struggling with depression all his life.

"To reflect rather than be angry"

Abraham believed that children who keep secret about their trauma and who lie instead of truthfully reporting the traumatic experiences

[15] "For the trend to self-destruction is present to a certain degree in very many more human beings than those in whom it is carried out; self-injuries are as a rule a compromise between this instinct and the forces that are still working against it" (Freud, 1901b, p. 181).

do so because of their abnormal disposition. As I have shown, in this matter Freud did not agree with Abraham. Adler, too, objected to Abraham's views. In the 27 November 1907 session of the Vienna Group—which Freud had opened with a reference to the publication of "The Experiencing"—Adler stated that "his experiences have been the opposite", namely that there were "non-neurotic individuals who have kept secret their sexual traumata" (Min 1, p. 252).[16] Abraham, on the other hand, was convinced that a child who was sexually seduced without consciously or unconsciously participating in the seduction "immediately found words in which to tell her mother what had happened" (1907a, p. 52). Those children were able "to speak freely", they did "not need to force out of their field of consciousness the recollection of that occurrence" (ibid., p. 55). As if a child ought to and indeed was able to tell the truth always and, if possible, right away. With a similar affect Abraham declares that children with an abnormal disposition readily gave in to temptations. Abraham's conscious sympathies—that much seems clear—lay with those children who are neither seducible nor seducers themselves. Those who he deemed abnormal he had little compassion for. With Abraham, abnormal children lose out.[17]

By way of comparison I want to call to mind how Freud talked about children who tell lies—even though Freud does not specifically refer to traumatised children. For example, the 1907 *Minutes of the Vienna Psychoanalytic Society* record the following: "Prof. FREUD: [...] As far as children's lies are concerned, it is by no means a matter of course for the child to lie; it is a matter of course to tell the truth" (Min 2, p. 203). On a different occasion Freud remarked that neglected children experienced "a breakdown of parental authority in the sexual respect" by, for

[16] This contrasts with Good's claim (1995, p. 1143) that in the 27 November session Freud did not specify which of the two works by Abraham he was referring to. Adler's response suggests the opposite: attendants knew quite well which paper Freud meant, that is, the one published on 15 November 1907 (Abraham, 1907a). Furthermore, Good's assertion that "virtually nothing was recorded regarding Abraham's 1907 papers" is inaccurate (Good, 1995, p. 1143). On 12 December 1907 Abraham's papers were the focus of the meeting whose minutes are entitled "Discussion on Sexual Traumata and Sexual Enlightenment" (Min 1, pp. 270–275).

[17] It is striking to read in Abraham's notes about the treatment of his seven-year-old daughter that he made her "confess that she masturbates" (Abraham, 1913, p. 6). A few lines down he writes: "I explained their [the self-reproaches] connexion with masturbation, which she again confessed to" (Ibid., p. 14). Abraham then expresses surprise that his daughter described her masturbating as "indecent", not taking note of the fact that he himself had described her communication as "a confession".

example "having witnessed actual sexual misbehaviour, especially on the part of the mother" (ibid., p. 516). Freud continues: "Another detail observed in our practice supports this view: the lying of children who in general do not lie and are by nature truth-loving. They tell lies from the moment when they see their parents lie" (ibid.).

Was Freud naive and maybe even in denial about the maliciousness of children? Did he grant them sexual wishes but turn a blind eye on their aggressivity, amorality, and dishonesty? It is, of course, possible that Freud did in fact hesitate to see children that way. But isn't the way in which he engages with their lies also convincing? His short paper "Two Lies Told by Children" (1913g) is a good example. Freud's introductory remarks might as well be directed at Abraham: "We can understand children telling lies, when in doing so, they are imitating the lies told by grown-up people. But a number of lies told by well-brought-up children have a particular significance and should cause those in charge of them to reflect rather than be angry" (ibid., p. 305). The passage has inspired the title of this chapter, because in it Freud describes a difference that I picked up studying Abraham's early paper and Freud's epistolary response. A difference that, to my mind, describes two distinct analytical attitudes. May Abraham forgive me for—in this case—finding the less sympathetic option in his 1907 paper, and attributing the analytic ideal to Freud's text.

Freud discusses children's motivation for lying in two brief case studies (1913g). Regarding the first one he concludes that the girl lied to her father because she could not admit—to herself and to her parents—how much she loved him. She was punished by him for lying and experienced the punishment as a "turning point" in her childhood; she became "shy and timid" and developed a number of idiosyncrasies which put a strain on her relationships (ibid., p. 305). In the second case, Freud believed that the persistent lying of a ten-year-old girl was caused by the fact that she could not bear the immense disappointment in her father. In her lies she made him more powerful than he really was. When she was younger, she had developed an "unusually strong attachment" to him. When she realised that he was "not so powerful or so distinguished" as she thought he was she could not tolerate this "departure from her ideal" and she began to brag about her father, in order "not to have to belittle [him]" (ibid., p. 308). Admitting her disingenuousness would have brought to light the hidden and forbidden love she felt for her father. In both cases, Freud argued, the lying occurred "under the influence of excessive feelings of love" (ibid., p. 305). Is it unfair to compare Abraham's short and early paper with Freud's position on the question of lying in children; and to use one as an example for the tendency to be strict and to judge impatiently, and the other one as an example for a kinder, more considerate attitude?

Concluding remarks

In 1907 Freud was far ahead of Abraham. For the past fifteen years he had been working on a theory of the aetiology of the neuroses and psychoses; he had revised neuropathological and psychiatric nosology; he had devised a new system for the classification of disorders according to their aetiology; and he step by step developed a new therapeutic procedure (May[-Tolzmann], 1996). He got lost often; sometimes he pursued ideas only to discard them later on. Eventually he arrived at a theory whose main features he held on to for the rest of his life. When Abraham approached him in 1907, Freud already had many years of observation and theorising under his belt. And yet, he patiently engaged with Abraham's first steps.

Abraham's "The Experiencing" had only a small share in the advancement of Freud's thinking. It is of course true that the Abraham of 1907 had not yet sufficiently understood all the factors that were at play in cases of sexual abuse. And we can assume that if Abraham were alive today, he would not express himself in the same way he did in 1907. And yet, even in 1907, analysts differed in the ways in which they made sense of their experiences. There were Stekel, Sadger, Adler, Rank, and Ferenczi (to name just a few). Great personalities and thinkers who not only developed new theories but who also thought about their patients' problems in their own ways. What was true then is true today. Psychoanalysis today incorporates various theories—not all of them compatible with one another—as well as different "approaches" and "techniques". It seems to me that the approaches analysts favour are more to do with their personality and less with the theory they feel beholden to. As much as psychoanalytic knowledge is grounded in its history, unfolding over time and gaining complexity, idiosyncratic factors are part of that history as well.

Stekel, whose work I have studied only partially has impressed me as a psychoanalyst who was first and foremost interested in his own thoughts, and who presented them proudly. For Stekel to analyse meant to show off his brilliant ideas. His patients' ideas played a minor role in his case studies. Sadger, whose early work I am more familiar with, belongs to a different "type" of analyst. He seemed to have had little interest in putting himself or his interpretative skills centre stage. His detailed case studies of analytic treatments present him as an analyst intent at making his patients "confess" infantile sexual wishes, especially those directed at the analyst (see Sadger, 1908a, 1910d; see also Chapter One). He was an early advocate of rigorous transference interpretations right from the very beginning of treatment—something that is not true for Stekel. And yet, up until 1910 both men's understanding of psychoanalysis was firmly grounded in Freudian theory.

It is also true that Abraham's "The Experiencing" offers too slim a basis to allow for more general statements about its author's approach. When I researched the reactions of some of Freud's disciples to "On Narcissism: an Introduction" (1914c), I was of the impression that in a number of papers Abraham took a position slightly different from Freud's (May[-Tolzmann], 1990, p. 701). Examples are Abraham's papers on depression, war neuroses, *ejaculatio praecox*, the female castration complex, tics, and the treatment of narcissistic disorders. What separated Abraham from Freud—it seems to me—was his greater ability to be in tune with his patients' "ruthlessness" and "aggressive wishes", "identifying more readily with the position of the attacked object and less so with the position of the attacker" (ibid., p. 706). In a subsequent study I argued that Abraham was able to come to an understanding of depression before Freud. Already in 1911 he was employing the imago of the "bad mother", a concept that for Freud did not possess the primary status it had for Abraham (see Chapter Two).

It makes sense to compare these findings with my reading of "The Experiencing". What speaks against such an undertaking is the fact that Abraham wrote "The Experiencing" very early in his career as an analyst, at a time when he had only begun to familiarise himself with Freud's theory. To put it differently, we ought to be careful when we interpret Abraham's "errors" and his idiosyncratic observations. However, what I do want to make a note of is that in my view "The Experiencing" indicates that Abraham was predominantly interested in the question of guilt, and that it was not easy for him to understand the traumatised child that lies and keeps secrets. This is of course not to say that Abraham really worked that way or that others experienced him that way. All we know is how he presented himself in his papers.

Engaging with "The Experiencing" made me think of analytic work in general. No group or school can claim to be immune to developing a kind of "catch the thief" mentality, where the analyst finds herself seeking to pin down the patient, arrest him, persecute him, telling and showing him what he did in an impatient, self-righteous, and bitter manner. There is a kinder attitude, characterised by thoughtful consideration and the ability to defer judgement and criticism. It is an ideal that Freud sometimes, in some of his papers, in some passages, measured up to. That being said, I wish for a psychoanalysis that finds its way back to thoughtfulness and to a kinder attitude that Freud's papers and letters sometimes speak to.

Translated by Bettina Mathes

CHAPTER FOUR

Karl Abraham's revolution of 1916: from sensual sucking to the oral-aggressive wish of destruction

It was Karl Abraham who introduced the concept of oral sadism into psychoanalysis. The concept can be found in its full-fledged form in "A Short Study of the Development of the Libido Viewed in the Light of Mental Disorders" (1924). It was to lead to major controversies soon after Abraham's death, and I would like to describe how it entered the psychoanalytic canon. In addition, I would like to show that Abraham's concept of oral sadism was the beginning of a change of course in psychoanalysis, creating divisions between psychoanalytic groups that have lasted to the present day.

It will become clear that Abraham was not simply the loyal disciple of Freud, whom he is generally considered to be, but also the founder of a new psychoanalytic approach. Like his contemporaries Ferenczi, Rank, Jones, and before them Jung and Adler, he succeeded in developing an original theory of psychic disorders and psychic development. I suggest that underpinning this theory stood his thesis on oral sadism.

Abraham's "The First Pregenital Stage of the Libido"

A few months after World War I broke out, Abraham volunteered for military service, and for the whole of 1915, in the time that remained apart from his work as a doctor in field hospitals in Berlin and East Prussia, he worked on the paper that was to lead to a change in psychoanalytic theory. Its title was "The First Pregenital Stage of the Libido" (1916–1917). The text matured slowly, "incrementally" and "in the course of seven or eight months", and was mainly written in Allenstein in East Prussia, where he had been transferred in March 1915.[1] Apart from the concluding passages, he had finished it on 28 December 1915, and declared it completed a few days later, that is, in January 1916 (F/A, pp. 321, 322). In December 1916, it appeared in the fourth volume of the *Internationale Zeitschrift für ärztliche Psychoanalyse*, and it received an award in 1918 (ibid., p. 386).

Already in June 1913, however, Abraham had given an unpublished lecture in Berlin that bore the title "Beobachtungen über die Beziehungen zwischen Nahrungstrieb und Sexualtrieb [Observations on the Relations between the Nutritional and the Sexual Instincts]" (Korr, 1913, p. 617). One year later, in March 1913, he told Freud that, as soon as he found the time, he would prepare his observations on "mouth eroticism" in a schizophrenic patient for publication (F/A, p. 179). However, other tasks had become more pressing: struggles with Jung, trying to obtain a professorship at the university, and working on the *Jahrbuch für psychoanalytische und psychopathologische Forschungen*, of which he had become editor in 1914. It was not until the beginning of 1915 that Abraham found an opportunity to continue his work on oral eroticism.

Abraham's interest may have been reawakened when he heard that Freud had introduced the "oral" or "cannibalistic" phase in October 1914, in the third edition of *Three Essays on the Theory of Sexuality* (Freud, 1905d/1915, p. 198). Previously, Freud had described the concept of oral eroticism in detail in the first (1905) and second edition (1905d/1910) of *Three Essays*. Now, however, in the third edition he added an oral *phase* to the anal phase (which he had introduced in 1913). He may have told Abraham about this when he visited him in Berlin on his way to and from Hamburg in September 1914 (F/A. p. 278); or Abraham might have seen this innovation described in January 1915, in the copy of the new edition of *Three Essays* that Freud sent him (ibid., p. 295). Whether or not Abraham was inspired by reading this, on 30 January 1915, he told Freud that he had started to write a small paper on the relationship

[1] F/A, pp. 297, 299, 307, 315, 318.

between hunger and libido (ibid., p. 297). This was the beginning of his work on "The First Pregenital Stage of the Libido" (1916–1917).

As previously mentioned, Freud had introduced the oral stage in the third edition of *Three Essays*. In addition, he explained his view of the newly introduced developmental stage in his case history of the Wolf Man (1918b, p. 106). Apart from an appendix, which he did not write until 1918, he began writing this text directly after completing his work on *Three Essays*, finishing it at the beginning of November 1914 (F/A, pp. 280, 282; F/Fer 2, p. 24). Ferenczi received the manuscript of the Wolf Man, but Abraham did not because Freud did not want to entrust it to the vagaries of the wartime postal service (F/A, p. 282).

Nonetheless, Abraham could have heard about the Wolf Man at the aforementioned meeting with Freud in Berlin in 1914. After that the two men did not see each other again until the war was over, and there are no indications that Abraham could have received the Wolf Man case from any third parties, so that, in all likelihood, he did not read it until January 1919, when it appeared in the fourth volume of the *Sammlung kleiner Schriften zur Neurosenlehre* (F/A, p. 390).[2]

It therefore seems very likely that when Abraham was writing "The First Pregenital Stage," he was not yet familiar with the longer, clinically based deliberations on the oral phase or the significance of the fear of being devoured that are included in the case history of the Wolf Man. It is, of course, difficult to say whether previous knowledge of this would have made Abraham alter his point of view. I suspect that it would not have; Abraham did not swerve from the course he had started in 1915 even after the war when he was once again in close contact with Freud and his writings. The new approach that he had developed in "The First Pregenital Stage of the Libido" had, I think, become so much a part of him, so much his possession, that he was subsequently more or less immune to theoretical views that were not congruent with this basic view.

There is no doubt, however, that, beginning in January or February 1915, Abraham knew that Freud had introduced "the oral or, as it might be called, cannibalistic pregenital sexual organization" (Freud, 1905d/1915, p. 198). It is important to emphasise this because there has

---

[2]Because of the prior publication of the Wolf Man's dream of the tree in which wolves were sitting (Freud, 1913d) in the *Internationale Zeitschrift*, Abraham would have been familiar with this while working on "The First Pregenital Stage". In this short text, Freud wrote about the meaning of devouring (*Auffressen*) but did not yet give any indications of the introduction of an oral phase.

been a lack of clarity—persisting to the present day—as to who originally developed the concept of the oral stage: Freud or Abraham.

This confusion may have been initially caused by Jones (1920), who—in the first issue of the *International Journal of Psychoanalysis*, of which he was editor—published for his English colleagues an authoritative overview on the development of psychoanalytic theory since the beginning of the war. He reported that Freud had introduced the anal phase in 1913, and then continued as follows: "Abraham has further shown that there exists a still earlier pregenital stage of development, which, from the prominent part played in it by the buccal zone, he calls the 'oral' or 'cannibalistic' one" (ibid., p. 165). Jones creates the impression here that Abraham had postulated the oral developmental stage of the libido, and that he, not Freud, had devised the terms *oral* and *cannibalistic*. Later, for example, in his biography of Freud, Jones did not repeat this mistake, but as far as I know, did not rectify it either.

Now that we have the complete correspondence between Freud and Abraham, I think there can be no doubt that it was Freud who introduced the oral stage, and that Abraham's contribution consisted in *developing a new perspective* on this in his paper on the first pregenital stage. The term oral-sadistic, however, seems to have been coined by Abraham a few years later in "A Short Study of the Development of the Libido" (1924), in which he suggested dividing the oral stage into two subphases: first, the *oral sucking phase*, followed by the *oral-sadistic phase* (ibid., pp. 450–451).

I cannot speculate as to whether and to what extent Freud later took over Abraham's suggestion of 1924, but I would like to point out that the term *oral-sadistic* (as well as oral sadistic) turns up only *once* in Freud's work, in a passage in the *New Introductory Lectures on Psycho-Analysis* (1933a), where he summarises Abraham's theory on the different stages (ibid., p. 99). Otherwise, we find only the term "oral" in his papers, sometimes together with "cannibalistic". However, Freud uses the adjective "sadistic" very frequently, in both his early and later works, but *only* to describe phenomena of the anal or sadistic-anal phase.[3]

[3] This statement is based on the *Standard Edition* as available through Psychoanalytic Electronic Publishing (PEP), version 9. Searching this electronic database for *oral-sadistic* and *oral sadistic* yielded the above-mentioned passage (1933a, p. 99). The related terms *oral-aggressive, oral aggressive,* and *oral aggression* do not show up in searching the *Standard Edition* in this database. The terms *oral aggressivity* and *aggressive oral* occur only once, in "Female Sexuality", both on the same page (1931b, p. 237). See Chapter Six, on the term *anal-sadistic*.

The important thing, of course, is not that Freud and Abraham utilised different words to characterise the instinctual aims of the oral stage, one using *cannibalistic* and the other *sadistic*, but that they viewed the psychic events at this stage differently. In my view, Freud's cannibalism is not the same as Abraham's oral-sadism.

Freud's introduction of the oral phase (1915)

The way in which Freud introduced the oral phase in the third edition of *Three Essays on the Theory of Sexuality* (1905d/1915) deserves closer scrutiny. On the one hand, this is important because these are Freud's last words on the subject. It was not so different with the anal phase: after writing an appendix (1917c), Freud did not return to the subject. In fact, after 1916, orality and anality were no longer areas of interest for Freud; he had no new ideas on these subjects, and his focus was moving in other directions.

It also seems to me that the alterations made in the wake of the introduction of the death and life instincts (Freud, 1920g), and with them a stronger emphasis on aggression, did little to change the concepts of orality and anality. Possible corrections would have been visible, for example, in Freud's last comprehensive paper, *An Outline of Psycho-Analysis* (1940a); but what we find there is a description of the oral stage that closely resembles that of 1915 (ibid., pp. 153–154). The only alteration—though a noteworthy one—was Freud's comment that sadistic impulses would "sporadically" turn up during teething (ibid., p. 154). I interpret his description of "sporadic" impulses to mean that there was no oral-sadistic "structure" or "oral-sadistic organisation" (comparable to the sadistic-anal organisation).

What does Freud say in that short passage of *Three Essays*, only eleven lines long, in which he introduces the oral phase? For elucidation, I will refer not only to that paper, but also to his description of the Wolf Man (1918b) and to "Instincts and Their Vicissitudes" (1915c), which Freud wrote in March 1915, right after finishing the third edition of *Three Essays* and his article on the Wolf Man (F/A, p. 302).[4]

The very first words of *Three Essays*, where Freud introduces the "oral or, if we so wish, cannibalistic" (1905d/1915, p. 198) phase, already

[4]Abraham was familiar with Freud's "Instincts and Their Vicissitudes" (1915c) when he wrote "The First Pregenital Stage of the Libido"; he had read it in April 1915 (F/A, p. 306).

express a certain caution toward the "cannibalistic". A few lines later he describes the oral phase as "constructed" (*fiktiv*). Its acceptance was "forced upon" us through the analysis of pathological phenomena; only "relics" of it could actually be observed, such as thumb sucking. In a similar vein, in the Wolf Man paper (1918b) Freud wrote that he had "been driven" to introduce an oral phase and that we cannot expect to see any "direct manifestations" of it, at least not in normal development (ibid., p. 106).

I consider these passages very important. I believe that Freud wanted to point out that the status of the oral phase was less firmly established than, for example, that of the anal phase. In "The Disposition to Obsessional Neurosis" (1913i), Freud described what events in the analysis of a certain patient (Elfriede Hirschfeld) had made him postulate an anal phase. Compared to this, the clinical justification for an oral phase was rather vague. Freud mentions "pathology", but does not specify the pathologic phenomena he had in mind, nor does the case of the Wolf Man provide much clarification.

As far as I can see, the partially "fictive" (in Strachey's translation: "constructed") character of the oral phase has so far been generally overlooked. Elsewhere, Freud spoke of the "vagueness" of instinctual drives, of "obscure" desires, and noted that the child can have only a vague sense of what it wishes; "words and thoughts have to be lent to the child"; indeed, "the deepest strata may turn out to be impenetrable for consciousness" (1909b, p. 41; 1918b, p. 9). In this context, it is remarkable that his bold and highly speculative study, "Overview on the Transference Neuroses" (1985a), written in the early summer of 1915, does not postulate an oral or cannibalistic developmental stage, although this might have been expected so soon after the recent introduction of the oral stage.[5]

All this seems to suggest that the instinctual aims of the oral phase—except for the "relic" of sensual sucking—were, according to Freud, accessible to consciousness only partially and then with difficulty. The grown-up, unlike the child, can be conscious of his incestuous and murderous wishes. If that happens, he will be frightened. However, as I

---

[5]In this paper, Freud develops the thesis that the first stage of the development of humankind created anxiety hysteria, then conversion hysteria and obsessional neurosis, and it was not until relatively late that depression and paranoia emerged (see, e.g., 1985a, p. 12).

understand Freud, cannibalistic wishes very rarely if ever become conscious for the adult, which is why he calls them "fictive".

Already in the first edition of *Three Essays* (1905d), Freud had stressed sensual sucking as the core phenomenon of oral eroticism (ibid., p. 179). There he described the autoerotic character of sensual sucking, of deriving pleasure from one's own body, which he saw as characteristic of infantile sexuality as a whole. True autoeroticism, however, occurs only when the pleasure derived from the breast is separated from feeding. It is not until sucking has attained a self-satisfying character in itself and no longer serves to relieve hunger that it is "really" sexual. This independence of sensual sucking from feeding—in other words, of the sexual instinct from that of self-preservation—is repeated almost verbatim by Freud in *An Outline of Psycho-Analysis* (1940a, p. 153); it is one of the basic tenets of his theory.

Whereas autoeroticism had already been introduced as a characteristic of the oral component instinct, the instinctual aim was an innovation introduced in the third edition of *Three Essays* (1905d/1915). Oral sexual activity now sought to achieve the "incorporation of the object" (ibid., p. 198).[6] This new determination gave rise to a number of questions, above all whether the incorporation of the object was not the very opposite of autoeroticism. Isn't object-related sucking opposed to sensual sucking, which does not require an object? In what follows, I will present my interpretation of Freud's numerous, often-ambiguous statements on devouring, incorporation, introjection, and identification.

It seems to me that there is a recurrent dimension to Freud's thinking, one of theoretical and practical relevance, in which autoeroticism and incorporation are not mutually exclusive. This line of thought is most tangible in "Instincts and Their Vicissitudes" (1915c), in the passage in which he describes incorporation as the "preliminary stage" of love or "a type of love which is consistent with abolishing the object's separate existence" (ibid., p. 138). Freud usually chose his words with great care, so I think it is no coincidence that here, where he describes the first developmental stage, he does not speak of destruction and annihilation, but of "abolishing the object's separate existence", which would

---

[6] Incorporation [*Einverleibung*], as Freud continues in this passage, is the "prototype of a process which, in the form of identification, is later to play such an important psychological part" (1905d/1915, p. 198).

be compatible with a preliminary form of love (ibid.). Although he does not explicitly point this out, the description indicates his awareness that *incorporation* and *love* are not immediately compatible. His answer was groundbreaking, enabling an approach to psychic processes whose logic was different from that of so-called adult experience. In this psychic area, the wellbeing of the (incorporated) object is of no interest; its separate existence is abolished without the incorporating subject experiencing this as aggression.

This is how I interpret Freud in these passages. That he does not consider incorporation to be a deliberately aggressive act can also be seen, I think, in his emphasising that, in the first developmental phase, we can speak only of "preliminary" forms of love, not of love or hate in their true sense, but rather of "unconcern or indifference" (Freud, 1915c, p. 133) toward the object. The child greedily grasping the breast when it is hungry, according to Freud, is otherwise indifferent, and on this level cannot be regarded as aggressive.

In this passage on the abolition of the separate existence of the object, Freud's reference to this kind of love as "ambivalent" (1915c, p. 138) is not a contradiction. It is characteristic of Freud's thinking that he does not always clearly differentiate between a genetic, that is, developmental, and a causal connection. When he says that devouring was a "model" for incorporation, for example, or that incorporation was a "precursor" or "prototype" for identification (as in the context of his introduction of the oral phase; 1905d/1915, p. 198), he means that one takes chronological precedence over the other, and that the earlier and later stages are connected in an unspecified way. The later phase is already contained in the earlier one without having yet become visible there. As I understand the passage mentioned above, ambivalence becomes perceptible later, and therefore must have been an incipient presence before, albeit not yet a noticeable one. This would also be compatible with Freud's observation that it is not until genital organisation has been achieved that love *becomes* "the opposite of hate" (1915c, p. 139).

The description of the so-called *purified pleasure-ego* that belongs to a phase somewhat later than the oral phase again serves to show what Freud meant by *introjection* (1915c, p. 136). Here Freud developed the idea, new at the time, that the early narcissistic-autoerotic ego emerges by making everything that is pleasurable its own, by "introjecting" it, and by rejecting everything that is unpleasurable.[7] In this way, what is pleasurable, or the pleasure-inducing object, becomes part of the ego. This psychic process as described by Freud does not have a deliberately or predominantly aggressive character; it is not directed *against* the pleasurable or the pleasurable object. Incorporation is seen as a natural expansion of the ego, which, in its autoerotic perception, sees itself as the embodiment of the pleasurable.

Freud has a similar view of the process of "replacing" and exchanging subject and object, which is characteristic of the narcissistic stage, and which he considers to be of significance in the etiology of perversion (1915c, p. 132). Again, this exchange, in which the subject feels as if it were the object, is not described as an aggressive process.

From this we can conclude the following: when we read Freud nowadays, we do so through Abraham's eyes, much more than we are aware of, and thereby tend to overlook certain aspects and meanings that are contained or also contained in his texts. When Freud speaks of *incorporation*—which, after "Instincts and Their Vicissitudes" (1915c), occurs mainly in *Group Psychology and the Analysis of the Ego* (1921c, p. 105)—it is worth remembering that he has an early stage of development in mind, one in which incorporation is neither an act of love nor one of aggression—at least from the point of view of the subject.[8]

Of course, I am not trying to say that Freud was not concerned with aggression in 1915. On the contrary, in "Instincts and Their Vicissitudes", in particular, it is dealt with in detail. However, at that time aggression occupied another position in the system. Aggressive impulses do not take place alongside libidinal impulses and do not have the same rank or status, but are always a subplot, a secondary motive, never the deepest and core motive. Never do they have a primary, non-reducible character. They are what needs to be explained and are not themselves an explanation.

A particularly impressive example of Freud's basic idea at that time of the relationship between sexuality and aggression can be found in the twenty-second chapter of *Introductory Lectures on Psycho-Analysis*

---

[7] This is the first time that Freud used the term *introjection*, coined by Ferenczi (1909), which pleased Ferenczi very much. In the third edition of *Three Essays* (1905d/1915), Freud used *Einverleibung*, not *Introjektion*—a differentiation lost in the English translation.

[8] Freud's and Abraham's different views of introjection do not fully unfold until later, in "A Short Study of the Development of the Libido" (Abraham, 1924).

(1916–1917). There Freud reviews the state of the theory of obsessive neurosis and discusses a very important finding, namely, regression to the stage of sadistic-anal organisation. As a result, "the impulse to love" must "disguise itself as a sadistic impulse" (ibid., p. 343). Freud continues: "The obsessional idea: 'I should like to kill you' […] means at bottom nothing other than: 'I should like to enjoy you in love'" (ibid., p. 344). The murderous desire, conscious and frightening as it is, is seen by Freud as a camouflaged desire to love. In a similar vein, he analyses the murderous desire directed toward the oedipal rival. This, too, is not primary, in his opinion, but serves the purposes of the libido—namely, the wish to be the sole possessor of the mother and to enjoy unimpeded autoeroticism.

The same is true, then, for the wolf that eats the grandmother and the little goats as for Kronos, who devours his children (1918b, p. 31; 1926d, p. 105).[9] For Freud, devouring always has a latent meaning that differs from its manifest meaning. In his view, myths, fairy tales, dreams, symptoms, and other manifestations of the psyche are always substitutes and compromise formations, and do not represent the unconscious as such. For example, he sees Little Hans's anxiety of being bitten by a horse as fear of the castrating father, which, because of partial regression, manifests itself as fear of being bitten by him (1909b, p. 123; see also 1926d, pp. 101, 124). The fear expresses itself through oral means. Little Hans does not altogether regress to the narcissistic or oral phase and is not affected by the mechanisms typical of this stage—such as, for example, narcissistic identification. His regression involves only the shape and specifics of the fear. The worst fear (that of being castrated) is replaced by one that is somewhat easier to bear (that of being bitten by a horse). Of course, Hans's fear of his father also has to do with his own aggressive impulses toward his oedipal rival but, as described above, these are not the "real" reason for it; instead, as Freud writes, "Hans's hostile complex against his father screened his lustful one about his mother" (1909b, p. 137).

The Wolf Man's fear of being eaten by a wolf is more regressive in character than Hans's horse phobia. The wolf phobia is revealed through Freud's analysis to be the wish for the passive love of the father (1918b, p. 104; see also 1926d, pp. 101, 124). Having observed coitus *a tergo* in his childhood, the Wolf Man believed that being loved meant being

---

[9] These are references to two well-known fairy tales: "Little Red Riding Hood", in which the wolf devours the grandmother, and "The Wolf and the Seven Little Goats", in which the wolf devours six of seven goats.

available to the father for anal intercourse and also meant having to be a woman, that is, castrated. This was extremely frightening, and so the wish was abandoned. What remained was the fear of the father that was then transferred to the wolf. In this fear, however, the original wish to be loved by the father makes a reappearance, albeit obliquely, because being devoured also means being devoured out of love. The libidinal, wishful idea of being devoured out of love, according to Freud, is a product of the regressive distortion of later, oedipal-passive wishes to be loved. Symptom formation (the fear of being devoured) is set in motion by later, passive wishes for love. So again, the primary wish is to be loved by the father, and this primary wish is what analytic work targets and tries to bring into consciousness; this is the true source of the symptom.

These examples are meant to show that, for Freud, infantile animal phobias in which the fear of being devoured is expressed are not caused by a wish to devour the object or to be devoured by it. Freud did not hypothesise along this line in the original publications of the cases of Little Hans (1909b) or the Wolf Man (1918b) or in his later, detailed postscript (1926d). Put differently, he did not regard the wish to devour the object as having dynamic effects. He resisted the trivial interpretation that a fear of being devoured by an animal reflected a wish for this to happen.

This touches on the central clinical question of how interpretation is to be carried out at all. It seems to me that, after World War I, the psychoanalysts in Freud's orbit developed a greater degree of arbitrariness, a tendency that can still be found today. Anything can stand for anything else, and any idea on how to interpret something is "right". This was not the case with Freud himself; he made a distinction between primary motives that have a dynamic effect and those that are of secondary significance. The rigor and discipline of Freud's analytic understanding grew with time. The more resistance he encountered in his disciples, especially against the concept of the oedipus complex, the more he found corroboration that infantile, already genital-centred eroticism was the dynamic core of symptoms, and that this was what analytic work was to home in on.[10] In this context, aggression was always of secondary significance.

---

[10] A good example of Freud's thinking in this regard can be found in a letter to Marie Bonaparte, which is included in Jones's biography of Freud (Jones, 1953–1957, vol. 3, p. 445). Here Freud argues against equating weaning with castration, and emphasises that only the fear of loss of the penis is dynamically effective, not the loss of the breast.

So much for Freud's concept of oral eroticism and the oral-cannibalistic phase as described in the third edition of *Three Essays on the Theory of Sexuality*. As I will elaborate later, Abraham's vision of the earliest developmental stage was different—particularly but not solely in regard to the position of aggression.

Freud's theory of depression: the sketch of 1915

Before I present Abraham's thesis on orality and depression as explicated in "The First Pregenital Stage of the Libido" (1916–1917), I would like to remind the reader of a further contribution of Freud's, namely, his theory of depression. Freud sketched it out in a manuscript dated 7 February 1915. He sent it to Ferenczi and asked him to pass it on to Abraham (F/Fer 2, pp. 47–49). At the beginning of March, Abraham confirmed that he had received the draft—and then did not comment on it for the next three weeks. It was not until March 31 that Abraham was ready to respond to Freud (ibid., pp. 303–306). His letter is of relevance to our deliberations here because it already contains the kernel of what was to become one of his main ideas. Furthermore, it shows that Abraham's "The First Pregenital Stage of the Libido" was a response to Freud's February 1915 outline of a theory of depression.

The short text under scrutiny here is not identical with the final version, namely, the paper that later appeared under the title "Mourning and Melancholia" (1917e). The focus of the draft is different—or, better, it shows the true focus of the later paper. This is not the place to consider the differences between the draft and the final version, and I will limit my comments to the draft. Abraham was familiar with it while he was working on "The First Pregenital Stage of the Libido", but not with the final version of "Mourning and Melancholia". Freud seems to have completed the latter on 4 May 1915 (F/A, p. 309). He thought that he had sent it to Berlin but was apparently mistaken, since in July, Abraham pointed out that he had not yet received it (ibid., pp. 313, 315). As far as we know, Abraham did not read "Mourning and Melancholia" in its revised form until three years later, in April 1918 (ibid., pp. 375–376).

With his new theory of depression, Freud entered an area that had previously been approached only by Abraham. He had been the sole theoretician to come closer to an understanding of depression (see Chapter Two). He had spoken about this subject at the congress in

Weimar in 1911 and published his first paper on it in 1912 (Abraham, 1912b). His primary thought was that repressed sadism played a crucial role in depression. (In 1912, sadism always referred to "general" sadism; at that time the distinction between anal and oral sadism had not yet been made.) Initially, Abraham's approach was not well received by his peers, including Freud (F/A, p. 154). In March 1915, when Abraham then read Freud's draft of "Mourning and Melancholia," he was put in an awkward spot; there was no ignoring that Freud had not gone along with "his" hypothesis, but had set off in a different direction.

After years of fruitless efforts, Freud had finally found his own answer to the question of which psychic mechanism distinguishes depression from other disorders. His answer was narcissistic identification, and this is what he proudly presented to his two most important disciples, Ferenczi and Abraham, in the draft. It was the first time that Freud used the concept of narcissistic identification; it had been outlined by Landauer (1914), but without Freud's metapsychological explication: that narcissistic identification with the object results from the removal ("Auflassen") of the unconscious cathexis of the object (F/Fer 2, p. 48).[11]

What Freud meant by this is that the object, because it is no longer cathected in the unconscious, ceases to be experienced as separated from the ego. After the removal of the cathexis in the psychic apparatus, it no longer exists as a separate object, so to speak, but is now part of the ego and is experienced as such without the ego being aware of this. The ego, therefore, does not know that it has feelings and thoughts that do not come from itself but from the object. In the text of February 1915, already we read that the shadow of the object "falls on the ego and obscures it" (F/Fer 2, p. 48); this was Freud's main finding on the etiology of depression. He regarded depression as a narcissistic disorder or ego disorder, and thus not primarily as one of libido development. Consequently, his draft begins as follows: "Dear friend, the mechanism of melancholia, which I present to you here, belongs to the beginning of an understanding of the *narcissistic* neuroses, which *we now* have to work out here" (ibid., p. 47).

It should be added that we have here (in the concept of narcissistic identification) a variant of the same psychic processes discussed above

[11] In "Mourning and Melancholia" (1917e, p. 249), Freud refers to Landauer's paper as the first publication of the concept of narcissistic identification.

in the context of incorporation: processes by which something that does not belong to the ego or subject becomes part of the ego. This is dealt with in "Instincts and Their Vicissitudes" (1915c), the text that Freud wrote right after the draft on depression.

Comprehension of Freud's new explanation of depression was not easy for either Ferenczi or Abraham; whereas Ferenczi was more or less able to take it in, Abraham initially found it extremely difficult to gain any understanding of the mechanism of narcissistic identification.[12] As he wrote to Freud in his moving letter of 31 March 1915, he himself had thought about the etiology of depression for a long time—and he was not able to agree with Freud. He could not help it; he had to stay true to his own ideas, and these continued to be that "repressed hostile feelings" (F/A, p. 304) were at the heart of depression. In the next passages of his letter, it becomes clear that, already at this point, he linked depression with oral eroticism and the wish for incorporation and destruction. He was not yet able to formulate a concise counterposition, however; this happened a few months later, in "The First Pregenital Stage of the Libido" (1916–1917).

After this, Freud and Abraham exchanged two letters on depression before Freud more or less terminated the correspondence on this subject at the beginning of July 1915 (F/A, pp. 308, 313). He wrote that he would be happy to continue to explain to Abraham how he viewed depression, but that this could be done "*properly* only if we met and talked" (ibid., p. 313, italics in the German edition), because, I think one can safely say, they had reached no agreement in their letters. The main impediment was not that Abraham could not understand that the self-reproach of the depressive person was actually aimed at the disappointing object (ibid., pp. 304, 311); this was merely secondary to Freud's main argument. The central point was the mechanism by which the object became part of the ego without the ego's knowledge: "the explanation of the illness can be derived only from the mechanism" (ibid., p. 309). This statement did not get through to Abraham. Discussing this in person was not possible because of the war, and their correspondence on depression stopped. Abraham and Freud continued to write to each other, but until "The First Pregenital Stage of the Libido" was completed in January 1916, the topic of depression was not again

[12] Ferenczi found it easier to adjust to Freud's new finding because of his own interest in the process of introjection, which he had introduced in 1909 (F/Fer 2, p. 50).

mentioned; Abraham completed the paper without having spoken to Freud again about their differences.

Up until 1915—or rather, until his writing of "The First Pregenital Stage of the Libido"—Abraham had closely followed Freud. In all his published papers and brief communications, he went to great pains to corroborate Freud's thoughts and perhaps to suggest additions. He invariably expressed his complete allegiance to Freud. Occasionally, one can detect the stirrings of ideas of his own; for example, on the significance of the mother and the so-called bad mother, and on the difficulties of separating from the parents and the mother. The general impression that remains, however, is that Abraham always moved in the greatest possible vicinity to Freud and set great store by Freud's approval. If this did not follow, he usually hastened to carry out corrections that would remove any of Freud's objections,[13] yet, as we have just seen, this was not always the case. The one point that he stuck to despite Freud's reaction was the significance he attached to repressed sadism in depression, and this was the aspect that he explored in greater depth in "The First Pregenital Stage".

Abraham's theory of depression (1916–1917)

In the very first lines of "The First Pregenital Stage", Abraham mentions the third edition of Freud's *Three Essays*, and then proceeds to give a detailed summary of Freud's description of oral eroticism, which still awaited "further investigation" (Abraham, 1916–1917, p. 251). Whereas clear observations were to be had regarding the anal phase, there was as yet "no clear picture, no direct view" of the "archaic condition" of the oral phase (ibid., p. 252). Abraham believed he could help address this deficit by naming phenomena that were psychopathological in nature:

> which goes to show that the instinctual life of the infant persists in some adults in a positive and unmistakable fashion, and that the libido of such persons presents a picture which appears to correspond in all its details to the oral or cannibalistic stage set up by Freud. (Abraham, 1916–1917, p. 253)

---

[13] For further examples of such objections from Freud, see F/A, pp. 87, 89, 154, 155, 156; see also May[-Tolzmann] (1990) and Chapter Two in this volume.

This was the first task that Abraham set himself in this paper: he wanted to report on normal, neurotic, and psychotic phenomena that could be comprehended as oral fixation and regression to the oral stage. Second, he wanted to show that the defence against regression to the oral stage led to typical depressive symptoms, and that this meant that the oral phase played a special role in the development of depression. Third, he intended to make a contribution to the problem of the so-called "choice of neurosis": he wanted to show in which way the etiology of depression distinguished itself from that of obsessive neurosis.

He had set himself an ambitious project, for "The First Pregenital Stage of the Libido" had the goal of making a substantial contribution to the understanding of psychic disorders and the theory of psychic development. In order to put Abraham's efforts into a clearer framework, I will return once more to the state of general developmental theory at the time.

Initially, Freud had only one general model of development. Like the concept of the oedipus complex, it dated from the 1890s and was one of his first basic ideas on the psychic system. In this model, development is viewed as advancing from autoeroticism to object-love. In 1911, it was extended to include the narcissistic stage, sandwiched between autoeroticism and object-love. Freud had based this hypothesis on findings reached in the investigation of male homosexuals and of psychosis.[14] The guiding principle of the model is the gradual intrapsychic constitution of the object as the precondition for object choice and object love. In childhood, an object can only be chosen if the narcissistic phase has been sufficiently overcome to allow libidinal impulses to be directed toward an object that is experienced as outside of and separate from the subject.

The general model of psychic development is the subject of dozens of letters in the correspondence between Freud and Jung, in particular regarding its usefulness in distinguishing neurotic from psychotic disorders, and in finding the difference between disorders that can be analysed and those that are not amenable to analysis.[15] Abraham (1908), too, was involved in developing and enhancing this model.

---

[14] The narcissistic stage had been introduced in 1909 at one of the Wednesday evening meetings of the Vienna Psychoanalytic Society (see Chapter One).

[15] This is discussed by Freud and Jung in dozens of letters; see, for example, Freud's outline of paranoia (F/Ju, pp. 38–40).

Its main and most practically relevant function consisted in differentiating between object-related psychic phenomena that were experienced as separate from the subject, and those in which this was not the case. All post-Freudian theories having to do with the gradual constitution of the libidinal object and the differentiation between objectal and pre-objectal experience (Spitz), the gradual intrapsychic separation of representations of self and object (Mahler, Jacobson), or the self-object relationship (Kohut) go back to this basic tenet of Freud's thought.

In "The Disposition to Obsessional Neurosis" (Freud, 1913i), this developmental model was divided into two submodels: one of libidinal development and another of ego development (see also Freud, 1911c). The distinction resulted from Freud's new insights into the etiology of obsessional neurosis, leading him to introduce a pregenital developmental stage that preceded the genital stage, as it was then called (later it became the phallic and the oedipal phase). In the pregenital stage, it was supposed, anal-erotic and sadistic impulses predominate. This enabled a new and more convincing distinction between hysteria and obsessional neurosis: whereas hysteria remains in the more advanced genital stage, merely regressing in regard to the object—that is, it reverts to the incestuous object—obsessional neurosis abandons the instinctual aims of the genital stage and replaces them with anal-erotic and sadistic aims (Freud, 1913i, p. 320).

The introduction of an anal stage created a new developmental model, that of libidinal development. An aspect of this was the oral phase, introduced in 1915 (the phallic followed in 1923). As of 1913, Freud insisted that, in order to understand the etiology of a psychic disorder, it was necessary to determine at which stage of ego development and of libido development it had fixated (1913i, p. 324; see also 1911c).

Abraham began his "First Pregenital Stage" (1916–1917) by presenting a number of normal and neurotic children and adults whose eating and drinking behaviours exhibited abnormalities, for example, children who did not want to give up the breast, and adults who replaced sexual with oral satisfaction (sections II through VI). The clinical material consisted of specific and manifest oral behaviour: eating and drinking and their libidinal significance.

One psychotic patient seems to have particularly impressed Abraham. Because of a lack of defences, his associations and memories were allegedly not distorted. The patient experienced the sucking of milk as extremely pleasurable, recalled that as a child he had wanted to bite into the breast of his nurse, and perceived milk as a "substitute for human flesh" (Abraham, 1916–1917, p. 257). The observations of this patient, as Abraham pointed out, pre-dated the third edition of Freud's *Three Essays*. In his opinion, they confirmed Freud's theory of orality and showed "to how great a degree Freud's theories are the result of direct observation, and how far they are removed from idle speculation" (ibid., p. 258).

Abraham emphasises that, in psychosis, due to the falling away of some "inhibitions", certain impulses are "expressed without resistance" (ibid., p. 254). Freud had also stated—before Abraham did—that the development of resistance is impaired in psychosis. But he did, for example, not treat Schreber's texts as undistorted material, but viewed them as the result of complex psychic defence mechanisms, whereas Abraham proceeded from the assumption that the utterances of psychotic patients allowed for direct observation of the unconscious.

For our purposes, these deliberations are of only secondary interest because the core of "The First Pregenital Stage of the Libido" lies elsewhere—namely, in the last two sections (VII and VIII). They make up just a few pages, but in my view contain momentous new material. Perhaps their special character becomes apparent only when Abraham's publications are read in chronological order; they certainly left a deep impression on me and were what impelled me to write the present chapter.

In Abraham's view two depressive symptoms are of greatest interest: a refusal to eat and a fear of starvation (1916–1917, p. 274).[16] According to Abraham, both show that orality plays a special role in depression. He explains that these symptoms develop because the libido of the patient has regressed to the oral phase. He continues:

> That is to say, in his unconscious the melancholic depressed person directs upon his sexual object the wish to incorporate it. In the depth of his unconscious there is a tendency to devour and demolish his object. (Abraham, 1916–1917, p. 276)

The libido of the depressive person is "predominantly hostile towards the object of its desires and endeavours to destroy it"; and, in contrast

[16] As he wrote to Freud, Abraham himself had a tendency to lose his appetite when he was in a depressed mood (F/A, p. 324).

to the wish of the obsessional neurotic, "the unconscious wish of the melancholic is to destroy his love-object by eating it up" (ibid., p. 277). This is why the depressive patient has guilt feelings: he reproaches himself for having wanted to orally destroy the object, which is why he eats nothing.

This is really an amazing idea—revolutionary, intriguing, and unsettling—and for the first time a major, original thought that Abraham developed on his own. In his draft of "Mourning and Melancholia" of February 1915, Freud had said nothing of the kind; he did not mention the oral phase with so much as a word, instead introducing narcissistic identification as the main mechanism in depression. No one had previously considered that guilt feelings might refer to oral wishes of destruction. In fact, as we know, in *Totem and Taboo* (1912–1913), Freud had found a completely different source for guilt feelings: the murder of the father, the oedipal father who hindered the son's sexuality and prevented his possession of the mother. For Freud, guilt feelings relate to murder and not to incorporation. In the totem meal and its realm of magical thinking, the adolescent son experiences incorporation as an approach to the father figure, as an identification with him; tender impulses are revived, leading to remorse over the murder (ibid., p. 141).

The differences we see here between Abraham and Freud are significant. They are hinted at in "The First Pregenital Stage of the Libido" and expounded in more detail in later works. In "The First Pregenital Stage", Abraham already writes, however, that oral wishes for destruction can also be seen in non-depressive, "normal" people—for example, in dreams (1916–1917, p. 179).[17] In his main work of 1924, Abraham will introduce, as mentioned, the oral-sadistic phase that begins with teething and biting. There he claims that ambivalence between love and hate can already be found at this stage, and that hostile impulses directed against the object predominate even at that time.

---

[17] Abraham reported the dream of an acquaintance in which there was a bowl on the table that also contained the legs of a child (1916–1917, p. 279). Still in the dream, the dreamer was horrified to realise that these were the legs of his little son. Abraham saw the dream as being the direct manifestation of an unconscious cannibalistic wish, similar to his understanding of the above-mentioned statements of the psychotic patient. He counted this as one of the "facts" that provided evidence for "Freud's theory of an early cannibalistic stage in the development of the libido" (ibid.). It is beyond the scope of this chapter to comment on the problematic nature of such an approach that focuses only on manifest content.

I am pointing this out in advance in order to highlight the beginnings of Abraham's new approach in "The First Pregenital Stage", an approach that he continued to pursue vigorously. At first, he presented a new view of the oral phase in "The First Pregenital Stage", and this was followed, at the beginning of the 1920s, by a new concept of the anal phase (Abraham, 1920, 1923). This phase, too, was reshaped, as the oral phase had been before. Further alterations involved the definitions of *object* and *object love*, which were included in Abraham's new model of psychic development in 1924.

I would characterise the changes that Abraham made as a tendency to emphasise the aggressive nature of the libido, and also a tendency toward reversal of the balance of power between aggressive and libidinal aims (see Früh, 2006, 2010). This, of course, changes the patterns and directions of interpretations in clinical work. If Freud's interpretations ultimately target the primary, pleasurable libidinal wishes, for Abraham, aggressive wishes have the upper hand.

The oral-sadistic wish to destroy the object by devouring it is conceived as a primary wish in Abraham's "The First Pregenital Stage of the Libido" and, of course, this stands in complete contrast to Freud's narcissistic identification. This is the case not only because the wish to destroy is an instinctual one and not a mechanism. Already in May 1915, Freud had expressed his misgivings about Abraham's lack of understanding of the meaning of "mechanisms" (F/A, p. 309); according to Freud, psychic disorders could not be explained solely by reference to a libidinal phase (fixation, regression), for one also had to be able to specify a particular mechanism by which to explain the etiology of the symptoms, which were characteristic of a particular disorder.

Freud's comments may not have convinced Abraham; at any rate, in "The First Pregenital Stage", there is no mention of a specific mechanism in the development of depression. Similarly, he does not attempt to distinguish depression from obsessional neurosis through separate mechanisms. His response to the problem of the "choice of neurosis" was the thesis that both neuroses shared the hostile attitude of the libido toward the object, and that they differed in the phase of libidinal development at which they were fixated; the desires of the obsessive neurotic were sadistic in character (meaning anal-sadistic), whereas the depressive person wanted to destroy the object orally by devouring (1916–1917, p. 277).

One could also describe the difference between Abraham and Freud as being that Abraham was mainly interested in drive aspects, and that his deliberations, on the whole, lay within the framework of libidinal development, whereas the model of ego development—to which both Freud (1914c) and Ferenczi (1913) had already made decisive contributions—remained alien to him. Perhaps the isolation into which Abraham had been pushed by World War I played a role in his preference for the theory of libidinal development. After September 1914, he did not see Freud or the other members of his circle for four years, and may have lost touch with some of the further developments of psychoanalytic theory, whereas in those same years Ferenczi had three analyses of high frequency with Freud and pursued related projects.[18] On the other hand, a life far removed from Vienna and from the possibility of exchanging ideas with colleagues may have had the positive effect of helping Abraham develop his own ideas.[19]

I see another difference between Freud's approach and Abraham's in that, for Abraham, the wish for destruction had a *purposively* aggressive character, whereas in "Instincts and Their Vicissitudes" (1915c) Freud had developed quite a different concept of early psychic development, as discussed earlier. He described a period in which one cannot yet speak of love and hate, but only of "preliminary" forms of both drives; it is the period of autoerotism and narcissism that precedes the phase of actual love for the object. None of this is to be found in Abraham's writing. For him, the destructive wishes for incorporation already clearly target an object very early.

Abraham was not alone at the time in this emphasis, and in the allocation of object relatedness to an earlier period. His altered view of development had far-reaching implications for analytic work. It could have furthered a technique based on the understanding of everything that happened in analysis is the manifestation of an objectal, object-related, neurotic transference. Excluded from such a practice was the

[18]See, for example, their correspondence on a phylogenetic theory that led to Ferenczi's genital theory (1924), and Ferenczi's assistance evident in Freud's *Beyond the Pleasure Principle* (1920g; F/Fer 2, p. 368).

[19]The "liberation" of Abraham's thinking in "The First Pregenital Stage of the Libido" may have been connected to the death of his father, just as Freud claimed was the case in his own development. It seems that Abraham informed Freud only of the illness of his father (F/A, p. 314), but not of his death on 20 November 1914. It is, of course, conceivable that Abraham sent Freud a telegram or letter that is no longer extant; similarly, it is also possible that Freud's answer got lost. All we know is that, five weeks after his father's death, Abraham told Freud he had now completed "The First Pregenital Stage of the Libido" (F/A, p. 321). The crucial passages that I describe as revolutionary are found on the last few pages of this text, and so may well have been written immediately after the death of his father.

narcissistic object that is experienced as part of the ego, and the non-aggressive constitution of an object that is separate from the ego.

All this is implicit in "The First Pregenital Stage of the Libido" and in the hypothesis of purposive, oral-aggressive wishes of destruction: the emphasis on aggressive impulses instead of pleasurable, primarily libidinal ones; the emphasis on an early, purposive object-relatedness at the expense of autoeroticism and narcissism; and the emphasis on drives instead of the ego.

These are the results of my study, and I would like them to be taken with a grain of salt. At times I place accents where there are in reality only gradations, and I stress differences where there are also similarities. I am also aware of the fact that Freud's and Abraham's writings are far from being unambiguous, and that they can be read in different ways, inevitably to some degree depending on the interests of the reader. In later studies, I hope to be able to show how Abraham continued to change Freud's theory, as he had begun to do in "The First Pregenital Stage".

Final remarks

Several disciples of Freud developed their own theories with their own focal areas, if not their own metapsychologies. This was the case for Abraham as much as for Jung, Adler, Ferenczi, Jones, or Rank. I do not think that Abraham intended to develop a theory that differed from Freud's; in fact, I doubt that he was fully aware of the differences between Freud's approach and his own. My impression is, rather, that he saw himself as carrying out and completing Freud's theory, since this motive dominates his main work of 1924.

Nevertheless, it appears to me that Abraham's basic ideas of the psyche and of psychic functioning were of a different character than those of Freud. They were taken up with enthusiasm by many analysts, including Abraham's English colleagues (e.g., Jones, Glover, Klein, Isaacs, Rivière), who ascribed an important role to early aggression and to the pregenital period in psychic development and the etiology of psychic disorders. Seen this way, Abraham had a great influence on the further development of psychoanalysis; in fact, we are only now beginning to take the full measure of how and to what extent he shaped our theoretical ideas and our clinical work.

Translated by Daniela Haller

CHAPTER FIVE

Towards Karl Abraham's "A Short Study of the Development of the Libido" (1924): August Stärcke's contribution to the theory of orality

All psychoanalytic theories leave room for interpretation. Freud's is no exception. Studying the history of psychoanalysis, I was impressed by how each of Freud's disciples understood and used their master's theory in their own ways. Ferenczi's focus was different from Freud's as was Abraham's, not to mention Jung—and they are just the most famous of the first generation of disciples. In a paper published twenty years ago, I discussed some aspects of these theoretical and clinical alternatives (May[-Tolzmann], 1990). I was especially interested in the history of narcissism, and the reception of Freud's "On Narcissism: An Introduction" (1914c) by the first generation of disciples (up to 1921). What I found was that Ferenczi remained relatively close to Freud's theory whereas Abraham stood in opposition to both Ferenczi and Freud. This constellation, it seemed to me then, was a harbinger of the differences that Kernberg and Kohut were to exchange in the 1990s.

I encountered Abraham again while researching the beginnings of the theory of depression (see Chapter Two). It was Abraham, and not Freud, who in 1912 came up with what proved to be an influential idea regarding the origins of depression: repressed sadism (Abraham 1912b). It being 1912, the distinction between "oral" or "anal" sadism was not made because the oral and anal stages of libido development had not yet been introduced. Freud, however, was not convinced by Abraham's idea. And this rejection, it seems to me, might have been an important incentive for Abraham to create his own theory. "A Short Study of the Development of the Libido" (1924), Abraham's opus magnum, is essentially a theory of depression with the notion of oral sadism, understood as a normal developmental stage, as its centrepiece.

I was furthermore struck by the fact that psychoanalysis owes the imago of "the bad mother (böse Mutter)" to Abraham. He invented the imago in his work on the painter Giovanni Segantini (Abraham, 1911), where he mentioned it in passing, but did not integrate it into his early theory of depression (1912b) or "A Short Study" (1924). And yet, the way he used the imago was compelling and stayed with his contemporaries. In the same paper I showed that the imago of the bad mother was another topic upon which Freud and Abraham disagreed. In Freud's theory the figure of the bad mother does not exist. For Freud the image of a bad mother is always a symptom, never a primary phenomenon. The same is true for the categories of good and evil, so important for Abraham and the variant of psychoanalysis founded by him, and rather marginal in Freud's theory. I found further theoretical and technical discrepancies between Freud and Abraham in Abraham's first psychoanalytic paper that explored the role of trauma in the aetiology and symptomatology of the neuroses (Abraham, 1907a, b; see Chapter Three).

In the course of the next two decades, as I was researching various aspects of the formation of psychoanalytic theories, I became increasingly convinced that Abraham played a much more important role in the history of psychoanalytic theory than we used to think. It seemed to me that his unique point of view resonated with many psychoanalysts, and significantly shaped psychoanalysis in Germany (and perhaps elsewhere). These findings contributed to my decision to study his work more closely, and to trace the development of his theory. In contrast to Ferenczi, whose works have been reviewed and discussed since the 1980s, not much attention has been devoted to Abraham.

One motivation for writing this chapter was a wish to find out more about my discomfort with certain tendencies in psychoanalysis today (May, 2009a). Reconstructing the history of psychoanalytic theory helps me to make sense of this discomfort. I want to find out more about what it is that I value and object to in Freud and other writers. My goal is to gain more clarity about what an acceptable psychoanalytic theory and practice would look like today. A second, more Freud-centred, motivation is to examine whether and in what ways I can accept Freud's conceptualisation of psychoanalysis, especially his emphasis on the primacy of the sexual but also other peculiar traits of his theory and clinical practice.

To make my project more manageable I will, for now, focus on the discussion of orality. I will give a brief summary of my paper of 2010 (b) before I present new material on the history of orality after 1916, precisely the period from 1916 to 1924, the year in which Abraham's "A Short Study of the Development of the Libido" appeared.

The history of orality up to 1916—an overview

The basic ideas about orality were, of course, introduced by Freud dating back to his work in the 1890s (see F/Fl, pp. 221, 278–282). Orality played an important role in the Dora case (Freud, 1905e, pp. 51–52). In *Three Essays on the Theory of Sexuality* Freud laid the groundwork for a theory of orality (1905d/1915, pp. 179–184, pp. 197–199). *Totem and Taboo* (1912–1913, pp. 140–146) expanded on the theory before the third edition of the *Three Essays* (written in the autumn of 1914, and published in 1915) presented a more or less final version of the notion of orality (1905d/1915, pp. 197–199). There Freud introduced the oral stage, a concept he also discussed in the case of the "Wolf Man" (1918b, pp. 106–107) written in October and November of 1914, right after the completion of *Three Essays*. Further additions can be found in "Instincts and their Vicissitudes" (1915c), finished in March and April 1915, as well as in "Mourning and Melancholia" (1917e), likely completed in May 1915, and published in the last issue of the fourth volume of the *Internationale Zeitschrift für Psychoanalyse* whose delivery was however delayed until the early summer of 1918.

By mid-1915 Freud's source of ideas concerning the development of a theory of orality was more or less exhausted. In *Group Psychology and the Analysis of the Ego* (1921c, pp. 105–110) he describes orality as a preliminary stage of identification (as he did in 1915) but this time his focus is on identification and he does not say anything new about orality. With one small but important difference (which I will come back to) the description of the oral stage found in *An Outline of Psychoanalysis* (1940a, p. 153)—to jump ahead for a moment—is almost identical to the one given in the third edition of *Three Essays*.

Unlike the development of the theory of anality, to which several of Freud's disciples contributed substantially, not one helped advance the theory of orality up to 1915. The disciples merely executed what their master was teaching. Not so Abraham. In 1916 he published an article entitled "The First Pregenital Stage of the Libido" (1916–1917) whose groundbreaking character remains hidden unless we dive into the stream of knowledge production from which Abraham's paper flows. It's just like in an analysis: a patient tells us that he has realised how much he hated or loved his father or mother. To an outsider this realisation may seem trivial, but for the patient in analysis this insight is a small revolution. Never before has he spoken, thought, and felt about his parents like this. He has gained access to thoughts and feelings that were previously closed to him. His whole internal world has changed. The history of psychoanalysis works similarly: we need to reconstruct Freud's development of a theory of orality to understand the revolutionary impact of Abraham's "First Pregenital Stage", which also marks a breakthrough in Abraham's development as a theoretician.

What, then, was the innovation that Abraham proposed in his paper "The First Pregenital Stage of the Libido"? What was new was a theory of orality that assumed aggressive wishes seeking to destroy the object by devouring it; Abraham also believed these wishes, characteristic of the oral stage, to be instrumental in the aetiology of depression; they were, in fact, the reason for the depressive's sense of guilt. In the same article Abraham moreover implied that they might be part of normal development, a suggestion that stood in opposition to Freud's view of the oral stage.

Even though the third edition of *Three Essays* categorised "incorporation" ("Einverleibung") as the instinctual aim of the oral-cannibalistic stage (1905d/1915, p. 198), the ways in which Freud described these psychic processes, especially in "Instincts and their Vicissitudes" (1915c), did not attribute a distinctly aggressive or purposefully destructive character to them. To the contrary, as Freud would have it, this developmental stage was characterised by a relative "indifference" to the external world (ibid., p. 139). Oral incorporation, Freud wrote, was a form of love "consistent with abolishing the object's separate existence" (ibid., p. 138). At this earliest stage of development love and hate did not yet exist as separate and fully formed affects. Neither did ambivalence. What did exist, Freud suggested, were "preliminary stages" ("Vorstufen") of those affects and conflicts (ibid.).

Freud made use of the category "preliminary stages" quite often. He used it to indicate that love, hate, and ambivalence did not exist from the very beginning; that they were developmental achievements that became possible as the child approached the oedipal stage. But of course, writes Freud, what develops into maturity must have existed in a germinal state, which means that love and hate and ambivalence were there from the very beginning in the form of "preliminary stages" of development. The preliminary stage is to the end result what the seed is to the flower: closely related and yet distinct.

In general (there are exceptions) Freud did not assume that the infant's psychic experiences are equivalent to love or hate, which is to say that at this stage in his development there is no ambivalence either. The infant's *behaviour* may look like love or hate and be experienced *by the object* as love or hate but in the infant's psychic reality it is not. And this was true for both oral and anal stages. The preliminary stage of love in the anal stage, Freud writes, "is hardly to be distinguished from hate in its attitude towards the object" (ibid., p. 139)—a remarkable statement. What Freud is saying is again that the infant's behaviour looks like hate but is not experienced as hate by the infant. "Not until the genital organisation is established," Freud continues, "does love become the opposite of hate" (Ibid.). While this is not the place to further discuss Freud's convoluted statement, I do want to mention that in Abraham's model of psychic development as presented in "The First Pregenital Stage of the Libido" and in "A Short Study" the category "preliminary stage" does not exist. For Abraham the wish to destroy the object seems to be "genuine" aggression—fully developed, intentional, determined, and experienced as an act of aggression by the subject.

This is not the space to discuss the ways in which Freud and Abraham's colleagues responded to his "The First Pregenital Stage of the Libido". As far as Freud was concerned, Abraham once again did not have much luck with his new approach. Freud had been unconvinced of Abraham's paper on the aetiology of depression (Abraham, 1912b), and he did not adopt his disciple's new description of the oral stage (1916–1917) either.

August Stärcke's imago of the infant as beast of prey (1921)

What, then, happened after Abraham's 1915/1916 advances into pre-oedipal aggressive instinctual impulses and guilt feelings? As far as Abraham was concerned—for a very long time, nothing happened at all. A number of lectures suggest that he continued to develop his notion of oral sadism (and the correlation between food and faeces, which I am not dealing with in this chapter; see Róheim, 1923b, p. 110; Radó, 1923, p. 380). But none of them was published. It took until 1924 before Abraham came forward with another publication on the topic—this time he left his mark! "A Short Study of the Development of the Libido", finished in 1923 and published in 1924 is a long, highly sophisticated paper in which Abraham introduces the "oral-sadistic" phase as successor to the "oral sucking" phase (1924, pp. 450–452). While his oral sucking stage was relatively similar to Freud's oral stage, the "oral-sadistic stage" was Abraham's own idea.

With the exception of Abraham none of Freud's other disciples contributed anything substantial to the theory of orality, both before and after 1916—until in 1920 the Dutch psychiatrist August Stärcke (1880–1945) entered the stage. Already in 1919 Stärcke had made an impact with a paper on the anal origin of persecutory delusions (Stärcke, 1919), and in September 1920 he surprised his colleagues again with two papers delivered at the International Psychoanalytic Congress held in Den Haag. The first paper was an audacious, anti-psychiatric statement on the relation between normality and mental illness. An expanded version was published as supplement to the *Internationale Zeitschrift für Psychoanalyse* (Stärcke, 1921b). The second, just as impressive, presentation dealt with the castration complex (1921a). The paper was published in 1921 both in the *Internationale Zeitschrift für Psychoanalyse* and in the in the newly founded *International Journal of Psychoanalysis*. In this work Stärcke presented new thoughts on orality; thoughts that aligned well with the ideas Abraham had put forward in his "The First Pregenital Stage of the Libido". To my knowledge Stärcke was not aware of the affinity of his work to that of Abraham, at least not initially. At any rate, in his paper he made no reference to Abraham, whereas Abraham referred to Stärcke. In his "A Short Study" he mentioned the Dutch psychiatrist's thoughts about the oral-sadistic (1924, p. 463) and the anal-sadistic phase (ibid., p. 489). In this sense, Stärcke paved the way for Abraham.

Aside from Stärcke there are three other authors whose work on orality predates and anticipates Abraham's "Short Study". They are Johan van Ophuijsen, James Glover, and Geza Róheim. Ophuijsen (1882–1950, a Dutch psychiatrist) and Abraham were on friendly terms since the Den Haag Congress. Abraham sent his daughter to him for analysis. In the autumn of 1922 Ophuijsen moved to Berlin for a while to undergo analysis and to participate in events organised by the Berlin Group (RB 2, p. 189; F/A, p. 708; Stroeken, 2009). As Ophuijsen later reported, sadism came up in a conversation he had with Abraham; they agreed that sadism was rooted in the oral stage and not in the anal stage, as Freud would have it. According to Ophuijsen this (in hindsight) "historic" conversation took place already in 1921 (Ophuijsen, 1929, p. 142). Abraham too mentions the exchange with Ophuijsen, and the part he had in his theory of oral sadism. There is a passage in "A Short Study", where Abraham describes the process by which "the child exchanges the sucking activity for a biting one". He goes on,

> In this place I should like to mention a private communication made to me by van Ophuijsen [...]. Psycho-analytic observation has led him to believe that certain neurotic phenomena are due to a regression to the age when the teeth were being formed, and furthermore that biting represents the original form taken by sadistic impulses. (1924, pp. 450–451)

Clearly, Ophuijsen has to be counted among the theorists of oral sadism even though at this point we are not able to say more about his ideas than the little that he and Abraham have disclosed.

The British analyst James Glover (1882–1926) and his brother Edward (1888–1972) had been in analysis with Abraham (Abraham, 1924, p. 448). According to Abraham, James Glover supported his view on oral sadism in a lecture given in London in May 1922. The lecture was never published. All we have is a short abstract written by Glover himself (J. Glover, 1922). In his summary Glover does not indicate whether he merely repeated Abraham's ideas (which he must have become acquainted with during his analysis with Abraham), or whether he made an original contribution to the theory of orality. In his few publications, James Glover, who died in 1926, did not comment on this. His brother Edward, who began publishing on oral sadism only after 1924, did not indicate that James might have had his own innovative thoughts.

And lastly there is Géza Róheim (1881–1953). In 1922, at the International Psychoanalytic Congress in Berlin, Róheim gave a paper entitled

"Nach dem Tode des Urvaters [After the Death of the Primal Father]" (1923b). Explicitly referring to Abraham's "The First Pregenital Stage of the Libido" (ibid., p. 94) Róheim suggested that ethnographic material supported the notion of an oral-cannibalistic stage as well as the idea that the sense of guilt originated in the oral stage. Upon Abraham's request Róheim stayed in Berlin and gave six lectures at the institute (RB 3, p. 199). Abraham felt quite stimulated by Róheim's lectures, and Róheim in turn was able to make more connections between his own work and Abraham's theory (F/A, p. 708; Róheim, 1923a, p. 390). In his "A Short Study" Abraham repeatedly refers to Róheim (1924, pp. 421, 426, 444, 447 fn. 1, 473). This is not the place to discuss Róheim's papers. The use of ethnographic sources to support assumptions about early infantile development raises a number of methodological questions that deserve a separate study. Moreover, it seems to me that Róheim was primarily concerned with collecting evidence rather than developing the theory further. Nevertheless, Róheim was part of the small circle of colleagues, formed in 1920, who were close to Abraham and who understood and supported his interests in developing a new theory of orality (others were Alexander, Radó, and Simmel). At this point in time the network was in its infancy, and so were Abraham's theory and his colleagues' theoretical contributions.

Everything seems to point to the fact that in the years between Abraham's "The First Pregenital Stage of the Libido" (1916–1917) and "A Short Study" (1924), August Stärcke (1921a) was the first psychoanalyst we know of who significantly altered Freud's concept of orality and its corresponding oral developmental stages and, it seems, he did so independently, without drawing on Abraham's research.

Stärcke had been interested in psychoanalysis from early on. He joined the Vienna Psycho-Analytic Society in 1911, and in 1917 he was one of the founding members of the Dutch Society (Spanjaard, 1955). He worked in a psychiatric hospital, but whether he also conducted psychoanalytic treatments is unknown (ibid.). Etchegoyen described Stärcke as a "lone genius" (1994, p. 176), and, besides Ophuijsen, as the most important Dutch analyst from the early days of psychoanalysis. Freud too held him in high esteem. When in September 1920, after the Den Haag Congress, Abraham suggested awarding Stärcke a prize for his two lectures, Freud readily agreed. Stärcke shared the prize with Róheim (Freud, 1921d).

Stärcke's starting point was his doubts about the castration threat as the origin of the castration complex. He had observed that more often than not male patients had no memory of the castration threat; and women, he argued, were not threatened by it because they could not be castrated (Stärcke, 1921a, p. 181). Based on a long dream of his own (which I cannot reproduce here; see Stärcke, 1921a, pp. 183–188), Stärcke suggested a different genesis of the castration complex. His dream, he found, spoke to the fear of losing the nipple or the breast. This fear, he argued, came developmentally earlier than the fear of losing the penis; it was therefore a "primary one" (ibid., p. 189) that was later "referred to the genitals" (ibid., p. 90). If the nipple is withdrawn before the infant is fully satisfied (a frustration that cannot always be avoided), he will experience the withdrawal as a castration. This withdrawal, and not the threat of losing the penis, Stärcke argued, was the "primitive" or primal castration ("Urkastration") for both boys and girls (ibid., p. 193). Just like "defecation in the infant was that situation from which [the imago of the persecutor] was derived" (ibid., p. 193; see Stärcke, 1919), nursing was the situation from which the imago of the *Urkastration* emerged (ibid.). Referring to Freud's hypothesis that the loss of the faeces was analogous to the loss of the penis (1917c, p. 133), Stärcke proposed the fear of losing the nipple as the actual origin and root of castration anxiety.

We acquire the castration complex at the oral stage, Stärcke wrote. But not only that: the guilt attached to the genitals and genital activity had its origin in the weaning situation as well. Why? Because the infant for whom sucking on the breast felt like eating up [feeding off][1] mother experienced weaning as a punishment (1921a, p. 195). Here was the beginning of the depressive patient's guilt feelings: it was true, once he had indeed eaten up mother. But this was not only true for the depressive. For Stärcke, all development began at the oral-cannibalistic stage: the sucking on the breast stimulates cannibalistic wish phantasies (Freud did not say that) which are accompanied by guilt feelings (Freud did not say that either); in that sense human evolution began from the cannibalistic phase as well (an assumption Freud definitely

[1] Translator's note: the German verb is "verspeisen" (eat up). The English translation of Stärcke's paper gives "feed off", which lacks the destructive/cannibalistic dimension of the infant's sucking.

did not share; see 1985a, p. 12). This is how Stärcke envisions the origin of the perversion of sadism:

> If I adhere to my belief that every erotic phantasy is based on a real experience, then it is evident that the basis for cruelty is to be found in the beast of prey which mangles its victim and thus creates fixed paths between gratification through taking nourishment, and the expressions of the victim's pain, humiliation, and seizure. (Stärcke, 1921a, p. 197)

The same comparison was true for the infant as well:

> We find the situation of the beast of prey in possession of its living victim roughly produced in the infant at the breast. If the mother during suckling has cracked nipples or pain due to other causes, then we have a real situation in which the child perceives expressions of pain in a person of whom he takes possession, and at the same time experiences most intense gratification. (Ibid.)[2]

I hope in this brief presentation of Stärcke's ideas on primal castration I was able to convey that he creates new imagery, and a new kind of psychoanalysis, whose elements are the baby at the breast—an image that in Freud's work holds no special significance—destructive oral impulses, purposeful aggression directed at an object at the first stage of development, and the guilt feelings that come with that aggression. In the world that Stärcke draws up for us the image of mother and baby is not an idyllic one. They pose a threat for each other: a baby that threatens to swallow mother, and a mother who believes that her baby is eating her up; a baby that feels bad towards mother, plagued by guilt feelings. Freud's "model scene", on which he erected his theory, looks very different. So does Ferenczi's.

The core phantasies that the theories are based on vary tremendously. But in no case are they grounded in "baby watching". Rather, they are the phantasies of the respective author, and every author has their own imagination. It may seem abrupt, but allow me to say this: the longer I study the history of psychoanalytic theories, the more I am convinced that the psychoanalysis of adults was never (and perhaps still isn't) fully

[2] For a more complete picture of Stärcke's sophisticated and interesting, at times broad and speculative, thoughts on the meaning of the oral stage, see his publications.

committed to understanding the developmental processes that take place in the first months of life. After all, analytic treatment of adults is not the most favourable place to start an exploration of our beginnings. There is a wish, it seems to me, to deposit into the baby our very own ideas about how adults relate to each other; and to, perhaps, ascribe to the infant what we have gleaned from our clinical experience with adults. Could it be that the theories of infantile development that we create serve as vehicles to describe what happens in the adult? Could it be that our theories of the psychic development of infants are ultimately theories of technique? As psychoanalysts it would be well worth our while to review and (where necessary) correct the blending of incompatible perspectives and standpoints. In addition, it would serve us well, I think, to consider infant research and the work of child analysts.

It is true that in his 1916 "The Pregenital Phase" Abraham had already described oral destructive impulses. But he did so with less determination and conviction than Stärcke, and he did not emphasise quite as vigorously as Stärcke did that these impulses were part of normal development. Moreover in 1916 Abraham avoided to qualify these destructive impulses as "sadistic"—most likely because Freud had attributed sadism to the anal, rather than the oral phase. Stärcke on the other hand, without much ado presented the oral stage as "the origin" of sadism (1921a, p. 197). In 1924, however, Abraham took his theory much further than Stärcke had taken his. In his "A Short Study" he posited a separate oral-sadistic stage of the libido based in teething and biting (1924, pp. 450ff). With the teeth comes the impulse "to destroy the libidinal object by devouring it" (ibid., pp. 451–52). As Abraham sees it, the impulse to love contains in it the impulse to destroy, which threatens the infant and makes him fearful.

Discussion: primal castration (Urkastration) and oral sadism

But what does all this mean? How to think about it? And, more importantly, what is there to think about? What difference does it make whether or not we define weaning as *Urkastration*; whether or not we assume the appearance of oral sadism in the first months of life? Well, for Freud it made all the difference, as I will explain in a moment.

But first, let me discuss Stärcke's *Urkastration*, that is, his thesis that weaning and the withdrawal of the breast before the baby is satiated are experienced as castration. Abraham partially adopted Stärcke's thesis; some, Jones among them (1923a, p. 324) fully embraced it, while others,

Alexander (1922, p. 22) for example, developed it further. Freud, however, let it be known that he did not share Stärcke's (and Alexander's) view; and he did so in a manner rather unusual for him, namely by addressing the issue in four different papers: the postscript to "Little Hans" published in 1923 (1909b, p. 7, fn. 2); the paper "The Infantile Genital Organisation" (1923e, p. 144, fn. 2), in "The Dissolution of the Oedipus Complex" (1924d, p. 175, fn. 4), and in *Inhibitions, Symptoms and Anxiety* (1926d, pp. 129–131). Since Freud's statements are of general interest and because they illustrate an important difference between his theory and that of several of his disciples, a brief summary of his position seems in order.

Freud's argument goes as follows: the term castration complex ought to be reserved for processes in the phallic stage because only then did the castration threat have pathogenic effects. Previous losses were just "preliminary stages" of the loss of the penis. A passage from the postscript of "Little Hans" (written in 1922, published in 1923) may serve as an example. Prompted by the work of Andreas-Salomé, Stärcke and Alexander, whose "contributions [further developed] the subject" (1923, p. 9), Freud added a footnote to the passage in which he introduces the castration complex:

> It has been urged that every time his mother's breast is withdrawn from a baby he is bound to feel it as castration (that is to say, as the loss of what he regards as an important part of his own body); that, further, he cannot fail to be similarly affected by the regular loss of his faeces; and, finally, that the act of birth itself (consisting as it does in the separation of the child from his mother, with whom he has hitherto been united) is the prototype of all castration. While recognizing all of these roots of the complex, I have nevertheless put forward the view that the term "castration complex" ought to be confined to those excitations and consequences which are bound up with the loss of the penis. (Freud, 1909b, p. 8, fn. 2)

To repeat myself: according to Freud the infant at the breast does not experience the loss of the breast or of the nipple as a castration but may experience it as such after the fact (*nachträglich*), at a later stage. For Freud, the baby's experience of loss is a preliminary stage, a root of the castration complex, and as such it must be distinguished from the castration complex proper. Weaning, Freud writes, provides the material for later experiences; it prepares the ego for castration (1926d, p. 130). Elsewhere, in a letter to Marie Bonaparte, Freud argued that before the phallic stage the loss of nipple and faeces had no dynamic impact because there was not yet an awareness of anatomical differences between the sexes, nor was the penis highly cathected yet. Bonaparte, who was in analysis with Freud, had told him about a paper by René Laforgue that had impressed her. Laforgue belonged to the group of analysts who, following Stärcke, emphasised the significance of weaning and oral erotism (Laforgue, 1926). Here is Freud's response to Bonaparte: "what is concealed behind it [=the trauma of weaning] is the denial of the castration complex" (quoted in Jones, 1953–1957, vol. 3, p. 445). Moreover, Freud continues, "the main objection to the theory"—the doctrine of the importance of weaning—"was clinical experience which shows the castration complex in a tangible form, but not the other [the trauma of weaning]" (ibid.). What we have here is Freud's technical and clinical argument against Stärcke's *Urkastration* as well as against Rank's birth trauma (1924). The following week Freud picked up the topic again, explaining to Bonaparte what he thought of those colleagues who overvalued oral erotism:

> Meine liebe Prinzessin: I am not surprised that the phrase "the eternal suckling" has somewhat impressed you. There is indeed something in it. Oral erotism is the first erotic manifestation, just as the nipple is the first sexual object; the libido is led along definite paths from these first position into the new organisations. But the question that interests us is not the genetic one, but the dynamic one. Even if the idea of losing the genital organ has a normal prototype, it is only with castration that the danger of loss becomes pathogenic: since only the penis carries the colossal narcissistic cathexis that corresponds with the importance of propagation. (Jones, 1953–1957, vol. 3, p. 445)

In this passage it becomes clear what Freud meant by the crucial importance of the oedipus complex: the primacy of phallic-oedipal sexuality. This conceptual narrowing was a slow and gradual process that began after 1920. It was, it seems to me, a response to the increasing emphasis his disciples placed on the pre-oedipal stages. "Pregenital primacy" (Praegenitalprimat) to use Simmel's later term (1933), was about to replace Freud's "genital primacy". Clearly, Stärcke's 1921 paper was instrumental in this move from the genital to the pregenital, but even more so was Abraham's theory of the development of the libido. In Abraham's theory each stage has its own dynamic, something Freud explicitly did not allow for. Here, it seems to me, we have an instance of Freud reacting to his disciples. He felt compelled to express his own thoughts more clearly, I suppose, and perhaps to understand them more clearly as well, as had been the case in his disputes with Jung and Adler. We have often wondered why the oedipus complex did not play a prominent role in Freud's papers before 1920, and why his (in the true sense of the word) "dogmatic" statements regarding the oedipus complex, including his final definition of the oedipus complex, date from after 1920 (Freud, 1923b). Now we are in a better place to understand why. Confronted with Stärcke's *Urkastration* and Rank's birth trauma, Freud understood that his disciples were about to depreciate the importance of both castration and oedipal complex, which triggered in him a move towards more radical, more dogmatic points of view. But it also set in motion a more thorough investigation of the pre-oedipal stage. His *Inhibitions, Symptoms and Anxiety* (1926d) is one example of this new engagement with the pre-oedipal.

Today, Freud's attitude towards Stärcke, Rank, and others is hard to comprehend. Most of us agree that the pre-oedipal is just as important as the oedipal—even though the training of the older generation of psychoanalysts, which I belong to, firmly rested on the dogma of the centrality of the oedipus complex. But let us forget our confusion for a while and try to understand how Freud envisioned psychic development.

In the beginning was "autoerotism" and "object love". They were the first two stages Freud conceptualised in his effort to develop a theory of psychosexual development. In 1911 he published papers on the narcissistic stage, followed by the anal-erotic sadistic stage (1913i), and the oral stage in 1915 (1905d/1915); later he added the identificatory stage (1921c) followed by the phallic stage (1923e). These developmental stages of infantile sexuality are not, it seems to me, of equal significance. Freud repeatedly described them as cover-ups for psychic processes in the oedipal stage, in line with his qualification of the erotogenic zones as "apparatuses subordinate to the genitals and [...] substitutes for them" (Freud, 1905d, p. 169). As though Freud was saying that in analysis these stages are relevant only insofar as they represent aspects of the oedipal drama in disguise. To put it this way may be an exaggeration given how much significance Freud attributed to anal (less so oral) erotism for the process of character formation: it translates into character traits, and through regression to the anal or oral stages symptoms are formed. In analysis, however, the only way to gain access to these stages is through the oedipal narrative (to borrow a word from contemporary literary theory) of which they form a part. Perhaps we can put it this way: according to Freud the oedipal constellation is the first time in our life that we take stock—of the romance with our parents, and the story of our own sexuality. The stories we create there we continuously revise throughout our lifetime. But it is this first stocktaking in the oedipal stage that, according to Freud, determines our continuing psychic development.

When I first started to study Freud's work, I did not look at his theory from this angle. Rather, it forced itself upon me, leaving me somewhat shocked. After all, I, like so many of my colleagues, don't think twice about including and exploring the time of pre-oedipal processes in an analysis. On the other hand we cannot deny that analysing oedipal forms of engagement is fundamentally different from analysing other material. Theories of the treatment of non-oedipal disorders, described as early, narcissistic, pre-objectal, structural, borderline-like, traumatic, and so on have addressed this difference. Without being able to elaborate on it, I want to say that—despite his dogmatism regarding the primacy of the oedipal complex—I agree with Freud. It has been my experience that in some cases it takes a long analysis, in even more cases it takes more than one analysis, before oedipal themes become analysable; and that when it happens, this piece of the analysis has the feel of reaching a climax, of achieving closure.

Furthermore, it seems to me that for Freud the processes that occurred in the anal and even more so in the oral stage remained more or less excluded from consciousness, hardly accessibly regardless of how much they may shape our phantasies and behaviour. In this Freud clearly differs from Abraham and other analysts. I believe that this may have been the reason why he (1905d/1915, p. 198) described the oral stage as being "constructed" ("fiktiv")—another surprise for me (see Chapter Four). One that makes sense in the broader context of how Freud understands psychic phenomena, be they symptoms, ideas, fairy tales, or myths. He doesn't just uncover oral or oral-sadistic impulses but sees them as surfaces behind which something else and something more important is hidden, that is, the sexual-oedipal material. Both layers are easily confused, the level of the unconscious wish and the level of the compromise and distortion of the symptom. Little Hans is a case in point. Rather than interpreting his fear of being bitten by a horse as a reversal of oral wishes, Freud saw it as a derivative of castration anxiety and oedipal wishes. The Wolf Man is another example: anal erotism is important only insofar as it marks the place of the Wolf Man's passive love wishes towards his father. The mainspring is not anal erotism but the love for the father, the disappointment by the Nanja, and so on. Obsessional-compulsive neurosis is yet another case in point: here oedipal love wishes are dressing up as anal wishes presenting themselves as vengeful impulses, anal-sadistic wishful phantasies and their corresponding defensive moves.

From the very beginning, long before he conducted analyses, Freud was convinced of the significance of the sexual element (May[-Tolzmann], 1996). He became interested in sexual aetiology in the 1890s working his way towards an ever more precise theory of sexuality: from traumatic sexuality, through intolerable sexuality and infantile sexuality to oedipal sexuality in *The Interpretation of Dreams*, eventually arriving at the polymorphousness of auto- and allo-erotic sexuality described in *Three Essays*. Despite the many revisions that his theory underwent, including the introduction of the death drive, Freud held on to his conviction that the sexual element was of the greatest importance. It was the cause for his break up with Adler, Jung, Rank, and Ferenczi. We have yet to fully grasp this momentous current in Freud's thinking—even though Freud himself may not have been entirely aware of what was the driving force behind it. No wonder we are still trying to figure out what sexuality really is, why it grips us so much, and whether it indeed does have such a grip on us.

Stärcke and Abraham (1924)

In the remainder of this chapter I want to address oral sadism. For Stärcke the infant was a beast of prey who experienced the sucking at the breast as a devouring of mother. Abraham developed his ideas about orality along similar lines. In 1924 he stated that there could no longer be any doubt about the existence of a developmental stage which was organised around wishes to swallow the object, wishes that gave rise to fear and guilt feelings (Abraham, 1924, p. 442). This is not the space to explore the evidence that Abraham offered to support his hypothesis. It found warm approval among his colleagues. Immediately after the publication of "A Short Study" and Abraham's lecture at the congress in Salzburg (1925b) other psychoanalysts assimilated the oral-sadistic phase and the guilt feelings it gave rise to into their vocabulary. By the end of 1924 the thesis of the infant's oral sadism was no longer considered an assumption, a hypothesis, theory or "superstructure"—it had become a "fact". This modification of the theory coincided with a transformation of psychoanalysis as a science and how it viewed itself. Whereas Freud (most of the time) worked under the reserve that what he was doing was formulating a theory, and that his statements on the nature of psychic development were assumptions, many of his disciples were less cautious. They regarded oral sadism as an incontrovertible given; and as such it was taught in the institutes in Berlin and London. Examples are Edward Glover (1924, 1925, 1932, 1933) who together with Ernest Jones dominated the London Institute; then there are Ophuijsen (1925, 1929), Fenichel (1925), Rank (1925), and Klein (1928, 1930). Famously, in the 1930s and 1940s oral sadism sparked an important controversy between the Vienna analysts and their adherents and Klein and her followers.

The ease with which oral sadism as a stage in the first months of life had come to be taken for granted stands in marked contrast to the many open questions that assuming a destructive wish directed at the maternal object entails. For example, and most importantly, how is it possible that a libidinal impulse also and at the same time seeks the destruction of the object? Trying to answer the question, I find myself caught in a maelstrom. If it is the infant's intention to bite mother, to cause her pain, and if he enjoys biting her, does this still count as a version of Freud's "sensual sucking" ("Wonnesaugen")? This is the question of questions: does predominantly aggressive satisfaction still satisfy Freud's idea of satisfaction? Moreover, is the satisfaction connected to infantile sexuality? Is aggressive satisfaction the satisfaction we can't get enough of, the satisfaction we chase after all our life, a goal we want to achieve, an experience we want to have? And finally, is there such a thing as a longing for aggressive satisfaction? Or could it be that Abraham's new theory is not at all concerned with longing, sexual excitation, and love?

In a footnote included in his *An Outline* Freud took the opportunity to revisit the question of the character of destructive impulses. He writes, "The question arises whether the satisfaction of purely destructive instinctual impulses can be felt as pleasure" (1940a, p. 154, fn. 1). Freud left the question unanswered, and I will have to do the same. I do not yet understand enough about the ways in which the introduction of the death drive and the aggressive impulse impacted Freud's theoretical system. And I am still mystified by the way in which Freud solved the conundrum posed by his new drive theory organised around the antagonism between Eros and death drive, which, in his own words "seems to explode the earlier construction of the successive stages of libidinal organisation" (ibid., p. 125): drives and impulses are never pure but "mixtures", Freud wrote. Hence "there is no need to revise our view of the organisations of the libido" (1926d, p. 125). *An Outline* confronts us with a similar conundrum. In the chapter entitled "The development of the sexual function" (1940a, pp. 152–156) Freud presents orality in much the same way he presented it in 1915 as if the revisions to drive theory he had made in the twenty-three years that separate the two texts had not happened. But this chapter also contains the small but significant digression I mentioned at the start: Freud now states that during the oral phase "sadistic impulses occur sporadically" (ibid., p. 154). Here Freud, ever so slightly, accommodated Abraham and others, without giving up his position: to concede that sadistic impulses occurred in isolation does not challenge the "supremacy" of sadism in the anal phase which Freud held on to in *An Outline*.

Perhaps a look at the developmental aims underlying Freud's and Abraham's theories will bring some clarification. Freud's theory revolves around the child's romance with early attachment figures—a story of love and disappointment—as well as around the story of his own sexuality. Then there is the progression from autoerotism to object love, that is, the capacity to direct libidinal wishes at a "foreign" object. This is not the story that Stärcke and Abraham tell. Both their theories, it seems to me, are concerned with the gradual mitigation of aggressive impulses and with the resolution of ambivalence. In the chapter "Origins and growth of object love", Abraham gives a detailed account of this process (1924, pp. 480–501). The developmental aim is to arrive at object love characterised by "care for the object" ("Rücksichtnahme auf das Objekt") and by the modification and renunciation of destructive wishes (ibid., pp. 488, 496). In Abraham's scenario development moves from an initial pre-ambivalent stage through a predominantly hostile attitude towards the object in the oral-sadistic stage to a predominantly friendly attitude towards the object in the post-ambivalent stage. Whereas in Freud's theory, to repeat myself, the subject becomes capable of choosing an object. The type of object relation that ensues depends upon how the oedipus complex is resolved: there are, for example, the narcissistic and the anaclitic type of object choice, and then there are the constellations Freud presented under the key word "necessary conditions for loving" ("Liebesbedingungen"). Whether the object was handled with care was the least of Freud's concerns.

In Abraham's theory the infant's increasing care for the object is, of course, the flip side of his idea that at the beginning of his life the baby is incapable of caring for the object. To put it differently, if the infant's and toddler's object relations are viewed as predominantly hostile and destructive—as Stärcke was the first to state—the question arises how in the course of development predominantly friendly relations become possible. To Freud, however, this point of view was foreign. He would have viewed it as anti-libidinal, in favour of the super-ego. Naturally, Freud supported the claim that we grow into reasonably civilised adults but his theory is not narcissistically invested in "morality", in that which is socially desired. In my view, we are at a cross roads, a nodal point where theory and practice meet. Just as morality is not a central concern in Freud's developmental theory, it does not play a leading part in his practice. Freud, it seems to me, was quite accepting of our idiosyncrasies and immorality, willing to meet the human weaknesses and vices of his analysands with sympathy and interest (regarding the opposite tendencies in Abraham see Chapter Three).

To conclude, in this chapter I have tried to shed light on the contributions August Stärcke made to the theory of orality. His ideas about the infant's oral-sadistic wishes show some affinity to Abraham's theory while at the same time differing from Freud's in several respects. Finally but importantly, I would like to issue a caveat: I am not as sure of my opinions as I may seem. All of us, I believe, often find ourselves on a sticky wicket, struggling to stay on top of the pressing and ever present bias of our own thinking.

Translated by Bettina Mathes

CHAPTER SIX

On the early history of anal erotism (1905–1924)

Having reconstructed the beginnings of the history of oral erotism (see the previous two chapters), I will now turn my attention to the early history of the concept of anal erotism. But first let me briefly recapitulate some elements in the psychoanalytic theory of oral erotism. In my research I found that the notion of a primary oral aggression made its first appearance very late, namely in Abraham's "The First Pregenital Stage of the Libido" (1916–1917), a paper he composed in 1916. At that time, more often than not, Freud tended to understand oral aggression as a symptom, that is, as a product of sophisticated psychic processes, rather than as a primary drive-impulse. Abraham's paper (1916–1917) only alluded to the primary oral-aggressive impulse; it presented more of an outline than a fully fleshed idea, similar to the imago of the "bad mother" he proposed in his paper on the painter Giovanni Segantini (1911) without fully developing it then. It was only later, in his "A Short Study of the Development of the Libido" (1924), that Abraham declared oral destruction the instinctual aim of a developmental stage, namely the oral-sadistic stage which he himself introduced into psychoanalytic theory (ibid., pp. 450–452). Abraham's oral sadism was well received and quickly gained followers. Many psychoanalysts began to take oral sadism for a "fact", and treated it as a tried and tested element of psychoanalytic theory.

What follows is an examination of whether the conception of anal erotism has a similar history. To do so, I will reconstruct the path that leads from the first edition of Freud's *Three Essays on the Theory of Sexuality* (1905d) to Abraham's "A Short Study" (1924). We will accompany Freud as he responds to the works of his disciples, and his disciples as they converse with each other. By doing so, the airtight theory starts to breathe, becomes more fluid and recognisable as a process, as a series of attempts at creating images and concepts that describe the development of the psyche and of psychic disorders.

It won't be possible to consider all the works relevant to the history of anal erotism. I have chosen publications that have prepared the way for Abraham's *Short Study* (Jones, 1913, 1918a, 1920; Stärcke, 1919; Ophuijsen, 1920), as well as two of his own publications, "The Narcissistic Evaluation of Excretory Processes" (1920) and "Contributions to the Theory of the Anal Character" (1923). Of Freud's works I am considering the first and third edition of *Three Essays* (1905d/1915), the "Rat Man" (1909d), "The Disposition to Obsessional Neurosis" (1913i), and "On Transformations of Instinct as Exemplified in Anal Erotism" (1917c). For lack of space other works will have to remain in the background (e.g., Freud, 1908b, 1912–1913, 1916–1917).[1]

Anal erotism: Freud in 1905

The theory Freud expounded in the first edition of *Three Essays* was the result of many years of work. The idea that infantile sexuality was primarily autoerotic formed one of the cornerstones of this theory (Freud, 1905d, pp. 181–183). Freud placed special emphasis on autoerotism, which he also highlighted in his summary of the *Three Essays*: "In childhood, therefore, the sexual instinct is not unified and is at first without an object, that is, auto-erotic" (Ibid., p. 233). According to Freud autoerotism was characteristic of the excitations belonging to the oral, and even more so to the anal zone whereas other sexual components—the

[1] For the same reason the following publications could not be included in the discussion: Andreas-Salomé, 1916; Brill, 1912–1913; Federn, 1913–1914; Ferenczi, 1911, 1911–1912, 1914b, c; Hattingberg, 1914; Hitschmann, 1913a, b; Jones, 1912–1913, 1914; Sadger, 1910a, 1913a, b.

scopophilic instinct, exhibitionism, cruelty, and so on—"from the very first involve other people as sexual objects" (ibid., p. 192). Despite these inconsistencies Freud held on to the idea of infantile sexuality as autoerotic. How important this notion was to him is apparent in his remark that "the infantile sexual instinct at first shows no need [for an object]" (ibid., p. 191). Just how uneven this aspect of the theory was, is quite obvious. Just as obvious is the fact that Freud regarded autoerotism as an essential element of infantile sexuality.

Autoerotism described the simple fact that the infant and toddler are able to stimulate the oral and anal zones without the help of another person or an object. In addition, autoerotism took into account the child's general and pervasive egocentrism—what Freud would later call narcissism. In Freud's view autoerotism and narcissism formed part of both normal and pathological psychic processes despite the fact that adult consciousness, for the most part, does not have access to them. Another important aspect of autoerotism was the fact that it was neither relating to nor directed at an object. When the infant refuses to empty his bowels, he, according to Freud, insists on his pleasure: "He is naturally not concerned with dirtying the bed, he is only anxious not to miss the subsidiary pleasure attached to defaecating" (1905d, p. 186). Initially, infantile experience was thus not oriented towards others; on the contrary, at the very beginning the infant did not take the other into account at all. Even though Freud significantly modified this view in the third edition of *Three Essays*, published in 1915, he did not give it up entirely. Lastly, anal and oral erotism lean on "vital somatic functions" (1905d/1915, p. 182). At the beginning, Freud argued, the satisfaction of somatic needs (hunger, excretion) was accompanied by pleasurable sensations at the erotogenic zones. Over time biological and psychic gratification separated. With regard to anality the attainment of pleasure was no longer tied to defecation but could now be achieved by withholding the contents of the bowels. Eventually, the anal zone only provided the excitations out of which anal erotism was "made".

Contained in Freud's notion of anal erotism as leaning on physical needs is the difficult question of how to define the contents and aims of component-drive erotism, that is, the relation between the body part that becomes an erogenous zone (e.g., the anus), its somatic-biological function (defecation), the aim of the drive, and the psychic meaning that is conferred upon the excitation of this zone. The term anaclisis underlines both the rootedness of the psyche in the body as well as its opposite: the independence and autonomy of the psyche. The fate of anal erotism, however, is not something that Freud concerned himself with very much in 1905. He assumed that all components of infantile sexuality will and must be repressed, sublimated or substituted by reaction formations; and that disturbances in the process of establishing defences against sexual satisfaction (shame, disgust, morality) could lead to the emergence of neurotic symptoms.

Last but not least, let's remember what the first edition of *Three Essays* says about aggression: "normal male adult sexuality," Freud writes, contained "an element of aggressiveness" (1905d, p. 157). Why? Freud assumed biological reasons: aggression was necessary in order to "overcome the resistance of the sexual object"—woman (ibid.). Perhaps, Freud speculates, sexual aggression had its origin in the instinct to master ("Bemächtigungstrieb"). In any case, Freud tells us, "the history of human civilization shows beyond any doubt that there is an intimate connection between cruelty and the sexual instinct" (ibid., p. 159)—even though Freud did not yet have an explanation of this connection "apart from laying emphasis on the aggressive factor in the libido" (ibid.). Sadism, Freud went on, "would correspond to an aggressive component of the sexual instinct which has become independent and exaggerated and, by displacement, has usurped the leading position" (ibid., p. 158). When this happened, love was being transformed into hate. "It is also through the medium of this connection between libido and cruelty that the transformation of love into hate takes place, the transformation of affectionate into hostile impulses" (ibid., pp. 166–167). Along with the other component drive impulses Freud considered cruelty to be part of every child's endowment. In the 1905 edition of *Three Essays* Freud did not mention a special connection between cruelty and sadism or oral and anal erotism.

Evidently, we have a problem here. On the one hand, Freud assumed close, if not "intimate" connections between the sexual pleasure and sadism; on the other, he wanted to separate sexual from non-sexual impulses. And then there was the hierarchy of drive-impulses in relation to the aetiology of the neuroses. "The energy of the sexual instinct," Freud stated over and over again, was "the most important and only constant source of energy of the neurosis" (ibid., p. 163)—a conviction he had reached and found confirmed in many years of clinical practice (as well as in his self-analysis).

Differences on how to distinguish sexual from non-sexual, especially aggressive drive-impulses and their role in the genesis of the neuroses led Freud to break with Adler (1911) and Jung (1913–1914). Needless to say, the break-ups did not solve the problem and it continued to be a topic of discussion for Freud and the group that had formed around him. Regarding anal erotism, Ernest Jones (1913) was the first to propose a new solution to the old problem. Freud disliked Jones's proposition but it did not provoke a conflict between the two men. To understand Jones's argument we need to know more about how Freud's theory of anal erotism evolved in the years between the first and the third edition of *Three Essays*.

Sadism and anal erotism: Freud in 1909

Those who have read the paper on the "Rat Man" will remember the cruel punishment in which the victim was forced to sit on a pot filled with rats. From the moment the "Rat Man" had heard of it, he was obsessed with the idea that the punishment was inflicted on people close to him. He tried in vain to ban the horrid image and other related obsessions from his consciousness. Regarding anal erotism—an idea that easily suggests itself in the Rat Man—Freud had a surprise in store for us. On the one hand, he described in some detail that anal erotism "had played an important part in his childhood" (1909d, p. 213), mentioning many examples of how it manifested in the patient's behaviour and phantasies. Freud's notes of the analysis with the "Rat Man" contain additional thoughts on anal erotism, such as "a most wonderful anal phantasy" and "'dirty' transferences" (1955a, pp. 287, 295). On the other hand, the long chapter entitled "Theoretical" of the published case study (1909d, pp. 221–249) makes no mention whatsoever of anal erotism. Instead Freud focuses on other component drives and he foregrounds sadism, especially its failed repression as the most important component (ibid., pp. 237–245). Freud did not see a connection between sadism and anal erotism—something that was soon to gain significance. How was that possible? How could Freud place so little importance on anal erotism? The same Freud who never tired of reminding us that the reasons for symptom formation were to be found in the individual's love life and sexuality. Had he not yet understood the significance of anal erotism for the aetiology of obsessive-compulsive disorders? Or was he afraid, given the outrage after the publication of "Character and

Anal Erotism" (1908b), to draw attention to the importance of anal erotism for fear of once again causing a scandal in the scientific community, as Mahony (1986, p. 158) has suggested?

I suspect there are additional reasons. It seems to me that in an analysis Freud was not interested in finding component drive impulses but in understanding how they were processed and used (see Chapter Five). The "Rat Man", for instance, used anal erotism to express rage and disappointment directed at the father, and in the transference directed at Freud. Envisaged this way, anal erotism belongs to another and "truer" story—a story created around the oedipal constellation, supporting Freud's claim that the component drives take a subordinate position in relation to of genital drives. Similarly, oral and anal erotogenic zones "serve" sexual satisfaction and are "apparatuses subordinate to the genitals" as well as "substitutes" for the genital zone (Freud, 1905d, p. 169). This, it seems to me, is the reason why in the theory chapter of the "Rat Man" Freud focused on the reconstruction of the oedipal situation, assigning little importance to anal erotism as the origin of obsessional neurosis. Instead Freud underlined the crucial role of sadism, which, he argued, expressed itself in the fear that other people will find themselves in harm's way. The Rat Man fought his sadistic phantasies, his thirst for revenge, and his death wishes towards the father, the friend, and the lover—all of which remained unconscious—with counter-responses and counter-actions. He acted as if he was about to commit an evil crime, which both frightened and tempted him—and yet he was not aware of his unconscious wishes. But, as Freud argued, what activated and kept the sadistic impulses alive were the demands of the sexual drive. This is how Freud put it: "The source from which his hostility to the father derived its indestructibility was evidently something in the nature of *sensual desires*, and in that connection he must have felt his father as in some way or other an *interference*" (1909d, p. 182). In other words, the sexual impulses are the driving force behind the never-ending hostility and the ambivalence of love and hate. They activate rage and a desire for revenge because they are tied to the phantasy that the father will forbid and reject the sexual impulses. Moreover, Freud went on, even though the sadistic impulses gave rise to terror and remorse, these feelings were not strong enough to suppress the sadistic impulses leading to a "*chronic* co-existence of love and hatred" (1909d, p. 239). Finally, Freud assumed constitutionally increased sadism that posed a challenge to repression.

To those of us wiling to accept Freud's argument thus far, going along with his claim of the primacy of sexuality, it must come as a surprise to learn at the end of the theory chapter that Freud asks us not to hold drive impulses responsible for the aetiology of obsessive ideas. "There are reasons enough for avoiding such a course," Freud warns us, "for we must remember that in every neurosis we come upon the same suppressed instincts behind the symptoms" (ibid., p. 240). Therefore, what is "characteristic" of obsessional neurosis "is not, in my opinion, to be found in instinctual life but in the psychological field" (ibid., p. 248). Is Freud saying that, after all, neither the sexual impulses nor the sadism they activate (and least of all anal erotism) are the decisive factors? He is, indeed! And he names the factor that he deems the most important: the "psychological" factor by which he means that due to regression "thinking replaces acting" (ibid., p. 244), and normal thoughts are experienced as obsessive ideas, that is, as ideas that could cause real harm which is why they are terrifying and need to be averted or prevented by countermeasures (mental rituals, etc.).

Let us be clear: to experience one's thoughts as actions with consequences in external reality, the "omnipotence of thoughts", which Freud mentioned for the first time in the "Rat Man" and expanded in subsequent works (1911b, 1912–1913), was in Freud's view not a manifestation of a drive-impulse but the modus operandi of the regressed ego. In the "Rat Man" Freud worked his way towards this "solution"—a solution in which Freud arrived at the astounding conclusion that instinctual life was to be regarded as secondary. In my view, this ability to remain open to new views, approaches, and unexpected perspectives is a quite remarkable characteristic of the way Freud the researcher worked.

From toilet training to hate: Ernest Jones, 1913

While Freud's disciples showed little interest in oral erotism, the opposite was true for anal erotism. One of the most important theoretical contributions came from Ernest Jones in a paper entitled "Haß und Analerotik in der Zwangsneurose" (1913). Jones' paper appeared in German in 1913; the English language version "Hate and Anal Erotism in the Obsessional Neurosis" was published five years later.

Jones, who met Freud in Salzburg in April 1908, and was almost immediately admitted to the inner circle, was a prolific writer as well as a serious theoretician, clinician, and organiser of psychoanalysis. Since at least 1910 he was interested in obsessive-compulsive neurosis, and he and Freud exchanged thoughts frequently. Their correspondence reveals that Freud took much interest in Jones' research on anal erotism; he encouraged his work and offered him his own thoughts (F/Jo, pp. 73, 77, 80).

In January 1913 Jones arrived in Vienna, where he participated in the session of the Vienna Society in which Freud presented the just-finished animism chapter from *Totem and Taboo* (Min 4, pp. 147–149). In the discussion Ferenczi mentioned his new, still unpublished treatise on the sense of reality (1913); a work that contained a theory of ego development that closely tied in with Freud's remarks on the omnipotence of thoughts ("Allmacht der Gedanken"). Back in Toronto Jones told Freud that he intended to write a paper "on the connections between the *Allmacht der Gedanken in der Zwangsneurose*, narcissism and the anal-complex (especially flatus)"—subjects which formed part of both Freud's and Ferenczi's work and about which he had heard them speak (F/Jo, p. 195).

Jones' paper was composed between the end of March and the end of April 1913 (F/Jo, p. 196). In May he presented the paper at the Congress of the American Psycho-Analytic Association (Jones 1913, p. 540, fn.1). At the beginning of June he once again travelled to Vienna and then Budapest, where he was in analysis with Ferenczi.[2] In September he attended the International Psychoanalytic Congress in Munich, where Freud presented on obsessional neurosis, and introduced the "sadistic-anal erotic" phase (1913i, p. 321).[3] In his paper Freud referred to Jones—something quite remarkable for Freud who used to be rather reluctant in mentioning his disciples by name. Jones' "Haß und Analerotik" appeared in the September 1913 issue of the *Internationale Zeitschrift für Psychoanalyse*; the following issue brought Freud's Munich paper entitled "Die Disposition zur Zwangsneurose [The Disposition to Obsessional Neurosis]" (1913i).

---

[2] Regarding Jones' analysis see, e.g., F/Jo, pp. 200, 204, 213; F/Fer 1, pp. 489–490; Freud's imposing advice to Ferenczi is remarkable: "Be strict and tender with him. [...] Feed the pupa so that a queen can be made out of it" (ibid., p. 490). At that time Jones was editing some of Ferenczi's work and translating it into English (Ferenczi, 1916).

[3] The journal *Luzifer-Amor* was first to publish Freud's summary of the paper he presented in Munich (Freud, 2011; May, 2011c).

The dates alone raise the question of how the two papers relate to one another. As far as Jones was concerned, his paper is closely connected to both Freud's and Ferenczi's work while at the same time suggesting important additions and significant modifications of the theory. One modification is to do with the meaning of anal erotism for the aetiology of obsessional neurosis. The very first sentence of this paper announces its author as an innovator in the field of anal erotism and obsessional neurosis: "In a recent contribution on the subject of obsessional neurosis [...] I laid stress on the remarkable prominence of the part played [...] by anal erotism", something Ferenczi and Seif were in agreement with (1913, p. 540).[4] While Freud in his discussion of the Rat Man's analysis (only) drew attention to the co-existence of love and hatred, he, Jones, had already underlined the meaning of anal erotism in his paper "Einige Fälle von Zwangsneurose [Some Cases of Obsessional Neurosis]" (1912–1913).[5]

In these first introductory sentences Jones lets it be known that it was he who first drew attention to the primacy of anal erotism in the aetiology of obsessional neurosis. On the one hand, this is not really a surprise, since for Freud anal erotism did not play a significant role in obsessional neurosis. On the other hand, it is not quite true that in the aforementioned paper (1912–1913) Jones reached the conclusion that anal erotism was a central factor in the aetiology of obsessional neurosis. What he did say was that obsessional neurosis comprised four leading "complexes"—the last of which was anal erotism. Thus the only thing that Jones could really lay claim to was the fact that he had included anal erotism as one of "the complexes".[6] The fact that no patient of his case studies suffered from obsessional neurosis—something he did concede (ibid., p. 602) and was openly criticised for by his colleagues (Min 4, p. 212)—further reduced the explanatory power of his paper.

---

[4] Though Jones expressed his gratitude to his colleagues Ferenczi and Seif, with whom he discussed the significance of anal erotism for obsessional neurosis, he did not mention any publications (1913, p. 540, fn. 4). Jones was in regular contact with Ferenczi and he and the psychoanalyst Seif, who lived in Munich, were close friends who had seen each other several times during that period (F/Jo, pp. 117, fn. 4; 154, 155, 158, 161).

[5] Jones' paper was not fully translated into English. The existing English translation is an abridged version of the much longer German text.

[6] The passage reads as follows: "It seems to me that in obsessional neurosis the main complexes, grouped around an incestuous core, are scopophilia, sadism, homosexuality, and anal erotism; in every single case that I examined those four stood out the most" (Jones, 1912–1913, p. 112).

The second thesis that Jones expounded in "Haß und Analerotik" addresses the relationship between the two components. Referring to the role of anal erotism in obsessional neurosis, he argued that "if, therefore, my finding [...] is correct," we have to assume "that there must be some inherent connection between hate and anal erotism, certainly in the obsessional neurosis, and perhaps altogether" (1913, p. 540). The fact that Jones speaks of hate rather than sadism, as Freud did, is of little significance. At the time both terms were used in a relatively unsystematic way.

For Jones, toilet training provided the link between anal erotism and sadism/hatred. Hatred did not only, and not in the true sense of the word, stem from the oedipal relationship to the father. As Jones saw it, toilet training put the child "in serious conflict with the outer world" (1913, p. 542). "Hate is to be regarded as an expression of disappointed or baulked love," wrote Jones; the child hated the person who interfered with his anal-erotic pleasure (ibid., p. 541). The proof Jones offered for his thesis was his analysis of a paraphrenic, that is, schizophrenic patient (ibid., p. 543). In his adult years the patient's "attitude towards his mother was one of open hatred" (ibid.). Because mother did not allow him to sit on the pot as long as he wanted to, "the conflict involved in the interference with anal erotism on the part of the mother, therefore, must be regarded as one of the important sources of chronic hatred" (ibid.). In Jones' view the hatred was caused by the disturbance of anal erotism; it was initially directed "towards the *Imago* of all later love-objects, the mother herself" (ibid.). Therefore, the co-existence of love and hatred had to have its roots in toilet training as well. The mother who was once loved is now hated: it is therefore "only to be expected that any one whose love towards the mother has from the beginning alternated with hate should show the same alternation towards all secondary love-objects" (ibid., p. 544).

Jones' third thesis, his notion of the "flatus complex", is a follow up on an earlier publication as well (1912–1913, pp. 587–594). One of his patients reported that thinking and speaking were like a liquid streaming out of him, entering other people's bodies and minds, allowing him to transfer his thoughts to them. Communications like this one gave Jones the idea that the phantasy of depositing one's thoughts into another person was a derivative of the infant's experience of flatulence. According to Jones the flatus complex was based on the omnipotence of thoughts, this peculiarity of infantile thinking that Freud had emphasised in the "Rat Man", and that he first attributed to the regressed and then later to the narcissistic ego—an idea that Ferenczi adopted from Freud (Freud, 1909d, p. 233; 1912–1913, pp. 86–88; Ferenczi, 1913).

To remind us of Ferenczi's ego theory of 1913: for Ferenczi the "sense of reality", identical to Freud's reality testing, derived from the infant's initial feeling of omnipotence and being one with the environment, which step by step grew into a more realistic perception of self and objects, and a sense of being separate from the environment. The erogenous zones did not play an important part in the theory of ego development. In the third stage of ego development, characterised by magical thinking, the child learned to give a signal in order to have his needs satisfied. Here is where Jones picked up in "Haß und Analerotik [Hate and Anal Erotism]", formulating a thesis regarding the symbolic meaning of the sound signals the child's ego learns to emit: "sounds accompanying anal activities play a part second only in significance to the voice itself, so that they constitute one of the chief means through which the infant retains its belief in its omnipotence" (1913, p. 546). In the unconscious the ego functions of thought and speech, Jones contended, were associated with flatulence—a thesis he was to expand upon in his 70-pages treatise entitled "The Madonna's Conception Through the Ear" (1914).

Jones' paper presented at least three new conceptual ideas about anal erotism: (1) its primary importance for the aetiology of obsessional neurosis, (2) the intimate ties between anal erotism and hatred, and (3) anal erotism as the bodily foundation of the omnipotence of thought.

Freud versus Jones, 1913

Freud wrote his conference presentation, later published as "The Disposition to Obsessional Neurosis", between the end of July and the beginning of September 1913 (May, 2011c). In one passage he refers to Jones' "Haß und Analerotik" (1913i, p. 321). As mentioned above, it was in this paper that Freud first introduced the sadistic-anal-erotic phase, inserted between narcissism and object love.

Neither in "Disposition" nor in later editions of *Three Essays* did Freud make mention of the flatus complex. In fact, the flatus complex, if I am not mistaken, does not appear at all in Freud's oeuvre, which seems to suggest that he was not convinced that this complex was a necessary addition to the theory. As for the circle of disciples, we know that Federn found the association between the omnipotence of thoughts and flatulency to be "quite doubtful" (Min 4, p. 212), whereas Abraham, in his contribution to the *Bericht über die Fortschritte der Psychoanalyse* [Report on the Progress of Psychoanalysis] (1914), at least acknowledged it as "new" (ibid., p. 353). Notably, Abraham's thoughts should later (1920) go in a direction similar to where Jones had gone.

Apart from the clinical evidence, assessed differently by different people, all participants were aware of the theoretical implications of Jones' flatus complex, which derived ego functions (communication, thought, speech) from drive-impulses, thus endowing the ego with a libidinal foundation. On the one hand, this tendency was in line with psychoanalytic theory; on the other, Freud and Ferenczi, whose work Jones was quite familiar with, had gone in a different direction: they conceptualised the ego and its functions as independent factors irreducible to drive-impulses, subject to development and therefore regression prone. Accordingly, in "Disposition" Freud repeated his demand that every theory of the aetiology of the neuroses and psychoses needed to account for both libido development *and* the stage of ego development in which any fixations may be assumed (1913i, p. 324). The flatus complex did not meet this requirement, fitting with Jones' tendency to not take note of the element of ego regression in general.

Even though he ignored the flatus complex, Freud did comment on the other two aspects of Jones's thesis. In the one and only passage in which he mentions Jones by name, Freud writes "The extraordinary part played by impulses of hatred and anal erotism in the symptomatology of obsessional neurosis has already struck many observers and has recently been emphasised with particular clarity by Ernest Jones (1913)" (1913i, p. 321). Among the "many observers" we might assume Brill (1912–1913) and Federn (1913–1914), and perhaps also Sadger (1913a). The slight irritation that I detect in this passage may be related to the fact that Jones created the impression that he had seen something that Freud had overlooked—an impression Freud would not leave unchallenged. By using the term "symptomatology" rather than aetiology he subtly downgrades Jones' paper from a work on the aetiology of obsessional neurosis to a contribution to the symptoms of obsessional neurosis. Jones' paper, Freud seems to be implying, "only" showed that the symptoms of obsessional neurosis—that is, the surface—manifested anal erotism and hatred. In my view, Freud's slightly irritated tone is due to Jones' tendency to declare impulses stemming from component instincts (anal erotism, hatred) as the cause (origin) of psychic disorders. We know that Freud had raised the same objection to Abraham's early deduction of depression from vicissitudes of libidinal-impulses alone (F/A, pp. 308–309).

Jones' proposition that anal erotism and sadism were intimately connected touched on a most sensitive issue: the place of aggression in Freud's theory. Jones knew that he was moving on thin ice. After all, Freud had just broken with Adler because of Adler's foregrounding of aggression. On principle, the third aspect of Jones's theory—deriving hatred from the prohibitions of anal erotism—was categorically unacceptable to Freud who rejected explanations of this kind (see Chapter One). For Freud, it seems to me, sadism was an elemental instinctual force; it was not the result of frustrations. In Freud's view, an instinctual force "had to be" a given which under certain circumstances could latch on to the sexual drive, act in its service and once again recede into the background, which is to say that as a given sadism could never arise more or less accidentally, by random causes. This would also explain Freud's remark in the meeting of the Vienna Group on November 1913, that he "knows nothing" about the origin "of hate in thwarted anal erotism, as assumed by Jones" (Min 4, p. 213). The pointed wording is not Freud's but Otto Rank's, who took the minutes at that meeting. It seems safe to assume that the entry conveys the tone of Freud's remark, or else it would most certainly not have been approved. The remark reveals how intolerable it was for Freud to think of hatred and sadism as "derived" from anal erotism in this way, or to assume a close bond between them.

In his own "Disposition to Obsessional Neurosis" Freud makes no mention of the "togetherness" of anal erotism and sadism. On the contrary: in Freud's account we are dealing with a more or less coincidental co-existence of two groups of drive-impulses that are opposed to each other. As Freud saw it, anal erotism and sadism emerged at the same time, namely at the stage of "sadistic anal-erotic" organisation (1913i, pp. 321, 323). Other than that, Freud's 1913 publication sees no connections between anal erotism and sadism—which did not mean that the two impulses could not coalesce, as they did in the case of the rat punishment or in beating phantasies, to mention the two most important examples that were instrumental in Freud's conceptualisation of the sadistic-anal stage.

What seems surprising to me is the fact that a PEP-Web (Psychoanalytic Electronic Publishing) search of Freud's *Gesammelte Werke*

(1940–1987) yielded zero hits for "anal-sadistisch" compared to twenty-three hits for "sadistisch-anal" (PEP, version 10, 2011).[7] And it is quite astounding that Freud's terminology as well as the issue it implies has gone unnoticed. The author of the index of the *Gesammelte Werke*, Lilla Veszy-Wagner, believed that Freud *alternated* between "anal", "anal-sadistic", and "sadistic-anal" (Veszy-Wagner, 1968b, p. XVII)—which is not the case. Accordingly, in the index the keyword "sadistisch" refers us to the entry on the "Anal (sadistische) Phase" (Veszy-Wagner, 1968a, p. 532), where all the passages in which Freud speaks of the "sadistisch-anale" phase are listed (ibid., p. 22). By contrast, the keyword "sadistisch-anal" that Freud preferred is *absent* from the index. And so Abraham's terminology—for it was of course Abraham (1924) who had coined the term "anal-sadistic"—found its way right down to the index of the *Gesammelte Werke*.

In Jean Laplanche and Jean-Bertrand Pontalis' *The Vocabulary of Psychoanalysis*, "sadistic-anal" is not a keyword either but "anal-sadistic" is (1967, pp. 35–36). Their answer to the question of how sadism and anal erotism relate to each other consists in a reference to the "biphasic functioning of the anal sphincter (evacuation/retention)" (ibid., p. 35). Here, for once, the authors don't do justice to Freud's thinking. Their presentation of the anal-sadistic situation is derived from Abraham.

In "The Disposition to Obsessional Neurosis", Freud found a new solution to the problem of how anal erotism and sadism were related to each other. He suggested that there was an analogy between the two impulses and the opposition between activity and passivity. Anal erotism lent itself to express passive-feminine love wishes whereas sadism derived from active impulses and was put in the service of active wishes; at a later stage the "antithesis" between activity and passivity becomes "firmly attached to that between the sexes" (1913i, p. 322). This was Freud's answer to Jones' thesis of the affinity between anal erotism and sadism; an answer he most likely found in his analysis of the

---

[7] www.pep-web.org search terms were "anal-sadistisch" and "sadistisch-anal" both with and without hyphen, and in all possible declinations. Addendum 2016: A search in the *Standard Edition* yields a similar result. The latest PEP version (2016) of the *Standard Edition* has twenty-four instances of "sadistic-anal" and three of "anal-sadistic" (1918b, p. 27; 1925d, p. 35; 1917c, p. 131). In all three cases "anal-sadistic" is a mistranslation. The German "sadistisch-anal" was translated as "anal-sadistic". As in the German index, the index of the *Standard Edition* erroneously lists "anal-sadistic", but not Freud's preferred "sadistic-anal".

"Wolf Man" where he made excessive use of it. In this analysis, Freud argued, it became clear that the boy's wish to be loved passively by the father, which stemmed from having observed the parents' copulate *a tergo*, was tied to the anal zone. Anal erotism had thus become the medium or the place to express passive-feminine wishes, which means it served to achieve several different aims: to find pleasure in filth, to express the wish to be loved by the father, or to express rage towards him, as described in the "Rat Man". In these instances we are presented with a fundamentally different conceptualisation of instinctual aims—one that is, compared to Abraham, less closely tied to organs and their functions.[8]

Federn (1913–1914) too had tried to create a bond between anal erotism, sadism, and activity. Since Abraham later would refer to Federn, let us recall his thesis. According to Federn, Freud's observation of the little boy's "obscure urges to do something violent" to his mother (1908c, p. 218) was a later manifestation of the earlier feelings associated with the activity of the sphincter during defecation, which suggested that the activity around the anus had "an active, hostile component" to it (Min 4, p. 212; Federn, 1913–1914, p. 42). Seen from today's perspective Federn's theory may seem unintelligible, but at the time his idea was explosive for it raised the question of the place of aggression in psychoanalytic theory. This was why Blüher, in a review of Federn's paper, registered a problematic "entanglement of Freud's and Adler's thoughts" (Blüher, 1914, p. 17). What is being negotiated here is precisely the issue of the priority of sexuality—an issue both Freud and his disciples struggled with, and that to this day continues to stay on the agenda.

When Freud introduced the sadistic-anal stage in "Disposition", much more was at stake than the importance of sadism or anal erotism. Freud occasionally talked about how much time had passed until it occurred to him to assume a "pregenital" stage (1913i, p. 321; 1917c, p. 127). It finally happened in the analysis of his obsessional patient Elfriede Hirschfeld (see Falzeder, 1994) when it occurred to Freud that the symptoms of her neurosis may be viewed as the product of an extensive regression whose cause Freud assumed to be her husband's impotence which she experienced as a devaluation of her

---

[8] On the relation between feelings regarding the erogenous zones and the corresponding "eroticism" see, e.g., Min 3, pp. 241–245; Jekels, 1913b.

own genital sexuality. The regression gave rise to the ascendency of pregenital impulses, among them sadistic and anal ones that were kept out of consciousness by reaction formations and other psychic mechanisms.

However, the predominance of these drive-impulses was not the decisive element in Elfriede Hirschfeld's regression. For an analytic understanding of her regression the fact *that* a regression had occurred is more important than the type of drive-impulses that became activated. Here Freud takes a view similar to the one he took in his analysis of the Rat Man. What brought about a transformation of ego-functions or of the personality as a whole were not defended against drive-impulses but the regression of the ego.

Furthermore, Freud argues, the regression does not imply a complete rule of pregenital instincts. Rather, the pregenital impulses are "place-holders" for the genital drives (1913i, p. 321); which is to say that the pregenital impulses do not pursue aims of their own. The sadistic desire for revenge, for example, is seen as mere surface, a symptom that deceived the ego into raising moral objections to terrifying sadistic impulses while misjudging their true content: "The obsessional idea 'I should like to kill you' [...] means at bottom nothing other than 'I should like to enjoy you in love'" (Freud, 1916–1917, p. 344). This elaborate concept, in which drive impulses such as sadism and anal erotism stand in for hidden genital impulses, has no place in Jones' theory, and it remained foreign to most of Freud's disciples as well.

Right after the congress in Munich, Jones wrote to Freud that he found his lecture "inspiring" (F/Jo, p. 229). He announced "a number of technical questions" which he however did not take up again, at least not in his letters (ibid., p. 233). Freud, it seems, did not inform Jones that the Vienna Group had discussed his publication on obsessional neurosis on 5 November 1913 and that he, Freud, had rejected Jones' thesis that sadism had its origin in anal erotism (Min 4, p. 212). It is possible that the differences between Freud and Jones disappeared from their written communications because another, more important, conflict pushed to the foreground: the accelerating controversy with Jung, then chair of the International Psychoanalytic Association. Freud and his disciples became absorbed in administrative strategising, and in writing papers "against" Jung. Scientific issues had to be put on the back burner and they played a minor role in their correspondence. It is however entirely possible that Freud would have dropped the argument with Jones regardless. At that point he had moved on to new topics, the most important of which was narcissism.

Nevertheless, the psychoanalytic community took note of the open questions concerning sadism and anal erotism. Hitschmann, author of the chapter on drive theory in the *Bericht über die Fortschritte der Psychoanalyse* [Report on the Progress of Psychoanalysis], summed up the discussion with a sense of humour: "the as of yet open questions regarding the relation between anal erotism and sadism (Federn [...], Brill [...], Jones [...]) are awaiting their final interpretation" (1914, p. 289). Concerning the priority of anal erotism in obsessional neurosis Jones insisted that Freud "confirmed" his (=Jones') conclusions (1918a, p. 420). He went on to repeat this not entirely accurate statement in a survey article written for the English-speaking audience of the *International Journal of Psycho-Analysis* (1920, p. 164). Abraham, by contrast, chose his words more carefully: "following on Jones' important investigation on 'Hate and Anal Erotism in the Obsessional Neurosis', Freud formulated an early pregenital organisation of the libido" (1923, p. 370). In addition, I have found that Freud, unlike Jones, underlined the significance of a non-instinctual factor—the development of the ego and its susceptibility to regression; he opened anal erotism to passive love wishes; emphasised the opposition of anal erotism and sadism (in contrast to Jones who assumed a kinship relation); and, as he had done before, drew attention to the component drives as surrogates, which is to say that with regard to the genital-sexual (or oedipal) drives they are of secondary importance.

Anal erotism, Freud 1914–1916

Modifications of his theory of anal erotism that Freud published after "Disposition" seem to be taken from his analysis with the Wolf Man (1918b). The study was written in the autumn of 1914 (with the exception of one insertion that makes no reference to anal erotism). In the autumn of 1914 Freud added his new ideas on anal erotism to the third edition of *Three Essays* (1915), in April 1916 they were added in "On Transformations of Instinct" (1917c), and between November 1915 and November 1916 they found entrance into the *Introductory Lectures* (1916–1917). It seems that after 1916 the early history of Freud's conceptualisation of anal erotism came to a halt. In my research on oral erotism I observed a similar timing. After 1916 Freud, for a long time, did not write anything that exceeded his theoretical achievements on the topic, including the *Lectures* (Freud, 1916–1917, pp. 315–319, pp. 326–330).

As previously mentioned, the most important innovation concerned the use of anal erotism for the gratification of passive-feminine wishes. In the "Wolf Man" Freud was able to show that in the course of psychic development anal erotism was drawn into the maelstrom of the oedipal constellation and certain infantile sexual theories and phantasies, which then allowed it (anal erotism) to gratify the wish to be loved by the father. This way anal erotism achieved a new significance, one that was not there from the very beginning, and one that gradually loosened its ties to the bodily functions of defecation.

Another addition to the theory of anal erotism from this period concerns the infant's experience of these anal processes. As Freud first explained in "On Transformations of Instinct" (1917c), the infant experienced the faeces in a narcissistic way, that is, as a valuable part of himself: he "either parts obediently with his faeces, 'sacrifices' them to his love, or else retains them for purposes of auto-erotic satisfaction and later as a means of asserting his own will" (ibid., p. 130). If the child experiences the giving up of his faeces as a gift, "as a token of affection", then, Freud argues, the baby has taken a step forward from autoerotism and narcissism to object-love (ibid.).

The differences between Freud and Jones are both evident and axiomatic. Where Jones interpreted the renunciation of anal gratification as the origin of hatred and sadism, Freud saw the infant's defiance as insisting on autoerotic and narcissistic gratification—a link he had established in "Character and Anal Erotism" (1908b) as early as 1908. In sum, where Freud sees narcissism, Jones sees sadism and aggression.

Another innovation Freud introduced in this small work was the developmental path from child to penis. In his analysis of the Wolf Man Freud had gained the impression that in the unconscious faeces and baby were perceived as equivalents (1917c, p. 128): at first the infant experienced his faeces as a part of his body; as soon as he developed the theory that eating produced babies, which were born through the anus, the child made a connection between "faeces" and "baby" (ibid., p. 131). Another link, Freud believed, led from faeces to penis. When the boy discovered the anatomical differences between the genders, he came to understand that the penis "must be a detachable part of the body", "something analogous to faeces" (ibid., p. 133). Thus, Freud proposed that initially the faecal stick was not experienced as a penis. Only later, through the rise of castration anxiety, did it become associated with the penis retroactively. Freud felt strongly about this developmental sequence and, at the beginning of the 1920s, vehemently countered some of his colleagues and former students. (More on this below.) Here we have yet another example of Freud proposing psychic links that could only be constituted by infantile experience, infantile sexual theories, and phantasies.

The last modification of anal erotism, the one I announced at the beginning of this chapter, refers to the intentionality and directionality of the child's experiences and behaviour. In *Three Essays* (1905), Freud reported that for the child the retention of the faeces served as "a masturbatory stimulus upon the anal zone"; in the third edition of *Three Essays*, he added that retention was also "to be employed in his relation to the people looking after him" (1905d/1915, p. 187). That the editors of the *Standard Edition* overlooked that the addendum was made in 1915 is most likely a coincidence. The oversight nevertheless fits the tendency to ascribe "object relatedness" to Freud wherever possible. Some of his disciples, Jones among them, found Freud's cautious approach irritating. In his Freud biography Jones stated on several occasions that Freud was reluctant to assume that the child's sexuality, especially in the first year of his life, was directed at an object (Jones, 1953–1957, vol. 1, p. 323; vol. 2, p. 261). In my view, Freud was not at all hesitant to endow the child with sexual wishes directed at objects. But his main concern lay somewhere else: with the child's (and the adult's) autoerotism and narcissism, which formed the main focus of all the amendments to anal erotism he added between 1914 and 1916. Freud believed them to be important discoveries, and it seems that he felt he literally needed to defend them against some of his disciples.

Anal erotism: Freuds disciples, 1918–1923

After 1916 Freud did not report new insights into anal erotism for a while—his disciples, however, did. Between 1918 and 1923, drawing on the article by Jones discussed above, they published a series of important papers culminating in Abraham's *Short Study of the Development of the Libido* (1924). In what follows I shall focus on publications that have close links to this study.[9]

---

[9] Ferenczi's contributions to anal erotism (1914b, 1914c), which as far as methodology and content are concerned, fall in line with Freud's theory, as well as Lou Andreas-Salomé's work (1916), will therefore not be discussed.

Ernest Jones: "keeping back" and "giving out" (1918)

Right after the end of the war Freud received the second edition of a volume of Jones' collected writings (Jones, 1918b; F/Jo, p. 330), which the latter had sent him. The volume contained three *new* papers; one of them entitled "Anal-erotic Character Traits" (1918a).[10] Jones asked Freud for his opinion on these papers (F/Jo, p. 332). Freud commented on two papers (ibid., pp. 334–335), leaving out "Anal-erotic Character Traits", the work which contained the previously quoted statement that Freud merely confirmed the links between sadism and anal erotism that Jones' had discovered (1918a, p. 420). It is possible that Freud did not comment on the paper because he was still annoyed with Jones.

In "Anal-erotic Character Traits" Jones made an attempt to give a systematic account of, as well as add to, the characteristics that Freud had described in his "Character and Anal Erotism" (1908a). Freud had only put them in a loose and provisional order: under "reaction formation against an interest in what is dirty and disturbing" (ibid., p. 172) he subsumed orderliness, cleanliness, and trustworthiness; avarice and parsimony were subsumed under the sublimation of anal interest in the faeces; defiance and obstinacy indicated, as mentioned before, an ongoing insistence on anal gratification.

Jones found the categories of "keeping back" and "giving out", which he had borrowed from Bertrand Russell, most suited for a regrouping (1918a, p. 428). Each category, he argued, was derived from an instinct—the "instinct to posses, and to create or produce" (ibid.), which he combined with two psychic mechanisms: reaction formation and sublimation, from which he extracted four types of personality distinguished by the choice of mechanism and the predominance of one of the two drive-impulses, "keeping back" or "giving out" (ibid., pp. 428–435).

Even though Jones' typology did not win broad recognition, the two basic impulses of "keeping back" (retain, hold on to, etc.) and "giving out" did catch on. Abraham (among others) drew on them (1923, 1924); Freud, however, did not adopt them, at least not until 1924, the period I am concerned with here. Which is not to say that Freud did not, here and there, make a connection between anal processes and collecting,

---

[10] It was translated into German by Anna Freud and published in the *Internationale Zeitschrift* (1919).

retaining, giving, but he did not limit anal erotism to this aspect. For Freud anal erotism was much more than that, it was a process that could acquire many different meanings.

August Stärcke and Jan van Ophuijsen: the faecal stick as love object (1919–1920)

At the same time that Jones worked on his "Anal-erotic Character Traits", two Dutch psychiatrists, August Stärcke and Jan van Ophuijsen, developed similar thoughts on anal erotism (Stärcke, 1919; Ophuijsen, 1920).[11] Their main thesis stated that the infant, equating the content of his bowels with his caregivers, experienced his faeces as persecutory.

Stärcke was concerned with offering a theory that could explain the curious transformation of love into hate that Freud had described in the Schreber case (1911c). In his study Freud had interpreted Schreber's delusion of persecution as a projective defence against homosexual desire: instead of feeling one's desire for the object, the object was perceived as hateful. Projection transformed love into hatred (1911c, pp. 62–65). Stärcke believed to have observed that patients who suffered from a delusion of persecution were secretly desiring *and* fearful of anal intercourse (1919, p. 231). It was "extremely probable", Stärcke wrote, that the phantasied persecutor once was the contents of the bowels which in the unconscious were identified with the loved object: "The scybalum[12] is the primary (real) persecutor; it commits anal acts of violence which are often at the same time acts of pleasure" (ibid., p. 232). Pain and pleasure, love and hate, Stärcke believed, were oriented towards the faecal stick. Toilet training intensified these affects making the child feel love and hatred both for his caregivers and for his faeces which he came to equate with his love objects (ibid., p. 233). Ophuijsen formulated a similar hypothesis with regard to neurotic patients who identified the "persecutor" (in dreams and ideas) with their faeces, a mechanism that had its root in the fact that the child must have felt persecuted by sensations at the rectum, the movement of the bowels among them (Ophuijsen, 1920, p. 238).

[11] At the meeting of the Dutch Psychoanalytic Society on 30 March 1919 both gave papers (Korr, 1920, p. 101) whose ideas were fleshed out in subsequent publications. Regarding Ophuijsen, see Stroeken, 2009; regarding his close personal ties to Abraham as well as his contribution to oral erotism, see Chapter Five.

[12] Scybalum = faecal stick.

It may well be that this is the first instance in the history of psychoanalytic theory in which the faeces are seen as equivalent to the love object, even though neither Stärcke nor Ophuijsen say whether this equation was a normal activity or a symptom (in the adult and the child). This new, modified notion of the object departed from the assumption that the (love) object had to be a person, at the most the breast, but in actual fact the term object almost always referred to the "mother" or an attachment figure. And while object love was not the only form of love—there was "thing love", and there were ideals that one could be in love with—the idea that the child experienced the contents of his bowels as a love object, rather than as a narcissistically cathected part of its own body, as Freud argued, had, to my knowledge, never been presented before—it would soon be adopted by numerous authors.

Problematic about this approach was the fact that the difference between narcissistic and non-narcissistic experiences seemed to be lost, or at the very least that non-narcissistic experiencing was reserved for the earliest period of the child's life. Freud had indeed assumed equivalence between faeces, baby, and penis but he thought of it as a developmental series that began with a predominantly narcissistic cathexis (of faeces, baby and penis) and ended in non-narcissistic object choice and object love. In fact, the transformation of autoerotism and narcissism into object love was taken to be the very core of psychic development.

Analerotism in the service of sadism: Karl Abraham, 1920

At the end of 1919, Abraham sent his paper "The Narcissistic Evaluation of Excretory Processes in Dreams and Neurosis" to Freud who responded with: "your contribution on the omnipotence of excreta amused me greatly" (F/A, p. 411). Abraham's paper was published within a few months, at the beginning of the following year. Its centrepiece was the dream of a female patient: She sat on a chair in front of a house situated by a lake. People were swimming and there was a boat on the lake. A gust of wind produced a huge wave engulfing the boat and its occupants (Abraham, 1920, p. 318). In Abraham's interpretation chair [*germ.* Stuhl = stool, faeces], wind and water symbolised anal and urethral erotism, and he understood the dream to be a manifestation of the dreamer's unconscious wish to eliminate her family (Freud would most likely not have stopped here but traced the symbols to the dreamer's hidden love wishes). Abraham found the dream surprising because he believed that *hostile* impulses were associated with anal and urethral erotism, which did not seem to fit Freud's assumption "that anal and urethral sensations are closely related to infantile impulses of love" (ibid., p. 319). On the contrary, as Abraham saw it, the dream showed that "functions and products of the bowel and bladder [were] used as vehicles of hostile impulses" (ibid.). Abraham went on: "it is rare to find those impulses so glaringly exhibited as in the example given above, where the functions of the bladder und the bowel are placed exclusively in the service of sadism, and urine and flatus appear as the instruments of a sadistic attack" (ibid.). The immense power that the dreamer ascribed to excretory processes was an expression of her "narcissistic over-estimation of the self" (ibid.). This over-estimation, wrote Abraham, seemed to be "more primitive" than the idea of the "omnipotence of thoughts"—in fact it was its "preliminary stage" (ibid.).

"The Narcissistic Evaluation of Excretory Processes in Dreams and Neurosis" is just four pages long but it contains a number of remarkable thoughts. To begin with, the paper reacquaints us with Jones' thesis about flatulency as the origin of the omnipotence of thoughts to which Abraham—just like Jones—believed to have found the somatic foundation: excretion. As Abraham saw it, excretion was the origin of narcissistic over-estimation. At the very beginning of his life the child believed in the omnipotence of excretion; the belief in the omnipotence of thoughts was a later development. In a paper published in 1923 Abraham added, "further experience has since convinced me that this is a regular and typical process" (p. 375). Initially, at least according to Abraham, narcissistic pleasure was associated with excretion, while Freud (and Ferenczi) understood the omnipotence of thoughts as an early function of the ego.

Referring to Federn's attempt at deriving sadism from defecation, Abraham argued that this view of anal erotism did not contradict Freud's. He stated that active and passive strivings were coupled with each other in defecation (1920, p. 321). Hence, the function of the bowels had both "passive" (as Freud had established in the "Wolf Man") and "active" elements. Which meant that as far as defecation was concerned activity and passivity were neither opposed to each other nor dissimilar but intimately tied to one another (ibid.) Abraham (implicitly) equated libidinal activity with sadism and he took the observation that the child "exhibits the same facial congestion, the same gestures, the same movements of the body" and "the same moaning sounds" whether it defaecates or throws a tantrum as evidence of the close association between anal erotism and sadism.

In this paper we witness Abraham trying to conceive of sadism and anal erotism as flip sides of the same coin, wooing us, with ever such new phrases, into recognising their relatedness, if not identity. We can assume that Abraham, who was familiar with Federn's paper, was aware that a lot was at stake in these sometimes-hairsplitting arguments, and he too tried to find words that would help to diminish the divergence from Freud's theory. So he spoke of "libidinal impulses of an active nature", knowing that Freud had conceived of activity (sadism) and passivity (anal erotism) as opposites. Interestingly, in his paper Abraham prefers "functions" of the bowels to "anal erotism". We can see why. While it was difficult to ascribe an inherently sadistic character to anal erotism, the functions of the bowels seemed to lend itself to such a point of view.

What, then, are we to make of Abraham's audacious thesis that bladder and bowel functions acted in the service of sadism? On the one hand, his thesis agrees with Freud's assumption that the excitations of an erogenous zone may be used for various psychic ends: the expression of rage is one of them. On the other hand, the idea that in normal development urination and defecation served sadism is not compatible with Freud's conception of anal erotism and infantile sexuality as first and foremost pleasurable experiences that were not primarily aimed at sadistic gratification.

The fact that Freud welcomed Abraham's paper, was "amused" by it despite the incompatibility with his own theory, seems to suggest that he chose to overlook the differences in their approaches. We know of other cases, Jung and Rank among them, in which Freud passed over dissenting voices hoping that his colleague would at some point be persuaded and agree with him. Rather than dramatise disagreements, Freud tended to play them down. He complimented and praised his disciples, expressed joy and delight even, until the controversy escalated to a stage where the differences could no longer be ignored, at which point ending the relationship would often be the only "solution". With Abraham, however, Freud did not break, perhaps because Abraham made every effort to make his theoretical interventions compatible with Freud's theory. Nonetheless, similar to "The First Pregenital Stage of the Libido" (1916–1917), the paper in which Abraham began to develop his own theory of orality characterised by the aggressiveness of the libido,

"The Narcissistic Evaluation" represents a move away from Freud and towards his own theory of anality, which he was to fully develop in "A Short Study" (1924).

En route to his book from 1924 Abraham composed another article on anal erotism ("Contributions to the Theory of the Anal Character", 1923), in which he closely followed Jones' 1918 paper, offering a host of new observations on the anal character.[13] At the beginning of this paper he tells the reader that "a problem of great theoretical importance will be very frequently alluded to in this study", that is, the issue of "the psychological connections that exist between the two impulses of sadism and anal erotism which we always mention in close association with each other, almost as a matter of habit. And I shall attempt the solution of this question in a later paper" (1923, p. 371), by which he meant "A Short Study of the Development of the Libido". This underlines, once more, how much importance Abraham placed on his attempts to find an answer to the question of the relationship between anal erotism and sadism. In fact, it was the main concern of his *opus magnum*.

This is not the place for an in-depth discussion of Freud's reaction to his disciples' contributions to anal erotism. A first glance reveals that he mentioned Jones' "Hate and Anal Erotism" and "Anal-erotic Character Traits" (1918a) only a few times, and that no mention at all was made of Abraham's "Narcissistic Evaluation" (1920) and "Contributions to the Theory of the Anal Character" (1923). The same is true for Stärcke's (1919) and Ophuijsen's (1920) articles on the anal origins of the delusion of paranoia.

The anal-sadistic phase: Karl Abraham, 1924

"A Short Study of the Development of the Libido" presents a new theory of psychic development. Its main purpose was to complement Freud's developmental model, which began with autoerotism and narcissism and opened out into object love (1924, p. 480). My discussion will focus on Abraham's modifications concerning anal erotism and their relation to sadism insofar as they draw and follow up on ideas

[13] The manuscript was completed in October 1922 and published in 1923 in the *Internationale Zeitschrift für Psychoanalyse*, vol. 9. The article seems to have been based on his presentation of the same title in the Berlin Group in January 1921 (Korr, 1921, p. 392); the text of the lecture has not survived. Relying on Jones (1926b), the literature erroneously dates the publication of Abraham's article back to 1921.

about anal erotism that were circulating in the group of disciples since the publication of Jones' 1913 paper—other aspects of Abraham's paper will have to remain unexamined. By 1924 Abraham had developed his own theory of the relationship between anal erotism and sadism. He was therefore repeating himself when he stated "that since Freud's discovery our clinical observation has confirmed over and over again the close relationship that exists between these two instinctual spheres; and yet we have never inquired into the origin of this special relationship" (ibid., p. 424). We would come one step closer to answering the question, Abraham argued, if we "took into consideration another piece of well-ascertained psycho-analytic knowledge", which is "that a complete capacity for love is only achieved when the libido has reached its genital stage" (ibid., p. 425). This, however did not answer the question as to "why, at a certain level of development, the sadistic impulses exhibit a special affinity precisely for anal erotism and not, for instance, for oral or genital erotism" (ibid.). In this, Abraham suggested, "the empirical data of psycho-analysis may be of use" (ibid.). Didn't it prove that both anal erotism and sadism each possessed two "opposite pleasurable tendencies" ("Lusttendenzen"): in anal erotism the pleasure of rejecting and retaining the object (anal erotism); and in sadism the pleasure to control and destroy the object (ibid., pp. 425–426, 428).

Apart from the fact that empirical observation alone doesn't prove or confirm anything, it is evident that Abraham adopted Jones' categories of "keeping in" and "giving out" and then adding two new ones that were meant to capture the two basic dimensions of sadistic experiencing: controlling and destroying.

The next step in Abraham's argument is quite confusing as he combines anal-erotic with sadistic impulses. He argued that two of the four pleasure tendencies—anal retention and sadistic control—were of a more or less conservative nature, while the two other tendencies—anal expulsion and sadistic destruction of the object—were of a more or less "destructive" nature (ibid., pp. 425–431). In a next step Abraham quite surprisingly equates the two conservative tendencies: the anal process of retention is said to be the same as the sadistic process of control (ibid., p. 428).

As confusing as this classification may seem at first glance, it is quite evident that Abraham no longer regards anal erotism and sadism as opposites; rather, he suggests that they are related, if not indistinguishable. The impulses, or "pleasurable tendencies, as he calls them, are *at once* anal-erotic and sadistic. Abraham replaces Freud's side by side or opposition of anal and sadistic impulses with an intrinsic togetherness that is not the result of a development (as Freud would have it) but a given, always already there. The possible connection between sadism and libidinal impulses has now become a fact, the rule, and the only option. Purely anal-erotic impulses were no longer conceivable. In other words, the new categories that Abraham introduced no longer referred to libidinal impulses but to impulses that possessed both anal-erotic and sadistic traits. Abraham achieved what Jones (1913) and Federn (1913–1914) had aimed at: a new conceptualisation of psychic development in which distinguishing between sexual and non-sexual impulses was no longer relevant, and the idea that sexual impulses were dominant impulses had become unrecognisable.

The second modification in Abraham's concept pertains to the relinquishing of the hierarchy between component and genital-oedipal drives that was at the heart of Freud's theory. Abraham's anal-sadistic impulses have fixed aims: they are oriented towards expulsion and destruction, retention and control. They are thus no longer part of "another" (hi)story; but they make history themselves, and in doing so they lose their ability to mask and substitute for the "real", which Freud had ascribed to them.

The third modification concerns the sadistic-anal stage, introduced by Freud in 1913. "We have been led on empirical grounds," Abraham writes, "to believe that there is a differentiation within the anal-sadistic phase which before had been supposed to be homogeneous" (1924, p. 481). Similar to the oral phase, the anal phase consisted of an early, primitive and a later, less primitive stage. Both, Abraham argued, were anal-sadistic. Abraham did not substantiate his reasons for introducing these substages, and instead referred, rather vaguely "to psycho-analytic experience and the direct observation of children" (ibid., p. 431), which supposedly proved that the destructive impulses were the earlier ones. In the first, most primitive anal-sadistic stage negative and destructive forces prevailed; consideration for the object did not exist, the aim was its total destruction. In the second, more object-preserving or conservative stage the aim was to control the object. In each stage (oral, anal, genital) the destructive tendencies had to be overcome anew, until the genital stage of post-ambivalency was attained. Only then did the individual achieve "a complete capacity for love" (ibid., p. 425), characterised by "tendencies which were friendly to their object" (ibid.). By contrast, the previous (oral and anal) stages were governed by emotions "which are destructive to their object" (ibid.). While a friendly attitude towards the object was characteristic of genital erotism, anal erotism was linked up with sadism (ibid.).

I think the differences between Freud's and Abraham's theories have become evident. While Freud held on to the primacy of the sexual, Abraham's "A Short Study of the Development of the Libido" (1924) insists on destructive, object destroying forces and impulses. In comparison, Freud's model was not primarily concerned with paving the way for the transformation of the destructive child into the loving child. Moreover, Freud's "object love" has very little to do with love in the sense of a loving or affectionate attitude. Development as Freud understood it, was a movement from egocentrism, autoerotism, and narcissism to object choice and object love, which is to say that in the course of psychic development the child acquires the capacity to direct his libidinous wishes at objects whose separate reality can be acknowledged and recognised.

As far as the meaning of "object" was concerned, Abraham drew on Stärcke (1919) and Ophuijsen (1920). But, referring to "the empirical data of psycho-analysis", he was more resolute than they were in arguing that the contents of the bowels were indeed equivalent to the "object": "Psycho-analytic experience has shown beyond a doubt, that," in the anal-sadistic stage, "the individual regards the person who is the object of his desire as something over which he exercises ownership, and that he consequently treats that person in the same way as he does his earliest piece of private property, that is, the contents of his body, his faeces" (Abraham, 1924, p. 425). And, "I assume that every psychoanalyst will be able to confirm this parallel from his own observation" (ibid., p. 426). In short, because the child experienced the contents of its bowels as an object, and the love-object as the contents of its bowels, the same impulses were directed at them.

Thus Abraham did not, in contrast to Freud, conceive of the faeces as a narcissistically cathected part of the body, not yet separated from the ego. As described in the section on Stärcke and Ophuijsen, this way of understanding anal erotism made autoerotic experience, so important for Freud, irrelevant to the theory of psychic development. For Abraham, Stärcke, and Ophuijsen anal erotism knows only one mode of experiencing: narcissism, in which drive-impulses are directed at objects that the subject experiences as separate from himself.

Conclusion

In my reconstruction of some aspects of the history of anal erotism between 1905 and 1924, I wanted to show that Karl Abraham has shaped our clinical and theoretical understanding much more than we are aware of, and that his theory differs from Freud's to an extent that we may not have expected. In this, the history of anal erotism has much in common with the history of oral erotism. What Abraham and the authors who were close to him share is a tendency to simplify, to level and to narrow down theoretical understanding and clinical frames of interpretation—so very different from Freud's highly sophisticated mind which over and again surprises us with unexpected turns that go beyond the established framework, and with his remarkable capacity for self-correction. It is of course also true that Freud's thinking is often inconsistent, and as a whole, it seems to me, based on preconceived convictions that he sought to prove in his self-analysis and in the work with his analysands. Up until 1924 these convictions include the primacy of sexuality, the secondary importance of aggressive-destructive impulses, the autoerotic and narcissistic, non-object related character of infantile experience, the inferior role and the "non-proper" character of pre-oedipal impulses as well as a sensibility for the effectiveness of non-instinctual, that is, ego-related factors. Freud's disciples struggled with their master's persuasions, confronting them with their own ideas and experiences, just as we too are challenged to form our own opinions about what it was that moved Freud, and how we want to think about it.

Translated by Bettina Mathes

CHAPTER SEVEN

Thinking up the death drive: remarks on Freud's research projects, his ambitions, and his vision of the primacy of sexuality

I

Beyond the Pleasure Principle (1920g) marks the beginning of Freud's late work, and the turn to the so-called third drive theory, in which he proposes the death drive and Eros as supreme instinctual impulses. The first drive theory concentrated on the conflict between sexual and self-preservative drives, the second drive theory focused on the opposition of narcissistic and object-libidinal impulses, and the third one revolved around the death drive and Eros as forces that worked against each other. Another innovation Freud announced in *Beyond the Pleasure Principle* was the definition of trauma as a breach in the "stimulus barrier" caused by "inflowing amounts of excitation" (1920g, p. 31). Furthermore, Freud introduced a new understanding of sadism, which he now, and for the first time, conceptualised as the death drive turned outward. Masochism, in turn, was equated with the death drive that remained within the psychic apparatus. Those are, briefly, the modifications that make up the third drive theory.

II

If we want to understand why Freud revised his theory in 1920, it will not suffice to say that the revisions came straight out of his practice. Even though there undoubtedly is a link between his new theory and his clinical experience, the path from experience to theory was neither apparent nor self-evident. And reducing Freud's motivation to both conscious and unconscious biographical factors is not fully convincing either.

Much has been written about the connections between Freud's life and his theories. Max Schur (1972), for example, offers a careful and persuasive account of the ways in which Freud's lifelong obsessive preoccupation with death and dying may be unconsciously motivated. Others have explained the formation of the third drive theory and especially the notion of the death drive with Freud's disappointment about the cultural regression triggered by World War I, his fear for the life of his sons, the deprivations of the post-war years, and the death of his daughter Sophie in January 1920.

As far as Sophie's death as cause for Freud's interest in the death drive is concerned, we have since learned that Freud had a draft of *Beyond the Pleasure Principle* already in March and April of 1919, a year before Sophie's death (May, 2013). This draft contains the core arguments of his theory of the death drive, which means we can dismiss the hypothesis, already drawn up during his lifetime, that Freud arrived at the death drive as a reaction to the loss of his daughter. Freud himself rejected the hypothesis in a letter to his biographer Wittels who in his biography had alluded to a link between the two. While a connection seems likely, Freud replied, "what seems true is not always the truth" (1924g, p. 287).

In what follows I will present additional factors that proved to be responsible for the theoretical innovations Freud made around 1920: his research projects—a clinical and a metapsychological theory—and his ambitions. They can be traced back to his papers of the 1890s.[1] The *first* factor pertains to Freud's research project to elaborate *a clinical, aetiological theory of the neuroses and psychoses* (May[-Tolzmann], 1996). Initially this project yielded Freud's early clinical theory

[1] Once all volumes of *Die Brautbriefe* [The Bridal Letters], the correspondence between Freud and Martha during their engagement, will have been published, we will be able to also take into account this period of Freud's life.

(1894–1896) which incorporated hysteria, obsessive-compulsive neurosis and anxiety neurosis, phobia as well as two kinds of psychosis: paranoia and amentia. This theory was replaced in 1896 by the so-called seduction theory that Freud revised in 1906 (Freud, 1906a). After that Freud never stopped in his efforts to advance and refine his project of an aetiological theory of the neuroses and psychoses. To give a brief overview, in the "Rat Man" (1909d) and the "Wolf Man" (1918b) he offers new insights into the compulsive neurosis; in "Little Hans" (1909b) he addresses the phobias; new ideas on the theory of homosexuality are presented in "Little Hans" and *Leonardo da Vinci* (1910c); the Schreber case further develops the theory of the paranoid and schizoid psychosis; "Mourning and Melancholia" (1917e) offers a deeper understanding of depression; and in "A Child is Being Beaten" (1919e) Freud turned to masochism. Freud subjected one clinical picture after another to a rigorous analytic examination aimed at the advancement of knowledge. In his view, every revision represented an epistemic gain.

It is easy to underestimate the significance of this project unless we realise that it serves as an organising principle in Freud's work. Every publication has its place; none can be understood without the ones that preceded and succeeded it. Envisaged that way, Freud's writings not only contain a wealth of "ideas"; more importantly, they are also an attempt to accumulate knowledge. This is why we cannot adequately understand the significance of Freud's theoretical contributions if we study a given text in isolation. We need to know the earlier positions that the text under consideration corrected, as well as the ways in which that same text was corrected by subsequent papers.

Freud's work on an aetiological theory of the neuroses and psychoses frequently contributed to a better understanding of normal processes as well. Dreams, jokes, the psychopathology of everyday life, normal psychosexual development, the origin of culture and morality—more than once Freud was able to reveal the normal in the pathological. Nonetheless, the focus of his interest had always been pathology, meaning psychic disorders, specifically those psychic disorders for which the patient sought help from a physician/analyst. Throughout his life Freud never lost sight of this focus. The neuroses and psychoses in both their clinical and theoretical aspects remained "the motherland"; they were "psychoanalysis itself" (F/Fer 1, p. 247; Freud, 1916–1917, p. 379). In his *Biologist of the Mind* (1979) Frank Sulloway went even further stating "that when

Freud himself ventured into neighbouring intellectual 'colonies' of psychoanalysis (anthropology, religion, sociology, etc.), he did so largely in order to clarify his most basic unsolved problems in the theory of the psychoneuroses" (ibid., p. 367).

III

Insofar as it offers an explanation of the origins of the traumatic neurosis, *Beyond the Pleasure Principle* is a contribution to the project of an aetiological theory of the neuroses and psychoses. From early on, since his time with Charcot, the clinical picture of the traumatic neurosis had been on Freud's mind. There was a time when he thought of it as the prototype of all psychic disorders. At the same time, Freud believed that the traumatic neurosis was "difficult to tackle" (F/A, p. 82). Even at the beginning of 1919, shortly before the completion of the first draft of *Beyond the Pleasure Principle*, Freud still held on to this opinion. And even after *Beyond the Pleasure Principle* he remained sceptical about the analysability of traumatic neuroses.

Let us, then, take a look at Freud's understanding of trauma in the months and weeks right before the completion of the first draft of *Beyond the Pleasure Principle*. In September 1918 Budapest hosted the International Psychoanalytic Congress, where several of Freud's disciples presented their findings on the aetiology of the war neurosis—the group of neuroses that by definition belonged to the traumatic neuroses. Understandably, they followed the theory available to them at the time, searching for sexual etiology, trying to understand traumatic neuroses in the context of the first and second drive theory. Freud did not present a paper on the war neuroses. As he himself states, he had never had a case of war neurosis in analysis. But there might have been other reasons for his silence. In my view, at the time of the Budapest congress Freud was still convinced that he had nothing new to say about the traumatic neurosis or the war neuroses. From a letter to Ferenczi we learn that only after the congress, at the end of October 1918 did "a new idea" occur to Freud; an idea he described as "a dream formation [Traumgebilde]" (F/Fer 2, p. 305). Freud published this new idea in his introduction to the congress proceedings; a small book entitled *Psycho-Analysis of the War Neuroses* (Freud, 1919d).

Freud likely wrote the introduction in February 1919, more than five months after the Budapest Congress, which is often referred to as the gathering that convinced the scientific community that psychoanalysis could indeed cure the war neuroses. In his introduction Freud emphasised that the traumatic neurosis presented "the most refractory material" (1919d, p. 209), and the least accessible to psychoanalytic treatment, if at all. Freud's "dream formation" suggested that the traumatic neurosis was caused by a conflict in the ego, between two parts of the ego. That is to say, that the cause was neither a conflict between sexual and self-preservative drives (an explanation in the spirit of the framework of the first drive theory) nor a conflict between narcissistic and object-libidinal impulses (an explanation drawing on the second drive theory). As Freud saw it, the ego, weakened by this conflict within itself, could no longer master the amounts of excitation breaking through its protective shield.

Interestingly, in *Beyond the Pleasure Principle* Freud did not elaborate on this intrapsychic ego conflict even though he began to work on the manuscript immediately after he completed his introduction to the volume on the war neuroses. Only later did Freud further develop his thoughts on this conflict within the ego, first in "The 'Uncanny'" (1919h), then in the theory of the Ego, Id, and Super-Ego (1923b) in which the two parts of the ego became the Ego and the Super-Ego. Perhaps Freud was not entirely satisfied with his notion of the conflict between two egos as an explanation for the overwhelming nature of the traumatic neurosis. Whatever the reason, the explanation Freud presented in *Beyond the Pleasure Principle* took the notion of the protective shield against excitation and tied it to a symptom: the return of the traumatic situation in dreams, where it is repeated with minimal distortion and symbolisation, untouched by the more sophisticated mechanisms of psychic defences. This new view on the return of the unpleasurable forms the main point of reference for Freud's new explanation of the traumatic neurosis. It also made him give up his then current basic model of psychic processes and led him to the notion of a "beyond" of the pleasure principle and eventually to the construction of a new, third, drive theory.

To put Freud's understanding of the trauma and the traumatic situation in theoretical language: trauma is characterised by external amounts of excitation breaking through the protective shield. These qualities of excitation overwhelm the ego, or, if there is not yet an ego, the protective shield of the rudimentary psychic apparatus. Where an ego has been formed, its functions will be seriously impaired due to the breach and because of the counter-cathexis that is set in motion and paralyses the ego functions. At the beginning of psychic development, in the pre-ego era, the trauma incapacitates the functioning of the psychic apparatus to such an extent that the regulatory process that governs mental functioning shuts down. In other words, the pleasure-unpleasure principle according to which we seek pleasure and avoid unpleasure no longer works, which is to say that traumatic activity takes place "beyond" the pleasure principle. In order for the regulative of the pleasure-unpleasure principle to work the qualities of excitation need to be "bound", so that mental functioning that is governed by the pleasure-unpleasure principle can begin, permitting the quality of mental functioning that is necessary for the conduct of a psychoanalysis.

I have used Freud's theoretical language; a language that mixes abstract and highly theoretical terms—excitation, apparatus, binding—with concrete, and experience-near language. One can easily lose sight of the distinction between the explanation and the object to be explained, between phenomenon and theory, between clinical observation and metapsychology. Even so, it is quite obvious that Freud regarded trauma and traumatic activity as a special condition that occurred before there was neurosis or conflict, and by doing so Freud advanced our knowledge of the traumatic neurosis. In *An Outline*, however, Freud seems to suggest that he was not quite satisfied with this explanation. Regarding the traumatic neuroses he writes, "their relations to determinants in childhood"—which is to say, their origins—"have hitherto eluded investigation" (Freud, 1940a, p. 184).

After Freud—to get ahead of myself for a moment—psychoanalysis has considerably advanced its understanding of the traumatic neurosis: beginning with the observation of infants and toddlers, followed by the engagement with the effects and consequences of the Shoah; the damage caused by the war in Vietnam; and, most recently, in the debates about sexual abuse. Bohleber (2000, 2007) and Krause (2012) present the most current research on the subject. In the course of the almost ninety years since the publication of *Beyond the Pleasure Principle*, Freud's assumption that there was a fundamental difference between the unanalysable traumatic neurosis and other forms of analysable neurosis has stood the test of time. After long and intense controversies, especially in the 1990s, most psychoanalytic schools now agree that trauma calls for a different therapeutic approach than psychic conflict, even though the language in which this difference is described may vary from school to school. Conversely it is also true that we are not giving full credit to Freud if we ignore the difference between the processes regulated by the pleasure-unpleasure principle and other processes not governed by this principle.

IV

The conceptualisation of a theory of mental functioning, the metapsychology I touched upon in the description of the protective shield, was Freud's *second* lifelong research project. Metapsychology forms the superstructure of Freud's clinical theory. It comprises terms such as ego, instinct (drive), unconscious, super-ego, psychic energy, cathexis, and protective shield. Despite Freud's attempt at designing one theory that could explain everything, metapsychology is less a unified theory than an assemblage of loosely connected theories and theoretical models. We thus speak of metapsychological "aspects" and specific "points of view", be they topological, dynamic, or economic. The prime examples of Freud's untiring attempt at unifying those aspects into a coherent theoretical model are the *Project for a Scientific Psychology* (1950a), and chapter seven of *The Interpretation of Dreams* (1900a). Other attempts can be found in "Formulations on the Two Principles of Mental Functioning" (1911b), in the metapsychological papers of 1915, and in *Beyond the Pleasure Principle*, a work largely dedicated to the metapsychological (economic-structural) discussion of trauma, which, as previously mentioned, heavily relies on theoretical constructs regarding the relation between excitations, energies and the psychic apparatus. After 1920 Freud continued his metapsychological efforts with undiminished energy, for example in *Group Psychology and the Analysis of the Ego* (1921c), *The Ego and the Id* (1923b), and other works.

With respect to the dynamic aspect, Freud felt compelled to change his definition of the drives. He came to realise that the repetition of unpleasurable situations in the dreams of traumatised individuals as well as the repetition of feelings of unpleasure in analysis did not fit his theory. Or, to put it differently, his theory was no longer capable of representing and explaining said phenomena. Before *Beyond the Pleasure Principle*, however, the changes he made were not forced upon him by clinical "observations". On the contrary, his new *evaluation* of the "observations" made it necessary for him to adapt his theory. Sometime before the spring of 1919 Freud realised that the unpleasurable events traumatised individuals repeated in their dreams and the feelings of unpleasure patients repeated in analytic treatment were not events that had once been pleasurable and had now become unpleasurable due to their conflictual nature, as his then valid interpretive framework would have it. Freud abandoned this framework in favour of a new theoretical construct that stipulated that events were being repeated, "which can never, even long ago, have brought satisfaction" (1920g, p. 20). What Freud is saying here is that there are psychic processes that have always been tied to vast amounts of unpleasure (fear, panic, psychic pain, etc.), psychic processes that have never been distorted or symbolised. They are not repeated and then analysed, as Freud describes in "Remembering, Repeating and Working-Through" (Freud, 1914g). They are not derived from conflicts, as the first and second drive theory would have it. In fact, the psychic processes in question take place outside the domain of the pleasure-unpleasure principle. They are governed by a drive that does not seek pleasurable satisfaction but rather the repetition of or return to earlier stages, and ultimately the return to an inorganic state. They are drives—Freud initially spoke of them in the plural—that push towards death; drives for which he coined the term death drives in the final version of *Beyond the Pleasure Principle*.

Once Freud had introduced the death drives into his theory, he was forced to alter his latest definition of the drives published in "Instincts and their Vicissitudes" (1915c). In his new theory the drives were no longer characterised by the pleasurable pursuit of satisfaction. Instead their most important quality was the repetition of an earlier state. If that state was initially pleasurable, the drives belonged to Eros, if it was initially unpleasurable (and remained such) it was an expression of the death drives.

The radical revision of his theory of mental functioning and of metapsychology that Freud achieved in *Beyond the Pleasure Principle* is characterised by a peculiar feature: while it is true that as far as chronology is concerned the third drive theory is indeed the third one, it did not invalidate the two theories that came before. The first and second drive theory remained valid, and the third one added to them. In *An Outline* (1940a) Freud alerts us to this peculiarity. It was in 1920, Freud tells us, that he arrived at the conclusion that the death drive and Eros were *the* two basic drives, and that the oppositions of sexual versus self-preservative drives and narcissistic versus object-libidinal cathexes (that is, the first and second drive theory) were to be subsumed under

Eros (ibid., p. 148). Freud thus kept the "old" theories and concepts, and added a new "third" layer to them. When the old theories operated and when the new one came into play, Freud did not specify. He left us alone with the imperfection of his theory. He seems to have believed that the lack of clarity would one day be dealt with. The drive theories are not the only example of Freud's approach to theory. He never completely gave up an insight, and he had great tolerance for ambiguity, hoping that he would be able to resolve it at a later time. His two theories of anxiety as well as the seduction theory are cases in point. It is now agreed upon that Freud never gave up the latter. Instead, he developed a new overarching theory in which the old one remained valid as one among several options.

So much for the state of metapsychology in *Beyond the Pleasure Principle*: Freud had decided to introduce new psychic functions and regulatory mechanisms, new drives, and a new definition of the drive because he was convinced that his previous metapsychological description could not do justice to the traumatic neurosis and the repetition of unpleasurable affects encountered in analytic treatment.

V

As is well known, when Freud introduced the death drive in *Beyond the Pleasure Principle,* he did not invent the term. Before him Stekel (Min 1, p. 177), Spielrein (1912), and Ferenczi (Andreas-Salomé, 1957, p. 172) had spoken of death drives. Moreover, questions of life and death were important subjects in the biological sciences of the time. And Freud followed these scientific debates with as great an interest as he did in the 1890s when he and Fließ designed and (for a time) collaborated on a research project dedicated to the theory of neurosis in which Fließ covered the biological part and Freud worked on the psychological section.[2] After Freud's breakup with Fließ, Ferenczi filled the latter's place, serving as interlocutor and collaborator (taking care

[2] We have to say goodbye to the idea that only the early Freud was interested in biology and medicine. Between 1915 and 1920 his interest in the biological sciences may well have intensified. How else are we to understand the many references to physiology, and the long passage entitled "Chemical Theory" that is part of the fifth edition of his *Three Essays on the Theory of Sexuality* completed in 1920? Other publications from this period contain discussions on the state and the significance of hormone research, e.g., "The Psychogenesis of a Case of Female Homosexuality" (1920a).

of the biological sciences) in Freud's third and ambitious project: "the conquest" of the other sciences. One outcome of this shared interest was the "Overview of the Transference Neuroses" (Freud, 1985a), this "phylogenetic phantasy", in which the neuroses and psychoses are derived from the history of geology and evolution. The so-called "Lamarck Project" was of a similar scope. In it Freud attempted to ground biology in psychoanalysis—no doubt an ambitious undertaking. He and Ferenczi had made plans to work on it in 1918 during their summer vacation in Csorbató. They never did. In a letter to Freud, written in October 1918, Ferenczi intimates that "ridiculous little irritations" between him and Freud prevented them from collaborating on the project (F/Fer 2, p. 297). He compared the vacation in Csorbató to the previous one in Palermo (1910), where personal intolerances caused the failure of the paranoia project they had planned to collaborate on. Some of Freud's notes from the summer of 1918, in which he already mentions death drives (*Todestriebe*), have survived (May, 2013, p. 239). It seems likely that Freud continued to work on the "Lamarck Project" on his own (ibid., p. 267), a result of which was the first draft of *Beyond the Pleasure Principle* with its "far-fetched speculation" and its "borrowings from biology" (Freud, 1920g, p. 24; 1923b, p. 12). Just like the "phylogenetic phantasy" Freud did not immediately publish his first draft of *Beyond the Pleasure Principle*. He kept thinking about it, revising it, and adding an entire new chapter in which he praised the superiority of the biological sciences. The final version of *Beyond the Pleasure Principle* was completed in July 1920, almost two years after his first mention of the death drives.

Freud's interest in applying psychoanalysis to the other sciences is reflected in a number of his works: for example, *Totem and Taboo* (1912–1913), *Group Psychology and Ego-Analysis* (1921c), and *Civilization and Its Discontents* (1930a). Rather than a contribution to an interdisciplinary conversation these works were designed to prove the superiority of psychoanalysis over the other sciences. We know of Freud's remark to Eugen Bleuler that psychiatry will be "conquered" sooner rather than later (F/Bl, p. 100). Other "targets", it seems to me, were sociology, psychology, philosophy, literature, and religion. In *Beyond the Pleasure Principle* his target was biology. And once again Freud had no intention of fostering a conversation between the two sciences. On the contrary, from the outset Freud saw psychoanalysis as fundamentally superior to the biological sciences. To give an example, Freud's lengthy discussion of biological research on mortality and immortality, and the evolution of sexual reproduction culminates in the conclusion that this research did not really matter because it was more than likely that there were forces "hidden" behind the ones that biology concerned itself with. Therefore, he had every right to propose ideas that stood in contradiction to biology: for example, the idea that sexual drives were there from the very beginning of life (even though biology postulated that they appear at a later stage of organic development); and the existence of death drives (even though many biologists assumed that single cell organisms were immortal).

VI

As I see it, *Beyond the Pleasure Principle* is situated in the space carved out by these aforementioned research projects and ambitions. In this dense and often enigmatic work Freud proposed a new approach to the understanding of the traumatic neuroses and thus made a contribution to clinical theory. With its introduction of new psychic processes, its regrouping of the drives, and its new perspective on their general traits, *Beyond the Pleasure Principle* modified metapsychology. Finally, *Beyond the Pleasure Principle* bordered on biology, taking objectives and arguments from it, wishing to impregnate them with psychoanalytic speculations, if not to offer an entirely new foundation. However, the strongest impulse motivating the revisions presented in *Beyond the Pleasure Principle* came from Freud's newly found assessment of the origin and function of the compulsion to repeat, specifically those cases which he deemed unanalysable, and which seemed to be subject to the work of the death drives, the agents of everything that resists change.

In my reading of *Beyond the Pleasure Principle* the turn in Freud's theoretical revisions is a volitional act, the result of a decision he took. In no way is the third drive theory a necessary outcome of clinical material. Rather, it is the sum of Freud's experiences. What he was concerned with was the scope of psychoanalysis and the applicability of psychoanalytic technique—a lifelong project for Freud. Already in the 1890s he had made an attempt at differentiating between psychic (analysable), and somatic (unanalysable) disorders. Twenty years later, Freud offered a fresh, updated summary based on new observations. This time narcissism determined analysability (1914c). The so-called transference neuroses were regarded as analysable whereas the narcissistic neuroses were not. Seen this way, *Beyond the Pleasure Principle* was yet another attempt at defining the boundaries and the applicability of psychoanalysis. This time, Freud synthesises the forces that are opposed to psychoanalysis into the notion of the "death drive": self-destructive, averse to change, seeking to regress to earlier stages of development, if not aiming at total destruction. The life affirming forces, open to change and to psychoanalysis, he allotted to Eros. It seems that throughout his life Freud held on to the belief that the death drive presented the most powerful obstacle to psychoanalysis (see 1937c, p. 243).[3]

A few years ago I studied Freud's patient record books dating from the years 1910 to 1920, the decade right before the composition of *Beyond the Pleasure Principle* (see Chapter Nine). At that time Freud had a small group of analysands each of whom he had seen for more than a thousand hours. Three of them have been identified: Sergej Pankejeff (the "Wolf Man"), Viktor von Dirsztay, and Elfriede Hirschfeld. Pankejeff returned to analysis with Freud after the war (and after more than a thousand hours). Freud observed that part of the transference was not resolved but still bound up in symptoms. What happened to Pankejeff after he left Freud is history. He surely benefitted from his analysis with Freud and from the treatments he underwent afterwards, but to say that he was cured would be inaccurate. Viktor von Dirsztay too had undergone more than a thousand hours of analysis with Freud. When the treatment ended in 1920, he continued with Theodor Reik but had to interrupt the treatment for frequent stays in sanatoriums. He took his own life in 1935. Elfriede Hirschfeld suffered from a compulsive neurosis. Her analysis ended in 1914 even though she was not "cured", as Freud himself noted. She was in need of further treatment.

These and similar experiences may have contributed to Freud's increasing doubts regarding the efficacy of psychoanalytic treatment. What is more, many of his disciples came out of their personal analyses just as neurotic as they were before. Freud's letters of the 1920s and 1930s are filled with complaints about the lack of progress they were making. Whether it was necessary to explain the limited effectiveness of psychoanalysis with the death drive is another question—I tend

---

[3] What struck me most during my latest stay at the Freud Archive at the Library of Congress, studying Freud's unpublished letters from after 1920, was how pessimistic Freud was about the effectiveness of psychoanalysis.

to answer it in the negative. Key is the "mechanism" (to apply one of Freud's terms to our context): the third drive theory was driven not by observations but by a new accentuation, a new emphasis. Even though Freud's decision to revise his theory did have an empirical basis, it was by no means grounded in "objective facts". The literature after Freud often creates the impression that psychoanalysis was developed from the ground up, meaning that psychoanalytic terms were derived from psychoanalytic practice, that is, from clinical experience alone (see, e.g., Abraham, 1924, p. 418, 431). Looking at it that way, we lose sight of the most important factor, that is, Freud's *decision* to shape his theory based on his subjective experience.

Freud's willingness to revise his theory over and over again is, it seems to me, unique among psychoanalysts. There are few psychoanalysts who developed a comprehensive theory and who replaced said theory with a series of new theories each different from the previous one. Each one of Freud's three drive theories—forming just one aspect of his oeuvre—represents a distinctive "grasp" on the ordering and evaluation of psychic disorders. With every theoretical turn Freud had the courage to admit to himself (and to others) that his theory was, in one way or another, inadequate. Even though Freud, it seems to me, had a tendency to downplay the extent and significance of his revisions, creating the impression that he was merely dealing with the "top of the whole structure (Überbau)" ready to be "replaced and discarded" anytime. This indifference (if that's what it is) does not quite fit the intellectual and psychic effort he put into developing the new theories, and the forcefulness with which he stood by them. Freud's apparent lack of emotional investment in his theories (especially metapsychology) points to the fact that he was well aware of how much they were influenced by his own authoritative decisions, and thus how random they were, but at the same time his indifference obscures how dear those decisions were to him.

VII

Elsewhere (May[-Tolzmann, 1996]), I have suggested that Freud's theorising is defined by his vision of the primacy of sexuality in the aetiology of psychic disorders. Long before he developed the psychoanalytic method or a theory of psychic disorders, that is, long before there was psychoanalysis, Freud was *convinced* to have found "the key that unlocks everything": sexual aetiology (F/Fl, p. 45). He believed that all neuroses and psychoses could be traced back to factors closely related to sexuality. Freud could be very impatient with colleagues who did not share his conviction. Well into the 1920s the role attributed to sexuality was the point of contention in each of his breakups with friends and colleagues (Jung, Adler, Rank).

Today I would like to add that Freud's vision of the singular importance of sexuality may have to do with highly cathected, early infantile affective experiences; experiences that were not open to modification. Convictions that rest on early experiences are non-negotiable, one clings to them tightly. Stemming from early infancy they are immune to experiences made in adult life. In *Beyond the Pleasure Principle* we can see this psychic structure at play. There is, for example, the passage towards the end of the paper, where Freud integrates sadism in his new theory by defining it as the death drive directed against the external world. The full weight of this seemingly insignificant remark becomes palpable when we add what Freud did *not* spell out: the fact that sadism is *once again* a derivative phenomenon, a secondary feature—a conviction Freud had always insisted on, especially when dealing with his "renegade" disciples. A similar kind of relief I hear in those passages in which Freud bestows onto Eros the power to divert the death drive outwards. In this model, if all goes well, Eros is stronger than the death drive; it is *the* decisive force in psychic life. Unless we take into account the emotional charge inherent in the notion of the primacy of sexuality, we will not adequately understand these (and other passages) in which Freud discusses the role of aggression in his theory. It is not a coincidence that Freud imagined himself (in relation to Adler) as the avenger of the "offended goddess Libido" (F/P, p. 48).

Despite his unwavering conviction of the primacy of sexuality, Freud spent his entire life as a scholar and psychoanalyst trying to prove that this vision was true, that his assumptions—as distant and immune to experience as they may have been—were accurate. Rather than derived from empirical clinical observation, Freud's efforts were guided by certain interests: first, to build an aetiological theory of the neuroses and psychoses and, second, to create a comprehensive metapsychological theory of mental functioning. His wish to "conquer" the established sciences—the third group of interests—has a different aim.

There, Freud's goal seems to have been dominance and power, rather than knowledge and scientific advancement.

That said, Freud possessed a remarkable openness to new experiences, which at first glance seems to contradict his tendency to hold on to preconceived ideas. In his efforts to better understand mental illnesses he more than once arrived at conclusions that turned out to be quite different from what he expected them to be. His research on the origin of obsessional ideas is a striking case in point. As he noted in the "Rat Man", their magical quality, and the overestimation of their power, was not so much an expression of the vicissitudes that drives undergo but rather a result of a regression of the ego (see May, 2011b). There are other instances where Freud draws unexpected conclusions. Even though he never went so far as to abandon his most basic assumptions, he did have an admirable willingness to accept partial results that disagreed with his theory.

Clinical theory is the sphere of Freud's greatest productivity and creativity. There he could give himself over to his unconscious, employing it to serve his projects, which means nothing less than the ability and willingness to tolerate findings he would not be able to (immediately) master with his theoretical toolkit. Even so, Freud regarded these findings as a legitimate outcome of his productivity and creativity. However, the more Freud's theorising moved towards metapsychology, the greater his distress. What made him refer to metapsychology as "a witch" (1937c, p. 225), and why describe his work in this area as "intellectual hell" (F/Fl, p. 421)? And why is it that many a passage in Freud's metapsychological works evokes similar feelings in the reader? Without having an answer to these questions, it seems to me that the agony that Freud experienced when working on his metapsychology was to do with the fact that he was reaching for the impossible: a unified theory containing all his ideas and findings, everything that was dear to him. Such a theory would have been the ultimate proof that his vision (rooted in early infantile experiences) was indeed irrefutable.

Translated by Bettina Mathes

PART II

FREUD AND HIS PATIENTS

CHAPTER EIGHT

Fourteen hundred hours of analysis with Freud: Viktor von Dirsztay

The Hungarian writer and Freud analysand Baron Viktor von Dirsztay (1884–1935) does not play a prominent part in the history of psychoanalysis. Nevertheless he is a figure who exerts a curious fascination that may stem from the fact that Dirsztay represents a link between two worlds which were hitherto assumed to be alien to each other: psychoanalysis and early expressionism in Vienna and Berlin. As will be shown, during his long analysis with Freud, Dirsztay was in contact with important artists of expressionism. His portrait was done by Oskar Kokoschka in 1911 (see Illustration 2) and he himself wrote two books that were illustrated by Kokoschka (Dirsztay, 1917, 1923).

According to the obituaries in the Viennese newspapers, Dirsztay led the bohemian, romantic life of the cafe literati, an eccentric aesthete, and art lover from a wealthy background. On closer acquaintance, however, he appears tormented and disturbed, a person whose life was full of difficulties. On 6 November 1935 he and his wife committed suicide and left on the kitchen table a note signed by both of them, with the words: "By consent" (Anon., 1935c).

We know next to nothing of the background to this double suicide. Press reports of his death state that Dirsztay could no longer bear the

Illustration 2. Oskar Kokoschka: Baron Victor von Dirsztay (1911). Sprengel-Museum Hannover. © Fondation Oskar Kokoschka/VG Bild-Kunst, Bonn 2009.

fact that his wife, who was undergoing psychiatric treatment, remained unimproved and in a bad condition. It is quite possible Viktor von Dirsztay himself had already been in a precarious mental state before World War I. As early as 1911 he was a ward of court, hence partly deprived of his rights, and from 1910 at the latest he was in analysis with Freud. The first period of analysis was also the period of highest frequency and lasted until July 1911; a second followed from 1913 to 1915 and a third from 1917 to 1920, so that Dirsztay belongs to that small group of patients who were with Freud for more than 1,000 hours (see Chapter Nine).

Psychoanalytic research has to date shown no interest in Dirsztay. In literary history, apart from the short study by Timms (1990, pp. 6–8), he appears only in footnotes (Lützeler, 1995, 2000; Sprengel & Streim, 1998, p. 579). Art history provides some biographical data, which, however, is frequently contradictory.[1] I found traces of Dirsztay in the autobiographies, diaries, and letters of Albert Ehrenstein, Hermann Broch, Walter Hasenclever, Theodor Herzl, Oskar Kokoschka, Karl Kraus, Arthur Schnitzler, and Herwarth Walden. But even in these sources Dirsztay remains an elusive minor figure. A clearer image of him emerges through unpublished correspondence. One series consists of a large number of letters to Karl Kraus, another of letters to the publisher Kurt Wolff.[2] Two manuscripts, also hitherto unknown, show another side of Dirsztay as a writer of comedies.[3]

Based on these limited and disparate finds, as well as on that of Dirsztay's analysis with Freud, I shall attempt to draw a picture of this Hungarian author. Obviously I cannot do justice to the demands of biography. I can only trust that the charm and tragedy of this life will justify my sketch. Aside from presenting Dirsztay as a person, I hope that it will show how close Freud and psychoanalysis were to the art scene of the time.

Family

Viktor von Dirsztay was born in Budapest and came from a Jewish family resident in Hungary. His father Ladislaus (1856–1921) was

---

[1] See Wingler & Welz (1975), Schweiger (1983, 1986), Winkler & Erling (1995), Schmidt & Dalbajewa (1996), Natter (2002).

[2] The correspondence between Dirsztay and Kraus is in the archive of the Wiener Stadt- und Landesbibliothek im Rathaus der Stadt Wien [Vienna Library in Vienna's city hall] and consists of 22 items (M09H, H.I.N. 176568); three further individual items are in the same place (H.I.N. 171274, 214783, 187381). The correspondence with Kurt Wolff consists of 14 letters and is part of the Wolff Archives at the Beinecke Rare Book and Manuscript Library, Yale University (YCGL. MSS 3, 2/47).

[3] This refers to the plays *Schlemihl oder die Romantischen* (handwritten note on the manuscript: "around 1925") and *Das Genie* (undated). Both are in the archive of the Österreichische Nationalbibliothek [Austrian National Library] (782352–D. The; Ser.n.19.417).

originally named Fischl.[4] On 3 September 1884 the father was raised to the peerage and became "von Fischl". No doubt as a result of the Magyarisation of family names at that time, he changed his name a few years later and called himself "Ladislaus von Dirsztay" (from 19 April 1889). Around 1899 he and his family moved to Vienna and on 30 November 1905 he was made a Baron, thus his name became "Ladislaus Baron von Dirsztay".[5] The children were also affected by the change of name; hence Viktor von Dirsztay was also born Fischl and only took the name Dirsztay from 1889 onwards.

Viktor's father was married at least twice. Viktor was supposedly born of the first marriage, in 1885, to Etelka Steinfeld (1860–1943). In 1892 his father divorced and married Georgine Plaut (1855–1928), a banker's daughter.[6]

Information on Viktor's date of birth is contradictory; it shifts between 1883 and 1889. The Vienna Stadt- und Landesarchiv refers to four different dates: first of all, 13 June 1884.[7] It must also remain unclear whether

---

[4] Dirsztay's father was born on 9 May 1856 and was thus only three days younger than Freud. According to information from the Wiener Stadt- und Landesbibliothek (= WSLA; Magistratsabteilung 8) on 31 December 2008, he died in Vienna on 4 June 1921. His body was consecrated at the evangelical church on Dorotheergasse in Vienna and "provisionally" laid to rest in the Zentralfriedhof (Anon., 1921a). Ladislaus v. Dirsztay must have converted to the evangelical faith. One of his brothers was Béla v. Dirsztay, a "philanthropist and art collector" living in Budapest (Anon., 1921b).

[5] His title is sometimes referred to as "Baron" as is customary in Austrian-speaking areas, sometimes as "Freiherr" which is the more habitual form in German-speaking areas. My reconstruction of the history of the family name is mainly based on the *Almanach des Ungarischen Adels* by Kempelen (1910; especially p. 33), which, after consulting various reference works, seems to me the most reliable.

[6] Etelka Dirsztay, née Steinfeld, married a second time in 1892 after divorcing Ladislaus and became Gräfin Zichy zu Zich (see website of the House of Zichy zu Zich). Georgine Plaut came from the banking house of H. C. Plaut: her marriage to Ladislaus v. Dirsztay was her third (Plaut, 2007, p. 168). Thomas Aichhorn has drawn my attention to the fact that Ernst Freud believed Viktor v. Dirsztay to be a nephew of Marie Ebner-Eschenbach; she dedicated her children's book *Hirzeprinzchen* (1890) to him (letter to Henry v. Witzleben of 13 November 1969). Possibly Ernst Freud was mistaken. For the printed dedication of *Hirzeprinzchen* reads: "To the mother of the Hirzeprinzchen/my beloved sister-in-law Gisela Gräfin Dubsky" (Ebner-Eschenbach, 1890). Gisela v. Dubsky was the wife of Viktor v. Dubsky, a stepbrother of the Ebner-Eschenbachs (Ebner-Eschenbach & Breuer, 1969, p. 185). Their son, Franz v. Dubsky, recounts in his memoirs that his aunt read the tale to him and that he had the feeling it referred to him (Bettelheim, 1920, p. 326; Dubsky, 1917). Hence Ernst Freud appears to have confused Viktor v. Dirsztay with Franz v. Dubsky.

[7] The WSLA (28 November 2006) answered the question of Viktor von Dirsztay's birth date as follows: "13.4.1884 (also recorded: 4.6.1884, 13.6.1883, 13.6.1888)". In the Gulyás Hungarian national biography yet another date, 1889, is given (Gulyás, 1943, p. 831).

Viktor grew up with his natural father or with his mother.[8] What is certain is that he had a sister Charlotte (1883–1942, who married De Menasce) and a brother Franz (1888–1956) who was later also active as a writer (F. Dirsztay, 1919, 1923, 1924, 1930); some sources also mention a further brother, Andreas.[9]

Viktor's father, Ladislaus von Dirsztay, was a rich man, a banker and retailer, Director of the Lemberg-Czernowitz railway, and imperial consul-general for Turkey.[10] Around the turn of the century he acquired an imposing three-storey palace, which is still standing today (Rennweg 25), in the Vienna diplomatic district, opposite the park and palace of Belvedere; he entrusted its interior design to the architect and co-founder of the Secession, Josef Maria Olbrich.[11] I have found out from Theodor Herzl's (1985, 1993) diaries that in his function as consul-general of the Ottoman Empire he participated in negotiations with the Turkish government over the acquisition of territory in Palestine.[12] During the years around 1900 he acted as a sort of intermediary between Herzl and the lower rank negotiators for Turkey. Herzl (1985) considered him "grotesque" and "absolutely comic" (pp. 50, 216). Once he spoke of him as the Turkish Consul-General von Dirsztay né Fischl from Pest and thus expresses a discrepancy between his status and his behaviour (ibid., p. 152). Elsewhere he is outraged by Ladislaus von

---

[8] In his childhood his grandmother may also have played an important role, since he dedicated his book *Das Lob des hohen Verstandes* (Dirsztay, 1917) to his "dear grandmother".

[9] Franz v. Dirsztay was adopted by Ladislaus (Kempelen, 1910, p. 33); hence he originates neither from a former marriage of Georgine Plaut nor from her premarital relationship with Ladislaus. Arthur Schnitzler mentions Franz v. Dirsztay in 1913 and 1928 in his diaries (Schnitzler, 1983, pp. 56–57, 70, 100; 1997, p. 119). Andreas (Andór) Dirsztay (1894–1944) is identified on the Plaut family internet site as the son of Georgine Plaut and Ladislaus v. Dirsztay (accessed 9 December 2007). He died in Auschwitz (Dokumentationsarchiv des österreichischen Widerstands: http://de.doew.braintrust.at/m17sm147.html; accessed 4 December 2007).

[10] Information about the father was collected from the following sources: Kokoschka (1971, p. 91); Wingler and Welz (1975, p. 109); Handler (1983, p. 4); Herzl (1985, p. 695); Winkler and Erling (1995, pp. 41–42). Ladislaus held the post of Consul-General from 1898 at the latest, as I deduce from Herzl's diary.

[11] On Olbrich see http://www.deu.archinform.net/arch/5.htm; accessed 12 March 2008. On the purchase of the palace see Anon. (1935c, 1935d). It may have been sold in 1918, since Ladislaus v. Dirsztay was no longer registered on Rennweg from 16 April 1918 onwards, but at Theresianumgasse 11/3 (WSLA, 31 December 2008).

[12] Ladislaus v. Dirsztay is mentioned in vol. 3 of Herzl's *Zionistisches Tagebuch* (1985), among others on the following pages: p. 50 with p. 695; pp. 152–153, 154, 156, 158, 160, 163–164, etc.; see also vol. 6 of *Briefe und Tagebücher* (Herzl, 1993, column 549).

Dirsztay's fondness for buying titles and orders, for bribing others and allowing himself to be bribed.[13]

These not very benevolent observations are of interest to us since his son Viktor also tried to gain advantage with the aid of money, though at the same time acting very generously with his fortune. In Dirsztay's comedy *Das Genie* [The Genius] one imagines meeting his father in the character of "Uncle Gyula, Petroleum Trade", a corpulent, ill-educated, wealthy old man, an endearing joker who speculates on the stock exchange and unashamedly seeks out the company of artists and intellectuals. He enjoys the company of the "genius", a well-known writer, while the latter is interested in him because he would like to pick up tips on buying shares. In the same humorous manner the overlapping of capital and art, money and poetry, is also depicted in *Schlemihl*. As I shall show, the darker and intolerable side of this contradiction comes to dominate, above all in the novel *Der Unentrinnbare* [The Inescapable One] (Dirsztay, 1923).

Oskar Kokoschka (1971, pp. 91–92), who was a friend of his and knew the family, dedicated one and half pages of his autobiography to Viktor von Dirsztay. We learn there that the Dirsztays supported him in his early career. Perhaps portrait commissions contributed towards that. Kokoschka painted not only Viktor but also his nephew, Jacques de Menasce, the son of his sister Charlotte.[14] Kokoschka saw the Dirsztays as "nouveau riche from Hungary without the faintest idea of the romantic aspirations" of their son. Viktor was musically very gifted and had a "complicated character". Kokoschka mentions a skin disease that tortured Dirsztay and nurtured his "wrath" (ibid., p. 91). In this connection he also comes to speak of the analysis with Freud:

---

[13] An example: "In the morning I was with Dirsztay, who read out to me the slanderous and threatening letters of the scoundrel Crespi [Eduard C., negotiator for the Turkish government]. This Dirsztay seems to be as dirty as he is rich, a Jew of the Apikorsim sort [= epicurean, freethinker]. For he is clearly letting Crespi do him favours in return for promising this levantine good-for-nothing to intervene with me on his behalf. For this service he probably wants to receive some award, if he is not actually doing business for it, he who receives an annual stipendium of hundreds of thousands of gulden" (Herzl, 1985 p. 282; entry for 29 May 1901).

[14] Portrait of Jacques de Menasce [www.smb.spk-berlin.de/jpg/1827_005.jpg; accessed 28 March 2006]. De Menasce (1905–1960) studied under Arnold Schönberg and became a concert pianist and composer. Kokoschka writes of the portrait: "A finely sculpted boy's face; the later generation of a robust family" (1971, p. 91).

> Freud himself, whom he consulted for years, could not heal him, for his disease came from his contempt of his family. [...] He suffered from world-weariness. I became aware of this when, from the upper floor of the palace in the aristocratic diplomatic district of Vienna where the family lived, Dirsztay mockingly pointed out a bundle of dirty washing left casually lying on the magnificent main staircase. On the ground floor, through the open door of the family drawing room, one could see fat bodies in underwear making noise, playing cards and drinking. That was what he thought of his family: an underworld. I understood his deep disgust with such a shameless exhibition of vulgarity; he was the prodigal son. (Kokoschka, 1971, p. 91)

First literary attempts, first analysis with Freud (1908–1911)

How Viktor spent his childhood and youth is not known. Obituaries mention the wealth that surrounded him (e.g., Anon., 1935a, 1935c). In 1904 he graduated from the Gymnasium [secondary school] in Mödling, a small town to the south of Vienna, after which he studied law and gained his doctorate.[15]

The first letter of Dirsztay's that I have found dates from January 1908.[16] It was addressed to an unknown friend and asks for a recommendation to Karl Kraus in whose journal, *Die Fackel*, Dirsztay wished to publish a text. Karl Kraus, the "master of the all-embracing style", was admired and revered "to the highest degree" in Budapest. Dirsztay's plea was unsuccessful; nothing of his appeared in *Die Fackel*.[17] During the following year Dirsztay applied to Kraus himself (letter of 9 May 1909) and sent him a poem "to the supreme judge", once again in vain. Both requests were written on notepaper of a Budapest hotel. Since Dirsztay speaks of a circle of Kraus admirers in

---

[15] It was the first *Matura* [school graduation exam] that took place at this school; nine students took part, of whom the only day pupil was Viktor v. Dirsztay [http://www.bgmoedling-keim.ac.at; accessed 28 March 2006]. The earliest proof of the doctorate is a visiting card to Karl Kraus on 8 March 1912. In 1909 it appears that Dirsztay had not yet graduated (see Dirsztay, 1909, p. 44).

[16] Dated 11 January 1908 (archive of the Austrian National Library, 782352–D. The; Ser.n.19.417).

[17] In the name register of *Die Fackel* there is no trace either of "Dirsztay" (even in a variant spelling) or of "Distriacus", a pseudonym that Dirsztay suggested to Kraus (letter of 11 January 1908).

Budapest, one can assume that his main residence was there during 1908 and 1909.

Budapest was where Dirsztay had his first literary success: in 1909 *Streichquartett* [String Quartet] appeared, a collection of comments, aphorisms and short atmospheric sketches. The small booklet was produced by the printer Samuel Markus.[18] The texts are in the first person and appear to be autobiographical. They too indicate that Dirsztay lived in Budapest at that time. Of himself he says, among other things, that he had been "confined to a general penitentiary for disturbers of the peace" and continues (1909, pp. 19–20): "I was assessed and found to be a lunatic. By comparison with the rigor that reigns here, my situation in my lunatic asylum is by no means so unfavourable." Possibly the lunatic asylum means a boarding school. Perhaps it is actually a psychiatric institution. What is certain is that two years later (1911) Dirsztay was "made a ward of court" (Schweiger, 1986, p. 47).

At the end of the year in which *String Quartet* was published, the name Dirsztay appears for the first time in Freud's correspondence. On 9 December 1909 a letter to Sándor Ferenczi states: "Dirsztay's [patient] parents were with me and proved themselves quite friendly to the treatment" (F/Fer 1, p. 110). It went no further than this single remark; in his letters Freud did not mention Dirsztay a second time.[19] It is only 26 years later, on the day of Dirsztay's suicide, that we encounter his name again, this time in Freud's diary: "† Victor Dirsztay" (Molnar, 1992, p. 192).

Possibly Freud came to Dirsztay via Ferenczi. This would explain Freud's communication about "Dirsztay's parents". That they showed a

---

[18] *String Quartet* is dedicated to Olga von Gomperz, of whom nothing further can be discovered (possibly: née Kohn, wife of Miksa Gomperz [Gulyás, 1992, p. 79]). The book consists of two chapters, of which the first, entitled "Wahrnehmungen, quasi scherzando" [Perceptions quasi scherzando], contains aphorisms and comments; the second has the title "Nachtgesang, Adagio" [Night Song, Adagio] and brings together three short pieces about meeting an admired and desired woman: "Verklärte Nacht" [Transfigured Night], "Liebesselige Nacht" [Amorous Night], "Sehnsüchtige Nacht" [Yearning Night]. The booklet gives the impression of a self-published text; perhaps it was produced without the collaboration of a regular publisher. Markus also printed texts for the Jewish community, among others the Rashi commentary of the Talmud.

[19] This assertion applies to the letters published up to 2009. Apart from that the name Dirsztay occurs in a letter of 22 July 1917, in which Freud informs his daughter Mathilde about the Basch family which was related to Dirsztay, and also in the codicil to Freud's will of 19 January 1919 in which he mentions a promissory note from "Dirszt" (see Freud, 2010).

favourable attitude towards the treatment could be understood to mean that they accepted the cost of the analysis. It is, however, worth noting that the parents did in fact come to Freud. Their son was in 1909 at least 21, possibly 25 years old; his Matura exam was already five years behind him. Was he so severely affected that he could not visit Freud alone? Or was the analysis begun, not at Dirsztay's own wish but at that of his parents? Or had they simply come to settle the financial side of the business? And the question arises: is the "Dirsztay" of Freud's letter and then of his patient record books really Viktor von Dirsztay and not his brother, his sister, or someone else in one of the numerous branches of this family?[20]

Here I can fall back on my research into Freud's patient record books (see Chapter Nine; see also Tögel, 2006). They show that in the ten years for which there are record books at our disposal, namely between October 1910 and December 1920, a Dirsztay was with Freud three times. Previously I only assigned the third analysis (1917–1920) to Viktor; for this I had sound evidence (May, 2007, pp. 49, 66–67). I can now say with certainty that the Dirsztay of the first and second periods is also Viktor. For Freud had a systematic and consistent manner of bookkeeping. When an analysis began with a patient who had the same surname as a former patient or as one who was already in analysis, both surname and first name would be entered in the record book.[21] Since Freud never, on any page of the record books, notes a first name with "Dirsztay", it must always be the same person. And since the Dirsztay of the third period can be unequivocally identified as Viktor, "Dirsztay" must always refer to him.

Thus the only question that remains open is when the analysis began. In October 1910, the first month of the patient record books that survived, Dirsztay was already with Freud. Did he begin the analysis then or earlier, some time after his parents' visit to Freud, that is, around December 1909? This question cannot be answered. We can

[20] One possibility, for example, might be Franz v. Dirsztay, who published an essay with the following (grammatically unclear) sentence: "Why am I imbued with Proust, Einstein and Freud only to fail so often at the most essential everyday adjustments?"

[21] For the sake of completeness I will mention an exception to the rule: when a married couple were successively or concurrently in analysis, only the surname is noted (thus with the Stracheys and the v. Freunds), presumably because Freud made the invoice out in the name of *one* of the couple. This exception cannot apply to Dirsztay because he only married after his analysis with Freud (1924).

only say that the first analysis began *at the latest* on 3 October 1910. It lasted until 8 July 1911 and during this period consisted of 297 hours (see Chapter Nine). From October 1910 Dirsztay had six, eight, sometimes twelve hours per week. At the end of February 1911 he broke off the analysis for two weeks, to take it up again in March and April with one hour daily; from May 1911 he mostly had one and half hours per day and from the middle of June 1911 two per day.[22]

As I have shown in a previous study (see Chapter Nine), such variable frequency is not unusual in Freud's practice. We can assume that Freud himself arranged the variations. We do not know why Dirsztay went into analysis at all, why he broke it off for two weeks in February 1911, or under what circumstances the first period came to an end. It could have been an agreed end or, just as likely, a breaking off.

After the first analysis: small publications, friendship with Oskar Kokoschka, breakdown? (1911–1912)

On 8 July 1911, when Viktor von Dirsztay had his last hour of analysis for the time being, we find his name for the first time in a correspondence between Oskar Kokoschka and Herwarth Walden, the editor of the Berlin art and literature journal *Der Sturm*. Kokoschka writes (Schweiger, 1986, p. 46):[23]

> Dear Herwarth Walden Doctor, After your letter I yesterday telegraphed. D[irsztay] who wanted to do less this time telling him that the old agreement has to stand and I assume that he will settle in the next few days. [...] D[irsztay]'s manuscript that I forgot to hand on has been sent on today.

---

[22] Precise details of the frequency and course of Dirsztay's analysis, which go beyond my previously published account are based on Freud's patient record books, kept at the Freud Museum London. An entry of one and half or two hours can signify that Freud visited the analysand, for example, in a sanatorium; or it could be that someone really did have one and a half or two hours analysis per day (see Chapter Nine).

[23] I quote Kokoschka's letters, not from the first edition of the correspondence (Kokoschka, 1984), but from the more reliable transcription by Schweiger, which is to be found in his study of the young Kokoschka (Schweiger, 1986, pp. 43–67). Both editions interpret the abbreviation "D" in Kokoschka's letter as "Dirsztay".

This letter brings us straight into the Vienna and Berlin art and literary scene before World War I.[24] Kokoschka had made Walden's acquaintance in February 1910, followed him to Berlin, lived with him, and supplied a large number of drawings for *Der Sturm*, whose first number appeared on 3 March 1910.[25] He remained almost a year in Berlin and returned in early 1911 to Vienna. There he acted as a kind of representative of *Der Sturm*, kept watch for Austrian authors and took charge of the distribution of the journal in the city. At that period both Walden and Kokoschka were poor. Walden repeatedly had to borrow money to be able to print and distribute *Der Sturm*. One of his most important sponsors at that time was Karl Kraus. The two writers had known each other since 1909 and held similar views on contemporary art. They shared their anger and their pleasure and helped each other as much as they could, above all through Kraus supporting Walden. The latter for his part set up an "office" for *Die Fackel* in his Berlin accommodation, where he sold his friend's journal.

Unlike the two young journal founders, Viktor von Dirsztay had money. Whether it came from his family or, less likely, whether he had already earned it himself, Dirsztay was evidently prepared to support Walden financially. This was what was meant by the "agreement" in Kokoschka's letter quoted above. Evidently the promised cash injection had not arrived or was at risk, so Kokoschka reminded Dirsztay of the agreement and requested him not to decrease the promised sum. Dirsztay's manuscript that Kokoschka promised to send to Walden must have been the poem "Pubertät" [Puberty] which was soon afterwards published in *Der Sturm* (Dirsztay, 1911a).[26] The publication of this poem and further small texts by Dirsztay played a significant part in the tragedy that unfolded over the following months between Walden and Kraus and at the end of which they parted company (see, e.g.,

---

[24] In this paragraph I closely follow the account of Schweiger (1983, 1986).

[25] During the first year of *Der Sturm*, twenty-eight of his pictures appeared as well as the drama *Mörder Hoffnung der Frauen* [Murder, Women's Hope] (Kokoschka, 1910–1911).

[26] It appeared in the issue of 3 July 1911: "The candle gutters where my star flames bright/ The eye grows clear, the heaven is blue velvet/tormented and inflated cloud shapes/compel me to keep my eyes open/darkness around—/From thousands of tears shed in vain/ you suddenly emerge from my yearning./A crossroad up above the ladder of heaven/All buds are thorns. I can get no further,/I fall. An arm sprouts out to reach me/I recognise you. In bliss of ancient days I saw you/how old are you? How young?—O happy/glide/ Now we touch ground./Already wood, earth and meadow sway/A Sunday surrounds the entire world."

Avery, 2002; Sprengel & Streim, 1998). How it came about cannot be reconstructed in its entirety, but enough is known that one can at least venture to recount the story—especially as Freud himself would have found out something about it, either at the beginning when Dirsztay was still in analysis with him (until July 1911) or later (1913) when he came to him for the second section of analysis.

Freud knew all those concerned: Walden, Kraus, and, of course, Dirsztay. In spring 1911 he had been in contact with Walden when he took part in a survey by *Der Sturm* on the projected ban on contraception in Germany (Freud, 1910–1911a; May, 2009b). He had known Karl Kraus personally since, at least, the plagiarism affair with Fließ in 1906 (Schröter, 2002). In 1910 Kraus again occupied the centre of his attention when he issued a temporary injunction against the sale of Fritz Wittels's (1910) *roman á clef, Ezechiel der Zugereiste* [Ezechiel the Newcomer] (Lensing, 1986, 1989; Timms, 1986). As a consequence of this affair, Wittels left the Vienna Psychoanalytic Society on bad terms with Freud. The trial against Wittels at Kraus's instigation began on 1 November 1910 in Berlin. Walden followed it, it was reported in the press, and the verdict was passed in February 1911: Kraus won. During these same months Dirsztay was in analysis with Freud. It could well be that during his sessions he spoke about the trial which his idol Kraus was conducting against the Freud pupil Wittels, or about his relationship with Kraus and Walden, about his financial support for *Der Sturm*, or about his publication plans, perhaps also about the fact that he would be painted by the young Oskar Kokoschka who was just becoming known in Vienna.[27] Something like this could have happened during the daily sessions, so that we see Freud here in close proximity to the artists of his time—not in direct contact but in that mediated form of contact produced by the analytic couch.

---

[27] It is not unlikely that Kokoschka's name was already familiar to Freud. For in January 1911 Kokoschka took part in the Hagen-Bund exhibition in Vienna and, unusually for a young and still unknown artist, he occupied two rooms. As Schweiger writes (1983, p. 165), he was singled out, negatively or positively, in all the reviews of the exhibition. I cannot here go into Freud's attitude towards contemporary art, expressionism in particular. As a representative example, see a letter to Pfister in which he expresses his aversion in a particularly humorous manner to this trend in art (p. 77).

Dirsztay's portrait (see Illustration 2) was done either in June/July or in the autumn of 1911.[28] It belongs to a series (1909–1911) that depicts friends and patrons of Kokoschka, among them Herwarth Walden, the writer Peter Altenberg, the architect Adolf Loos, the Swiss sexologist August Forel, the Berlin lawyer Hugo Caro who acted on behalf of the poor, and Tilla Durieux, the Berlin actress and wife of Paul Cassirer. Viktor von Dirsztay's elegant, somewhat blasé and stylised appearance fits well in this company and in that of the Vienna and Berlin literary and artistic cafés like the *Größenwahn* [Megalomania], where some of those depicted circulated and were so amusingly described by Walden (1911) in *Der Sturm*.

To return to Dirsztay's contacts with *Der Sturm*: after Kokoschka had appealed to him not to reduce his payments to Walden, we find in a letter of the following day (9 July 1911) that Dirsztay wanted to publish another text in *Der Sturm*.[29] It seems that Karl Kraus "liked" the text, which should appear, as Kokoschka writes, in the "next number, by my word of honour. With God's help it will go. Incidentally D. will commit more money in spring, a very fine person, for the time being a ward of court" (Schweiger, 1986, p. 46). Again there is talk of Dirsztay funding *Der Sturm*, though at the same time that the sponsor is a ward of court, that is, not legally in charge of his own affairs.[30] How did it come to this? Who had set the process in motion and conducted the concomitant assessment, according to which either reckless spending or some sickness equivalent to a mental disorder would have to have been diagnosed? His parents? Were they not in agreement with the way their son spent the family money, or was Dirsztay really suffering from some grave disorder?

---

[28] Winkler and Erling (1995, p. 41) suspect autumn, Spielmann (2003, p. 112) June or July 1911. The latter thinks that the portrait was shown in Karlsbad (1 July to 15 August 1911). Incidentally, at the time of the exhibition Freud was there on a cure and could therefore have seen the picture. The portrait (98.5 × 73 cm, oil on canvas) was first in Dirsztay's possession and in 1925 was bought by a Dresden gallery (details of its provenance are in Winkler & Erling, 1995, p. 41), perhaps in connection with his increasing impoverishment after World War I. On the portrait, see also Timms (1990, pp. 6–8) and Soussloff (2006, pp. 44–45; further bibliographical information in Winkler and Erling (1995, p. 42).

[29] This may have been a collection of aphorisms that appeared there in September (V. Dirsztay, 1911b).

[30] The expression used is "Kuratel" which is a term in Austrian law and denotes, according to *Meyers Konversations-Lexikon* (1888), guardianship over someone "totally or partially incapable of managing their affairs e.g., a lunatic or a notorious spendthrift" (vol. 10, p. 338).

The letter that Dirsztay wrote to Karl Kraus a week later, on 15 July 1911, sounds depressed and full of longing. The analysis had ended seven days previously; Freud had travelled to Karlsbad for a cure, and on 13 July Kraus had gone to the sea bathing resort of Ostend. The young Dirsztay wrote to him there, in a somewhat affected manner:

> Unhindered by the awkwardness of a face to face notification, *I am eager*, today on the first evening of your absence whose *crippling effect has already begun* to make itself felt and the intense feeling of *abandonmen*t by all good spirits—more than that: *by the best spirit*, leads me—*to show you my gratitude* for every thought you ever had and for every sentence you have ever written down.

He signs the letter "Küppe", his nickname, and puts his wish to be nearer to Kraus directly into action by travelling likewise to Ostend.[31] Viktor's father also made himself known to Kraus in Ostend. He sent him a telegram thanking him for "efforts in the interests of my son" and requested Kraus to "maintain his benevolent care for him"—where "care" is certainly not meant in a material sense but rather in that of spiritual support.[32]

The next thing we hear of Dirsztay is a suggestion that Kokoschka sent to Walden at the end of August or the beginning of September 1911. He wrote to his holiday address in Norway (Schweiger, 1986, p. 46):[33]

> Dear Herwarth Walden Doctor. What are you doing at the North Pole? Very cold? Give Strindberg my greetings. Dirsztay has the following offer for you 200 mark for [his] complete works to be printed with short excisions in the shortest time. Obligation to pay in advance word of honour from me that you will print everything

[31] "Küppe" is also the name of a minor character in *Das Genie*, a "young, totally unknown writer". That Dirsztay travelled to Ostend can be deduced from Kokoschka's letter to Walden on 20 July 1911 (Schweiger, 1986, p. 47).
[32] The telegram is in the Kraus File at the Vienna Library.
[33] The faulty punctuation is part of Kokoschka's original style. It is preserved in Schweiger's transcription (in contrast to the 1984 edition of the correspondence). Schweiger dates the undated letter to summer 1911. From the correspondence since published between Kraus and Walden (Avery, 2002) it follows that Walden left Berlin on 27 August and returned there on 10 September (pp. 355, 358–359). As one can now say more exactly, Kokoschka's letter must therefore fit into the time between these two dates.

> with small excisions (if you don't do it then Budapest is lost for me, where he has rich relations and I an exhibition in January). So wire answer. I think you can print the Jewish novel abbreviated without any problem, and of the aphorisms 1/3, don't you agree. He needs money from his people and therefore he has to plead high literary honours. Of course many of his circle will subscribe to the journal. So telegraph when you want and you will have the money in a few days. But be sure to print it, yes? With warmest greetings, yours O Kokoschka.

This letter is unequivocal evidence of Dirsztay's attempt to induce Walden, by means of financial contributions, to print his texts.[34] It seems that Dirsztay was hoping to receive money from home if he could prove that he was successful as a writer. Kokoschka's interests were also involved. He promised himself support from the Dirsztays if they could be put in the right mood by publishing their son's work. As far as Walden was concerned, he was still in dire need of money; for example, he did not know how he could pay the rent of the Berlin accommodation (Avery, 2002, pp. 360, 364). It is therefore not surprising that Walden accepted Dirsztay's offer and published the aphorisms which the latter submitted in July, in the third September number of *Der Sturm*, under the title "Wahrnehmungen" [Perceptions] (Dirsztay, 1911b).[35]

Shortly afterwards we hear from Kokoschka that Dirsztay was "incapable of paying now", but could "on the first again" (Schweiger, 1986, p. 48). Thus he had made further financial undertakings and he could not fulfil them. Perhaps he sent more money to Walden in early October, for his satire "Unser Photo" [Our Photo] was published in *Der Sturm* from the second October edition on, in four succeeding numbers

---

[34] I cannot say what work is meant by "the Jewish novel". Unlike the editors of Kokoschka's letters (see Kokoschka, 1984, p. 331; Schweiger, 1986, p. 46), I do not think it refers to *The Inescapable One*, which, as I deduce from Ehrenstein's (1987, p. 198) statements, would only have been written around 1921. Apart from that, the 129-page *The Inescapable One* could hardly have been shortened to the length that was normal for publication in *Der Sturm*.

[35] The four aphorisms that appeared in *Der Sturm* had been extracted by Dirsztay from his *String Quartet* (Dirsztay, 1909, pp. 26, 33, 35, 37). Perhaps Walden did not publish them immediately because Kokoschka had written to him on 20 July 1911 (Schweiger, 1986, p. 47): "If you publish it now, he [Dirsztay] requests not at the same time as my drawings, because his people from whom he wants to extract something will notice that not literature alone etc."

(Dirsztay, 1911c).[36] This publication may again have come about through a financial contribution. At any rate Walden wrote to Kraus at this time that the chances of *Der Sturm*'s survival had "somewhat improved" (Avery, 2002, p. 373).

During publication of "Unser Photo" Dirsztay appears to have suffered a breakdown. Kokoschka wrote to Walden on 13 October 1911 that their sponsor appeared to be "in the lunatic asylum"; he would find him and speak to him (Schweiger, 1986, p. 48). At any rate things did not look good because Dirsztay was a ward of court, which of course meant that he was not free to dispose of his wealth. A month later, on 15 November 1911, Kokoschka reported to Walden that Dirsztay had left Vienna "with great debts" and without leaving any address (Schweiger, 1986, p. 49). Reassuringly he adds: "The man is *certain* because he is my friend."[37]

What had happened? We do not know whether Dirsztay was really taken into psychiatric care. But he might well have found out that his revered Karl Kraus had not liked his latest text ("Our Photo"). A Kraus letter to Walden on 21 October 1911 states this clearly (Avery, 2002, p. 375):

> On the other hand—I have no alternative, I have to tell you this—I was *shocked* by the last St[urm]. As you know, under no circumstances am I in favour of sometimes being only human for reasons of artistic politics. I must confess, such swill as this sketch "Our Photo" is not permissible. Nothing so dilettantish and humourless appears, even in the papers you are attacking. After all one should not make it so easy for the enemy.

Thus began the estrangement between Kraus and Walden, which, within a few months, led to the end of their friendship. Walden agreed with Kraus that the quality of Dirsztay's text left something to be desired (Avery, 2002, p. 376), but Kraus did not stop criticising: "One should make every sacrifice for art, but she herself should not be one of them."

---

[36] The content of "Unser Photo": a correspondent and photographer of the *Freie Neue Presse* (obviously the *Neue Freie Presse* is intended) is sent to heaven to photograph God and reports on meeting God and the angels.

[37] Both editors of the Kokoschka letters read: "The name is certain" (Kokoschka, 1984, p. 25; Schweiger, 1986, p. 49). Having seen the letter for myself in the Sturm Archive of the Staatsbibliothek Berlin, I suggest the above reading.

(p. 377) Dirsztay was a "totally original and droll person "but he could not write". Kraus stuck to his reproach that Walden had let himself be corrupted. At the end of December 1911 he informed him that he wanted to break their connection (pp. 393–394). The publication of Dirsztay's text was explicitly one of the incidents to which he referred. Kraus announced that he wanted to give up the *Die Fackel* office run by Walden in Berlin. *Die Fackel* should no longer appear in Germany; he wanted no further collaboration with *Der Sturm*. Walden made counter-offers and defended himself: "You are unjust against 'Sturm'. What I managed without means far outweighs the Dirsztay." At any rate he was "taken in" by the latter (pp. 395–396). Finally, in *Die Fackel* of June 1912, Kraus distanced himself publically from Walden and from the Berlin art world (Kraus, 1912). Afterwards the two exchanged a few letters but their friendship was over.

Thus, in 1911 after the end of his analysis, Dirsztay had, albeit by dubious means, achieved publication in *Der Sturm*. Short texts by him appeared in six issues during 1911.[38] He would have also learned that Kraus did not rate his literary ability and took exception to the way that Walden had let himself be bribed. Nevertheless Dirsztay kept faith with Kraus. In January and in March 1912 he declared his delight over the new issue of *Die Fackel* and sent his idol sweets from Budapest.[39] He also seems not to have been discouraged in his literary ambitions for he informed Kraus on 8 March 1912 that he had "a great plan to realise". When he attained his goal, he would "again live for a longer time in Vienna"—from which one deduces that his main residence at the time was still in Budapest. In October of the same year he sent Kraus a humorous postcard from the world premier in Stuttgart of Richard Strauss's *Ariadne auf Naxos*. He could not follow the opera well: "For a fact disturbed me greatly. Namely, having arrived from a great distance and by coincidence sitting together, were Vanderbilt from New York and myself from Pest and so I had to continually calculate how many times I went into him with no remainder."[40]

---

[38] In his 18-volume bibliographic *Index des Expressionismus*, Raabe (1972) does not include any of Dirsztay's texts that appeared in *Der Sturm*.
[39] Letter of 2 January 1912; visiting card of 8 March 1912.
[40] Postcard of 25 October 1912. In obituaries (Anon., 1935c) and in Kokoschka's autobiography (1971, p. 91) there are mentions that Dirsztay himself was a good piano player and worshipped Richard Strauss and Gustav Mahler. Kokoschka tells the story that, after Caruso had boxed his ear, Dirsztay went for days without washing his face (1971, p. 92).

Second analysis with Freud, enraptured by Kraus, "treatment finished for good" (1913–1916)

Soon afterwards, in May 1913, Dirsztay went back into analysis with Freud, this time for two and a half years.[41] He had an hour daily until summer 1914, mostly one and a half hours daily in autumn 1914, again mostly one hour daily from spring 1915 until the end of his analysis on 31 December. With the exception of a single day it seems that he never missed an hour. In April 1915, when Freud's practice had shrunk, he was one of the three patients who remained: "I still have three patients, all Hungarian and aristocrats" (F/Fer 2, p. 56).

We know almost nothing about Dirsztay's life between 1913 and 1915. In late 1913 he again appears as a benefactor: for the *Internationale Schwarz-Weiß-Ausstellung* [International Black-White Exhibition] in which Kokoschka also participated. Among its initiators was the painter and graphic artist Erwin Lang who was a friend of Dirsztay (Schweiger, 1983, p. 229). Dirsztay helped the exhibition with a "generous contribution of 1000 Kronen" (1983). Another friend who makes an appearance during these years is the author and poet Albert Ehrenstein who published in *Die Fackel* and *Der Sturm*; his *Tubutsch* (1911) was illustrated by Kokoschka.[42] Ehrenstein (1915) dedicated to Dirsztay a long, impressive, and gloomy poem entitled "Entwandlung" [Dischange].[43]

Dirsztay was certainly in contact with Karl Kraus again during these years, at least by letter. During the pause in analysis in summer 1914 (on 9 September) he sent him a postcard from Bad Ischl: he felt himself "cut off from any conversation as never before in [his] life" and he had "never before experienced so distressingly what it means to be

---

[41] At the beginning of the second analysis Dirsztay was living in the family palace on Rennweg, then from 2 July to 14 November 1913 in Waaggasse, then again on Rennweg (WSLA, 28 November 2006).

[42] A postcard of 20 June 1913 to Ludwig von Ficker, publisher of the literary journal *Brenner*, also indicates a relationship between Ehrenstein and Dirsztay. It was signed, among others, by Dirsztay, Ehrenstein, Kraus, Loos, and Georg Trakl [http://www.literaturnische.de/Trakl/briefe2.htm; accessed 28 March 2006].

[43] Drews (1969, p. 53) reports that it was written on the day of the assassination of the heir to the throne at Sarajevo (29 June 1914). It begins with the lines: "Als ich ganz zernichtet war,/vor Nacht und Hölle und Pest und Erde/verging im dunkel tosen-den Raume,/erschienen die Dinge,/Trost zu schütten über den Gram." [When I was totally reduced to nothing,/in the face of night and hell and plague and earth/passed away in the dark raging of space/things appeared/to pour down comfort upon the grief.]

distanced from any sort of intellectual culture"; he longed for a visit from Kraus.

How essential Kraus was for Dirsztay becomes evident from a distressed letter right after the end of the second analysis. The last hour took place on Friday 31 December 1915. Already on Saturday Dirsztay sent Kraus a telegram: "Am in terrible state [...] phoned you in vain last night."[44] The long letter, which begins as follows, must have come about soon afterwards:[45]

> Dear Mr Kraus, I am calling you in a moment of recognition such as I have hardly before experienced, in which the atrocious stupidity, the atrocious bestiality, the atrocious ugliness of life has dawned on me as never before. I am more and more possessed by the conviction that never before has human mind been as convinced of this fact as you are and that no previous writer and probably also none that will come after us has been able to describe it as definitively as you.

Since he had last seen Kraus, he had fallen into a rapture, a "Faustian urge for knowledge" had "feverishly gripped" him. Then he "awoke" and now saw everywhere the "wretchedness and stupidity" of people:

> As I am aware of supersensory connections everywhere and each becomes a symbol for me, so I never emerge from the depths of boundless despair and dejection. The spectral eeriness of this mad phantom existence torments me to the core and I tremble at the animal faces perpetually appearing to me, no less than at my own manifestation that is a mystery to me. The strangest metaphysical problems haunt me day and night, questions that I cannot find studied anywhere, that before me seem never to have been asked. How delivered I would feel if you could explain these things, if you were only here again!

---

[44] The telegram was mailed from Munich where Dirsztay wanted to recover for a few days. Kraus was not available because he spent New Year in Venice with Sidonie Nádherný v. Borutin (Canetti, 1974, p. 26).

[45] It is undated (handwritten note by the archive: 1916).

He was delighted by the latest *Die Fackel*. Kraus's poems, "Eeextraausgabeee—!" [Eeextraaa-!] (Kraus, 1915b) and "Elegie auf den Tod eines Lautes" [Elegy on the Death of a Sound], were "the most extraordinary thing" he had read lately. He had been unable to tell Kraus himself or to attend his latest reading because:

> [It] took place a week before the end of my five year long *treatment* and this time was so *critical* that, except at great risk, I could not seek any distraction. So with a heavy heart I had to remain absent. From the beginning of this year my treatment is ended for good, without my having until now any clear sense of its result; the success should slowly make itself felt during the course of the year, after its ground had been prepared for many years. This is more or less the situation. My greetings to you and my thanks to you for everything. I once more belong to life, having seen a higher form of existence during the hour I was writing to you. I will end; the wavering forms approach already and everything continues on its way.

The "five year long treatment" can only refer to analysis with Freud. Other events fit: Kraus's poems appeared in *Die Fackel* on 30 December 1915 (Kraus, 1915c), the reading took place on 21 December.[46] It is alarming that, to use Schreber's phrase, Dirsztay had to take up "nerve-connection" with Kraus only a few days after the last hour of his second analysis, just as he had after the end of the first. In imaginary contact with the admired man he felt alive and elevated, but he had the feeling he should not really seek his proximity. Must it not have been hard for him that Kraus had such a sceptical attitude towards psychoanalysis as he had once more made clear in the October edition of *Die Fackel* (Kraus, 1915a, pp. 132–133)?

Five short communications from Dirsztay to Kraus survive from 1916.[47] They came, among other places, from the Semmering and from Bad Ischl. Once Dirsztay included an extract from the spa list in which

---

[46] See the back cover of *Die Fackel*, no. 413–417.

[47] Letter of 27 March 1916; postcards of 30 May 1916 and 25 October 1916; card with handwritten note: July 1916; Telegram of 31 December 1916. The postcard of 30 May 1916 is a photo of Dirsztay.

he had for a joke signed himself "Dr. Dirsztay, Mystic"; on another occasion he expressed his enthusiasm for a Kraus poem (Kraus, 1916b). Twice gifts are mentioned which he sent to Kraus who had returned them. Kraus seems to have felt under pressure from him.

The first book: Lob des Hohen Verstandes *(1916–1917)*

The centre of Dirsztay's life in 1916 must have been the preparation for the publication of his first book, which appeared in 1917 under the title *Lob des Hohen Verstandes* [In Praise of High Intellect].[48] Possibly he wrote the manuscript during the second analysis. At any rate it was finished by early 1916 and sent to the Leipzig publishing house of Kurt Wolff; Ehrenstein appears to have mediated in this (Göbel, 1977, p. 777). There was much to-ing and fro-ing between author and publisher before the book came onto the market. In this instance as well, Dirsztay offered a sum of money in return for publication. But Wolff declined the offer and instead suggested to Dirsztay that he buy Kokoschka's drawings and put them freely at the disposal of the publishing house.[49] Dirsztay agreed and thus a method was found that did not at first sight look like bribery.

From the correspondence with the Kurt Wolff publishing house one gathers that Dirsztay had the impression they were not working speedily on his manuscript and that the editing was bad. He offered extra payments to the typesetters and the director of printing, Georg Heinrich Meyer (Göbel, 1977, pp. 693–704), and he rallied his friends to put pressure on Wolff. A humorous letter of 16 July 1916, written by Hermann

---

[48] Dirsztay adopted the title from a poem in the Arnim-Brentano collection *Des Knaben Wunderhorn,* about the contest between a cuckoo and a nightingale judged by an ass. Gustav Mahler had set it to music in 1896. The popular version by Hoffmann von Fallersleben and set to music by Karl Friedrich Zelter is well known: "The cuckoo and the ass,/they had a quarrel/which of them sang the best" [Der Kuckuck und der Esel,/die hatten einen Streit./Wer wohl am besten sänge].

[49] Wolff wrote to Dirsztay on 16 May 1916: "You suggested to the publishing house that you were willing to pay yourself the costs of the publication of your work. On principle I cannot accept such an offer. On the other hand I would gladly accept it if you were to acquire from Mr Kokoschka a set of illustrations for the manuscript and put these gratis at the disposal of the publishing house". The letter is to be found in the Wolff file, as are all subsequently quoted extracts from this correspondence (see note 3).

Sinsheimer and signed by Kokoschka, Loos, Oskar Maurus Fontana, and Paul Stefan, begins as follows:[50]

> The author of *In Praise of High Intellect*, soon to appear in your press, today read out to the initially serious and then highly amused undersigned what he modestly wished to write and what literary nonsense your surely highly educated literary board had amassed and accumulated, in the book that is yours or also not your book, that is his or also not his book, in Dirsztay's or not Dirsztay's book.

But most letters from Dirsztay to Wolff sound different, namely despairing and demanding. They are in part written in pencil, in nervous, sketchy handwriting and with many corrections. Dirsztay wanted better paper, another format, translations into many languages, prepublication copies, and more advertising in order to "compensate for his great lack of fame" (undated letter). Finally Wolff requested him (on 27 July 1916) not to send any more letters and telegrams, which did nothing to speed things up but rather would only "bring about disturbance and nervousness in the business". But Dirsztay did not cease harassing Wolff. In summer or autumn 1916 he again suffered a "breakdown" and submitted to a rest cure (undated letter to Meyer). Further delays in publication occurred, perhaps also because of difficulties caused by the war: paper became expensive and in short supply, censorship was increased, directors of printing, among them G. H. Meyer, were arrested (Göbel, 1977, p. 769).

On 15 October 1916 Dirsztay sent his "absolutely final" letter to Kurt Wolff. Here is a lengthy quote that shows Dirsztay's touching, tragicomic side:

> Since there is little interest in the publishing house for my affair and they clearly gave me to understand how little value, perhaps justifiably, was put on my modest writing, I can no longer apply to them; also because a correspondence with me is being conducted which, while not lacking an unbusinesslike, humoristic tone, does not seem suitable for this purpose. I consider it my duty to communicate this to you in this final letter; since to be treated as a joker and grumbler

---

[50] Sinsheimer was made artistic director of the Munich Kammerspiele in 1916; he attracted great interest in expressionist plays (Petzet, 1973, pp. 115–118). Oskar Maurus Fontana was an Austrian writer and journalist; Paul Stefan wrote on music and was co-editor of *Der Ruf*, a journal of Austrian expressionism (Schweiger, 1983, pp. 221–222).

> after having written a work with serious intentions seems to me all the more unjust insofar as the writer of those letters, of which I already have a collection, seems to be unacquainted with the contents of my book. I think I have paid for my mistake, which stemmed from ignorance and ill health, by the long months that I had to wait, and I cannot accuse myself of much more; it would not be difficult to prove to you that I am not in the wrong, were it not against my nature to harp upon this long delay, which I now want to bury and be no longer heard from, though that may mean condemning myself to wait even longer. You may be inclined to give my words no credence, since your information can only come from one side; nevertheless I feel relieved at least to have given you some indications in these lines of what oppresses me.

In the spring of 1917, *In Praise of High Intellect* appeared in large format and in an edition of 200 copies (Göbel, 1977, p. 1336).[51] It consists of no more than twenty-eight pages and includes six lithographs and a drawing by Kokoschka. Kurt Pinthus, an expert on expressionism, found the book "very confused".[52] I have not found any further commentaries or criticisms.

Parts I and III of *In Praise of High Intellect* consist of aphorisms, maxims, and reflections; it deals, among other things, with the unconscious and its counterpart, the intellect. Most interesting is Part II, entitled "Enträtselung" (Solution, 1917, pp. 11–14). Its subject is a decompensation and it offers an insight into Dirsztay's mental life. What he describes in this chapter is obviously based on his analysis. Freud's conceptual and interpretative frames of reference are recognisable everywhere. Two instances can demonstrate this. In the first (ibid., p. 11), a man leaves his house, goes out into the snow and loses the sense that his body belongs to him:

> With clairvoyant inspiration he felt himself wrenched from eternity and placed in this landscape; he lost his ego—thought himself a phantom, not knowing how it happened that a stranger—he touched himself, felt ice-cold face, alien limbs—stood at this moment there in the snowy landscape [...] Now he no longer understood that he had once been

---

[51] Dirsztay dedicates it to the memory of his "dear grandmother". It was printed in a 33.8 × 25.4 cm format (Wingler & Welz, 1975, p. 108).

[52] Pinthus's remark is to be found in a letter addressed to "Henry", probably Henry v. Witzleben (LoC/SFP, 29/5).

> able to feel an inner connection with this body leaning on a stick, or that he had assumed that this body was himself, of the same essence as his innermost essence, this mysterious self. [...] Recognizing this, an endless fear of existence seized him; his heart stopped beating.

In another place (p. 12) Dirsztay describes how a man threatened by the dissolution of his ego seeks help from his father and by thinking of his father. In these lines one hears Freud even more clearly; at the same time they illuminate Dirsztay's longing and love for men like Karl Kraus, for example:

> Irrefutably in these moments, feeling abandoned by everything and floating in space in utter deprivation, he experienced a heartfelt need to cling to something that existed, to take refuge on a firm point from the monstrous, menacing nothingness, from the cemetery silence of the universe. He tried to conjure up his father's image. Had he not, his whole life through, preserved a childlike trust in him, recognised his elevated mission which, according to celestial law, had called him into existence? Now that the ground was trembling beneath his feet he had the right to appeal to his father to comfort him, to console him and protect him with paternal love. That even the father could do nothing, that no help could be expected from him, now he had to understand this, for one day nobody would know that a sacred bond had once existed between them. This bond itself did not bind them, it was undone, was too transient to be able to survive his and his father's existence. Nothing seemed real any more, he himself was an illusion.

The man finally returns home and comforts himself by looking at the starry sky, feeling uplifted by God: "bathed in the shimmer of starlight and the sound of angels" harps, wafted in eternity by "clouds of God's breath, sheltered and protected by God's cloak" (ibid., p. 13).

Munich (early 1917), Dr Teuscher's sanatorium in Dresden (summer and autumn 1917)

After finishing work on *In Praise of High Intellect*, in late December 1916 Dirsztay again turned to Kraus in a long letter:[53]

[53] Letter of 27 December 1916 from which the quotes in this section are taken.

> Since I last spoke to you, dear Mr Kraus, I have again endured much pain on my way of the Cross. I will spare you and myself a detailed account of my fate, which includes all the woes of creation and which will either end in nothing or will attain a high goal; if I were to try to depict in words even a fragment of what occurs hourly in my soul, the report would soon break the bounds of a letter and expand into a biographical novel whose composition would in the end become my duty.

After long consideration he had obeyed his "inner voice", the "sole nurse of all woes", and had decided "to say farewell to his previous idle way of life and to begin a new way of life in a strange city, among strangers and strange circumstances, to speed up my cure through the greatest sacrifices". He would take up the post of literary manager at the Munich Kammerspiele theatre.

Probably one can take Dirsztay at his word that he had never sought any regular work before. The Kammerspiele theatre was at the time under the direction of Hermann Sinsheimer, whom we have already encountered as Dirsztay's mediator with Kurt Wolff. Money might play a part this time as well, since Dirsztay wrote Kraus in the same letter that, finding the theatre in a crisis, he had "contributed a modest capital sum".

Separation from his idol once again concerned Dirsztay, and once again it was not possible, for inner reasons, for him to speak to the revered man:

> Many times I have sought the way to you in order to bid you farewell and to be able to speak *to you once more before my parting*. After a hard battle, however, I had to give that up for, believe me, the parting *would have become too difficult for me* and at the last minute I might have thrown over everything I had so painfully brought together. Thus the only thing that I might have brought here as a beautiful memory, *a last talk with you*, dear Mr Kraus, had to be set aside despite all my longing and I must do without the sight of you for who knows how long. [...] However difficult it is, I do not intend coming to Vienna for a long time and at any *rate I intend to take precautions against it* lest I weaken and fall prey to temptation. With great longing and admiration [...]

We do not know whether Dirsztay really took up the post at the theatre and, if so, for how long. He could only have been half a year at the most in Munich, because by the summer of 1917 he was in a sanatorium, namely Dr Teuscher's institution at Weisser Hirsch, a district of Dresden.[54]

Albrecht Scholz (2003, 2004) has shown that this sanatorium served as a refuge for many artists during World War I. The director of the institution and the doctors in charge adopted an attitude that "combined pacifism and human dignity and thus enabled those of an artistic nature to lead their own lives. Without this support the artists would have come to grief during the war" (Scholz, 2003, p. 15). There was another legendary place closely connected to the sanatorium: the Felsenburg Pension. The sanatorium patients went there to convalesce. Scholz describes the Pension as a "temple of expressionism" and the source of many artistic activities during World War I (2004, p. 352).

Not only Dirsztay, but also his friend Oskar Kokoschka, were among the artists who stayed at Dr Teuscher's sanatorium and at Felsenburg in 1917 (Scholz, 2003, p. 17). The sanatorium doctors declared him unfit for military service and he stayed at Felsenburg, with intervals, from December 1916 to 1918.[55] At the same time as Dirsztay, Walter Hasenclever was at the sanatorium. He had also been declared unfit for service and spent an entire year at the Dresden refuge (2003). Dirsztay presented him with a copy of *In Praise of High Intellect* with the following dedication: "To my dear Walter Hasenclever in true devotion and unending stellar friendship your

---

[54] This follows from a postcard Dirsztay wrote to Adolf Loos (no date). On the front is a photo of Viktor v. Dirsztay. The card has until now been wrongly attributed to Kokoschka, which is, however, out of the question on the grounds of the unequivocal sender's address: "Dr. Victor Frh. von Dirsztay, Sanatorium Teuscher, Weisser Hirsch" as well as because of the similarly unequivocal signature "Yours Dirsztay". In this card Dirsztay asks Loos for his reaction to his book and tells him that "in autumn" he would return to Vienna. He wrote this handwritten remark on the photo: "Beauty passes, nothing remains! Ponem est omen. The born minister of the (unpleasant) exterior!" "Ponem" is a Yiddish term for facial expression or appearance (with thanks to Thomas Aichhorn).

[55] Kokoschka's famous painting *Die Freunde* [The Friends] (1917–1918), among others, was done at the Weisser Hirsch: it shows the duty doctor Dr Fritz Neuberger, Walter Hasenclever and other patients. Kokoschka was writing stage plays at the time, such as *Der brennende Dornbusch* [The Burning Bush] (Kokoschka, 1917), which was premiered in Dresden in June 1917 with the lead played by Heinrich George who was living at Felsenburg (Scholz, 2003, p. 17). On 8 October 1916 in Dresden there was the first performance of Hasenclever's *Der Sohn* [The Son] (Rühle, 2007, p. 309). These are only examples of the plethora of artistic productions that owed their existence to Dr Teuscher's Sanatorium and Felsenburg.

Victor Dirsztay—Weisser Hirsch in September 1917."[56] He gave him Freud's *Psychopathology of Everyday Life* (Freud, 1901b) whose fifth edition appeared in 1917. From the gift's dedication one deduces that Dirsztay was planning a further analysis, for the "Master of this book" can only mean Freud:

> To my dear Walter Hasenclever at a moment of great need when under torture I decided, as a shipwrecked man, once again to spend a period of intense work with the Master of this book, in melancholy farewell mood and in the clear knowledge that I am still stumbling in darkness and far from myself, your poor, faithful sanatorium room neighbour, hoping you will think of him now and again! V. D., 27.10.17.

As Dirsztay reports here, after the stay in Dresden he took up the analysis with Freud again. From 3 December 1917 we find him once again inscribed in Freud's patient record books.

Third analysis with Freud (1917–1920), enquiry about a fourth (1920)

The third period of Dirsztay's analysis lasted for two and a quarter years (see Chapter Nine).[57] Freud generally worked for six hours per week with him, for long periods of nine hours and for shorter ones of five and three hours. From the beginning of February 1920 Dirsztay no

---

[56] A transcript of this and the following dedications quoted here is to be found in the Freud Archives (LoC/SFP, 29/5). There is also a photo of Dirsztay with an inscription dated 4 August 1917, that once more comments on his "unpleasant exterior": "Walter Hasenclever in friendship! 4/8.17.—V. Dirsztay. Traveller, stop here, what you see here is Dirsztay— a whisper in your ear: "e ain't no goy! E's a diplomat!" Further, there is an undated congratulation from Dirsztay to Hasenclever on his being awarded the Kleist Prize (1917).

[57] During the analysis Dirsztay lived firstly in the family palace on Rennweg, then (17 February 1918 to 10 July 1918) in the Hotel Bristol; during the summer interval in 1918 he went to Ischl and was continually registered in Vienna from 11 November 1918 onwards until his death (WSLA, 28 November 2006). It is highly likely that he took no part in the war. From the beginning of the war until the end of 1915 he was with Freud in analysis; in 1916 he was occupied with the publication of his book; in 1917 he was in Munich and Dresden; at the end of 1917 his analysis in Vienna continued and lasted until 1920.

longer had any regular hours, but only two isolated consultations, one in February and the other in early March.[58]

Apart from that we know hardly anything about Dirsztay's life during the third analysis.[59] It seems that things continued to go very badly for him, at least for a time. In a letter of 30 October 1918 he congratulated Kraus on the publication of the 500th issue of *Die Fackel* and depicts his mood.[60] His state was "unbearable", he could "no longer appear in society", he had to stay away from Kraus's readings and wanted to remain alone with his misery: "You can imagine, my dear Mr Kraus, how much of a struggle it costs me to have to stay away from your readings—*the days on which you read are the darkest for me!*"

In this letter as in the previous ones, his suffering, caused by forbidding himself contact with Karl Kraus, is clearly evident. Consequently, I consider it possible that Freud hoped to solve the riddle of masochism in his work with Dirsztay. In the letter to the "dear Baron" of June 1920 cited below, he himself speaks of his "masochism". It could therefore be that the insights into the etiology of male masochism, which Freud portrays in "A Child is Being Beaten", go back to impressions from Dirsztay's analysis, among other things.[61] Freud understands a man's masochism as an expression of a feminine attitude, as a regressive distortion of the wish to be loved in a passive feminine manner

---

[58] During the time of the analysis there was a two-week stay in the Cottage Sanatorium (22 May 1919 to 9 June 1919; WSLA, 28 November 2006). Freud noted one hour daily in his record book during both weeks. Perhaps that means that Dirsztay had to pay the hours or perhaps that he came each day to Berggasse from the sanatorium.

[59] It may have been in 1917 or 1918 when a scene occurred which Alma Mahler-Werfel (1960, p. 129) describes in her autobiography without giving any indication of its exact date. She reports that one evening in her salon, after nearly all the visitors had gone: "The least significant was left: Baron Dirsztay. He had come at the wish and request of Oskar Kokoschka and he claimed that Kokoschka was still in love with me and wanted to come to me on some sort of human terms, whichever they might be. Baron Dirsztay felt that I owed this to Germany's greatest painter! Kokoschka was living at the time with a woman, but remained true to me. He could only paint me and whenever he began starting another, it was my picture which emerged"; Dirsztay told her: "You are his ideal and everything else pales beside it." The fact of his acquaintance with Kokoschka suggests that this Baron Dirsztay is probably Viktor. But Viktor's brother Franz, who moved in Viennese artistic circles too, is also a possibility (see above, note 10).

[60] Dirsztay dates it 30 October 1917. That must be a mistake since the 500th number of *Die Fackel* was produced one year later, at the end of October or beginning of November 1918.

[61] The work dates back to early 1919 (see Strachey, 1955b, p. 177). On male masochism, see pp. 196–200; compare also Freud, 1924c, pp. 161–162. A conjecture by K. R. Eissler on Dirsztay's sexual masochism would also be relevant (LoC/SFP, 21/13).

by the father (Freud, 1919e, pp. 196–200). When one knows Dirsztay's writings, one is reminded of his characters, for example, of the legation secretary in *The Inescapable One* who insists that his superior should be, and remain, "Master", as well as of the explicit master-slave relationship of the two parts of the ego that forms the hub of this novel.[62]

One can only briefly indicate here a further parallel between Freud's theory and Dirsztay's mental problems, namely the concept of the superego or, alternatively, the doppelganger. In "The 'Uncanny'" (Freud, 1919h), a short work from the first half of 1919, Freud discusses for the first (and last) time the phenomenon of the doppelganger.[63] He was able to base it on Rank's preliminary work (Rank, 1914), but went far beyond it when he interpreted the double as a "second" ego opposing and criticizing the first, containing both infantile narcissistic ideals as well as repressed drive representatives. Freud's description of the regressive confusion of two selves, with the result that "he is in doubt as to which his self is, or substitutes the extraneous self for his own"—all this reads for lengthy passages as though it were tailored to fit Dirsztay (Freud, 1919h, p. 234; pp. 234–235). Conversely the latter's description of the doppelganger in *The Inescapable One* (Dirsztay, 1923) exactly matches Freud's portrayal of it in 1919.

The third period of Dirsztay's analysis finished at the beginning of February and in June the baron was once more in a sanatorium, this time in the private clinic for nervous disorders at Mariagrün near Graz. From there he turned to Freud, asking whether he could undertake a further, fourth analysis. This can be deduced from Freud's reply of 10 June 1920, the only letter of his to Dirsztay that has survived.[64] As I shall report below, Dirsztay later disposed of this letter, selling it to an autograph dealer. It reads as follows:

> Dear Baron,
>
> At long last a reasonable letter with a definite, even answerable question; almost normal except of course the fee offer which I gratefully decline.

---

[62] Schlemihl, eponymous protagonist of the Dirsztay play, wants to be servant and page of the woman he admires; moreover, the keyword "Masoch" occurs in this play.

[63] Freud was possibly already working on "The 'Uncanny'" in March 1919, but certainly in May; he finished the work in July (F/Fer 2, pp. 354, 363). That was the month of Dirsztay's two-week stay in the Cottage Sanatorium (see earlier note); perhaps a decompensation in the above-mentioned sense (pp. 43–44) had taken place.

[64] LoC/SFP, 21/13. Dirsztay's address, Mariagrün, evident from the envelope.

Now it can be said with certainty that the process has not been lost, that there is a chance that continuing the task may lead to a satisfactory resolution of the conflict. The maintenance of what has been thus far achieved prevailing against your masochism, speaks unmistakably in favour and your present suffering will, I expect, greatly assist in wearing down your resistances when the analytical work is resumed.

However this cannot happen before early October; until then, take advantage of the sanatorium as a summer residence and as one more Purgatory. After all, one must make sacrifices, there is just no other way. What is worthwhile and acceptable in one's deepest wishes can be obtained later.

With kindest wishes for your appointment, respectfully yours
Freud
P. S. *Do not spoil the effect of the first letter with a second!*[65]

Some things about this letter are unclear, for example, what is meant by "process" [Prozeß]. Does it mean the analytical process or a legal one since Freud subsequently speaks of an "appointment" [Termin]?[66] The reason why Freud declined Dirsztay's offer of a fee must surely be that it was too high. Our baron was perhaps hoping once again that he could assist the fulfilment of his wishes through a financial contribution.

---

[65] Lieber Baron.

Endlich einmal ein vernünftiger Brief mit einer bestimmten Frage, auf die man antworten kann, fast normal bis auf das Honorarangebot, das ich dankend abweise.

Es läßt sich also mit Bestimmtheit aussprechen, daß der Prozeß nicht verloren ist, daß man Aussicht hat, die Aufgabe durchzuführen und mit einem guten Ergebnis aus dem Konflikt herauszukommen. Die Erhaltung der bisher erreichten Überwindung Ihres Masochismus spricht unverkennbar dafür, und Ihr gegenwärtiges Leiden wird nach meiner Erwartung das Meiste dazu beitragen, Ihre Widerstände mürbe zu machen, wenn die analytische Arbeit wieder aufgenommen wird.

Das kann aber erst Anfang Oktober geschehen; bis dahin bedienen Sie sich des Sanatoriums als Sommeraufenthalts und weiteren Fegefeuers. Entbehren muß man nun einmal, da giebt es nichts anderes. Was an dem sehnlich Gewünschten wertvoll und zuläßig ist, wird auch später zu haben sein.

Mit freundlichsten Wünschen zum Termin
Ihr ergebener
Freud
P. S. *Nicht die Wirkung des ersten Briefes durch zweiten verderben!*

[66] Translator's note: "Prozeß" also means "trial", "Termin" also means "judicial hearing". Perhaps hints of a public disagreement between Dirsztay and his wife mentioned in the obituary in the *Pester Lloyd* (Anon., 1935b) might refer to such a trial.

The reference to the "maintenance of what has been thus far achieved prevailing against your masochism" attracts one's attention. Obviously Freud felt that the long analysis had resulted in a significant change. Apart from that, the occurrence of the term "masochism" here is evidence, as noted above, for the supposition that Freud may have been thinking of Dirsztay, among others, in his discussion of the genesis of masochism. All in all, this is not so much a neutral as a humorous, paternal-advisory letter to the long-term analysand, whose first literary success in *Der Sturm* Freud had accompanied, as he had, perhaps, the birth of his first book and the course of his many friendships with artists and writers like Kokoschka, Walden, Loos, Ehrenstein, and Hasenclever.

Hence Freud would have been prepared to take Dirsztay on for a fourth period. Perhaps he numbered him among those patients of whom he later said that one had to keep them "for their entire life in analytical care" (Freud, 1933a, p. 156). But it seems that it never came to a resumption of the analysis: the patient record book for October, November, and December 1920 includes no corresponding entry. We do not know whether the analysis was continued in January 1921 because Freud's patient record books are extant only until the end of 1920. Thus we cannot say whether the three periods and more than 1,400 hours were all that Dirsztay had with Freud.[67] Apparently Freud found him pleasant and also interesting enough to keep him on so long, while Dirsztay, after more than 1,400 hours, still felt that he needed Freud.

Analysis with Theodor Reik, second book: The Inescapable One *(1921–1923)*

Directly after the letter from Freud reproduced above, we are surprised to find Dirsztay, whom until now we have only seen in contact with men, as the admirer of a woman, the fashion journalist Ea von Allesch (see, primarily, Severit, 1999). The "Queen of the Café Central", as Broch's biographer Lützeler (1995, p. 192) calls her, was older than Dirsztay and already had a grown daughter. The relationship between her and Viktor von Dirsztay had progressed so far by the summer of 1920 that he had

[67] The first period lasted at least 297 hours, the second 663, the third 529, so that gives at least 1,489 hours (see Chapter Nine). Exact figures cannot be presented because it is not known whether Dirsztay had any hours before October 1910 and, if so, how many.

proposed to her several times.[68] That aroused the jealousy of Hermann Broch who was having a relationship with von Allesch at the time (see Broch, 1995, pp. 39–40, 81, 107–108; Lützeler, 1995, p. 186).

Dirsztay's relationships with women also feature in Arthur Schnitzler's diary. On 5 May 1921 he noted in Munich (Schnitzler, 1993, p. 176): "Baron D[irsztay] […] wavers […] between two women, puts on an act; quite a funny figure." The previous day he had written:

> In my hotel. Baron D[irsztay] who had already followed me on the street sends me a letter; we walk up and down in front of the hotel; he is in psychoanal. treatment, first with Freud, now with Reik, who advised him to speak with me;—for the last 20 years "double self" is liberating himself through a novel; one self is a rake (in the novel a consular attaché), elegant,—this is what I remember,—the other his daemon;—battle between them. He makes a comic impression, literati-like, slightly self-ironic, not entirely unsympathetic. (Schnitzler, 1993, p. 175)[69]

Thus in May 1921 Dirsztay was in analysis with Theodor Reik. Probably Freud sent him there. Reik had little analytic experience at the time and was only 33 years old, around Dirsztay's age. Since receiving his doctorate in 1911, he had, however, worked a great deal on literary themes, among others on Flaubert and Schnitzler. He was well acquainted with the latter, respected him, and, as the diary entry quoted above indicates, had recommended Dirsztay should speak with him and get advice on his literary work (Urban, 1975). The fact that Reik was interested in the phenomenon of masochism may have been decisive for the referral to him. He had already portrayed the background to his own masochism in his first clinical paper in 1914 and had traced it back to unconscious

---

[68] In a footnote to Broch's diary, Lützeler (1995, p. 109, n. 3) writes: "Dirsztay seems to have made Ea von Allesch the offer of a nominal marriage to her daughter from her first marriage, Ella Rudolph, who was then twenty-five years old. That would have made it possible for Dirsztay to live together legally with his 'mother-in-law' Ea von Allesch even without an official separation from Johannes von Allesch." Lützeler (2000, p. 44) considers that the figure of the "Englishman" in Werfel's (1929) novel *Barbara oder die Frömmigkeit* was a condensation of Werfel and Dirsztay.

[69] When one knows Freud's steady practice, which was only interrupted by a few holidays, one asks oneself how Dirsztay was in Munich on a Wednesday and Thursday (5 and 6 May 1921) while being in analysis with Reik. Perhaps analyst and/or analysand took advantage of 5 May (Thursday), which that year was Ascension Day, as a holiday.

guilt feelings. The self-revelatory article appeared anonymously in the *Internationale Zeitschrift für Psychoanalyse* (Anon., 1914).[70] That Reik considered himself "masochistic" may go back to remarks of Freud, who had several times drawn his attention to his inclination towards "masochistic guilt feelings" (Reik, 1956, p. 634).[71] Karl Abraham, to whom he went for a few months of analysis in the summer of 1914, agreed with Freud: Reik indulged a "pleasure in suffering" (F/A, p. 256). Later Reik wrote articles and books about masochism and the unconscious need for punishment, for example, the monograph *Aus Leiden Freuden* [Masochism in Modern Man] (1940). As indicated in the Appendix, I consider it possible that Reik was referring to Dirsztay's analysis in these publications.

Reik was thus familiar with masochism from his own experience. This would have made him suitable as an analyst for Dirsztay. But maybe masochism was not alien enough to him. This thought comes to mind when we hear the reproaches that Dirsztay later directed against psychoanalysis. They are not explicitly directed at Reik—his name does not occur any more than does Freud's. Dirsztay's accusations are aimed quite generally at analysis and at a "bungler" whom he felt had "destroyed" him (see below). I should make clear in advance that I cannot answer the question of what drove Dirsztay to make this accusation. Nevertheless I have looked for possible grounds and the analysis with Reik comes into question, as does the one with Freud.

It is not known when the analysis with Reik began and when it ended. We only know from Schnitzler's diary that Dirsztay was being treated by Reik in May 1921. A further important event of the year 1921 was the death of his father: Ladislaus von Dirsztay died on 4 June 1921

---

[70] That the anonymous article was by Reik can be deduced from clear evidence and the easily deciphered information that it contains (see Sherman, 1978; Reik & Zohn, 1978). Possibly a remark of Freud's in May 1914 refers to this text: "You know, I would never have written the article, but I do not feel I have the right to alter anything in it" (Reik, 1976, p. 102; only in the German edition). The contribution towards psychoanalytic technique, which Reik (1915) published the following year although at that point he still had no patients (!), is largely based on his own analysis (Sherman, 1978).

[71] Freud obtained a post at Heller's bookshop for Reik in 1913. When Reik had a row with his boss, Freud wrote to him in early 1914 "Perhaps you have to conquer in yourself a streak of masochistic guilt feeling which sometimes compels you to spoil favourable opportunities" (Reik, 1956, p. 634). Freud expressed himself in a similar way in June 1914: "I know that you are again successfully engaged in spoiling for yourself as many opportunities as possible. All this because of a few people whom you would like to kill! Too much repentance!" (ibid., p. 635) See also Freud's letter of 15 July 1914 (ibid., p. 636).

in Vienna (Anon., 1921a, 1921b). Unfortunately we cannot reconstruct the son's reaction to the death. Father figures play a central role both in his life and in his understanding of himself.

In the diary entry cited above Schnitzler mentions a novel through which Dirsztay was trying to liberate himself from his "double self". This refers to *The Inescapable One* (Dirsztay, 1923), which was finished in summer 1921. In August 1921 Dirsztay's friend Albert Ehrenstein (1987, p. 198) had applied to Stefan Zweig who worked at that time for the *Neue Freie Presse*. He was sending Zweig:

> five scenes by poor Dirsztay; perhaps you could get some of it printed in the N. Fr. Pr.?!—he is after all a baron and also a member of "society". Dirsztay has also written an interesting novel which I unfortunately cannot place anywhere. In his illness he believes he would be cured if he were "famous". As a maniac he threatens to move in with you for a fortnight on Kapuzinerberg, if you don't print him in the N. Fr. Pr. Joking aside, I think the publication would help him—and the theatre too, for which he has written longish scenes.

The *Neue Freie Presse* did not accept anything by Dirsztay, but Kurt Wolff, who had already printed his first book, did. In early 1922 Dirsztay sent Wolff the manuscript of *The Inescapable One*. In April Ehrenstein again interceded for him and demanded a reaction from the publisher (Wolff, 1966, p. 239):

> One more request: Dirsztay has once again been well illustrated by Kokoschka (7 drawings); let the Wolff readers not ponder endlessly over his novel *The Inescapable One* which I have cut down fairly well, but recommend it for acceptance. Dirsztay is celebrating […] his fortieth birthday on 13 May. The novel really turned out well—could Wolff or the Hyperion publishing house not afford him a little pleasure? […] O.K. did his work out of charity, not for any material advantage, Dirsztay compensated him: to the extent that a poor rich man from the pre-war period could reward him.[72]

---

[72] If Dirsztay really had his fortieth birthday in 1922, he would have been born in 1882, which has not been confirmed from any other source. Apropos of "Wolff or the Hyperion publishing house": both publishers were owned by Wolff at that time (Göbel, 1977, pp. 816–817).

This letter contains the first inkling of what World War I signified for Dirsztay and his family, namely financial ruin. Dirsztay was now a "poor rich man" and would never recover from the economic decline.[73] In the few testimonies concerning his life in the 1920s and 1930s, he is seen as being in straitened circumstances.

After many difficulties, which we will not go into here, the 129-page novel *The Inescapable One* appeared in the spring of 1923. It bears the dedication: "To Dr. Theodor Reik in gratitude".[74] On the front cover of the book there is a Kokoschka drawing of a head. I am of the opinion that it is Dirsztay's head. Similarly the consular attaché and his alter ego, the *Inescapable One*, bear Dirsztay's features in Kokoschka's illustrations. Probably the novel includes biographical details, as the obituaries indicate (Anon., 1935a, 1935c). The protagonist, the consular secretary, also brings to mind, by his very occupation, Dirsztay's father, the Turkish consul-general.[75]

Even more than *In Praise of High Intellect*, *The Inescapable One* is the literary response to a long analysis. Through and through, every sentence of the novel is stamped and formed by psychoanalytic interpretative schemes. Again there is a decompensation at the centre. The consular secretary suffers grave damage to the unity of his ego or "self", as it is generally referred to in the book. He no longer knows what or to whom his self belongs and encounters part of his self in another character, the Inescapable. The borders between himself and the other are ill defined. Sometimes he is the other and sometimes vice versa, and even in encounters with other men he is threatened by loss of identity. In the end the Inescapable kills himself and the consular secretary is united with him in death.

---

[73] Possibly other events contributed towards Dirsztay's impoverishment. Risky speculation on the stock exchange plays a part both in the novel of 1923 and the two plays.

[74] I have found no information about the size of the edition. An official note of Wolff's on 9 November 1922 indicates that he wanted to rescind the contract with Dirsztay. From it we learn that Dirsztay had to pay 50,000 marks for the publication costs and the reproduction of the Kokoschka pictures, and put 10,000 marks at the disposal of the typesetters, printers, and bookbinders.

[75] The remark of the consular secretary that his parents had soon separated and remarried could also be autobiographical (Dirsztay, 1923, p. 11). Further one cannot rule out the possibility that what Dirsztay writes about the secretary applies to him, namely that he "had no more feeling" for his father and mother "since early childhood" (1923). That could mean that Viktor was brought up somewhere else after his parents separated, perhaps with the grandmother to whom he dedicated his first book, perhaps at a Catholic boarding school.

It seems that Dirsztay's novel was hardly noticed, and not reviewed. Schnitzler (1995, p. 61) noted in a diary entry that *The Inescapable One* was "snobby" and "weakish". Edward Timms (1990, pp. 6–8), who devotes several pages to an examination of the novel, considers it to be dealing with the repression of Jewish identity. I see it as a significant document in the history of psychoanalytic theory. As mentioned above, one can read it as a correlate of the so-called structural model, as the clinical basis of Freud's (1923b) introduction of the superego.

"Soul murder" (1924–1930)

After the publication of *The Inescapable One*, Dirsztay's traces are lost. Clearly he continued literary work since he left behind manuscripts dating from the years after 1923: *The Genius* and *Schlemihl or the Romantics*.[76] Both comedies remain unpublished.

In 1924 Dirsztay married Klara Unreich who was 35 years at the time.[77] They divorced six years later, "only for reasons of civil law" as was reported in the *Neue Freie Presse* (Anon., 1935c), whereas the *Pester Lloyd* speaks of "painful differences" which arose "between the spouses" and were "much discussed" (Anon., 1935b). The marriage appears to have been childless.[78]

A year after the marriage, on April 26, 1925 Dirsztay wrote a distressed letter to Karl Kraus. During the last few years he had not been in contact with anyone and for some time he had walked up and down

---

[76] *Schlemihl* may have been written around 1925 (see above, note 4), but could be later since the manuscript bears the address "Plenergasse 24", which was where Dirsztay was registered only from 1929 on. It is not known when *The Genius* was written. In both plays identities dissolve in a humorous manner. As indicated, the stockbroker in *The Genius* has a liking for the writer, who for his part develops an interest in shares. The leading role in *Schlemihl* is doubled: on the one hand, Dr Schlemihl, an unemployed writer who has a guardian and loves a woman whom he does not dare approach; on the other hand, Max, a hard-working young stockbroker who loves the same woman as Schlemihl. At the end the young men shake hands as they realise that they can only survive together.

[77] Born on 3 January 1889 in Lemberg; married on 22 January 1924 (WSLA, 11 November 2006). In Viennese obituaries she is described as a former bank clerk (Anon., 1935c, 1935f); in the *Pester Lloyd* obituary (Anon., 1935b) as a former actress. Eissler, who remembered seeing Viktor v. Dirsztay with his wife as guests of his parents, stated that she was a former dancer (LoC/SFP, 21/13).

[78] In none of the obituaries are children mentioned. Also Dirsztay's remark to Kraus's lawyer in 1931, that he had to take care of a "second person" (see below) argues against the presence of children.

every evening in front of Kraus's house because he had a "terrible secret" to confide:

> What I have to say and report is, however, so monstrous, so different from anything which has ever taken place, that it is infinitely difficult for me to bring it to light. For I fear that people will hardly understand me—also I shy away from the unspeakable ill that would be reported and in its description *conjured up again, from the very beginning to the sad end.*—It can only be comprehended thus, that for many years I have been totally lost, dead, without the slightest sign of life for anyone—relations or friends.
>
> Nobody knows—not a soul guesses—*what has happened here* and I had to remain silent—*more dead than the dead in the grave.*

He wanted to try to reveal the secret to Kraus. It was much worse than "even your imagination could envisage". He had been kept going by the wish:

> to bring the incomprehensible that happened here to people's knowledge and *to summon them to atone for the crime* that for year after year has been committed against me in public daily and hourly.
>
> And now I have pronounced the word: it is a matter *of a crime*—an infamous soul murder which has been allowed to be practised upon me in full view of everyone unhindered for year upon year.—I was so bewitched, so entangled and blinded was my soul that it was *only one year ago that the fearful enlightenment came to me* and it has been only such a short while that I have understood what happened here!—More than that I cannot and do not wish to betray in this first message—I am not yet capable. *I am still not used to writing—no less than speaking*—for I have had to remain silent for too long—for too long I have been dumb.—And only now, in the last few weeks—the urge has grown ever stronger and more irresistible—*though it may have come too late and in vain*—to initiate *a revered person* into the secret.

His admiration for Kraus remained unbroken:

> During that time, as concerns your work, I followed everything with the same burning admiration with which, as you will remember,

> I did in those distant times, when I was happy and near to you.—I did not miss a single reading—I was always hidden in some unseen place—*full of longing to seek you out and tell you everything.*—But I never had the heart to do it and had to sink back, silent and uncomplaining, into oblivion.—If I saw you at one time or other, since I could not avoid that exact street—*I had to jump aside, to hide myself*: an inevitable, complete confession would have seemed so terrible to me.
>
> Now it seems that my strength is at an end—I can no longer remain silent—*do not want to remain buried*—I cannot determine when the day will come that I speak to you as to the First Man—*but I feel that it is no longer distant!*

How should one understand this letter? Dirsztay speaks of a crime, an "infamous soul murder", which was committed against him in public for years on end, and at the same time that he had something to confess—and cannot say what. This brings to mind the consular attaché in *The Inescapable One*, who wants to "pour himself out" into another man and asks himself if this is permitted (Dirsztay, 1923, p. 106). Even the formulation that he is "more dead than the dead in the grave" has a counterpart in *The Inescapable One* (p. 111). Dirsztay's sense of life was therefore the same or similar to when he wrote the novel, before the summer of 1921. Apart from that, it seems he was "bewitched", "entangled", and "blinded" before he recognised the truth, before he had the "fearful enlightenment". To whom does the bewitching refer: to Kraus, to Reik, to Freud, to his wife, or to someone else with whom he was in love? Did he suffer a psychosis? Or did something unheard of and scandalous, something that shook his foundations, occur in his analysis or in his family?

Perhaps his experience "a year ago" corresponded to something he had already always feared and which he now "understood". Dirsztay was no longer just in a bad way but was convinced that he had been damaged, that a real crime had been committed against him. A decompensation such as he had experienced several times already may, on this occasion, have been caught up in a delusional formation. The trigger might have been the death of his father, but other events are also possible candidates: perhaps he had been disinherited, robbed of all his means; perhaps his wife had publically exposed him? Something must have happened that he experienced as annihilation or withdrawal of his innermost essence and as betrayal of his love. Perhaps something similar happened to him as to the characters in *The Inescapable One* and *In Praise of High Intellect*: they are seized by horror and threaten to lose consciousness if they lose their soul, their ego, their self, their identity (in being together with other men). Schreber too had accused his doctor Flechsig of soul murder. The comparison with Schreber is not unfitting insofar as Dirsztay's hints display that "vagueness and obscurity" that, according to Freud, are marks of the delusional formation (1911c, p. 38). So if Dirsztay had suffered a shift in the direction of paranoia, he could have held Freud and/or Reik responsible for the soul murder. Six years later (in 1931) Dirsztay explicitly asserts that he had been "destroyed by analysis" (see below).

Before I examine this question, I should like to recapitulate what we know about Dirsztay's life in 1924, the year of his "fearful enlightenment". In January he married, from March to June he was in Budapest, and in June he returned to Vienna.[79] It is not clear whether he was still in analysis with Reik in 1924.

However, in 1924 Reik found himself at the centre of public attention. On 10 October 1924 the first charge against him for quackery was registered. Shortly afterwards, on 20 October, Wilhelm Stekel issued a strong warning in the *Wiener Montagszeitung* against lay analysis (Anon., 1924) and in December, Kraus (1924) commented in *Die Fackel* on Stekel and the problem of lay analysis. In February 1925 Reik was banned from practising.[80] If Dirsztay was still in analysis with him, the ban could hardly have remained unknown to him, for it would have meant that his analyst would have had to terminate their sessions. If the analysis had already finished, Dirsztay might have heard from friends and acquaintances that Reik had been forbidden to practice analysis. It would not be surprising if he were disturbed by these events. They could have led to a sudden change in his feelings, even to the conviction that he had been badly treated by Reik and/or Freud, and (perhaps

[79] WSLA, 28 November 2006.

[80] The best account of this affair is Fallend (1995, pp. 130–140). Stekel's statement appeared in an article entitled "Officialdom against Psychoanalysis", which reported that a psychoanalytic ambulatorium that Stekel and other doctors wanted to open had not been permitted by officials (Anon., 1924). The decision was very strange, according to Stekel, because at "other" clinics—without naming it he was referring to the ambulatorium of the Vienna Psychoanalytic Society—non-doctors, people without a profession and "half-cured neurotics" were working and constituted a great danger for patients.

even financially) destroyed by them.[81] In *The Inescapable One*, Dirsztay had written how the admiration that the consular attaché had felt for Gustav Mahler had suddenly turned to coldness. The attaché's soul was no longer willing to bear the "excess of admiration" (Dirsztay, 1923, p. 68). Perhaps something similar had happened in relation to Reik and/or Freud, but perhaps there were other occurrences that gave Dirsztay the feeling of having been psychically "murdered".

"Destroyed by analysis": Dirsztay's end

Even during the following years Dirsztay did not lose the conviction of soul murder. In 1930 he wrote a short letter to Kraus "out of *deep misery* the secret of which shall in the near future *be exposed*". In a second letter, also of 1930,[82] he asks Kraus to give him manuscripts, "a few words in verse", or a few pages from the *Last Days of Mankind*. Illness prevented him from "personally being able to see" the revered man. Kraus should leave the manuscripts with the concierge for him to pick up. He would do without any "accompanying words" which would "only bring tears to his eyes *in memory of those happy days* when I could be near you and everything I deeply admired and loved was not yet lost!"

We do not know whether Kraus fulfilled Dirsztay's wish. But it is certain that during this time Dirsztay sold Kraus manuscripts. His last surviving letter is dated 28 February 1931 and is addressed to Dr Oskar Samek, Karl Kraus's lawyer. In it Dirsztay is defending himself. He admitted that he had sold the antique dealer Heck a manuscript that he received from Kraus "about fifteen years ago". He was living "in illness and poverty" and was turning his "belongings into money" because he was in need and had "also to take care of a second person". Consequently he had parted from prized possessions that were "extremely dear" to him, namely a manuscript of Richard Strauss, and also the "Dying Man", a poem by Karl Kraus (1916a, p. 67).

In the next issue of *Die Fackel*, which appeared at the end of March 1931, I believe that Kraus is alluding to the forced sale. He reports that in the latest autograph catalogue of the Vienna antique dealer V. A. Heck,

---

[81] The charge against Reik was dropped in the summer of 1925. In 1926 there was a second charge, which was discussed in the press, and on which Freud (1926i) commented publically, as did Kraus (1926, p. 36).

[82] Both letters are undated and the note "1930" is added in another handwriting.

he discovered that "a verse manuscript of mine, 3¾ sides—which I had not sold nor intended to—was apparently worth 740 Swiss francs". This referred to the manuscript of his "most famous dramatic poem written in dialogue form" (Kraus, 1931, p. 53). This description could correspond to "The Dying Man" (which Dirsztay had sold Heck). Kraus continues that the antique dealer Heck was also advertising his aphorisms. This referred to five lines only, costing 36 Swiss francs: "Exactly the same as 'two complete sides' by the founder of psychoanalysis" (Kraus, 1931). That Kraus refers to Freud is confirmed by the lines that he quotes from the antique dealer's catalogue; they are known to us for they originate in the (two-sided) letter that Freud wrote to Dirsztay on 10 June 1920![83] Thus Freud's letter had in the meantime come to Heck and was offered there for 36 francs.

But how had the letter arrived there? This question can be answered: in the business archives of the Heck company there is a note that in 1929 "Dr. Hirschfeld (Dirsztay)" had sold the antique dealer two items; one of Freud's and the other of Kraus's.[84]

Kraus made use of the advertised Freud letter to mock psychoanalysis once again. His commentary (Kraus, 1931, p. 53) refers to Freud's remark that Dirsztay's suffering would contribute towards "wearing down [his] resistances":

> I gather from this how much psychoanalysis is worth—at least its practice which I consider to be the Jewish quack herbalism of the soul—and the patient was quite right not to let his resistances be worn down, but to protect himself by selling the prescription.

It remains unknown whether Dirsztay really gained any advantage from the small sum that Freud's letter brought him. The quoted letter of February 1931 to Kraus's lawyer leads one to doubt it. It shows him under great pressure. Part of his need was surely material. The press reports that appeared after his suicide unanimously state that he

---

[83] The catalogue text (Heck, 1930, p. 10) extends from "The maintenance" to "is resumed" (p. 49).

[84] Bernfeld bought Freud's letter on 8 February 1934 so it is probably through him that it came to the Library of Congress. With thanks to Frau Dr. Uta Schweger, the co-owner of the antique dealer V. A. Heck (Wien I., Kärntnerring 14) for her kind generosity allowing me to look over the business records; also for her permission to publish the above-mentioned information.

was living in very modest circumstances. Naturally his life was made more difficult by his mental suffering, namely by the conviction that he was victim of a soul murder. In a letter to Samek he gives a more exact report than hitherto of what had happened to him. There was nothing left for him:

> but to vegetate *a long time* more in my need […] until I am released from this life, in which case—as you should know—I have prepared for *Karl Kraus* himself (in the form of a bequest) *the exact explanation* of my tragedy (*destroyed by analysis*) together with the declaration of my *awe and love* (for about the last 15 years)—an *admiration* which I have described *in this very* document as the only gain of this life of mine that has been annihilated by a quack. (My case is clearly described in this document.)

Dirsztay's "bequest" that was to have explained everything does not appear to have survived in Karl Kraus's literary heritage—at least not in the files concerning Dirsztay—so the Samek letter is our only indication of it. There he states that he was "destroyed by analysis" and the source of his tragedy was a "quack". The dating to a time "about 15 years ago" is new. These were the years around 1916 when Kraus gave him "The Dying Man" as a present and after he had finished his second period with Freud. It remains curiously unclear whether Dirsztay means that it was his destruction through analysis that began fifteen years ago or his admiration for Kraus or both. Perhaps both aspects are connected? Perhaps Dirsztay felt that his love for Kraus was threatened by the analysis and believed he had to choose between Freud and Kraus, who were by no means good friends. In the end all of this remains speculation. We have to reconcile ourselves to not being able to explain at whom Dirsztay's accusations were aimed and how they should be interpreted. A delusional process may be involved as much as a real experience, and a combination of both is not out of the question.

Four years after this letter, on 6 November 1935, Viktor von Dirsztay together with his ex-wife committed suicide. The *Neue Freie Presse* (Anon., 1935c) reported the news in the evening edition of the same day: when the sister of Dirsztay's wife had rung at the door it had not been opened. She smelled gas and called the police who opened the door. The two were found lifeless; on the kitchen table lay a note with the words "By consent". Baroness Dirsztay had suffered from a nervous illness, had been certified, and had repeatedly spent time in mental institutions. A few days before the suicide, she was released from the "Am Steinhof" institution. Dirsztay could no longer bear the fact that her condition was not improving. The Viennese obituaries agree that the illness of his wife was the motive for the double suicide. The couple had lived on the best of terms after their divorce. On the other hand, the author of the obituary in the *Pester Lloyd* expresses his surprise at the Viennese versions and, as has been mentioned, points to "painful differences" between the couple (Anon., 1935b).

Several reports highlight Dirsztay's popularity and humour, his love of music, his reverence for Gustav Mahler and Richard Strauss, as well as his respect and admiration for Freud. In the *Neue Freie Presse* he is represented as an "enthusiastic Freud disciple" and a "follower of Siegmund [sic] Freud" (Anon., 1935c, 1935f); the *Reichspost* even entitled its report "Tragic End of a Freud Disciple" (Anon., 1935a). The report was followed by a separate small obituary under the title "A Viennese Original". I should like to end my sketch of the life of Viktor von Dirsztay with a quotation from this sympathetic obituary:

> For this Baron Dr. Viktor Dirsztay was an aesthete. The whole world knew him as such and was on more or less intimate terms with him. Of course the concept expressed as "the whole world" needs to be defined. This was the world of opening nights at the theatre, of grand concerts, of the more adventurous art exhibitions and of the café tables where difficult problems were worked over with great zest. In this world Baron Dirsztay was at home. Some saw in him a passionate partisan of every new artistic and intellectual trend, others, less sympathetic to his attitude and work, an extravagant original.

* * *

Appendix

Viktor von Dirsztay in Theodor Reik's work

In one of Reik's books I noticed a vignette about a forty-one-year-old writer called Viktor who was in other ways similar to Viktor von Dirsztay. I then consulted other Reik publications in search of Dirsztay's traces. My results are, of course, not entirely serious in their intention for, strictly speaking, I do not know whether Reik's descriptions were really based on Dirsztay. However, sometimes the similarity is very strong; one then becomes aware that it could be helpful to know of it. That applies, of course, not only to Reik's but also to Freud's publications. As soon as one can identify the patient under discussion, one's perception of the text changes. I believe that it gains in comprehensibility. The decisive factor is not that one knows the real name of the analysand but that one knows what else is known about them, in other places or in the writing of other authors. If, for example, we know the Wolf Man only from Freud's (1918b) work—and not also from the accounts by Mack-Brunswick (1928) and Gardiner (1971), let alone from his own memories—we have a weaker, more abstract image of him. The differing views enrich the image and at the same time contribute towards making one aware of its subjectivity and specificity.

The episode quoted above about "Viktor" is in Reik's *The Haunting Melody* (Reik, 1953, pp. 127–128). The Viktor described there had a stepmother and brothers and suffered from severe mood changes:

> reaching from depressions in which he was almost apathetic, to hypomanic states in which he made himself the butt of many, sometimes excellent jokes. He described his emotional situation as a battlefield of opposite forces, and felt best when those antagonists in him had arrived at an armistice. [...] He oscillated in his emotions from those of a sinner in despair and atonement to those of a saint who feels superior to others, and but rarely succeeded in reaching the state of a person ready to make compromises between his own impulses and the demands of society.

Often his mood would switch abruptly "from depression to an almost humorous self-mockery". He said, for example:

> "I don't know why I am punishing myself so cruelly. All this because I have killed a few people in my thoughts? When you think of the millions murdered during the war, the number of persons I killed does not even need consideration". This kind of sorry humour in which he looked at his troubles and emotional difficulties from a bird's-eye view also appeared in his writings.

What Reik writes here and elsewhere about Viktor *could* apply to Dirsztay. The remark quoted about death wishes brings to mind a place in *The Inescapable One* where similarly formulated guilt feelings are traced back to death wishes (Dirsztay, 1923, p. 118).

The case of "Viktor" appears in two more of Reik's publications, namely in an article on masochism (Reik, 1939) and in *Aus Leiden Freuden* (Reik, 1940). In both publications the case was not named "Viktor" (perhaps to conceal Dirsztay's identity, which may no longer have seemed necessary in the later *Haunting Melody*). In "The Characteristics of Masochism" (1939, p. 56) Reik reports on a man in middle age who had previously engaged in masochistic sexual practices but had given them up during the analysis. This led to a change in his character. His sexual masochism became "desexualised", "social" masochism, which consisted primarily in making fun of himself. In this connection Reik compared the analysand to a Schlemihl [Transl. = "an unfortunate person" (Yiddish)]—which naturally brings to mind Dirsztay's comedy of the same name. The reference is as follows:

> He went much into society and greatly amused his friends and associates by retaling [sic] many experiences in which he appeared as the boob or the poor fish. He produced a constant stream of witticisms—killing ones moreover more than not—which made unmerciful fun of his own stupidity, tactlessness or egotism. Generally he simply played the clown whose job it is to make others laugh at himself. Out of the sexual perversion had arisen, so to speak, a social one. His masochism had persisted in assuming the role of a Schlemihl, a self-deriding wit. The self-depreciation had become a social mask.

Reik also speaks of this case in *Aus Leiden Freuden* and, moreover, in several places, at times repeating the article of 1939 word for word (cf., 1940, pp. 27–28, 106, 249–251). Thus he reports that during walks through the streets in the evening the analysand had phantasised being a sex murderer. If he was with a girl, "sometimes the impulse" took him "to turn a tender movement into a brutal, hurtful one" (p. 251). We find this in *The Inescapable One* again. The consular secretary walks through the town and feels as if he were a sex murderer (Dirsztay, 1923, p. 87). He visits a woman friend, wishes to be tender to her, and is afraid of being rough, which so frightens him that he rushes away (p. 88).

Finally there is a letter that Freud wrote to Reik in January 1938. There he writes about a "D." (Reik, 1956, p. 118): "I have nothing against your remark about the influence of analysis on D.'s perversion. I can no longer recall that the passage you note in V. 365 refers to D."[85] Reik elucidates the letter as follows:

> I asked Freud for permission to quote certain passages from his paper on masochism contained in Vol. V of his *Gesammelte Schriften*. The passage concerns the case of a masochist who had been under Freud's psychoanalysis for a long time, and whom Freud had referred to me for continuation of the treatment. (Reik, 1956, p. 656)

This "masochist" too *could* be Dirsztay, who had been first with Freud, then with Reik. The article in the fifth volume of the *Gesammelte Schriften* refers to "A Child is Being Beaten" (Freud, 1919e): its page 365 corresponds to page 196 in the *Standard Edition*, where the dynamics and etiology of male sexual masochism are mentioned. While Freud could not confirm that the passage referred to D., he had no objection to Reik's explanation of "the influence of analysis on D.'s [or S.'s] perversion". That could refer to the alteration of sexual into social masochism mentioned above, which would fit Freud's remark in his letter to Dirsztay, that he had largely overcome his masochism (see above).

But what did Reik want Freud to agree to in 1938? In which of his own works did he want to refer to "A Child is Being Beaten"? I believe it was in *Aus Leiden Freuden*. For in this book Reik discusses Freud's theory of masochism at length. He felt he had new insights to offer that went beyond Freud (cf., 1940, pp. 249–260). He saw the main starting point of masochism in the pre-oedipal relationship to the mother and not, as Freud, in the attitude of passive love towards the father in the oedipal phase.

Not only masochism but also the dissolution of the unity of the ego and its splitting into various parts were key words, as I have shown above, that could refer back to the analysis of Dirsztay. Reik (1923) discusses the splitting of the ego, for example, in *Der eigene und der fremde Gott* [One's Own and the Foreign God], a book that is based on articles and lectures from 1920 and 1921. Among other things he describes how different ego components and identifications—at that time there was not yet any concept of the superego—battle each other. In this connection

---

[85] "D." in the German text becomes "S." in the English edition (Reik, 1956, p. 118).

he reports details known from *The Inescapable One*. He speaks, for example, of a compulsive neurotic patient in front of a theatre, "which he would not allow himself to visit, standing against a streetlamp with outstretched arms" and in a "passive feminine" attitude thinking of "Christ on the cross" (1923, p. 114). In *The Inescapable One* the consular secretary adopts the same crucified posture at a streetlamp (ibid., p. 14). If the man Reik mentions is Dirsztay, then in his youth he would have been sent by his father, "after many vain attempts at education", to a "seminary" (ibid.), so that the "lunatic asylum" that Dirsztay speaks of in *String Quartet* (1909, p. 19) might also refer to this boarding school. Similarly, the remark about the consular secretary in *The Inescapable One*—that he had grown up without any "feeling" for his parents—could also refer to his period in a boarding school. The "wickedness" of the young man, according to Reik (1923), had given way to a "self-tormenting masochism" which "forbade any pleasure and, through stubborn obedience to it, made life impossible". Sometimes the patient pursues "any pleasure", "throws money around, and plays all sorts of foolish and mad tricks that must arouse the father's displeasure". At these times he is "active and masculine; he himself is then the father in whose place he has put himself and he wants to be successful, pleasure-loving and scrupulous like his father". At other times, and ones which have "greater significance for his neurosis, he denies himself the slightest pleasure, any enjoyment in life, and lives ascetically". This too could correspond to Dirsztay, both the extravagance with money and the efforts mentioned several times above not to see his beloved Karl Kraus and not to attend his lectures.

This brings to a close this brief foray into Reik's work. To repeat: I do not know whether Reik really means Viktor von Dirsztay in the quoted passages. If he does, then this case appears to us in a somewhat different light.

Translated by Michael Molnar

CHAPTER NINE

Freud's patient record books (1910–1920): on the duration and frequency of thirty-six of Freud's analyses

The patient record books

What we know about Freud's analytic work has come from his case histories, his technical papers, and scattered remarks in his correspondence, as well as from reports from his analysands.[1] There did not seem to be any documentary evidence that directly reflected Freud's working-day situation. This was, however, as Christfried Tögel pointed out

[1]Since the original version of this chapter appeared in 2006 and 2007, several texts have been published that offer additional insight into the biographies of the analysands: Arthur Fischer-Colbrie (Walder, 2010), Emil Oberholzer (von Planta, 2010; Schröter, 2010); Anton and Rózsi von Freund (Huppke & Schröter, 2011); Kata Lévy (Freud, 2012), and Victor von Dirsztay (May, 2010a, 2011b). Furthermore, valuable new source materials have become available to Freud scholars, for example, the complete correspondence between Freud and Abraham (2002), Bleuler (2012), Groddeck (2008), Lévy (2012a), and Pfister (2014), as well as with his daughter Anna (2006), which also contain information relevant to the analyses presented. This new material has been taken here into account only where corrections in the text were proven necessary.

In this chapter, two texts were combined that were originally published separately (May, 2006b and May, 2007). During the merger, the term "patient calendars" was replaced by "patient record books". The new wording makes it clear that Freud did not note in these books the hours he had arranged with the patients, but rather that he entered only the hours he had held.

to me, not the case. He drew my attention to Freud's patient record books, copies of which are in the Freud Museum in London.[2] Their existence, as I subsequently learned, was known to a few insiders but until now they have not been mentioned or used in a publication, although they are freely accessible.[3] Chris Tögel kindly provided me with copies of the record books.

In these record books Freud made daily entries of the patients he had seen—no more and no less. We can therefore see exactly how many hours a week his patients came and over what period of time. There are three books altogether that cover the decade between October 1910 and December 1920. There are no gaps in these books and they thus provide us with new opportunities to gain more extensive and precise insights into Freud's therapeutic practice.

The patient record books were small notebooks called *Grubers Ärztliches Tages-Notizbuch* with preprinted pages. There was a double page for each month; on the left-hand side the patients' names were written in a column; on the right there was a row of 31 boxes, one for each day of the month, which could be ticked if the patient was seen that day. The last column on the right was for the notation of fees (see Illustration 3).

The three patient record books comprise approximately 100 pages (see Illustration 3 for a sample page) and include hours for about 130 analysands. The exact number is difficult to determine because Freud usually just noted last names. He seems to have only added a first name if he had previously been treating a patient with the same last name. Freud made a vertical stroke in the box for the day in question, one stroke for one hour, two strokes for two hours, one and a half for one-and-a-half hours, and so on. In the box for his fees he sometimes wrote down the total number of hours a patient had had in a month. Apart from the name of the analysand, the strokes in the record books, and occasional monthly totals there are no further notations in the record books. Nonetheless they provide a unique window into

---

[2] At the same time I received Tögel's information I discovered on the website of the Freud Museum an entry "mottled notebooks" in the archive section and learned that these were the record books in question. The exact descriptions are: "Mottled notebook 1: patient attendance figures Oct. 1910–July 1913"; "Mottled notebook 2: patient attendance figures Oct. 1913–Jan. 1918"; "Mottled notebook 3: patient attendance figures, Jan. 1918–Dec. 1920".

[3] See Tögel, 2006. After completing this chapter I discovered a passage in Freud's *Diary* where the record books are mentioned although without a description of what they comprised (Molnar, 1992, p. 298).

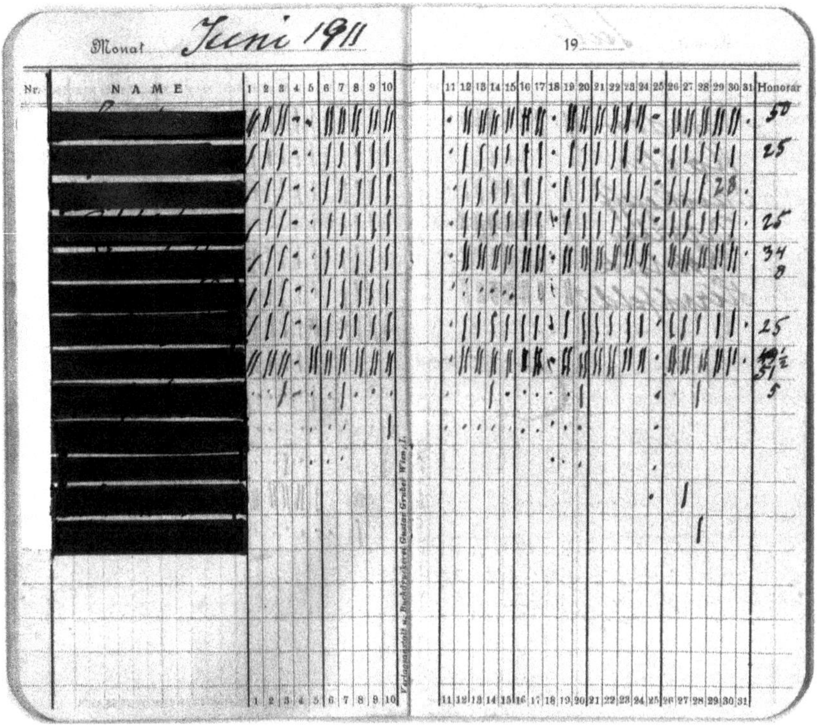

Illustration 3. Freud's patient record book: June 1911. Freud-Museum London. In the entries for June 1911 the 1st of June falls on a Thursday, the 4th and 5th were Pentecost Sunday and the Monday holiday; subsequent Sundays were the 11th, 18th, and 25th.
The patients found in lines 1 and 8 had two hours daily, the patient in line 5 had two hours daily only in the second half of June. The patients in lines 2, 3, 4, 6, and 7 had one hour daily, the remaining patients in June had an hour only occasionally.

Freud's work as a psychoanalyst in the period between 1 October 1910 and 31 December 1920.

Confidentiality of patient data

I deliberated over the question of how to deal with the data for a long time. I consulted colleagues and eventually reached a solution that, albeit far from perfect, seemed to be the best possible in the circumstances: providing individualised information on the number of hours of analysis *without*, however, *revealing any new names of patients.*

The published correspondence of Freud with Ferenczi and Jones as well as the many contributions to Freud's biography and the history of psychoanalysis have provided the names of a number of women and men who were in analysis with Freud. Quite a few of these include detailed descriptions of the course of treatment in which the complete name of the analysand is mentioned, for example Loe Kann, Elfriede Hirschfeld, Elma Palos, or Tatjana Nacht. Some analysands have themselves written about their analyses with Freud, such as Helene Deutsch (1973), Sergei Pankejeff (1971), or Adolph Stern (1922). In these cases—but only in these cases—I have found it acceptable to mention the duration and frequency of the analyses. In short, only if there already is a published description that *explicitly* and *unmistakably* states that Mrs X or Mr Y was in analysis with Freud have I included this person in the group of analyses that I am presenting here.

This still does not absolve me from the responsibility involved in using patient data. On the one hand, it is important not to make patient data from analyses public; on the other hand these details have already been published. This creates a dilemma. The strategy I have chosen is not perfect in that I have taken advantage of breaches of data protection perpetrated by others. It is also arguable what really constitutes a breach (see Fichtner, 1994; Schröter, 1995). Without discussing the principles here, I would like to point out that other researchers have proceeded in a similar fashion: for example, Hirschmüller in his edition of the Freud-Bernays (2005) correspondence. He too used the names of patients whose history "had already been made public" (p. 200); this was also the practice of Schröter and Meyer-Palmedo in their edition of Freud's correspondence with Eitingon (F/E, 2004) and Anna Freud (F/AF, 2006).

The alternative would have been to posit that never and under no circumstances should Freud's patient record books have been examined nor should the number of hours of this or that analysis with Freud and its weekly frequency ever have been published, even if its course could already be followed quite accurately in letters. This position cannot be dismissed out of hand, but I do find it overly rigorous. A further possibility would have been to provide information only about groups of patients and to re-encode the data of individuals. One would have to undo the revelation of names, by for example giving a new abbreviation for Loe Kann to hide her identity, such as "Mrs A". This procedure would, of course, have meant that none of the already published information using the analysand's real name could have been used. Quite apart from that, any coding of that kind could easily be undone with the help of the correspondences and other published sources, thereby reducing these efforts to a futile gesture.

What does a stroke in the patient record books denote?

Freud entered all analytic sessions—with the exception of those he gave his daughter and those that took place during his vacation. This was the case for two treatments (Jan van Emden, Kata Lévy). In all likelihood he only noted sessions with patients in analysis but not contacts with patients who came to the regular consulting hours of his practice. What Freud did when the analysand did not appear is not quite clear, although there are some indications that these hours were not entered. It should at some point be possible to clarify this with the help of the account notebooks. For the time being, the "number of hours" refers to the strokes in the record books and not, strictly speaking, to the hours held.

A stroke in the record book most likely stood for a time unit of slightly less than sixty minutes.[4] Freud probably had a short break between sessions as can, for example, be deduced from a remark he made in a letter to Ferenczi when he was looking for a new apartment, "I wish you a beautiful place to live, so that you, dear friend, each time between two [analytic] hours, can go over to where your wife is keeping house" (F/Fer 2, p. 334). Not infrequently one-and-a-half, sometimes two, and occasionally three strokes are noted per day which probably corresponds to one-and-a-half, two hours, and so on as can be seen in Freud's correspondence where "two hours daily" is mentioned several times.[5]

Freud's working day

In the period between 1910 and 1914, Freud saw between nine and eleven patients every day. His working week continued from Monday to

---

[4] One indication for this is that David Forsyth, who underwent a first period of analysis with Freud in 1919 and then wrote a book about the psychoanalytic method of treatment and the establishment of a practice in which he stuck closely to what he had experienced with Freud, recommended a fifty-five-minute hour (1922, p. 30).

[5] For example, Freud writes to Ferenczi: "I will thus reserve for you two hours a day" (F/Fer 2, p. 130; see also pp. 125, 129). Referring to his analysis Anton v. Freund also speaks of "double sessions" (see Huppke & Schröter, 2011, p. 65).

Saturday, each a full working day. Very rarely Freud also had an appointment on Sunday. This heavy daily workload seems to have been quite usual at the time; at various times Jones reported seeing ten patients daily, as did Abraham (for example, F/Jo, p. 358; F/A, p. 148). After the beginning of World War I, Freud only had between two and five patients per day, and for more than two years his practice stayed at this low level. Starting in 1917, the number of patients increased again, and by January 1918 it was back to about nine to ten daily hours. In the years leading up to the war Freud's daily workload of nine to eleven hours meant that he had up to sixty-six hours of analysis per week; this would amount to approximately 250 hours per month. After the war, Freud worked a little less than before (approximately 200 hours per month).

Freud's working year

The year was clearly structured. His work began on 1 October, corresponding to the academic year, and ran to the beginning of July the following year, a good nine months. He did not work on 25 or 26 December or on 1 January, nor did he work for between one and three days at Easter and Whitsuntide. Christmas Eve, New Year's Eve and all other days were normal working days. There seem to have been only two normal weekdays when Freud's practice was closed: 6 January 1913 and 29 January 1916. We know that he was ill on the latter of these dates because he had noted influenza in his diary[6] but it is not clear why he did not work on 6 January 1913, which was the day of the Epiphany.[7]

His summer vacation usually began in the second week of July and lasted until the end of September, a little less than three months. In the war years Freud worked longer in the summer, up to the middle of July, and ended his holidays earlier in September. After the war he extended the period in which he worked in July by one to three weeks.

---

[6] My thanks to Ernst Falzeder. On 1 January 1913, Freud had written to Anna that he could not shake his cold (F/AF, p. 61). Perhaps that developed into a more serious infection. In November 1931, he told Eitingon, that he had to break off a session because he was not feeling well and that this had only happened to him once in his life (F/E, p. 768).

[7] In a letter (to Anna) dated 1 January 1913 he speaks of the "today or at least on the 6th [Jan] end to the holidays" (F/AF, p. 61). Meyer-Palmedo points out that the Freud family "complied with the Christian holidays customary in Austria" (F/AF, p. 57, German edition). Regarding the Epiphany and Freud's practice, however, this only applies to the year 1913.

Otherwise Freud never interrupted his work during the "season", that is, between the beginning of October and the beginning of July. The psychoanalytic congresses always took place during his holidays and he participated in no other congresses. There evidently was no reason for him to cancel hours, no professional or family commitments that interrupted the continuity of his work. Nowhere in the patient record books is there a trace of his daughter Sophie's death on 23 January 1920, of which he did not hear until two days later (Sunday 25 January). Because of travel restrictions Freud could not attend the funeral in Hamburg (on 28 January) and his working schedule remained unchanged for the whole week. On 20 January 1920, a few days before Sophie's death, Anton von Freund had died. The usual session of Margit Dubowitz who was a friend of von Freund's did not take place on 22 January, on the day of the funeral nor did that of another patient, possibly because Freud cancelled it in order to attend.[8] More irregular timetables in the practice occurred only at the beginning and at the end of the working year. Many patients did not start their analyses on Freud's first working day in October but often came a few days or weeks later. Similarly, each year several patients stopped their sessions one or two weeks before Freud's summer vacation began.

Of the approximately 130 women and men who went to Freud for treatment and appeared in his patient record books between 1910 and 1920, a large majority were "genuine" patients; only about twenty were or became analysts. In this period Freud still mainly had a *regular analytic practice*, whereas later most of the analysands were colleagues who wanted to become analysts (F/W, p. 33; F/A, p. 481; RB 4, p. 170).

Selection of thirty-six analyses

Out of the approximately 130 analyses, I excluded all those that were entered on the first days of the record books, that is, from 1 October 1910, as they could have been ongoing treatments and I did not want to include fragments without knowing what part of the whole analysis they constituted. The only exception was if I could find evidence of an earlier begin of analysis from another documented source. I followed the same procedure for the other end of the ten-year period of the record books, that is, for those analyses that had hours entered up

---

[8] This is what the words "We buried him on 22 January" (F/Bi, p. 150) may have referred to.

to 31 December 1920, where we do not know whether or how long they may have continued. I have therefore only included analyses whose beginning and end are clearly demarcated in the record books and in other sources.

As mentioned above I then selected those analysands who had already been clearly and explicitly identified in the literature at some point. An additional requirement was convincing *verification* outside the patient record books that the analysis had actually taken place *at the time* for which it was recorded in the books. This was necessary in order to make sure that names had not been confused. That means that I have only chosen an analysis for this investigation if I knew from letters or other documents when it had taken place. If this was not possible, the analysis was considered "unverified" and was not included.[9]

To summarise the criteria for inclusion:

- The existence of the analysis must have already been included in a publication.
- The time period of the analysis (or the section of the analysis) must be verified by a second document apart from Freud's patient record books.
- The beginning and end of the analysis must fall within the period of the record books (October 1910 to December 1920); if this is not the case, the dates of the beginning and/or the end of the analysis must be verified by other documents.

These criteria were met by thirty-six men and women. I have divided them into two groups: One consists of seventeen analysands (five women, twelve men) who were "analysts". For practical reasons I included in this group anyone who had been a member of a psychoanalytic association, regardless of whether the membership began before, during or after the analysis with Freud.[10] The second group consists of

[9] That is why I have, for example, not included two short sections for "Vest" (no first names) that are recorded in Freud's patient record books. This could have been Anna von Vest, who had already been with Freud between 1903 and 1904 and who resumed treatment in 1925 (Goldmann, 1985), but it could just as well have been somebody else who happened to have the same name.

[10] There are two further names where it is not clear if they refer to the analyst of this name or to someone else who happened to have the same name; in a third case membership in a psychoanalytic association could not be confirmed with certainty. For these reasons these three cases were not included in the further investigation. I also excluded two analyses that were not yet completed by the end of December 1920, among them that of James Strachey.

nineteen "patients" (ten women, nine men), analysands who were not members of a psychoanalytic association at any point in their lives.

Of course these two groups do not constitute proper representative samples, neither for all the men and women Freud saw between 1910 and 1920 nor for all the patients he saw in all of his practice.[11] We have to therefore be cautious regarding conclusions on "the" patients and "the" way in which Freud worked.

I will first present the analyses of seventeen "analysts" in the chronological order in which they came to Freud. I will then discuss the duration and frequency of this group of analyses. In a further step I will describe the analyses of nineteen "patients". Afterwards the duration and frequency of the analyses of "patients" will be compared with the analyses of the "analysts". Observations on Freud's analyses of psychotic patients will be reported in an Appendix and conclude this work.

Seventeen "analysts" in analysis with Freud

The group of "analysts" consists of the following women and men: Jan van Emden, René Spitz, Arnold Stegmann, Emil Oberholzer, Ludwig Jekels, Eugenia Sokolnicka, Sándor Ferenczi, Erszébét Révész, Anton von Freund, István Hollós, Helene Deutsch, Margit Dubovitz, David Forsyth, Claud Dangar Daly, John Rickman, Kata Lévy, and Adolph Stern.[12]

Nine of the seventeen women and men were already members of a psychoanalytic society when they came to Freud: Stegmann, Oberholzer, Jekels, Sokolnicka, Ferenczi, Hollós, Deutsch, Forsyth, and Stern.

---

[11] How my selection may have distorted the results is hard to say. Treatments with a frequency of less than six hours a week, particularly those of one or two hours appear underrepresented. There are not any among the nineteen "patients" or seventeen "analysts", however they can definitely be found in the total group of 130 men and women.

[12] The analyses are mentioned *inter alia* in the following: van Emden's, Sokolnicka's and Spitz's analysis with Freud can be found in Mühlleitner (1992, pp. 84, 304, 311), that of Stegmann in Müller & Hermanns (2001, p. 23). The treatment of Oberholzer is discussed in the letters between Freud and Jung (F/Ju, p. 511), that of Hollós and Dubovitz in Freud and Ferenczi's correspondence (F/Fer 2, pp. 272, 344). The analyses of Jekels and Révész have been mentioned by the editors of the German (not the English) *Minutes of the Vienna Psychoanalytic Society* (Min 2, p. xviii, German edition; Min 1, p. xxiii, German edition). We know of the treatment of Daly and Rickman from the correspondence between Freud and Jones (F/Jo, pp. 364, 373) and that of Kata Lévy from Roazen's *How Freud Worked* (1995, pp. 143–165). Jones mentioned the analysis of Anton von Freund (1953–1957, vol. 2, p. 196). Freud himself published the fact that Forsyth and Ferenczi were his analysands (1933a, p. 48; 1933c, p. 228). Helene Deutsch (1973) and Adolph Stern (1922) themselves described their analysis with Freud.

Van Emden, von Freund, and (in all likelihood) Révész became members during their analyses. Spitz, Dubowitz, Daly, Rickman, and Lévy joined afterwards.

Seven analysts came from Hungary, whereas Holland, India, the USA, and Germany had one representative each, and Switzerland and Great Britain had two. Of those in the immediate Viennese circle, two went to Freud—Deutsch and Jekels.[13] There were more doctors (thirteen) than non-doctors (four). Most were around forty when they started their analysis, there was a small group of thirty-year-olds, and nobody was older than fifty.[14]

The knowledgeable reader will notice that a few names are missing, first and foremost that of Anna Freud who started a first series of sessions with her father in 1918.[15] Her analysis does not appear in the patient record books. Although it has been claimed that W. R. D. Fairbairn, Theodor Reik, and Karl Landauer were in analysis with Freud between 1910 and 1920, their names do not appear here either.

As far as Fairbairn is concerned, a "Färbern" turns up once in the *Minutes of the Vienna Psychoanalytic Society* but in contrast to Fallend's assumption (1995, p. 200) this was not the analyst W. R. D. Fairbairn.[16]

---

[13] Jekels had moved to Vienna in 1911. Mühlleitner und Reichmayr state that until 1938, twenty-two members of the Vienna Psychoanalytic Society had had an analysis with Freud (1997, p. 1073). Among them there were some residents of Vienna, including Jekels and Deutsch, but the number is certainly small. Of the most important students only Ferenczi went to Freud. In 1914 Jones went to Ferenczi for a short time; Jung probably underwent analysis with Moltzer (Falzeder, 2000, p. 52); Abraham was not with anyone in analysis.

[14] Age when starting analysis: Spitz: 24; Révész, Rickman, and Oberholzer: 29; Sokolnicka: 30; Dubowitz: 31; Deutsch: 34; Daly: 36; Levy: 37; v. Freund: 38; Stegmann: 39; Ferenczi and Stern: 41; Forsyth: 42; Emden: 43; Jekels: 45; Hollós: 46.

[15] According to Young-Bruehl, the first section took almost four years and was conducted with a six-hour frequency in the autumn of 1918 (1988, pp. 103–139). Rothe and Weber note that the analysis had been terminated in November 1921 (Andreas-Salomé & A. Freud, 2001, pp. 708, 750).

[16] Fallend suspected that the participant in the meeting of the Vienna Psychoanalytic Society of 2 June 1920 called "Faerbern" actually was the English analyst W. R. D. Fairbairn and that this Fairbairn had also received a confirmation from Freud that he had given him thirty-five hours of analysis (1995, pp. 200, 376). My research, however, has concluded that the certificate was issued to a "Dr. R. Fairbairn". There is also an invoice from Freud for "R. Fairbairn" and Freud's address book includes an entry for a "R. C. Fairbairn" (personal communication from Christfried Tögel). That means that a "W. R. D." does not turn up anywhere, whereas a "R. Fairbairn" turns up three times. It is an equally persuasive counter-argument that none of the biographers of W. R. D. Fairbairn, including his daughter's biography (Scharff & Birtles, 1997; Sutherland, 1989), makes any mention of an analysis with Freud, although there would hardly be reason to conceal it.

From what we know it was not until around 1930 that Reik was in analysis with Freud, and not in 1913 (see Leitner, 2001, p. 268).[17] And finally, in contradiction to what Brecht, Friedrich, Hermanns, Kaminer, and Juelich (1985, p. 56) and Rothe (1991, p. 15) wrote, Landauer either did not have regular analysis with Freud or it took place after December 1920.

Questions regarding Freud's analyses of "analysts"

My evaluation of the patient record books will focus on the question of the *length and frequency* of the analyses. This is not a purely historical question but has implications for our work today. Our own experience is not enough to modify or correct our work; we must also actively concern ourselves with history and the circumstances and considerations that make us work differently today. Deliberations on the history of psychoanalysis will not, of course, tell us what to do but they will help us to see more clearly how and why analytic practice has changed over the course of time and what unintended developments may have ensued. In a first step we need to establish how Freud worked. Then we will be better equipped to look at later developments and to assess whether we find them desirable and wish to support them.

I was also interested in the *motives* of "analysts" in being analysed by Freud in the pre-institutional phase of psychoanalysis when there was no training analysis in the present-day sense of the word. Freud had initially recommended self-analysis (1910a, p. 32). It was necessary in order to deal with "counter-transference":

> We [...] consequently require that he [the doctor] shall begin his activity with a self-analysis and continually carry it deeper while he is making his observations on his patients. Anyone who fails to produce results in a self-analysis of this kind may at

[17] Reik wrote (1956, p. 214) that one summer when he was taking a holiday from Berlin in Vienna, he called on Freud at his holiday residence outside Vienna and had several sessions with him. He reported his symptoms of fear to Freud and compared these with his experiences at the front in World War I (ibid., p. 213). This is one of several reasons why the analysis must have taken place after 1918. Since in April 1928 he decided to move back to Berlin, which he then proceeded to do (F/E, p. 599), the sessions with Freud would probably have been during a vacation in 1928 or during a later vacation.

> once give up any idea of being able to treat patients by analysis. (Freud, 1910d, p. 144)

Two years later, in "Recommendations to Physicians Practising Psychoanalysis" (1912e), Freud modified this advice. Self-analysis was "enough for many people, but not for everyone who wishes to learn analysis" (ibid., p. 116). It was necessary that "everyone who wishes to carry out analyses on other people shall first himself undergo an analysis by someone with expert knowledge" (ibid.). In this context Freud did not yet speak of "training analysis" but it is the first passage where he recommended the analysis of the analyst *by someone else*. This can also be seen in a remark to Oberholzer who at that time wanted to be treated by Freud. On 1 March 1912 Freud wrote to him that he would "soon" publish the requirement that every analyst needed to be analysed (Schröter, 2010, p. 104). The publication he was referring to was clearly the "Recommendations" that appeared in June 1912.

In "Recommendations" Freud had said that self-analysis may suffice for some people but not for all, and these individuals will need an analysis by someone else. It is therefore not "surprising" and "contradictory", as Leitner (2001, p. 304) and Falzeder (2000, p. 40) seem to think that in 1914 Freud wrote that for a "good dreamer and not too abnormal" a person self-analysis is enough (1914d, p. 20) and a little later in the *Lectures* recommended, as he had done previously, "studying one's own person", and added that one "advances much further if one is analysed oneself by a practised analyst" (1916–1917, p. 19). Freud was consistently of the opinion, at least in the years between 1910 and 1920, that self-analysis was sufficient for some, but not for others.[18] We know that when Bernfeld wanted to start working with patients in 1921, Freud told him to go ahead and not wait until he was first analysed (Bernfeld, 1962, p. 463).[19] This example is a (late) illustration that at this time Freud still regarded self-analysis as well as analysis by someone else ("Fremdanalyse") as appropriate preparations for

---

[18] Leitner (2001) has many interesting references to comments that Freud's disciples made on the significance of one's own analysis by someone else (see, for example, p. 304).

[19] Bernfeld was probably the last analyst of the International Psychoanalytic Association who entered into practice so informally.

practical analytical work.[20] In the last decade of his life, however, he emphasised the limitations of *both* methods in gaining self-knowledge (Freud, 1937c).

In the years between 1910 and 1920 Freud's recommendations had no binding character, and even a motion that Hermann Nunberg put forward at the congress in Budapest in 1918 was shelved.[21] Nevertheless, after 1920 an obligatory training analysis quickly became the rule, without any centralised decision having been made. At the congress in Bad Homburg in 1925 it was already taken for granted (Korr, 1925, p. 515). Up until 1920, however it was still the case that the future analyst *could* undergo an analysis but did not *need* to. Membership in a psychoanalytic society at that time was linked to another criterion, namely evidence of an interest in psychoanalysis that usually had to be substantiated by a lecture. Whether the member had undergone

---

[20] The idea of an *obligatory* training analysis seems to have come from Jung not Freud, a fact that has been pointed out recently (Leitner, 2001, p. 213; Shamdasani, 2002, p. 9; Roazen, 2002, p. 73; Falzeder, 2004, pp. 144, 153). Freud had in fact written: "I count it as one of the many merits of the Zurich school of analysis that they have laid increased emphasis on this requirement, and have embodied it in the demand that everyone who wishes to carry out analysis on other people shall first himself undergo an analysis by someone with expert knowledge" (Freud, 1912e, p. 116). It has so far remained unclear where this requirement of the Zurich School was set down. Jung's *Fordham Lectures* of autumn 1912 are out of the question because they were conceived in the spring of 1912, held in September 1912 and not published until 1913 in German (1913, p. 414), and in English in 1914 (Jung, 1913–1915, p. 429). Was Freud referring to the "lay association" founded in Zurich in February 1912 whose members had to be analysed before they could join (F/Ju, p. 487; Korr, 1912, p. 480; Korr, 1913, p. 635)? It is clear that the concept of an obligatory training analysis was part of the tension and the split between Freud and Jung. It was among others things part of accusing each other of being neurotic and therefore requiring more analysis (F/Ju, p. 509). For more deliberations on the context in which training analysis emerged see Falzeder (2000; 2004).

[21] The report on the general assembly in Budapest said: "On Dr Nunberg's motion regarding the modalities of accepting new members into the International Psychoanalytic Association or their local group no decisions will be made for the time being" (Korr, 1919, p. 56). This event has often been considered the birth of training analysis. Nunberg himself reported that once during a meeting of the Viennese group he had said, "that every analyst ought to be analysed" (1969, p. 35). Later the following happened at the Budapest Congress: "Freud suddenly announced that I had an important statement to make. Taken by surprise, I had to improvise, and made the motion that every analyst be analysed. This was opposed by Rank and Tausk [...]. It was only in 1926, [...] that this motion was carried. It was then that the training analysis was introduced" (ibid.)—a date (1926) given by Nunberg and certainly based on a distortion of memory.

analysis was beside the point.[22] This is why I will call the analyses that I describe in the following pages "learning analyses" and not "training analyses".

What moved these men and women to go to Freud—the wish to be healed or the wish to learn analysis or both? I will explore this as well as the kind of relationship Freud maintained with his analysands apart from the medical-analytical one. On the whole I will disregard the biographies of the analysands, some of whom had important functions in the psychoanalytic movement, and their achievements as psychoanalytic authors.[23]

The analyses will now be presented in the order in which they began.[24]

Jan van Emden

Freud had met Jan von Emden (1868–1950) in Holland and on 12 May 1911 he wrote to Jung: "In a few days I am expecting the visit of a splendid colleague, Dr. van Emden" (F/Ju, p. 422). From Monday 15 May to Saturday 8 July *two* hours per day are entered into Freud's record books for van Emden. Since Freud worked six days a week, this meant an analysis of twelve hours per week.

Freud was proud of his Dutch student "who is teaching himself PsA and will then practise it on patients" (F/Fer 1, p. 286). "Things seem to be stirring in Holland", he wrote to Ferenczi. Two months later Freud mentioned his new student to Ferenczi again: van Emden was becoming very "attached" to psychoanalysis and wanted to make it "his life's calling"; he and his wife would accompany Freud on his vacation in Karlsbad, to receive "an hour [...] on an afternoon walk" (ibid., p. 294). And this is exactly what happened as Freud then reported from Karlsbad: "Dr. van Emden is continuing his course in PsA with me" (F/Ju, p. 434). Based on Freud's proposal (Min 3, p. 281) van Emden was elected a member of the Vienna Psychoanalytic Society in October 1911 after the first section of his analysis (May–July 1911). Van Emden returned to Vienna

[22] Anna Freud's wording in her appreciation of Nunberg was even more radical. She wrote about Nunberg: "He had joined the VPS in 1914, at a time when members were not 'admitted', as they are today, but themselves decided to join on the basis of their previous publications and scientific convictions" (1969, p. 135).

[23] For more biographical information on those analysts who were members of the Vienna Psychoanalytic Society see Mühlleitner (1992).

[24] More detailed information about the course of the analyses can be found in May (2006b, Appendix, German edition).

the following three summers. In 1912 and 1913 Freud usually worked with him six hours per week, in 1914 it was mostly twelve hours. Hours during Freud's vacation take place again one last time in 1912 (F/Fer 1, pp. 387, 395, 403). In 1913 Freud cancelled the vacation sessions saying that as "pleasant company as they [the Emdens] are", he needed to be "analysis-free" during his vacation (F/Fer 1, p. 499).

The hours Freud gave in Karlsbad in 1911 and 1912 have not been noted in his record books; perhaps he did not put them on his bill. For my purposes these vacation sessions are of course a problem because they suggest the possibility that similar sessions of this kind may have take place. After looking into this quite carefully I can say with some confidence that between 1910 and 1920 of the group of seventeen analysands only van Emden and Kata Lévy received hours from Freud during his vacations that were not noted in his record book. We can, of course, not be completely certain on this point but on the whole Freud was happy to write quite openly about such things in his letters.

Freud entered a total of 245 hours for van Emden in his record book. This makes this analysis the longest that Freud carried out with a colleague and disciple between 1910 and 1920, even if the instructive afternoon walks in Karlsbad are not included. Freud quite often worked in sections, that is, in separate periods of analysis. In 1924, for example, Emden was hoping for another section—"an hour of analysis every day for four weeks"—which, however, he did not receive because Freud lacked the time.

The little we know about van Emden's analysis suggests that it was primarily, at least initially, intended to serve learning and teaching purposes. We could therefore call it an early "learning analysis". Since Freud stresses the element of "teaching" in van Emden's analysis we can assume that it will have contained decidedly didactic elements.

Freud's readiness to work in sections is particularly striking in Emden's analysis. This may have been an arrangement that was convenient for Freud personally; in addition it met the external requirements of his non-Viennese clients. It is likely that van Emden and most other analysands coming to Vienna were not able to take much time off from their professional duties so that a fractionated analysis was the only feasible option for therapy or learning. Another feature that van Emden's analysis shares with some of Freud's other cases, is the close friendship that developed between the Freuds and the van Emdens during the analysis and continued for years afterwards. It is also quite typical that van

Emden took part in *all* the meetings of the Vienna Psychoanalytic Society during his analysis as well as translating Freud's Clark Lectures (1910a) into Dutch.[25] Later (1917) he was a founding member, and for many years the chair, of the Dutch Psychoanalytic Society (F/Ju, p. 350).

René Spitz

After the record of van Emden's long analysis we can no longer say that it was Spitz who had the first "learning analysis" with Freud (as, for example, Leitner, 2001, p. 161).[26] In the period between 1910 and 1920 Spitz was the *second* future analyst who approached Freud for an analysis. On 2 October 1911 Ferenczi announced the visit of the twenty-four-year-old doctor René Spitz (1887–1974) from Budapest who requested to be reserved "one hour a day" (F/Fer 1, p. 301). Freud's record book shows that the first session of "Dr Spitz" took place soon after that, on Tuesday 10 October; the treatment initially was six hours per week. Four weeks later Freud wrote to Ferenczi: "Dr. Spitz made a bit of a play of grandiosity and was penalized for it by being deprived of three hours, and since then he seems to want to take it more seriously [...] Still, he is quite nice" (Ibid., p. 317). The record book shows that as of 20 November, Spitz only received two to three hours per week. The analysis ended on 20 December. According to Freud's patient record book it did not last "about one year", as Spitz later said, but a little more than two months, from October to December 1911; it comprised forty-six hours.[27]

Compared to van Emden's analysis, that of Spitz was very short and with far fewer hours per week. We do not know, however, if it was prematurely terminated or had always been planned to only last that long. The few indications we have suggest it was a "learning analysis". In a later

---

[25] This statement can of course only refer to those evenings for which attendance lists are available. According to these lists, van Emden had taken part in a Vienna Psychoanalytic Society meeting on 31 May 1911 as well as in the "get-together" on 28 June 1911 (Min 3, p. 266; only in the German edition) before he became a member. In the following years he attended the meetings in April and May 1912 as well as in May and June 1914.

[26] Regarding the analyses of doctors that Freud carried out before 1910, see Falzeder (2000, 2004).

[27] In an interview (1965) Spitz said that he had been in analysis with Freud in 1910/1911 (Archives of Columbia University New York). It can, however, be excluded that he began his analysis in 1910 because it was not until August 1911 that Ferenczi asked Freud if he could take Spitz (F/Fer 1, p. 300).

oral history interview[28] Spitz said that, before he called on Freud, he had already carried out analyses and had among others treated a schizophrenic patient. He had wanted to go to Freud in order to learn how to analyse. An obituary on Spitz echoed this and noted that he saw himself as the first training analysand "since a chief motive, in addition to his personal reasons for seeking analysis, was to learn how to be a psychoanalyst" (Steele, 1975, p. 3).[29] That it was an analysis that not only served learning purposes but, as it developed, also touched on Spitz's problems can be seen in Freud's comment a few weeks after the analysis began: "Dr. Spitz is very interesting; the window dressing is over, and he is behaving quite properly neurotic, with strong resistances" (F/Fer 1, p. 309).

An interesting aspect of this analysis is Freud's reduction of Spitz's hours. Apparently Freud had, at least at this time and in this case, taken this measure for therapeutic purposes. However the analysis of low frequency—in Freud's work a frequency of less than six hours—is, as can be seen later, not just a deviation from the norm, but a type of its own.

Spitz is one of the few analysands of the group of "analysts" who did not take part in meetings of the Vienna Psychoanalytic Society during his analysis. The most likely reason was that he was not a member and apparently did not want to attend as a guest. It was not until fifteen years later (1926) that he became a member.

Arnold Stegmann

Stegmann (1872–1914) has become part of psychoanalytical history because Freud mentioned him as a researcher in the case of Schreber (1911c, pp. 6, 46). In November 1911 he came to Vienna from Dresden together with his wife. Stegmann had been a member of the Berlin Psychoanalytic Society since 1910—in 1912 his wife Margarete also joined the group—and had already published several psychoanalytical

[28] See previous note.

[29] In the interview Spitz reports that Ferenczi told him that Freud would not take him because he was not ill enough; Freud would only treat people who were ill. This is perhaps why Freud wrote to Ferenczi, after he had received the inquiry regarding Spitz: "If Dr. Spitz is to be taken seriously, I am ready. But that is a condition for treating him; otherwise it would be too unpleasant to take on a physician as a patient. Since you recommend him warmly, it certainly seems to be in order" (F/Fer 1, p. 300). I see Freud's comment on it being "unpleasant" as meaning that it would be embarrassing to treat a doctor because it implied that the doctor had neurotic problems (see on this question Leitner, 2001, p. 161).

papers before he began his analysis with Freud.[30] He was the only analyst from Germany who came to Vienna to be treated by Freud in the period from 1910 to 1920. Freud's patient record book indicates that starting on Monday 20 November, "Stegmann" came for analysis for exactly four weeks and had one hour daily. That makes his analysis one of the shortest in our sample (a total of twenty-four hours).

Unfortunately there are only two comments regarding Stegmann's motivation for seeking analysis, neither of them from him and both dating from *after* his analysis. In March 1912 Freud described the situation with Stegmann as follows: "First he married, then he came to me, then he told himself that the reverse would have been more rational" (F/Ju, p. 495). In April of that year Freud spoke to Ferenczi about the "miserable course" of the Stegmanns' marriage, adding that "Stegmann has acted unbelievably crazy and counted on something quite unfulfillable" (F/Fer 1, p. 371). From a letter to Abraham in 1913 we learn that the Stegmanns divorced (F/A, p. 185). It seems likely that Stegmann went to Freud in order to deal with problems connected to his marriage. There is no indication that it may have been a learning analysis, but of course this possibility cannot be excluded.

During his analysis Stegmann and his wife took part as guests in all meetings of the Vienna Psychoanalytic Society (Min 3, p. 320). It is not clear why he withdrew his membership from the Berlin group in 1912, soon after his analysis, whereas his wife joined the group at this time. Stegmann fell in World War I.

Emil Oberholzer

Emil Oberholzer (1883–1958) joined the Zurich group in 1911 and in 1919 co-founded the Swiss Psychoanalytic Association, whose chair he remained for many years. His analysis had a format similar to Stegmann's and very likely was mainly for therapeutic purposes. Freud wrote to him on 1 March 1912: "I certainly approve of your plan, and will myself, in a publication, endorse that each analyst should have undergone an analysis himself. So if you think that you are in need of my help, I will be only too happy to give it to you" (Schröter, 2010, p. 104). Seeking analysis was "nothing to be ashamed of among ourselves" (ibid., p. 105). If need be, he would interrupt the sessions of another

[30] On this and other biographical details, see Müller and Hermanns (2001).

patient to make hours available to Oberholzer. At the same time, Freud said that he was "in the embarrassing situation that I have to ask for a fee also from colleagues" and could therefore not treat Oberholzer free of charge, a reminder of the custom that doctors did not request a fee when they treated colleagues (ibid.).[31]

On 30 May 1912 the patient is to arrive shortly: "on Monday I am expecting Oberholzer [...] for treatment" (F/Fer 1, p. 377) and on the Monday in question the first hour with "Oberholzer" is entered in Freud's patient record book. For four-and-a-half weeks Oberholzer had one hour every day (twenty-six hours altogether). The analysis ended immediately before Freud's summer vacation began on 3 July.[32] Freud considered this length insufficient, as he wrote to the analysand's fiancée a few weeks after the analysis had started: her husband-to-be had "very serious disturbances" and "5 weeks are unfortunately not sufficient a time to bring about a change" (Schröter, 2010, p. 106). He made similar comments to Jung: "Oberholzer has come to me for analysis, unfortunately a very abbreviated one" (F/Ju, p. 511). It becomes clear here that Freud considered a treatment of five weeks too short but nevertheless carried it out.

As with Stegmann none of the published sources on Oberholzer mentions learning as the motivation for his analysis. I therefore assume that it was primarily therapy ("Kur") whereas Falzeder believes that Oberholzer was looking for the "experience of a proper 'training' analysis" (Falzeder, 2000, p. 52). I do think that in those years the term "Kur" that Freud frequently chose was increasingly being used for a therapeutic analysis as opposed to analysis whose prime purpose was instruction in the psychoanalytical method.

The forthcoming publication that Freud referred to in his letter to Oberholzer was, as already mentioned, the paper "Recommendations to Physicians" (Freud, 1912e). The analyses of van Emden, Spitz, and/or Stegmann may have contributed to Freud's modifying his opinion on the prerequisites for the work of an analyst and he was now recommending analysis by someone else.

---

[31] This may also have been the background to Freud's previously quoted remark about the impending analysis of Spitz that it was "unpleasant" for him to "take on a physician as a patient".

[32] During Oberholzer's analysis no meetings of the Viennese group took place (F/Fer 1, p. 377; Min 4, p. 102) so the question of his participation is irrelevant.

Ludwig Jekels

From 1909 onwards Ludwig Jekels (1867–1954) was a guest and as of April 1910 a member of the Vienna Psychoanalytic Society. In 1908, if not before, he was in personal and increasingly cordial contact with Freud. In 1910, some members of the Freud family spent a few holiday weeks in his home (Freud & Bernays, 2005, p. 255). Czarnecki reports that in 1912 Jekels sold his sanatorium in Bistrai in what was then Silesia, moved to Vienna in the autumn, and then started analysis with Freud (2004, p. 24).[33] This corresponds to Freud's patient record books where the entries for "Jekels" begin on Tuesday, 15 October 1912.[34]

Jekels's analysis lasted for exactly one "season", that is, from October 1912 to July 1913. The frequency varied but was usually five hours, from Monday to Friday so that Jekels had an extra day to his weekend (175 hours in total). We do not know why he underwent analysis and for the time being we have to make do with the comment that he had gone to Freud "initially for treatment reasons" (Mühlleitner, 1992, p. 170).[35] It lasted nine months and was the longest analysis so far in our group of "analysts" (175 hours altogether).

Before his analysis, Jekels had translated the *Five Lectures* (Freud, 1910a) and *The Psychopathology of Everyday Life* (Freud, 1901b) into Polish, written an introductory text to the theories of Freud, and been actively engaged in various ways on behalf of psychoanalysis in Poland.[36] During his analysis he also regularly took part in the meetings of the Vienna Psychoanalytic Society as had van Emden and Stegmann.

---

[33] According to Czarnecki he was registered in Vienna as of 2 November 1912. In the minutes of the Vienna Psychoanalytic Society, the list of members of 9 October 1912 records him as already living in Vienna (Min 4, p. 97; only in the German edition of the *Minutes*).

[34] Jekels may already have been in analysis with Freud in 1908 because Czarnecki referred to a two-month stay in Vienna that was registered with the authorities (2004, p. 24). Wittenberger and Tögel also mention an analysis in 1908 (RB 1, p. 236).

[35] Colleagues who had known him longer (for instance Bergler, 1955) considered Jekels to be depressive. During his analysis he published various small items in the *Internationale Zeitschrift für Psychoanalyse* of which one referring to a doctor may have been about himself (Jekels, 1913a). Freud included it in the fifth edition of *The Psychopathology of Everyday Life* (1901b, pp. 188–191). In the parapraxis described there, a doctor tragically lost his wife and subsequently developed a neurosis and later underwent treatment. This corresponds with Mühlleitner's report that Jekels' wife committed suicide in 1905 (1992, p. 170; ditto Czarnecki, 2004, p. 23).

[36] He translated Freud's *Psychopathology* together with Helena Ivanka; it was published in 1912. For more on his publications and other activities, see Czarnecki (2004).

Eugenia Sokolnicka

The analysis of Eugenia Sokolnicka (1884–1934) is dealt with extensively in the correspondence between Freud and Ferenczi. From it we know that Sokolnicka had been in analysis with Freud before she went to Ferenczi in 1920 in order to "complete" her analysis with him (F/Fer 3, p. 8; cf., Mühlleitner, 1992, p. 304). Now we have precise data: the analysis with Freud began on 19 March 1914, lasted for not quite three months and, like most of the treatments described so far, it was six hours per week (a total of sixty-eight hours).

When Sokolnicka came to Freud at the age of thirty, she was already a member of the Zurich Psychoanalytic Society.[37] We do not know her reasons for undergoing analysis. Ferenczi later speaks of a "character analysis" (F/Fer 3, p. 48, see also p. 23), and his detailed descriptions of Sokolnicka's treatment show that her analysis with Freud had had an unhappy end. It seems that it was discontinued by Freud because, as Sokolnicka phrased it, he did not "like to accept money from poor people" (ibid., p. 23). Another time she was harsher in describing what she assumed was the reason: Freud had not continued her treatment "because of inability to pay" (ibid., p. 49).[38] In his letters to Ferenczi after the analysis, Freud made several disparaging remarks about Sokolnicka, but considered her to be a gifted analyst (ibid., p. 29); Ferenczi's comments were milder and kinder (e.g., ibid., pp. 48–50).

During her analysis with Freud Sokolnicka regularly took part in meetings of the Viennese group as a guest (from 8 April to 3 June). She became a member in Vienna in 1916, and was an active supporter of psychoanalysis in Poland. She went to Paris after her treatment with Ferenczi where she was the only analyst for a long time and co-founded the Paris group. In 1934 she committed suicide.

Sándor Ferenczi

As is generally known, for a long time Ferenczi (1873–1933) tried to undergo an analysis with Freud, but to no avail.[39] His first attempt was a letter in December 1912: "I am also a case in need of treatment—but

---

[37] See Korr, 1912, p. 549.

[38] According to Ferenczi, after her analysis had been discontinued she tried to commit suicide (F/Fer 3, p. 49; see also Leitner, 2001, p. 389).

[39] From the extensive literature on Ferenczi's analysis see, for instance, Dupont (1994), Hoffer (1996), and Falzeder (1996).

there has been undeniable progress to the extent that I am conscious of that fact" (F/Fer 1, p. 450). This was written in response to Jung, whom Ferenczi accused of demanding that analysts be analysed, but not being able to tolerate this himself. When he wrote to Freud in December 1912, Ferenczi acknowledged: "It was and is my intention, to be granted time (hours), to go into analysis with you—perhaps two weeks (maybe three), for now" (Ibid.). A little later he talked of a whole month, whereupon Freud answered that he feared "the danger of personal estrangement" (ibid., p. 482), and that four or six weeks "would be much too insufficient" (ibid., p. 481). It was not until the following year (1914) that they started working together. After World War I had begun, Ferenczi was able to take four weeks off and Freud then agreed to a very short analysis—a decision that was possibly facilitated by the dwindling of Ferenczi's practice to two patients (F/Fer 2, p. 11).[40]

The general course of Ferenczi's analysis is on the whole already well known: three sections that each lasted between two and four weeks. This is what we find in Freud's patient record books and we can correct a few details. In the first two sections Ferenczi had two hours daily, as has always been assumed. Since the record books also contain entries for Sunday, the first section that began in October 1914 would have consisted of an analysis of fourteen hours per week.[41] As we know, Ferenczi was called up for military service and the analysis had to be broken off after three-and-a-half weeks, a turn of events that he found very upsetting (F/Fer 2, p. 39). Nevertheless he emphasised the therapeutic effect of the treatment: "Despite its incompleteness, I note daily it was nonetheless able to change my neurotic attitude, which has been evident for a number of years" (Ibid., p. 40).

The second, three-week section did not take place until two years later (1916). Now Ferenczi received thirteen hours per week since an additional hour took place on Sunday. After this section came to an end as previously agreed, Ferenczi thought he had become a person "who

---

[40] After the first section, Freud wrote: "if war hadn't come, you wouldn't have had any reason to spend your vacation in Vienna and I might have had reservations about taking you on" (F/Fer 2, p. 33).

[41] Dupont (1994) claims the analysis began on 26 September. Conversely, we find that Ferenczi's letters and telegrams indicate that he wanted to begin the analysis on Wednesday 30 September, but he missed his train, so that the first session did not occur until 1 October (F/Fer 2, pp. 18–19). This coincides with the entries in Freud's patient record books.

is less interesting, but more normal" (ibid., p. 132). However, he perceived the termination of the "doctor-patient relations" as a "shock" (ibid., p. 133). Two weeks later he told Freud that he was still suffering from various symptoms and would like to have another two weeks to devote "to terminating or completing the treatment" (ibid., p. 135). This suggestion met with Freud's "full approval" (ibid., p. 137).

Initially Ferenczi wanted to have the third section during Freud's vacation and travelling time (ibid., p. 130), but then abandoned the plan, presumably after Freud's objections. On 15 September he wrote, "I ask you to reserve three hours per day (1 1/2 +1 1/2 or 1+2) for me. I don't dare to ask for four" (F/Fer 2, p. 140). Freud fulfilled his wish. In the record books three hours daily (except for Sunday) are entered for this third section that lasted from 29 September to 13 October. At this time, apart from Ferenczi, Freud had only one regular analysand (in addition to one or two patients who only rarely appeared).

Ferenczi's analysis with its thirteen to eighteen hours per week was special. No other analysand who was with Freud between 1910 and 1920 received a denser analysis. The analysis however was very short in duration and only lasted a total of eight-and-a-half weeks; the total number of hours (131) is roughly the average in our seventeen-person sample.

For Ferenczi the wish for therapy prevailed and it was not slaked by the three sections. He appeared to have wanted a continuation and went through "tormenting times" with a flare-up of psychic and somatic symptoms (F/Fer 2, p. 151). Freud wrote "You know that I consider your attempt at analysis finished—finished, not terminated, but rather broken off because of unfavourable circumstances" (Ibid., p. 153). He more or less advised against continuing; it would only serve resistance. As we know from their correspondence, Ferenczi continued to send detailed self-analytical notes to Freud but did not go back to analysis with him; later he went to Groddeck.

Ferenczi had taught himself analysis (after a short introduction with Jung) and had already been working as an analyst for several years before he went to Freud for treatment. He was, as we know, not only a member of the Vienna Psychoanalytic Society (since 1908) but also headed the group that he had founded in Budapest. In his letters to Freud there is never any mention of a lack of confidence in his ability to analyse. There was much mention, however, of his somatic and psychic complaints and of standstill in his self-analysis. For this reason Ferenczi's analysis is to be regarded more as a "therapeutic" than a learning analysis.

Erszébét Révész

In November 1916, immediately after the last section with Freud had come to an end, Ferenczi announced the arrival of the twenty-nine-year-old Erszébét Révész (1887–1923):

> A very respectable and apparently clever physician, Fraeulein Dr. Révész [...] would like—in order to learn analysis—to be analysed by you herself (two hours a week). She actually came to me with the request (she wanted to do it here in Budapest, not until after the war). But I motivated her to go to you and ask you, if possible, to fulfil her request. She seems worth it to me." (F/Fer 2, p. 159)

Starting in December 1916 the name "Revesz" appears in Freud's record books. The treatment, consisting mainly of three hours per week, was continued until the end of June 1917. After the summer break in 1917 "Revesz" no longer appears among the patient names and does not turn up again until March 1918. That the person in question was actually Erszébét Révész can be deduced from Freud's comment of 17 March 1918: "I was able to take on Révész again, she should already serve you as an assistant in the autumn" (F/Fer 2, p. 273). We do not know why Révész interrupted the analysis for a year. It may have been the case that Freud treated another patient and had her wait until hours were available again (this would fit the entries in his record book). After the interruption, Révész continued the analysis until June 1918. Again she received three hours per week.

It is surprising that, of all the analyses, this one was consistently three hours per week, although its declared purpose was learning the psychoanalytic treatment method because almost all the other analyses of the seventeen members of psychoanalytic societies were mostly six hours. We will later encounter this phenomenon a second time. Perhaps Révész was a "slight case" because in 1913 in a paper on the practicalities of treatment Freud wrote that for such cases three hours were sufficient (1913c, p. 127).[42] In spite of the consistently low frequency,

---

[42] Freud continues: "Any restrictions of time beyond this bring no advantage either to the doctor or the patient; and at the beginning of an analysis they are quite out of the question. Even short interruptions have a slightly obscuring effect on the work. We used to speak jokingly of the 'Monday crust' when we began work again after the rest on Sunday. When the hours of work are less frequent, there is a risk of not being able to keep pace with the patient's real life and of the treatment losing contact with the present and being forced into by-paths" (1913c, p. 127).

Révész's analysis was not particularly short. It comprised 128 hours and initially lasted more than six-and-a-half months, and then in the second section more than three-and-a-half months.

Freud had a high opinion of Révész's analytical abilities (F/Fer 2, p. 325) and that is probably why he called her a future "assistant" of Ferenczi. The term "assistant" turns up several times in Freud's correspondence at the time and, analogous to the way this was used at universities and hospitals, it referred to younger analysts who were considered to be suited to the treatment of patients. This underlines the learning aspect of Révész's analysis.

Like many of the analysands discussed here Révész frequently took part as a guest at the meetings of the Vienna Psychoanalytic Society during her treatment by Freud. Starting in April 1918 she was registered as a regular member.[43] It is hard to elucidate when she joined the Hungarian Psychoanalytic Society, so we do not know whether she already was a member when she called on Freud; at any rate in December 1918 she appeared as a member of this group.[44] She seemed to have a well-frequented practice (F/Fer 2, p. 331); among others she had Sándor Radó in analysis, whom she later married. Révész went to Ferenczi for a second analysis and died following surgery in 1923.

Anton von Freund

Freud had known Anton von Freund (1880–1920) since 1915 when his wife came for treatment (F/Fer 2, p. 95). Freund was the co-owner of a brewery in Budapest, had a doctorate in philosophy, and was the first non-physician in the group of seventeen. Freud was drawn to him, and later became very fond of him (see, e.g., ibid., pp. 207, 367; Freud, 1920c).

Anton von Freund required surgery because of cancer and was operated on in 1917. In February 1918 he was taken to Vienna because of a transient psychotic state. Freud's diagnosis was post-operative

---

[43] Révész was present at all meetings of the Vienna Psychoanalytic Society between 7 March and 6 June 1917 and then again starting on 12 December 1917. On 17 April 1918 she is "listed without any information on her election", as the editor of the *Minutes* commented (Min 4, p. 311; only in the German edition of the *Minutes*). I suspect that Révész became a member after a presentation that she had given in January 1918 because a similar procedure had been carried out with Helene Deutsch, who had given a presentation the same evening and was subsequently elected a member (ibid., p. 308; only in the German edition of the *Minutes*).

[44] She may have been elected in March 1918 (Korr, 1919, p. 59).

psychosis and the next day, Wednesday 20 February, he began von Freund's treatment (ibid., pp. 269, 272).[45] After two weeks Freud considered the psychotic symptoms to have faded and he began a "regular analysis" (ibid.). In April he wrote that his analysand "will be cured of his excursion into psychosis" and had become "a half-way analysed neurotic" (ibid., p. 341, see Appendix).[46] At the end of June, after four months of analysis, von Freund returned to Budapest and resumed work at his firm.

This first period of analysis is notable because of its high and changing frequency. Initially von Freund had two hours a day; after about two weeks, in no particular order, one-hour days alternated with two-hour days. Towards the end of this period von Freund again received two hours daily. There is no indication of the reasons for this change in frequency.

At the end of September 1918, the International Psychoanalytic Congress took place in Budapest and von Freund played an instrumental part in organising it. Ferenczi, who at that time was briefly president of the International Psychoanalytic Association, appointed von Freund as his secretary. Before the congress Freud and Anna spent part of their vacation in a house that belonged to the family of his patient (F/Fer 2, p. 289). During this time Freud wrote to Abraham:

> Materially we shall be strong, we shall be able to maintain and expand our journals and exert an influence, and there will be an end to the begging we have had to do heretofore. The man whom we shall have to thank for this is not merely a wealthy man, but a man of sterling worth and high intellectual gifts, who is greatly interested in analysis; he is in fact the sort of person whom one would have to invent if he did not already exist. (F/A, p. 381)

Here Freud refers to the foundation that von Freund was planning on behalf of psychoanalysis. His sponsorship testified to his interest in

---

[45] In February 1918 his wife gave birth to a son; subsequently v. Freund's crisis developed (F/Fer 2, p. 265).

[46] The letter that contains this is dated 1 April 1919 (F/Fer 2, p. 341). I suspect that the year is not correct because of the first sentence in which Freud wrote: "Easter Monday is so peaceful" (ibid.). In 1919 Easter Monday was not on 1 April, but it was in 1918! Second, in this letter Freud described v. Freund's condition but v. Freund was not in Vienna in April 1919 (but was in April 1918). Therefore I conclude that the letter has to be dated 1 April 1918.

psychoanalysis and would have played a role in his admission into the Viennese group. It is not possible to elucidate when exactly von Freund became a member. What we do know with certainty is that his name was included in the list of members of the Hungarian Psychoanalytic Society in 1918 (Korr, 1919, p. 53).[47]

In the same year (1918), on Christmas Day, von Freund arrived in Vienna for the second period of analysis. We do not know what the immediate reason for this may have been. Again his treatment consisted of twelve to thirteen hours per week. Whether it ended in February or in March is not quite clear.[48]

After he returned to Hungary and during the Hungarian Soviet Republic, von Freund lectured and was involved in the organisation of psychoanalytic training in Budapest and treated at least one patient (F/Fer 2, pp. 359, 361). His health deteriorated and in June 1919 metastases were diagnosed. In the autumn he came to Vienna one last time, this time to stay in a sanatorium. Freud visited him there frequently; no further hours are noted in the record books. Anton von Freund died in January 1920.

Von Freund's analysis is notable in several respects. It was begun during an episode that both Freud and Ferenczi called "psychotic" (see Appendix). In addition—as with Ferenczi and van Emden—it was an intense analysis with a very high frequency of twelve and thirteen hours per week, and a comparatively high number of total hours (at least 256).

---

[47] Perhaps he was elected in March 1918. Freud called him "a member of your society" in April 1918 (F/Fer 2, p. 341; see the note above). In the *Minutes* of the Vienna Society he is listed as a member on 19 November 1918 (Min 4, p. 296). On 5 and 12 June 1918 he took part in the meetings of the Vienna Psychoanalytic Society as a guest (Min 4, p. 313; only in the German edition of the *Minutes*).

[48] In Freud's record book there is an entry "Freund" through to the end of March 1919, although v. Freund certainly was not in Vienna after 17 March, as Freud writes on that day: "I miss Rank very much, and also Freund in another sense, but similarly" (F/Fer 2, p. 335). A day later Ferenczi reports from Budapest: "Toni is cheerful again and totally with us. Of course, for the time being, only a beer brewer" (ibid., p. 336). Nevertheless, there are session entries in Freud's record book throughout all of March. The interim published work of Huppke and Schröter (2011) on Anton v. Freund confirms that the analysis only continued until mid-February 1919, in which case sessions were noted in the record book that did not take place; presumably v. Freund paid for the sessions that were not actually held. Due to these uncertainties, only confirmed sessions are noted in Table 1, namely those up to and including 13 February 1919.

Again, as with Ferenczi, in the case of Anton von Freund analysis, friendship and a professional partnership were closely linked. He helped Freud in the war years with food, made his house available for vacations, and was a generous sponsor who supported the psychoanalytical movement financially. The complicated relationships of von Freund's life are also reminiscent of Ferenczi: in 1915/1916 Freud had von Freund's wife in analysis; immediately after treating Anton, he treated his lover, Margit Dubovitz; and had already analysed Anton von Freund's sister, Kata Lévy, in 1918.[49]

István Hollós

The analysis of István Hollós (1872–1957), co-founder of the Hungarian Psychoanalytic Society is the shortest analysis that Freud carried out with an "analyst" between 1910 and 1920. It seems to have been exclusively for therapeutic purposes.[50] Freud wrote: "His work inhibition, which I studied in nine hours, is probably based on the fact that he has brought things far enough against his father. He came to me in order to establish, that I, too, when looked at from close up, am not worth much" (F/Fer 2, p. 272). Freud's record books shows that he saw Hollós between 4 and 13 March (1918) for one hour daily.[51] Directly after the treatment Ferenczi remarked: "He reacted to the last, somewhat harsh analytic cycle with you with a small depression and jealousy mania which he recognizes as such and is, however, mastering. I advised him to take a small follow-up treatment with you as soon as possible" (F/Fer 2, p. 280).[52]

From 1912 Hollós was an active member of the Hungarian group and, after Ferenczi's death, its chair. He was also involved in translating *The Interpretation of Dreams* into Hungarian (F/Fer 2, pp. 45, 277). We do not know if he was satisfied with or had to be satisfied with so few hours of analysis. None of Freud's comments suggest that the analysis was discontinued. Together with the analysis of Stegmann and Oberholzer,

---

[49] At the same time Ferenczi had Margit Dubovitz's husband in treatment as well as later on Anton v. Freund's wife and his sister.

[50] This is perhaps why Lévy (1957) does not mention the analysis with Freud in his obituary of Hollós.

[51] On 13 March Hollós took part in the Wednesday meeting of the Vienna Psychoanalytic Society as a guest (Min 4, p. 310; only in the German edition of the *Minutes*).

[52] The German "*Eifersuchtswahn*" should perhaps be translated not as "jealousy mania" but as "delusional jealousy". In June 1918 Hollós came once again for three sessions, which I had overlooked in the original publication of this chapter (2006b).

described earlier, it forms a group of short therapies or short analyses that Freud carried out.

Helene Deutsch

In the case of Helene Deutsch (1884–1982) the entries in Freud's record books come as a surprise because this analysis, which began in December 1918 and ended in November 1919, mainly took place at a frequency of three hours per week. This low frequency is astonishing since the daily hour was almost always the rule in virtually all of the cases presented here. The only exceptions so far have been Jekels (five hours) and Révész (three hours per week).

Is it really possible that Freud had Helene Deutsch in only a three-hour analysis, or did he perhaps only note half the hours in the record books and leave out the other half because he did not charge them? Although we cannot exclude this, there is no evidence for it either. In her autobiography (1973) Deutsch does not mention the frequency of her analysis nor does Roazen's biography (1985) provide any information on this, although both books give a detailed description of the treatment.[53] Should the treatment have actually been three times a week, Deutsch may not have had the courage to admit this at a time when this was considered to not meet the *minimal standards*.

A closer look at the course of the treatment shows that in the first three weeks Deutsch had an hour every day; then the three-hour analysis set in. Both the three hours and the change in frequency would correspond to Freud's above-mentioned comment: "For slight cases or the continuation of a treatment which is already well advanced, three days a week will be enough" (Freud, 1913c, p. 127). In addition in this text he had suggested taking the analysand "at first provisionally, for a period of one to two weeks" (ibid., p. 124). It may well be that after this provisional period he concluded that Deutsch was a "slight case". Her description of the end of her analysis seems to confirm this; Freud had told her: "You do not need any more; you are not neurotic" (Deutsch, 1973, p. 133). Another explanation would be that Deutsch only wanted to come for three hours (with Freud's

[53] Roazen describes the analysis with Abraham (e.g., 1985, Chapter IX). Unfortunately, when reading this author, it becomes difficult to distinguish which opinions are his own and which are those of Deutsch.

agreement) because she did not have more time for the analysis; she was working as a doctor at the Wagner-Jauregg clinic, and, as of the end of 1918, in a neurology department under Karplus, and her son was barely two years old.

According to Deutsch's own account it was a colleague (possibly Erszébét Révész) who made her think of having an analysis (1973, p. 130). Deutsch had become a member of the Viennese group in 1918 and, as she wrote in her autobiography, she asked Freud about the possibilities of a training analysis in August (ibid.).[54] During her analysis that began in December 1918 she of course continued to take part in the meetings of the Vienna Psychoanalytic Society (Fallend, 1995, p. 335). The sequence of first being a member of the Viennese group, and then undergoing analysis, which might later have been seen as improper, was glossed over by Deutsch in her autobiography.

In Freud's record book the first entry for "Dr. Deutsch" is for Monday 2 December 1918 which roughly corresponds to her account of the analysis having begun in "the autumn" (Roazen, 1985, p. 151). The analysis continued until 14 June 1919 and was resumed in October 1919 after a summer break of three-and-a-half months; it ended at the beginning of November in 1919. Deutsch wrote that her analysis lasted "about a year" (1973, p. 133) which is the case if the summer break is included; without counting the break, the analysis lasted seven-and-a-half months. That puts Deutsch into the group of "longer" analyses (112 hours).

Helene Deutsch emphasised that her analysis served as training:

> My analysis was a didactic one, and thus a part of my professional training [...] Though Freud's personality and my personal relationship with him were of the greatest importance to me, I was motivated by professional goals when I went to him not only as a patient but also as a candidate. (ibid., pp. 133–134)

Freud had been both her training analyst and the supervising analyst for her cases (1973, p. 135). We know she was treating Victor Tausk and

---

[54] Starting in November 1917 Deutsch took part in the meetings of the Vienna Psychoanalytic Society as a guest and on 13 February 1918 she was elected as a member after she had given a presentation on a paper by Andreas-Salomé on 30 January (Min 4, pp. 304, 309; only in the German edition of the Minutes; Deutsch, 1973, p. 140).

a member of the Freud family during her analysis, which shows that Freud respected her as an analyst. Deutsch wrote that the "unorthodox" aspect of her analysis had been that "it began with a certain personal relationship to Freud (the donation of the milk, for instance)" (ibid., p. 131). Here she is referring to the story of the goat's milk that she brought to the sessions for the Freud family.

As we know, Freud terminated Helene Deutsch's analysis because he needed the hours for another patient (the "Wolf Man"), and he deemed that she no longer needed the analysis.[55] Deutsch responded to the termination with "the first depression of my life" (1973, p. 133), and four years later went to Abraham in Berlin.[56] At the end of her treatment, Freud had told her: "You will now be my assistant" (Ibid.). As mentioned above, this is also what he had called Erszébét Révész. Both young women had come to him to learn analysis; he considered them both to be talented analysts, and, judging from the entries in his patient record book, both received three hours per week.

Margit Dubovitz

Like most of the Hungarian patients, Margit Dubovitz, about whom we know very little, came to Freud via Ferenczi.[57] At the beginning of January 1919 Ferenczi inquired about the possibilities of an analysis for her and wrote: "There is probably no other way out for her. The treatment should determine whether she stays with her family or not" (F/Fer 2, p. 324). This probably referred to the situation with Anton von Freund whose extramarital companion she was. Her husband was in analysis with Ferenczi, and Anton von Freund was with

---

[55] As Freud's patient record books shows, the second section of the Wolf Man did, in fact, begin on 11 November 1919, after Deutsch had had her last hour on 10 November.

[56] On 3 May 1923 Abraham wrote to Freud: "My analysand from Vienna (Frau Dr D.[eutsch]) presents no easy task, but I expect good results. The same is true of Radó [...] Neither analysis is easy, but it is a question not only of getting rid of two neuroses, but of freeing, for our cause's sake, two unusual talents from their inhibitions" (F/A, p. 469). Abraham evidently saw Deutsch's treatment differently from Freud as we can also see in his letter to her husband Felix Deutsch: "I *hope* we will get by with less than one year, which certainly is not long for such a difficult analysis" (Roazen, 1985, p. 222; italics by K. A.).

[57] The dates of her birth and death are unknown; nothing can be found in Harmat (1986), Mészáros (1998), or in the Freud-Ferenczi correspondence. The editors state that Dubowitz's brother was the politician Ernö Garami (F/Fer 2, p. 309). I have used the spelling of her name that the editors of the correspondence used. In the record books Freud spelled her name as "Dubowitz" and "Dubovicz".

Freud (ibid., p. 200). Freud initially could not take Dubovitz on because he had no free hours: "She shall have the next free hour, whether [it comes] in weeks or months. Try to hold her off until then; otherwise I would advise her to go to Frau Dr. Révész, whom I believe capable of much" (Ibid., p. 325). At the end of January Freud still had no hours available and he expressed his reservations to Ferenczi about how useful an analysis with him would be (ibid., p. 329). Perhaps he found the circumstances too tangled and complicated, but we cannot be sure of this because he took Dubovitz on as a patient two months later.[58] The name "Dubowitz" appears for the first time in Freud's record books on 6 March 1919. Apart from the last month, the analysis took place six times per week (a total of 170 hours). We have a comment on its course by Ferenczi in June 1919; he had found Margit Dubovitz "very much changed. She seemed to have overcome her suicidal tendencies" (Ibid.).

In the autumn of 1919 when Anton von Freund was taken to Vienna in an advanced stage of his illness, Freud wrote: "The direction of the sick-bed is in the hands of Margit, who is behaving splendidly, keeping Kata under control and maintaining Rószi. She probably won't collapse herself until afterwards" (Ibid., p. 371).[59]

Margit Dubovitz's treatment was over in January 1920, three days after Anton von Freund's death.[60] In 1922 she appeared once in the *Korrespondenzblatt* of the *Internationale Psychoanalytische Vereinigung* as a guest of the Budapest group (Korr, 1922, p. 393). In 1929 she became a member of the Hungarian Psychoanalytic Society and was then actively involved in psychoanalytic training.[61]

---

[58] At the beginning of January 1919, Freud wrote to Ferenczi: "I don't consider his presence in Vienna to be a contraindication to the treatment of Frau Dubovicz; for I could certainly restrain him, but I would have no influence on her if they were here together. So it is a good thing that it isn't working now" (F/Fer 2, p. 325).

[59] Kata (Lévy) was Anton v. Freund's sister, Rószi his wife.

[60] In February 1920 Freud wrote to Kata Lévy asking her about the whereabouts of Dubovitz; she had not come back to him although she had initially wanted to complete her analysis with him (F/L, p. 34). In the patient record book there are entries for a six-hour analysis from 4 October to 9 December for "Dubowitz". Freud writes to Ferenczi during this time: "The Dubowitz woman upbraided his character, the way he is supposed to have shown himself in the difficult times in Budapest" (F/Fer 3, p. 38). As it is unclear whether *Margit* Dubowitz is meant, I have not included the sessions that began in October 1920 in Table 1.

[61] See the corresponding entries in *Korrespondenzblatt* since 1929. In 1930 Ferenczi put her in charge of a child guidance clinic (F/Fer 3, p. 389).

What we can deduce from this very sparse information is that Dubovitz in all likelihood first came to Freud for therapy, that this probably comprised more than one section, and that the former patient later developed an interest in psychoanalysis and in working as a psychoanalyst.

David Forsyth

In the *New Introductory Lectures on Psychoanalysis* (1933a) Freud himself published the fact that David Forsyth (1877–1941), an English doctor and a founding member of the British Psychoanalytical Association (1913), had been in analysis with him:

> One autumn day in the year 1919, at about 10.45 a.m., Dr. David Forsyth, who had just arrived from London, sent in his card to me while I was working with a patient. (My respected colleague from London University will not, I feel sure, regard it as an indiscretion if in this way I betray the fact that he spent some months being initiated by me into the arts of psycho-analytic technique.) (Freud, 1933a, p. 47)

Freud goes on to write that Forsyth had received "instruction in analysis" and was the first foreigner who had come to him after the war (ibid., p. 53). Forsyth apparently approached Freud directly, so it was not until afterwards that Jones learned of the analysis: "He told me that you were going to analyse him, which naturally aroused my jealousy, though do not fear that I shall not be able to control this" (F/Jo, p. 350). Forsyth already had much psychoanalytical experience and had a senior position at London University.

The patient record books shows that his first hour was entered for 6 October 1919. The analysis was six hours per week and lasted until the middle of November (thirty-eight hours). During the weeks that Forsyth spent in Vienna he took part in at least one meeting of the Vienna Psychoanalytic Society as a guest and also met Freud socially, who called him "a very notable personality" (Fallend, 1995, p. 183; F/A, p. 407).[62] Then he returned to London, "deeply impressed with your technique",

[62] From October and November 1919 only the minutes of one meeting of the Vienna Group are to be found (2 November 1919; Fallend, 1995, p. 183). On this evening Forsyth was noted as a guest. The convivial get-together with Freud can be inferred from the following entry referring to Forsyth from 19 November 1919: "He had just replaced Jones, but Ferenczi was still there. Hence a time of lively psychoanalytic fellowship" (F/E, p. 170).

as Jones reported to Freud, and wrote a book on the technique of psychoanalysis (F/Jo, p. 357; Forsyth, 1922).

Freud wrote to Eitingon that Forsyth had "worked on his analysis" (F/E, p. 170). This is a term that turns up several times in Freud's writings. It is no longer used, emphasising as it does that the analysand is actively engaged, unlike other terms such as "entered" or "underwent" analysis.

Claud Danger Daly

Daly (1884–1950) came to Freud via Jones who had treated him a few years previously (F/Jo, p. 364). He then, according to Jones' account, decided it was cheaper to be analysed in Vienna than in London and wanted analysis with Freud. Daly was a captain in the British army in India and was able to take a year off. Freud thanked Jones for the patient: "You are providing well for my medical income" (Ibid., p. 368).

According to the patient record book, Daly's treatment began on Monday 12 February 1920 and was regularly six hours per week; it ended in January 1921 (ibid., p. 405). We know from Freud's correspondence with Jones that it lasted exactly the year that Daly was on leave (ibid.). Daly's analysis is therefore quite long and, among those in our sample, it is the longest, only interrupted by the summer holidays. The total number of hours is quite high, too: by the end of December 1920, 221 hours had been noted in the record book. Daly later (1925) went to Ferenczi for treatment and in the 1930s once again to Freud (F/Fer 3, p. 209; J.R., 1950, p. 291).

Daly was not a doctor and probably only carried out a small number of analyses, but he did publish several psychoanalytical-ethnological papers (J.R., 1950). In the 1920s he turned up as a member of the Indian Psychoanalytical Association—one of the rather rare examples of membership based on an interest in *applied* psychoanalysis.

Freud kept Jones up to date on the development of the analysand, as he had done with Ferenczi with the patients he had sent. Freud's comments were not very flattering (F/Jo, pp. 380, 405; see also F/Fer 3, p. 212). At the end of the treatment he told Jones about Daly's plan to work as an analyst: "His mind is still set on practising analysis himself after having served his term in India. He may become qualified in the course of some years for practical educational work" (F/Jo, p. 405). The "practical educational work" probably meant that Daly might at some time be able to work as a non-medical analyst.[63] That Daly did not take part in the meetings of the Vienna Psychoanalytic Society may have been because, like Spitz and Dubovitz, he was not yet a member of a psychoanalytical organisation; he may also not have been sufficiently proficient in German.

John Rickman

Jones had first told Freud about the twenty-nine-year-old John Rickman (1891–1951) in the following words: "A clever man, a doctor [...] extremely interested in psa of which he already knows something, and begs me to ask you if you can take him for analysis in the first week of April" (F/Jo, p. 364). This aroused Freud's curiosity, much more than had been the case with Daly (ibid., p. 368). The first entry for "Rickman" in his record book was for Thursday 15 April 1920. The analysis was six hours per week and went until the end of July. Unlike other years, Freud worked longer this year, because he had several patients from abroad whose fees were not affected by inflation, which helped him over the difficult post-war years.

The duration of Rickman's analysis would clearly have been determined from the outset, as would have a number of analyses where I did not specifically mention this. Viewed from a contemporary position, Freud's pragmatism and "lack of rigour" in this point may seem astonishing. When Rickman returned from Vienna, he became an associate member of the British Psychoanalytical Association (ibid., p. 391). In the following year he went back to Freud for a second period of analysis (ibid., p. 443), and in 1922 he became a full member of the British society in which he played an important role (King & Steiner, 1991).[64]

The treatments of Dubovitz, Daly, and Rickman show a change in the character of the analyses in that they took place *before* membership in a psychoanalytic society. Many factors would have contributed to this change, including the new training institutes whose establishment, it might be said, turned psychoanalysis upside down. One no longer

---

[63] Jones, too, was reserved about Daly's possible future role as an analyst: "I am not too enthusiastic about his becoming an analyst" (F/Jo, p. 417).

[64] In 1928 Rickman went to Ferenczi (F/Fer 3, p. 345) and later to Klein for analysis (Payne, 1952, p. 54). We do not find any evidence of his presence at the meetings of the Vienna Psychoanalytic Society until the second section (Fallend, 1995). As with Daly, language problems at the beginning may have been the reason for this.

became an analyst because one was interested in psychoanalysis and had developed a commitment to it but because one had received the training. Of course, the obligatory analysis of the analyst would not have become established if Freud had not recommended it but, to make this the norm, institutions were probably necessary.

Kata Lévy

In the course of time a cordial friendship developed between Freud and Kata Lévy [-Freund] (1883–1969), the sister of Anton von Freund. The Freund family helped the Freuds in the difficult years during and after the war, and there was much goodwill and affection in other respects, too. In the summer of 1918 when Freud was spending a few weeks in a house that belonged to Kata Lévy, he got to know her better and suggested analysis (Lévy, 1990, p. 53).[65] She was thirty-seven years old at the time, married to Lajos Lévy, who had co-founded the Hungarian Psychoanalytic Society, and was the doctor and the friend of Ferenczi. For Anna Freud, Kata Lévy was a kind of motherly friend or older sister (Young-Bruehl, 1988, p. 195).[66] According to Lévy's recollections she first did not want to accept Freud's suggestion because he was on vacation, but he responded by saying that he wished to do her brother a favour who had so much wanted her to benefit from analysis (Lévy, 1990, p. 53). We know from a letter that Freud wrote in September 1918 that Lévy was receiving hours during his vacation, that her treatment had progressed, had then stagnated and that it would be resumed in Vienna (F/AF, p. 146).

Freud's patient record books for September 1918 show *no* hours for Lévy, as was the case with the hours that van Emden received in Karlsbad which were not noted either. We do not know why Freud did not enter the vacation analyses. It may have been, as we suggested before, because he did not charge the analysands for these. After the summer 1918 we do not find Lévy in Freud's record book either since,

---

[65] The page numbers of Lévy's paper refer to the German edition in 2012. According to Roazen (1995, p. 153) Freud told her, he had just started the analysis with Anna and would therefore want to have another female analysand.

[66] Roazen (1995, p. 160) refers to her as "teacher for defective children", Young-Bruehl (1988, p. 79) as a "social worker". Thomas Aichhorn (Vienna) made me aware that both statements must be incorrect, as neither profession yet existed. Kata Lévy had no professional training in the strict sense. Later, she became an analyst. See now F/L.

as he had written to her, he had no vacancies (F/L, p. 24). It seems that her analysis was not resumed until April 1920. In this month Freud informed Lévy that he could now take her and in this month her name appeared in the record book (ibid., p. 37).

I therefore assume that Lévy had a few hours during Freud's holiday in September 1918 and resumed her analysis in spring 1920. The long interruption was in all likelihood a result of the revolution that broke out in Hungary in the spring of 1919. For several months any contact or travel between Budapest and Vienna was barely possible. It was also at this time that Anton von Freund's health seriously deteriorated so that he was taken to a clinic in Vienna. Kata Lévy accompanied her brother who died in Vienna in January 1920. It was not until afterwards that she continued the analysis (Roazen, 1995, p. 157).

On 1 May 1920 there is an entry of the first hour for "Lévy". The analysis took place three or four times per week until the middle of June, after that six times per week. It was over on 28 July and comprised sixty-two hours. In this case we happen to know why Lévy at first received so few hours. Freud had written to her that initially he would only be able to give her the three hours that he was "taking away from another" (F/L, p. 38) This is reflected in the record book insofar as when a patient stopped in the middle of June, Lévy was able to come six times a week for the remaining seven weeks up to the summer holidays.[67] The two to three weekly hours at the beginning of the treatment were declared as a temporary stopgap arrangement by Freud and not as the regular frequency. After the three-month period of analysis, Freud let her know that he was relieved that he could "simply be cordial" again "without the didactic roughness of the analysis, without having to conceal my cordial friendship for you, which you would nonetheless not have been in doubt of" (ibid., p. 38).

After the summer holidays in 1920, Lévy did not go back to analysis, but returned a few years later for a second section (Roazen, 1995, p. 161). She "diligently" attended the sessions of the Budapest group in 1921 and began to treat patients (F/Fer 3, pp. 51, 202; Korr, 1923, p. 247).

---

[67] Roazen (1995, p. 154), Appignanesi & Forrester (1993, p. 379), and Leitner (2001, p. 381) write that Freud did not charge Lévy a fee.

In 1927 she appeared with a paper as a guest at the Hungarian Psychoanalytic Society, and in 1928 became a full (non-medical) member.[68]

Lévy's development seems to have been similar to that of Margit Dubovitz. Neither became members of a psychoanalytical association until several years after the analysis. The impression we get is that Lévy initially came to Freud because of personal problems. Like Dubovitz she did not take part in the meetings of the Vienna Psychoanalytic Society during her treatment.[69] I assume the reason was that both women were not yet members of a psychoanalytical society nor intended to become so at the time.

Adolph Stern

Stern (1879–1958), who had been a member of the American Psychoanalytical Association since 1915, was the first American to come to Freud after the war. After the International Psychoanalytic Congress in The Hague (1920) he began his two-month analysis of moderate length (sixty-two hours). It began on Monday 3 October and ended on Wednesday 8 December 1920. Stern did not take part in the meetings of the Vienna Psychoanalytic Society, probably because of the language barrier.

When he returned to the United States, Stern wrote a paper about his experiences (1922): He had travelled to Vienna in order to get an idea of how Freud worked; Freud considered it necessary that the analyst be analysed; in rare cases self-analysis was sufficient; the analysis of an analyst was no different from that of a patient; it took place six days a week "until well along in the treatment" (ibid., p. 22); compared to the three hours a week that were usual in the United States, daily analysis had the advantage that the total duration of the analysis was shorter.

Stern's description is interesting because it seems to indicate that Freud's views on the analysis of the analyst and on the frequency were

---

[68] Korr, 1927, p. 369; 1928, p. 429. Earlier she was mentioned as a guest in the Hungarian Society once in 1923 (Korr, 1923, p. 247).

[69] The minutes of the Vienna Psychoanalytic Society from 1919 to 1923 (Fallend, 1995) were less carefully taken than before so we cannot be sure that a guest may not occasionally have been inadvertently omitted. However, both Lévy and Dubovitz's absence is so consistent that this cannot be a coincidence.

the same in 1920 as they had been before the war (Freud, 1912e, 1913c). His intervening experience of analysing analysts had apparently not changed his opinion.

Freud was not particularly taken with his analysand: "Dr. Stern [...] was uninteresting, nothing special" is what he wrote to Ferenczi (F/Fer 3, p. 43).[70] Stern later had another analysis, with Frink, and was at various times president of the New York and the American Psychoanalytic Association.

Freud's analyses of "analysts": duration of analyses and frequency of sessions

Table 1 summarises data on the duration and frequency of the seventeen analyses.[71] In the calculation of the *duration* of the analyses, I distinguished between the "duration of treatment in months or weeks" and the "time between the first and the last hour". This distinction is necessary in those cases in which the analysis was not carried out in one piece but was given in several sections, often separated by long intervals.

In order to assess the *frequency* with which Freud treated his analysands, I checked every single week in order to see how the weekly total had come about, that is, if sessions had not taken place because of public holidays or short vacations, if the beginning or end of Freud's working season had been mid-week, or other reasons why his practice might have been closed. I drew on Freud's correspondence and other published sources that might contain references to arrangements affecting the hours of analysis. This detailed and time-consuming approach was important. Had I simply looked at the number of hours and ignored the background circumstances I would have reached very different and somewhat erroneous conclusions.

---

[70] Similarly in a circular letter: "Dr. Stern who was with the professor after the congress benefited personally but otherwise was not a very interesting person" (RB 2, p. 87).

[71] The treatments generally begin at the frequency that was then maintained for a long time (or through the whole analysis). It seems that Freud either did not conduct any preliminary talks or did not note them in the record books. The first possibility is supported by his comments in "On Beginning the Treatment" where he considers long preliminary talks inadvisable and recommends beginning immediately with a trial treatment over one to two weeks (Freud, 1913c, p. 124).

Table 1. Number of hours, frequency, and duration of Freud's analyses (training analyses) of seventeen "analysts"; that is, men and women who were or became members of a psychoanalytic association (between 1910 and 1920).

Name	*Start and end of analysis*	*Hours for each section*	*Total hours*	*Weekly frequency*	*Duration in months*[1]
Jan van Emden					
Section 1	15.5.1911 to 8.7.1911	92		12 hours	
Section 2	2.4.1912 to 24.5.1912	41	**245**[2]	6 hours	6¼
Section 3	2.6.1913 to 5.7.1913	35		5–7 hours	
Section 4	25.5.1914 to 10.7.1914	77		12 hours	
René Spitz	10.10.1911 to 21.12.1911		**46**	2–6 hours	2½
Arnold Stegmann	20.11.1911 to 16.12.1911		**24**	6 hours	1
Emil Oberholzer	3.6.1912 to 2.7.1912		**26**	6 hours	1
Ludwig Jekels	15.10.1912 to 4.7.1913		**175**	5 hours	9
Eugenia Sokolnicka	19.3.1914 to 12.6.1914		**68**	6 hours	3
Sándor Ferenczi					
Section 1	1.10.1914 to 24.10.1914	47		14 hours	
Section 2	14.6.1916 to 6.7.1916	43	**131**	14 hours	2½
Section 3	29.9.1916 to 13.10.1916	41		13–19½ hours	
Erszébét Révész					
Section 1	13.12.1916 to 27.6.1917	81	**128**	3 hours	10
Section 2	14.3.1918 to 28.6.1918	47		3 hours	

Anton v. Freund					
Section 1	20.2.1918 to 28.6.1918	173		Alternately 6 and	
			256[3]	12 hours	6¼
Section 2	25.12.1918 to mid-Feb. 1919	83		5–14 hours	
István Hollós	4.3.1918 to 8.6.1918		**12**	6 hours	½
Helene Deutsch	2.12.1918 to 10.11.1919		**112**	3 hours	7½
Margit Dubovitz	6.3.19 to 26.1.1920		**170**	6 hours	7
David Forsyth	6.10.1919 to 18.11.1919		**38**	6 hours	1½
Claud Dangar Daly	9.2.1920 to 31.12.1920		**221**[4]	6 hours	9
John Rickman	15.4.1920 to 28.7.1920		**89½**	6 hours	3½
Kata Lévy	1.5.1920 to 28.7.1920		**63**[2]	6 hours	3
Adolph Stern	3.10.1920 to 8.12.1920		**62**	6 hours	2

[1]Duration without interruptions due to Freud's holidays and excluding time between the sections.
[2]Excluding hours during Freud's vacation.
[3]Hours up to and including 13 February 1919.
[4]Hours up to and including December 1920.

Short analyses

The most surprising finding of the study is the short duration of Freud's analyses (Table 2). Neither the analyses consisting of only one period, nor those with several periods, lasted longer than eleven months, even *including* Freud's summer vacation. If the vacation months are subtracted, then the longest analysis was for a period of ten months (Révész); and a considerable number (seven out of seventeen) were shorter than three months. This would be in keeping with Freud's comment in 1913 that an analysis would take "half a year or whole years"—periods that at the time he characterised as "long" (1913c, p. 129).[72]

One might try to understand the comparatively short duration of these analyses by noting that *after 1920* treatments generally became longer, possibly because it was not until then that Freud realised how much time was required to remove the symptoms and change a personality. However, in the seventeen cases presented here (1910–1920), the duration did not increase between 1910 and 1920, as can be seen in Table 1.

Table 2. Duration of Freud's analyses (training analyses) of seventeen "analysts", that is, men and women who were or became members of a psychoanalytic association, measured in months, without interruptions due to Freud's holidays and excluding time between the sections (between 1910 and 1920).

Duration of analyses in months	*Name*	*Number*
Less than 3 months	Hollós, Ferenczi, Spitz, Stegmann, Oberholzer, Forsyth, Stern	7
3 to 6 months	Sokolnicka, Rickman, Lévy	3
6 to 9 months	Deutsch, Dubovitz, v. Emden, v. Freund	4
9 to 10 months	Jekels, Daly, Révész	3
Sum		17

[72] Hitschmann expressed himself similarly in his *Freud's Theories of the Neuroses*, which is known to have been drafted in close consultation with Freud and whose views were in part reproduced verbatim: "Freud claims to need long periods, six months to three years, for an effective treatment" (1911, p. 127). This statement refers to "very severe" cases. With "less difficult cases, the treatment time would be reduced accordingly" (ibid.).

Another possible explanation for the short duration was that the group of seventeen only consisted of analysands who already were, or were soon to be, analysts and who might therefore have suffered from less serious disturbances than "genuine" patients. This is a question we will address again later. We will then also examine whether the short duration was because most of the seventeen analysands had to come to Vienna and the interruption of their livelihoods and the separation from their families could not be maintained over very long periods.

A few points are clear at the moment. First, the duration of the analyses had nothing to do with membership in a psychoanalytic society during the analysis or years later. Second, the motivation for the analysis did not seem to have had an effect on its duration: some "learning analyses" were relatively short (Forsyth, Rickman, Stern), others long (van Emden, Révész, Deutsch); and some "therapeutic" analyses were short (e.g., Oberholzer, Stegmann, Hollós) and others were longer (Dubovitz).

High number of hours, high weekly frequency

In relation to the short duration Freud's analysis of "analysts" comprised a relatively high number of hours, due to the *high weekly frequency* (see Table 3). By comparison, today's training analyses are considerably longer but take place at a much lower frequency.

Table 3. Duration of the analyses (training analyses) of seventeen "analysts", that is, men and women who were or became members of a psychoanalytic association, measured in number of sessions (between 1910 and 1920).

Number of hours of the analyses (training analyses)	*Name*	*Number of analysands*
Less than 50 hours	Spitz, Stegmann, Oberholzer, Hollos, Forsyth	5
50 to 100 hours	Sokolnicka, Rickman, Lévy,[1] Stern	4
100 to 150 hours	Ferenczi, Révész, Deutsch	3
150 to 200 hours	Jekels, Dubovitz	2
200 to 250 hours	Van Emden,[1] Daly	2
250 to 300 hours	Anton v. Freund	1
Sum		17

[1]Excluding hours during Freud's holidays.

Apart from Spitz, Deutsch, and Révész, all seventeen "analysts" had at least six hours per week, which conforms to Freud's much-cited words that an analysis usually takes place "six times a week".[73] The six-day working week was the rule at the time. In addition it would have reflected Freud's vitality and the intensity with which he worked. On the other hand, Will pointed out that in spite of the six-day working week, patients at the Berlin Psychoanalytic Institute were only seen "three to four times weekly, in severe cases more often" (in 1920–1922; see Eitingon, 1922, p. 511).

Freud worked at an even higher frequency with three of the seventeen "analysts": van Emden, Ferenczi, and von Freund had twelve and more hours per week. It was already known that the last section of Ferenczi's analysis consisted of eighteen and nineteen-and-a-half hours per week, but as we see here this was not really an exception.

In the group in question, analyses that comprised twelve or more hours per week were only the case in treatments that took place in sections, that is, separate time periods. It may be that Freud wanted to make the best possible use of the limited time available; on the other hand he did not always provide more than six hours for all analysands who had come to Vienna for a short time for treatment. The three-hour analysis is surprising (Révész, Deutsch). As mentioned before, Freud suggested this "for slighter cases or a treatment which is already well advanced" (1913c, p. 127). Nonetheless this was not integrated into the training guidelines that were developed in the mid 1920s in Berlin and Vienna. The most likely reason for the three hours could have been that Freud considered the two young doctors analytically talented and not very neurotic. One-, two-, and four-hour treatments were not the case in the group of seventeen "analysts".

Analyses in separate periods and multiple analyses

Freud's treatment of analysands in separate periods of analysis would at least in part be due to the difficulties of some of his colleagues to leave their work for extended periods. In these cases the duration of the analysis would probably have been agreed on beforehand. In any case Freud was prepared to work in sections and for predetermined periods, which shows his pragmatism: his willingness to do what was possible, even if it

[73] Regarding frequency see Rotmann (1988), Pollak (2001), and Will (2003, pp. 117–134).

was not what was most desirable. In addition Freud himself reduced the frequency (Spitz), abruptly terminated treatments (Deutsch), and permitted interruptions (von Freund) when he considered it appropriate.[74]

It is interesting in this context that more than half of the seventeen analysts underwent *more than one* analysis: Oberholzer later went to Pfister, Helene Deutsch to Abraham, Daly to Ferenczi and a second time to Freud, Ferenczi to Groddeck, Lévy a second time to Freud, Révész to Ferenczi, Rickman a second time to Freud, then to Ferenczi and to Payne, Sokolnicka to Ferenczi, and Stern to Frink (to compare this with the group of "patients", see below).

Analytical and extra-analytical relations

In recent years there have been a number of publications pointing out that Freud was not, strictly speaking, "anonymous" and was quite visible as a private person to his analysands.[75] My research confirms this. Freud had been personally acquainted with or had been a friend of many of the seventeen "analysts" discussed in this chapter before their treatment: first and foremost with Ferenczi but also, for example, with Jekels, von Freund and Lévy. Occasionally he knew the spouses and close friends of his analysands and took them on as patients, too. During treatment he maintained cordial private relationships with a number of his analysands, spending vacations in houses that belonged to them or their families, receiving their visits during his vacation and also occasionally giving them extra hours during this time. Intermingling analysis and friendship was probably not unique to Freud: we know of similar individual examples with Ferenczi, Jones, and Abraham.[76] Freud also had no qualms about working contacts with his analysands. Many of them (twelve out of the seventeen) took part in meetings of the Vienna Psychoanalytic Society during their analysis.

I would hesitate to say that Freud did not take his own "rules" very seriously. Freud's disciples may have misapprehended what he had actually meant. In 1913, for example, Freud wrote: "Special difficulties

---

[74] See also Eitingon's report on the practice of "fractioned" analyses at the Berlin institute (1922, p. 512).

[75] See Lipton (1977, 1983), Cremerius (1984), Momigliano (1987), Lynn & Vaillant (1998), and Couch (1999).

[76] According to Roazen, Helene Deutsch frequently visited Abraham during her analysis and spent time with his family (1985, pp. 194, 197).

arise when the analyst and his new patient or their families are on terms of friendship or have social ties with one another" (1913c, p. 125). I would not interpret this as a "prohibition" as such, but rather as an observation of the special problems that may arise in these circumstances. That we work differently today has, to my mind, more to do with our fear that too much contact with the analysand would be too taxing and therefore be detrimental to our work. In addition, Freud regarded it as crucial, both for himself and for his analysands, to draw a clear demarcation line between their "real" relationships and their relationships within the analytic situation. In the summer of 1916, when he was expecting Ferenczi to come to his second period of analysis, he wrote:

> Since you want it that way—and if your fate permits, I will thus reserve for you two hours a day from the middle of June on. I also hope to see much of you otherwise, and you should at least have one meal with us daily. Technique at least will require that nothing personal will be discussed outside the sessions. (F/Fer 2, p. 130)

He made similar comments to Kata Lévy whose brother Anton von Freund was taken to Vienna to continue his analysis on the next day: "As of tomorrow, technique will take the place of friendship, to his advantage I hope" (F/L, p. 26).

Concluding comments

Dealing with the small group of "analysts" who came to Freud in the years 1910–1920 puts us in touch with a world that disappeared long ago. This is the case for the teaching or learning analysis that played a minor role during this period. What counted was a proven commitment to psychoanalysis. The majority of the seventeen women and men presented here had already *before* their analysis founded local groups in the cities where they lived, propagated psychoanalysis in their medical associations, at universities and to the larger public, translated Freud's texts (into Dutch, Polish, Hungarian, and English) and often published in psychoanalytic journals. Until about 1918/1919 these activities were the prerequisite for their membership in psychoanalytic societies. In short, they first became interested in psychoanalysis, thereupon joined a society, and might then have entered analysis either to "learn" analysis or to receive help with personal problems.

The way in which Freud worked also belongs to the past. He saw his teaching or learning analysands daily for short periods, while maintaining amicable or collegial relations with them and their families outside the sessions. His contacts to colleagues were short, intense, and interwoven with a great deal of real friendship and working relationships. Freud may have perceived these circumstances as encumbrances of his therapeutic work but he seemed willing to put up with them. Freud's approach to the analysis of colleagues may convey how he envisaged the analysis of future or already "complete" analysts at the time (1910–1920): to take place for a predetermined time, to be an impetus, an intensive stimulant. That also meant no long-term accompaniment and no extensive in-depth exploration. In the next section we will see how this compared with the analysis of analysands who primarily and explicitly came as patients.

Nineteen "patients" in analysis with Freud

The following deals with Freud's analysis of "patients". To distinguish this group from the one previously examined, analysands are considered to be "patients" if they were at no point in their lives members of a psychoanalytic association. In order to be included in the group presented here, the analysis also had to meet the following criteria: it would have to have been mentioned in a publication at least once and corroborated by a source other than the patient record books. In addition the analysis (or one of its sections) would have had to begin after October 1910 and be completed before December 1920.

This is the case for nineteen analysands (ten women, nine men). I will list them in the order that they came to Freud: Elfriede Hirschfeld, Sergej Pankejeff ("Wolf Man"), Victor von Dirsztay, Claire von Wallentin-Metternich, Tatjana Nacht, Elma Pálos, Loe Kann, Bruno Veneziani, Lucy Hoesch-Ernst, Karl Mayreder, Aranka Schwarcz, Rózsi von Freund, Arthur Fischer-Colbrie, Rudolf Kriser, Georgina Weiss, Margarete Rie, Julius Hering, Bieber (first name not known), and George M. Young.[77]

---

[77] It seems remarkable to me that ten of the nineteen "patients" were under thirty years old when they began the analysis with Freud: seven were between nineteen and twenty-five, three between twenty-six and thirty years. Only four patients were between thirty-one and forty; one was fifty-nine years old. Among the "analysts", however, there were only a small group of young men and women, while the majority were older than thirty years.

Elfriede Hirschfeld

Freud perceived Hirschfeld (1873–?) as a "pleasant, over-considerate, shrewd and distinguished personality" (F/Bi, p. 132).[78] She came from Frankfurt, had married a rich man, and had been referred to Freud by Jung (F/Ju, p. 175). We know her name from the correspondence between Freud and Ferenczi (F/Fer 1, p. 146) and from Falzeder's detailed description (1994). Her analysis is the subject of several of Freud's letters to Jung, Pfister, Binswanger, and Abraham.

Starting on 11 October 1910, "Hirschfeld" can be found in Freud's record book. We know, however, that she had begun the treatment two years earlier (F/Ju, p. 175). In 1908, Freud wrote to Jung that the patient who had just arrived for treatment was a "very serious case of obsessional neurosis, improvement is bound to be very slow" (ibid.). Hirschfeld had already been suffering from a severe obsessional neurosis for ten years.

From October 1910 to July 1911, she came to Freud every day with the exception of a two-week holiday. In this section of her analysis she received between nine and twelve hours per week (a total of 392 hours).[79] In the summer holidays she called on Oskar Pfister in Zürich, as had been agreed with Freud, and stayed with him until the beginning of December 1911 (F/Ju, p. 473; F/P, p. 80, German edition, 2014). She wanted to go back to Freud who initially was somewhat reluctant but took her back at the end of December and began a second period of analysis (F/Ju, p. 474; F/P, p. 86, German edition, 2014). He then learned that Hirschfeld had also consulted Jung in Zürich. Her report on the talk with Jung led to considerable tension between Freud and his Swiss disciple (Falzeder, 1994).

Hirschfeld stayed with Freud from December 1911 to January 1914 (approximately 810 hours). The second period was usually eleven-and-a-half hours per week. We do not know how the analysis was terminated. The gradual decrease of hours in the last weeks makes it

[78] For more biographical details, see Falzeder (1994), who provides a birth date of "around 1873" (p. 299); see also Leitner (2001, p. 202).

[79] Again it was not always easy to decipher the boxes so that the exact number of hours cannot be provided. In Hirschfeld's case (and only in her case), Freud occasionally noted the hours not by means of a stroke but by putting numbers in the box, e.g., "4" or "8". I believe that the figures correspond to the fee in Austrian Kronen (forty or eighty, that is, one hour or two), which can be deduced from the monthly sum of hours that Freud often entered at the end of a line.

seem likely that the end had been agreed upon. A special feature of the second period of analysis was that for one week Hirschfeld had two analysts (in June 1912). Freud had asked Pfister to comply with the patient's wish and to come to Vienna to help with a "withdrawal process," which probably was a reference to Hirschfeld's attempt to give up some of her obsessional behaviour (F/Fer 1, p. 386; F/P, p. 93, German edition, 2014).

A few months after the end of the second period, Hirschfeld returned to Freud: starting at the end of June 1914, her name appears again for a period of two weeks with an entry of usually one-and-a-half hours per day (a total of seventeen). We do not know why she started analysis again. On the last day before his summer holidays, Freud wrote to Abraham that Hirschfeld was coming to Berlin and might consult him (F/A, p. 255). He requested that Abraham not turn the patient down, but to let her feel that someone who was not familiar with her case could not "intervene" (ibid.).[80] The wording might be an indication that Freud believed Hirschfeld would return in order to continue the analysis after the summer break. However, Hirschfeld does not appear in the record book after that, so she may have broken off her treatment with Freud in July 1914.

When Hirschfeld called on Binswanger one year later (1915), Freud wrote the following to his colleague:

> She is a case of obsessional neurosis of the severest kind who was *nearly* analyzed to the end, has proved incurable and has resisted all efforts because of particularly unpropitious extreme circumstances and is supposedly still dependent on me. In fact, however, she has been running away from me ever since I let her into the real secret of her illness. Analytically useless to anyone. (F/Bi, p. 132)

The patient was admitted to Binswanger's sanatorium and later on tried to get further treatment, also from Freud, who refused a continuation (F/Bi, pp. 133, 155, 160, 165; Falzeder, 1994, p. 306).

Around 1,200 hours have been entered for "Hirschfeld" in Freud's patient record book. Should the patient have already received six hours a week before October 1910, this would amount to approximately

[80] In July 1914, Abraham spoke with Hirschfeld; after that, she apparently did not get in touch with him again (F/A, pp. 262, 281).

1,600 hours. Hirschfeld's analysis lasted almost six years, if Freud's summer vacations are included (October 1908 to July 1914). It was not a continuous analysis, but was interrupted three times for weeks or months within the period of the record books that we have. Consequently, Hirschfeld had only twenty-nine months of treatment between October 1910 and December 1920, whereas Pankejeff, for instance, had forty months of treatment within a shorter time span. On the other hand, Hirschfeld had one-and-a-half or two hours daily over long periods, thereby achieving a greater number of hours than Pankejeff.

Freud ascribed the fact that the intensive work with Hirschfeld did not lead to the desired changes to the severity of her disturbances and the "particularly unpropitious" circumstances of her life (F/Bi, p. 132). This might have been a reference to the infertility of her husband (Freud, 1941d, p. 186; Falzeder, 1994). Of course, Hirschfeld also stayed in analysis and in Vienna for so long because she could afford to do so, and that Freud liked her would have contributed to his keeping his "main client" and "grand patient" for so long (F/Fer 1, pp. 146, 386). He may also have expected to gain some insight from his work with her. As we know, some aspects of his theory derive from her analysis, even if the treatment itself failed as therapy (Falzeder, 1994; Grubrich-Simitis, 1993, pp. 209–211).

Victor von Dirsztay

The name of Victor von Dirsztay (1884?–1935) turns up only once in Freud's correspondence, in a letter to Ferenczi on 3 December 1909: "Dirsztay's [a patient] parents were with me and proved themselves quite friendly to the treatment" (F/Fer 1, p. 110; see Chapter Eight). Dirsztay is listed as a patient in the index of that volume (ibid., p. 436). We come across the name a second time as an entry in Freud's diary on 6 November 1935: "Victor Dirsztay †" (Molnar, 1992, p. 26). According to the editor Michael Molnar: "It is possible that Freud noted the death of the Austrian writer Victor Dirsztay (1884–1935) because he had once been one of his analysands" (Ibid.).[81]

---

[81] In the German edition of Freud's diary, the year of birth is given as 1884 (1992, p. 341); according to Schmidt and Dalbajewa, it was 1882 (1996, p. 204). The former date is more likely because a newspaper report of 7 November 1935 stated that von Dirsztay was fifty years old when he died (Anon., 1935e, p. 9).

A Google search of the name "Dirsztay" yields a portrait of a man with the same name, Victor von Dirsztay (1884–1935), who was painted by Oskar Kokoschka in 1911.[82] The painting shows a slim and elegant figure, pale, with circles under his eyes, and a cigarette in his hand. A foray into library catalogues showed that Kokoschka had illustrated two of Victor von Dirsztay's books (1917; 1923) with lithographs.[83] In his autobiography, Kokoschka commented: "Even Freud, to whom he went for years, could not heal him" (1971, p. 91). This remark confirms that the man portrayed in the painting actually was the von Dirsztay who had been in treatment with Freud.

Dirsztay's expressionist works depict men whose experience of life is agonising and who eventually commit suicide. Dirsztay's life ended like that of his protagonists: he committed suicide together with his former wife. The *Wiener Zeitung* of 7 November 1935 reported: "Tragedy of the Dirsztay Couple" (no. 308, p. 9). The deceased had been a *bel esprit*, a musician, and a writer. He came from a Hungarian family and, as the son of the director of the Lemberg-Czernowitz Rail Company, had spent his youth "surrounded by wealth". He had been "an original, witty and extravagant socialiser who had enjoyed great popularity" and was counted as "one of the enthusiastic fans of Sigmund Freud". In recent years, he had been suffering from "severe depressions" (ibid.).[84]

All this makes clear that Victor von Dirsztay was once a patient of Freud's, but it has not been equally clear whether all three sections entered into the patient record books under the name of "Dirsztay" (sometimes also "Dirsztai") refer to Victor. More detailed research has however confirmed his identity (May, 2010a). We can therefore say that the total number of hours according to Freud's record book entries

---

[82] www.thecityreview.com/kokosch.html (2002) [accessed 12 January 2006]. The painting is in the Sprengel-Museum, Hanover. Kokoschka also painted a portrait of Jacques de Menasce (1905–1960), a nephew of von Dirsztay who later became a pianist and composer. It now belongs to the *Neue Nationalgalerie* in Berlin. Google also provided a link to the autobiography of Alma Mahler-Werfel, including a passage in which she described how Kokoschka had sent a "Baron Dirsztay" as a messenger to tell her that he still loved her (1960, p. 128).

[83] Dirsztay published a few smaller pieces (1911a; 1911b; 1911c) in the art periodical *Der Sturm*, which was edited by Herwarth Walden and in which many drawings by Kokoschka appeared (see May, 2008).

[84] Winkler and Erling (1995) describe the Dirsztays as a poor family that had become rich in one generation (p. 41; see also Kokoschka, 1971, p. 91). They state that Victor von Dirsztay was born as Anton Fischl. His father, Laszlo Fischl, married his second wife, the Baroness Georgine Dirsztay, in 1885 and had been given the title in 1905 (ibid.).

amounts to 1,489. Should the Dirsztay mentioned in a letter to Ferenczi in 1909 also be Victor, the analysis would have comprised approximately 1,700 or 1,800 hours, making it the longest in our group.

Sergei Pankejeff, the Wolf Man

Kurt Eissler revealed the name of the "Wolf Man", Sergei Pankejeff (1887–1979), immediately after his death (McLaughlin, 1980, p. 103). The analysis was described by Freud (1918b), Mack-Brunswick (1928), and by Pankejeff himself (1971).

In January 1910, Pankejeff travelled to Vienna in the company of the doctor and later analyst Leonid Drosnés. He was suffering from various obsessional symptoms and was, as Freud wrote, "entirely incapacitated and completely dependent upon other people" (1918b, p. 7). Pankejeff was a student at that time, twenty-three years old and very wealthy. The analysis began in February 1910.[85] The entries for Pankejeff in Freud's record books start on 3 October 1910, and until July 1911 the treatment was mainly six hours per week. In the two following years, Pankejeff continued to receive six hours per week, occasionally more. As is generally known, Freud had determined when it was to end (July 1914), which happened to coincide with the weeks leading up to World War I.

He had told the patient "at the beginning of a year's work"—as we now know, this was in October 1913—that "the coming year was to be the last one of his treatment, no matter what he achieved in the time still left to him" (1937c, p. 217).[86] At the end of this first four-and-a-half year section, Freud considered the cure to have been "radical and permanent" (ibid.).

In 1919, five years after the termination of the analysis, Pankejeff travelled to Vienna and visited Freud. They agreed on a "short re-analysis"

---

[85] Pankejeff arrived in Vienna in January 1910, and after a few talks with Freud decided to embark on an analysis (1971, p. 155). The editors of the Freud-Ferenczi correspondence believe that the treatment had already started in January 1910 (F/Fer 1, p. 134). Strachey's opinion was that it had begun in February (1955a, p. 3). What makes Strachey's version more plausible is a letter Freud wrote to Ferenczi on 13 February 1910, in which he said, "A rich young Russian whom I took on because of compulsive tendencies admitted the following transferences to me after the first session" (F/Fer 1, p. 138). This remark is unlikely to have referred to a session that had taken place quite a while ago, and so I will assume that the first hour was in February.

[86] In the same text, Freud wrote that he later also used the determination of the termination of the analysis, as he had done with the Wolf Man, in other cases (1937c, p. 218).

in the late autumn, which apparently Pankejeff himself had initially not considered necessary (1971, p. 128). Freud recommended it in order to deal with "a piece of the transference which had not hitherto been overcome" (1918b, p. 122).[87] The second period began on 11 November 1919, was for six hours per week, and ended on 17 March 1920. Freud considered this to have helped the patient: since its completion, "the patient has felt normal and has behaved impeccably" (ibid.). A few years later, Pankejeff went to Freud again for help, and was referred to Ruth Mack-Brunswick, with whom he resumed his analysis (1926).

The first section with Freud comprised somewhat more than 1,000 hours (1,067), and the second ninety-eight hours (a total of 1,165). In the absence of a record book for the period between February and October 1910, I would estimate about 120 hours for this time, resulting in a total of around 1,280 hours. The first section lasted four-and-a-half years, including Freud's vacation, and the second, four months.

Freud saw the severity of the disease as the reason for the long duration (1918b, p. 10). The first years had "produced scarcely any change" and had "necessitated an excessively long process of preparatory education" (ibid., pp. 10, 104). Nevertheless, there had been partial success. The analysis had helped the patient to regain "a large amount of his independence, to awaken his interest in life and to adjust his relations to the people most important to him" (1937c, p. 217). The fact that the analysis could be carried out for so long was in no small part due to the "external circumstances" (1918b, p. 10), by which Freud must have meant Pankejeff's financial situation that allowed him to pay for the analysis and stay in Vienna for a long period of time. Had circumstances been less favourable, the treatment, as Freud wrote, would probably have been given up after some time. Freud also mentioned the "patience, adaptability, insight, and confidence" of the patient and his family as factors that made the long duration possible (ibid.).

Claire von Wallentin-Metternich

The shortest of the analyses presented here was that of Claire von Wallentin-Metternich (1878–1934). On Sunday 5 November 1911, Freud wrote to Ferenczi: "A 'countess', who has been in the news much lately,

[87] According to Mack-Brunswick, the Wolf Man had returned to consult Freud in 1919 because of his "hysterical constipation" (1928, p. 289).

is supposed to enter treatment tomorrow" (F/Fer 1, p. 309). In their commentary, the editors of the correspondence said that the person in question was probably Claire Wallentin-Metternich and that was actually the case (ibid., p. 317). The first entry for "Walentin" in Freud's record book was for Saturday 4 November for half an hour, so most likely an introductory session. Starting on Monday 6 November 1911, regular treatment began to be recorded in the record book, with a variable number of hours per week. This analysis comprised forty hours and was terminated after less than two months.

In a letter shortly after the beginning of the treatment, Freud wrote to Ferenczi that his "most interesting patient [...] Wallentin-Metternich" was with him, "unfortunately only for a short time" (F/Fer 1, p. 317). This makes it seem likely that the short duration was clear from the beginning or early on during the analysis. Furthermore, we can deduce from Freud's remark that he himself considered the duration "short" but that this did not prevent him from beginning an analysis with this young woman who was a well-known actor (Eisenberg, 1903, p. 1088).

Tatjana Nacht

We know of the analysis of Tatjana Tamara Nacht (?–1934), who resided in Berlin, from Neiser's dissertation (1978). Her analysis is discussed in the correspondence between Freud and Eitingon, who was a friend of Nacht's husband, Albert Nacht (F/E, pp. 64–77; 80). Nacht was suffering from a severe and chronic obsessional neurosis. After being briefly treated by Eitingon, she was supposed to come to Freud in the middle of October 1911, but then did not turn up, so that he gave the hours to someone else and told the patient he would try to see her at some later point. He hoped he would have an available hour at Christmas or New Year (F/E, p. 64). To Eitingon he wrote of his objections against treatment in Vienna:

> If the husband of the patient is not very rich, I would advise against an attempt in Vienna. Experience has shown that cases like the one you described only change very slowly in analysis and demand a long treatment. Accommodation will be very difficult because the patients have nothing to occupy them when they are on their own. We do not have a psychoanalytic sanatorium here. (Ibid., p. 67)

> A week later, he told Eitingon that he could take the patient after Christmas, but only on a "trial basis"; not much therapeutic success was to be expected in this case (ibid.).

The first entry in the patient record books for "Nacht" is on 26 December 1911. The analysis was six hours per week and ended 29 June 1912, just before Freud's summer vacation (151 hours). Freud initially found working with Nacht very interesting: "No other treatment has given me so much pleasure—if I ignore the therapeutic standpoint. The way things are going is ideal, the case has almost been solved" (F/E, p. 71). He added that the patient comprehended much but did not feel anything, and "with the help of the great resistances (disbelief) lets nothing touch her" (ibid.). At the end, Freud considered the outcome to have been only a partial success (ibid., p. 75). In Vienna, the patient had been "removed from the scene of her problems (Berlin)" and could not "*be convinced by experience*" (ibid., p. 76; italics in original).

Freud had apparently agreed that the patient could stay with him until the summer and was then to return to Eitingon. When she was back in Berlin, Eitingon described her transformation as "enormous" (F/E, p. 76), but soon afterwards remarked that her condition was "variable", to which Freud responded that he "at least had the gratification to find my prognosis confirmed that such a vast improvement achieved in so short a time cannot last. An honourable testimony for the analysis whose continuation she has been avoiding" (Ibid., pp. 80–81). This comment refers to Nacht's unwillingness to continue her analysis with Eitingon. In 1920, we then hear that she had not in a good state for some time and that she had inquired whether she could have a further period of analysis with Freud (ibid., p. 195). Freud hesitated to take her and recommended that she continue her treatment with Eitingon (ibid., p. 196). Shortly afterwards, she became Abraham's patient (F/A, p. 426; RB 1, p. 207).

It is noteworthy that Freud described the duration of the analysis as "short" although it lasted six months. This has, of course, to be seen in relation to the severity of the disorder. Here we also have evidence that Freud initiated trial treatments, as he was to recommend shortly afterwards (1913c, p. 125). It is also of interest that he regarded it as disadvantageous that the treatment did not take place in the patient's usual context of relationships (see Freud 1916–1917, p. 461).

Elma Pálos

We know the background to this treatment: Ferenczi had fallen in love with Elma Pálos (1887–1970), the daughter of his friend Gizella, and in her analysis he had approached her in a way "which I can no longer put forth as the benevolence of the physician or of the fatherly friend" (F/Fer 1, p. 318). He wanted to marry Elma, only to soon realise that she required an analysis that he was no longer able to provide (ibid., p. 324). Freud "took over" Elma, albeit with great reservations, and began the treatment on 8 January 1912, as we can see in his record book ("Pálos"). It was consistently six hours per week, comprised seventy-seven hours, and lasted until 5 April 1912.

As he often did when a patient had been referred, Freud kept his colleague (in this case Ferenczi) informed on the course of the analysis. Nowadays, this strikes us as somewhat strange, whereas Freud evidently did not consider it to be a breach of confidence (see Lynn and Vaillant, 1998). After three weeks, he reported, "Today I was able to observe the first sign of her ability to take part in independent thinking, with an excellent insight right away" (F/Fer 1, p. 340). By the middle of March, he found that the patient had made considerable progress and considered terminating the analysis at Easter:

> I would like to send her home for Easter. Now some new but quite different difficulties have set in. We are really in the narcissistic stage in which she behaves very self-sufficiently and actually refuses help. She no longer plays the part of the good patient at all. She is now herself, and I am curious how far I can bring her in these four weeks. (Ibid., pp. 356–357)

Then he continued and explained the good course of the analysis, "I believe it went so well only because she was so utterly indifferent to me. Now I value her more, naturally, and want to keep a close watch on the danger that is connected with that" (Ibid.).

Shortly afterwards, as Freud wrote to Ferenczi, the analysis started to stagnate. He nevertheless wanted to stop at Easter, also because he had three new patients who were about to start their treatment (F/Fer 1, p. 360). Elma had "brought out several quite surprisingly intelligent insights, but she doesn't want to get into the experience with you and doesn't seem to want to finish with me; i.e., because of the transference [she wishes] to extend her stay past Easter, which I don't want to do. So I am cooling off noticeably again" (Ibid., p. 74). Freud stuck to his plan; the last hour is entered on his last working day before the Easter break. Pálos returned to Budapest and continued her analysis there with Ferenczi (ibid., p. 369).

In this case, it was Freud who terminated the treatment after three months. It seems that there were two reasons for this: on the one hand, there had been good progress; on the other hand, he saw strong resistances.

Loe Kann

The name of Louise ("Loe") Dorothea Kann (1882–1944), a very wealthy Dutch woman, turns up in the correspondence between Freud and Jones (F/Jo, p. 12).[88] From 1906 onwards, she was in a relationship with Jones and called herself "Jones"; this was the name that appeared in Freud's record books. It is possible that she had at one time been Jones's patient (ibid., p. 63). During the congress in Weimar (1911), Jones asked Freud to take her into treatment (ibid., p. 117). Jones's biographer, Vincent Brome, wrote that Kann suffered from compulsions and mood swings (1982, p. 37). Freud mentioned sexual anaesthesia (F/Jo, p. 181).[89] Before and during the analysis, Kann was ill several times and had to undergo a number of operations. She had become addicted to morphine, possibly as a result of her ailments and operations. Nevertheless, Freud took her into treatment.[90]

On 16 June 1912, two weeks before Freud's summer break, Kann turned up for "preliminary treatment". She received one hour daily

---

[88] The date of birth and death are according to http://treefic.com/preview/treefic/billjones?a=biog&s=572 [accessed 20 November 2006].

[89] On the subject of Kann and her analysis, see also Brome (1982, pp. 37–39, 50, 64, 83–89; 104); Appignanesi & Forrester (1993, pp. 226–239); Leitner (2001, pp. 220–228); and Maddox (2006, p. 96).

[90] Leitner (2001, p. 221) has pointed out that Freud's statement about the problematic compatibility of psychoanalysis and physical disease went back to an idea of Ferenczi's and dated from the time in which Kann's analysis began. Freud wrote, "Combined treatments for neurotic disorders which have a powerful organic basis are nearly always impracticable" (1913c, p. 137). Leitner poses the question, "Did he already know this before Loe Kann's investigation?" (2001, p. 222) My response is that although Freud advised against carrying out an analysis in such infelicitous circumstances, this did not stop him from trying. As was often the case, he was not dogmatic but simply said that such treatment could "usually" not be carried out.

until Freud's vacation began. After the holidays, her analysis was continued at six hours per week. Kann rented an apartment in Vienna and moved in with her maid (Maddox, 2006, p. 202).

Since the analysis was discussed in about fifty letters between Freud and Jones, there is copious information about its course. Jones, for example, regarded it as "resistance" when his life partner complained in her first months of analysis that the analysis was "an attack on her personality"; Freud would not believe what she said and would twist everything "until she is quite confused in her mind" (F/Jo, p. 173). In February 1913, Kann threatened to break off the analysis after Jones had confessed that he had been unfaithful. "It was a tremendous shock at first. She got the old pains [...], raised the morphia [...] and renounced treatment," Freud wrote to Jones. He continued:

> You remember, she identified PsA, your and my own person and so she had to break off with all three of them. Yet there was a thread left undamaged between her and myself. I got hold of it and persuaded her to go on not for your sake but in her own interest. She agreed and it came to be right. (Ibid., p. 191)

Six hours continued to be entered into the patient record book for these days, which *could* mean that Kann did not really interrupt her analysis but kept on coming to the sessions.

After the summer holidays of 1913, she then did actually interrupt the analysis. The background to it: in October 1913, Freud expected to find Kann in his practice (F/Jo, p. 227), and heard that she would be coming a few days later (ibid., p. 227). Shortly afterwards, he received the message that Kann was postponing her departure again and would be in Vienna on 21 October at the earliest. She had not been able to finish furnishing Jones's consulting rooms in time and requested that Freud "reserve her some hours" (ibid., p. 229). Freud acceded to her request. However, when the analysand once again changed her plans and announced that she would arrive on 18 November because, as Jones wrote, she first wanted to rest and do some errands, Freud no longer reserved hours for her (ibid., p. 231f).[91] Should another patient stop,

[91] According to Maddox, Kann offered to pay Freud for the hours she had missed in October, November, and December (2006, p. 112). Since no hours for "Jones" are entered in the record book during these months, it could be an indication that Freud did not always charge a cancellation fee.

which could well be the case soon, she could then have these hours (ibid., p. 240).

Kann was furious with Freud, stayed in London, became ill, and finally arrived in Vienna at the beginning of December. Freud gave her "two hours a week to help her in clearing the darkness of the last London events and freeing herself again from Morphia" (ibid., p. 247). This is exactly what we find in Freud's record book: in December there are entries for three hours in one week, and two weeks with two hours each for "Jones". On 14 December, Freud found Kann "in a deplorable condition" and "nearly inaccessible [...] doesn't understand what we want her to do or find" (ibid., p. 249). At the beginning of January 1914, Freud wrote to Jones: "Loe has just given in and will take a daily treatment" (ibid., p. 252). In a letter to Ferenczi on the same day, he wrote, "From today on I am going to work more energetically on Loe" (F/Fer 1, p. 529). This is exactly what we find in the record books: starting from 3 January, six hours per week are again regularly noted for Kann.

An explanation for a second gap of two weeks at the beginning of June 1914 can again be found in the letters. During this time, Kann got married to a man whose acquaintance she had made during her analysis and whose last name also happened to be Jones (Herbert Jones).[92] Freud and Rank were present at the wedding in Budapest, and Ferenczi, who had had Ernest Jones in analysis the previous year, joined them as a translator (F/Jo, p. 285). Freud agreed with Ernest Jones that Loe Kann was a "jewel": "She must be judged for herself, measured by a standard fitted to her only self" (Ibid.). Shortly before the end of the analysis he admitted, "as for Loe, the morphia campaign has miscarried; in the trial to get loose from it she developed such a misery that it could not be followed up in the short time before us" (ibid., p. 289). A complicating factor of the treatment was that the reason for her somatic complaints and pain had remained unclear—or, as in Freud's laconic commentary to Ferenczi: "mixed case always unpleasant" (F/Fer 1, p. 539). On 10 July, the day of Kann's last session, Freud wrote to Jones:

> I will take leave tomorrow from Loe. She recovered instantly after taking more morphia and I see no way to wrench it from her at the moment. She has become no believer in Psa. as yet, but she is

[92] In 1938, they were divorced, according to Wilsey, because of Kann's addiction to morphine (2002, p. 14).

> charming with all her faults, which are more than outweighed by her excellent qualities. There is light and shadow. (F/Jo, p. 292)

This is how this analysis (392 hours) ended. Although Loe Kann remained addicted to morphine, and although she had tried Freud's patience and did not become convinced of psychoanalysis, the treatment seems to have ended on amicable terms (F/AF, p. 271).

Bruno Veneziani

The entries in Freud's patient record books between October 1912 and May 1913 for "Veneziani" refer to Bruno Veneziani (1890–1952), the brother-in-law of the writer Italo Svevo. Fallend (1995, p. 375), Esman (2001), and Roazen (2005, pp. 92–96) have reported on his analysis.[93] Before Freud, Veneziani had been in analysis with Sadger (F/A, p. 446). Veneziani had a total of 187 hours with Freud. The number of hours per week varied considerably in this case, between four and seven hours. We do not know how the analysis ended. Judging from Freud's remarks, it would certainly not have been to their mutual satisfaction.

After his analysis with Freud, Veneziani went to Reitler and Tausk, then in 1914 to Abraham and later to Groddeck (1921, 1922, 1923).[94] After that, Weiss kept him in "treatment that was limited to supportive therapy" (F/W, p. 28). In his letters to Abraham, Freud described the patient as "a bad case", "an enigma", and said that nobody had been able to bring about any changes (F/A, p. 283). Abraham came to the same conclusion after a few weeks: the patient "will very soon leave treatment; there is no getting at his narcissism" (ibid., p. 448). Nor did Groddeck find any possibility of helping him (F/G, p. 88). According to Weiss, Veneziani was "an addict and led a very turbulent life" (F/W, p. 27).

In 1920, Weiss asked Freud if he would take the patient for a second section (ibid.). Freud refused, saying that Veneziani was not suitable for an analysis because he did not suffer from a conflict between his ego and his drives; he did not have a "normal" character or an ego that could work together with the analyst; he was too narcissistic and

---

[93] More literature about Veneziani can be found in Fallend (1995) and Roazen (2005); see also the case of "Dr. A" in the letters between Freud and Eduardo Weiss (F/W, pp. 24–29).

[94] The information about the treatment in Groddecks Sanatorium comes from Fallend (1995, p. 375).

self-satisfied; his homosexuality was not the issue (ibid.). Veneziani, incidentally, is the only one of the group of nineteen patients who may have wanted to join the Vienna Psychoanalytic Society.[95]

Freud's comment that Veneziani "had tasted psychoanalysis" with him (F/W, p. 39) has less to do with the duration of the treatment than the twenty-two-year-old's approach to it. Nonetheless, Freud worked with him for eight months, and it is of special interest that, like Loe Kann, whose analysis began at the same time, Veneziani suffered from problems of addiction. Freud nevertheless took him as a patient and apparently needed so much time to discover that the patient was not suited for analysis.

Lucy Hoesch-Ernst

So far we have known little about the analysis of Lucy Hoesch-Ernst (1864–1944). Her name occurs in the Freud/Jones correspondence, where her treatment is also mentioned (F/Jo, p. 213). Jones announced her in July 1913 as "a very troublesome lady" whom he had met in Canada:

> She is a German psychologist, who has read most of the psa literature, and is sure she knows everything. She is a woman of 48, with very disagreeable character traits, and in a miserable current situation, with little chance of future happiness. (Ibid., p. 213)

Shortly afterwards, Freud received a letter from her and offered her an appointment after his summer vacation (ibid., p. 214).

Lucy Hoesch-Ernst had written a doctoral thesis on a psychological subject at the University of Zürich (Hoesch 1906). She came from Düren and was married to the American doctor George R. Ernst.[96] The first entry in Freud's record book, on 30 October 1913, is for one hour for "Hoesch Ernst" (later usually just "Hoesch"). The analysis began at six hours per week and was interrupted for a week in December. Later

---

[95] Fallend discovered an entry in the minutes of the Vienna Psychoanalytic Society of 7 April 1920 that he believed was a reference to Veneziani: "Dr. Venetiani has applied for membership. Will be asked to send a paper" (Fallend, 1995, p. 197). Since neither the name Veneziani or Venetiani turns up in any of the membership lists of the society, the applicant probably thought better of it.

[96] www.matrikel.unizh.ch/pages/0.htm [accessed 15 June 2006].

in the same month there was a longer break of four weeks up to 18 January 1914. We have not come across any similarly long interruption of an analysis during Freud's working year. It is not clear whether the patient took a holiday, was ill, or had discontinued and then resumed her analysis. After this break, the frequency of hours varied (from four to six per week). The analysis ended on 18 March; the treatment (without the five-week break) comprised sixteen weeks and came to a total of eighty-five hours.

We do not know why the treatment was terminated. All we have is a comment Freud made on 19 March 1914: "Lucy Hoesch-Ernst left me yesterday for my relief. She is a heavy burden" (F/Jo, p. 270). After that, the patient is no longer mentioned in the correspondence between Freud and Jones. Since Freud described her as a "heavy burden", was relieved when the analysis came to an end, and at no point reported on any progress or positive development, one gets the impression that the analysis had not been entirely satisfactory for either Freud or the patient.

In his autobiography, Jones mentioned Hoesch-Ernst, using her full name, and called her a "stormy petrel" (1959, p. 252). She came from a well-known family in the Rhineland and had been "strongly anti-German" in World War I (ibid.). Research has shown that in 1915, Hoesch-Ernst had been one of the main initiators and supporters of a pacifist journal, the *Internationale Rundschau*, that appeared in both English and German editions until 1918 (Meylan, 2004). Contributions by Rosa Mayreder, the wife of Freud's patient Karl Mayreder, and, for example by Romain Rolland, Annette Kolb, and Bertrand Russell, were published there, as were articles by Hoesch-Ernst and Jones himself.[97]

Karl Mayreder

Karl Mayreder (1856–1935), an architect who had founded and now occupied the chair for urban development at the University of Vienna, had a comparatively short analysis with Freud (Anderson, 1988, pp. 11, 36). He had been suffering from a severe depression since 1912 and had

[97] For the first volume Jones wrote an article "Krieg und Sublimierung" [War and Sublimation] (1915). In a letter to Ferenczi Freud complains, that though Jones mentions his article "Thoughts for the Times on War and Death" (Freud, 1915b) in a footnote, the entire essay was nothing but an "unconcealed rendering" of his (Freud's) own article, which had been published in April 1915 (F/Fer 2, p. 98).

already consulted several doctors (ibid., p. 24). On 16 January 1915, he ran into Paul Federn who "urged him" to "go to Professor Freud" (Mayreder, 1988, p. 151). The Mayreders were familiar with Freud. Mayreder's wife Rosa was a writer, feminist, and pacifist, as well as being a friend of Freud's former patient, Emma Eckstein. Among other things Rosa Mayreder had written a review (1906) of the first edition of the *Three Essays on the Theory of Sexuality* (Freud, 1905d).[98] After her husband had talked to Federn, she got in touch with Freud and made an appointment, and on Wednesday 20 January 1915 she and her husband visited Freud. As Rosa Mayreder wrote in her diary, her husband's treatment "already began the next day" (1988, p. 151). This corresponds to the entry in Freud's record book. The first entry for "Mayreder" is on Wednesday, the next on Thursday. There is also an entry for an hour for the fifty-nine-year-old on Friday and on Saturday. In the following week, he had five hours, and after that always four hours per week. The treatment lasted ten weeks and comprised forty-one hours.

On the last day of treatment, Freud wrote to Abraham: "I am working slowly and steadily on the papers for Imago and the Zeitschrift, and have found confirmation of the solution of melancholia in a case I studied for two months, though without visible therapeutic success, which, however, may follow" (F/A, p. 302). Since *no other* treatment terminated in this month (March, 1915), there can be little doubt that Freud was referring to Mayreder. Rosa Mayreder also wrote that his short analysis had not helped her husband. She may have welcomed its termination because in her diary she noted that Fritz Eckstein (Emma E's brother) had advised her not to leave her husband "longer than Easter with Freud" (1988, p. 155). The treatment did in fact end a week before Easter. Freud might have had the Mayreders in mind when he wrote soon afterwards in the *Introductory Lectures*, "in psychoanalytic treatments the intervention of relatives is a positive danger and a danger one does not know how to meet" (1916–1917, p. 459).

There are several entries in Rosa Mayreder's diaries regarding the analysis of her husband. She was disappointed and considered Freud to be "clever in the art of interpreting" and a "monomaniac of his system", rather than a "scientific observer" (1988, pp. 160–161). She wrote that

---

[98] On Rosa Mayreder, see Anderson (1992). The Mayreders are considered significant up to the present day in Austria, as reflected by the fact that their portraits were on the 500 Schilling notes of 1997.

her husband's severe depression lasted until his death (1935). Various treatments in a sanatorium and the consultation of numerous doctors, including Adler, Federn, Steinach, and Wagner-Jauregg, had not led to any real improvement.

An interesting point about this treatment is its beginning: just one preliminary talk with the patient *and* his wife was sufficient for Freud, and this was what he went on to recommend (1913c, p. 184). The frequency was also unusual since mainly four sessions per week did not take place among the analyses of the analysts. We do not know the reason for the reduced frequency; perhaps Mayreder's commitments at the university did not allow him to come more often. Freud would not have lacked the time, since his practice had shrunk considerably in the first months of the war.

Aranka Schwarcz

Aranka Schwarcz (1895–?) turns up in the correspondence between Freud and Ferenczi. There we can read that she came from Szolnok, Hungary, and that Ferenczi sent her to Freud (F/Fer 2, p. 83).[99] We do not know why this young woman sought treatment. In his letter of October 1915, Freud called her his "only new acquisition" (ibid.). In the record books, the first entry for "Schwarcz" appeared on 4 October. Apart from her, Freud only had two patients with six hours per week at that time and an additional two who came one or two hours per week.

Until the middle of April 1916, "Schwarcz" regularly received six hours per week (183 hours). We do not know why she terminated the treatment after six-and-a-half months. A few months after the analysis, Schwarcz approached Ferenczi, who sent her back to Freud: "I have also directed Fräulein Schwarz [sic] from Szolnok to you. It is better if she continues the work with you. I also noticed her hesitation and am only supporting my own wish with my decision" (F/Fer 2, p. 140). She evidently did not immediately resume her treatment because an entry for "Schwarcz" does not turn up in Freud's record book until October the next year (1917). That this entry actually referred to Aranka Schwarcz again seems highly likely based on the registration documents in Vienna, according to which she stayed in the city for exactly the same

[99] The date of birth, 11 December 1895, is according to WSLA; information received on 26 November 2006.

period that Freud entered her in his record book.[100] The second period lasted until March 1918 and again was six hours per week (127 hours).

Rózsi von Freund

We have known of the analysis of Rózsi von Freund (1887–?), the wife of Anton von Freund, who had come to Freud via Ferenczi since the publication of the Freud/Ferenczi correspondence (F/Fer 2, p. 96).[101] However, we do not know why she sought treatment.

At the end of the first period, in June 1916, after eight-and-a-half months of analysis, Freud explained himself to Ferenczi, "Frau von Freund will undoubtedly turn out well. It was difficult, instructive work; one couldn't have done anything in a shorter time" (Ibid., p. 131).[102] It seems that Freud thought that the treatment, which was usually two hours daily, could now come to an end (399 hours).

One year after the end of the analysis, Rózsi von Freund returned to Freud in November 1917, this time for only eight weeks and with a "normal" frequency of six hours (a total of forty-two hours). She was pregnant at the time (her son was born on 6 February 1918), as had been the case during the first period of her analysis (her daughter was born on 22 October 1916).[103] We know from a letter that Freud later wrote to Anna, he considered Rózsi von Freund to be a difficult if not intractable case (F/AF, p. 272). Anna in turn mentioned the "terrible moods" von Freund had been suffering from (ibid., p. 139).

---

[100] Aranka Schwarcz was registered in Vienna from 14 October 1915 to 24 April 1916, and again from 29 September 1917 to 18 March 1918 (WSLA, documentation received on 26 November 2006); see also F/Fer 2, pp. 259, 260, 361, 363, 364.

[101] I take the year of birth from the commentary of Meyer-Palmedo, who provided her maiden name of Bródy (F/AF, p. 201, German edition). Rózsi is the familiar abbreviation of Rozsália, and is unusual and inappropriate in formal speech (as Laszlo Kruppa kindly pointed out to me in a personal communication on 12 November 2006). In this chapter, I nevertheless continue with the name Rózsi because it has become the one commonly used when referring to her.

[102] This remark confirms that the person referred to in the patient record book entries with "Freund" and "v. Freund" in this time and in the previous months was Rózsi von Freund; see also Ferenczi's letter of December 1915 in which he called Rózsi von Freund Freud's patient (F/Fer 2, p. 95).

[103] The dates of birth are according to F/Fer 2, pp. 150, 267. Rózsi von Freund was registered in Vienna from 2 November 1917 to 21 December 1917, exactly the period in which sessions for "Freund" were entered in the record book (WSLA, documentation received on 26 November 2006). This is why I consider the second period of analysis to be verified.

Arthur Fischer-Colbrie

The analysis of twenty-year-old Arthur Fischer-Colbrie (1805–1968), a student of German literature who later became known as a poet, began on 13 November 1915 and lasted until the summer holidays of 1916, with mainly six hours per week (179 hours).[104] Goldmann drew attention to this analysis and to Fischer-Colbrie's relationship to Freud (1985, p. 271). The analysis was apparently meant to continue after the summer holidays since Freud later wrote to the analysand: "I would like to take you back again, I too am not happy about the uncompleted treatment" (quoted in Walder, 2010, p. 126). That this did not initially come about was in all likelihood because Fischer-Colbrie was called up for military service.[105]

In October 1918, Freud offered him a place. Fischer-Colbrie, however, became ill, and it was not until January 1919 that he came for the second section. He was probably one of the two "returnees" whom Freud mentioned in his letter to Ferenczi of 1 January 1919 (F/Fer 2, p. 321). There were 140 hours entered in Freud's patient record book between January and July 1919, usually six per week, so the young man received a total of 319 hours. There were three interruptions of about one week each when there were no entries for him; we do not know whether he was ill, or had to attend to his university studies, or was on holiday during these breaks.

Why Fischer-Colbrie wanted an analysis is also unknown. In a medical certificate of the summer of 1917, Freud listed various neurotic symptoms, including anxiety and obsessional ideas.

A special feature of this analysis that Goldmann has already drawn attention to is that Fischer-Colbrie's charm apparently led Freud to use the familiar "du" form. Freud wrote to him:

> Your sense of humour is contagious. So we will continue the treatment on a first name basis and you will have the opportunity to kick your heels in the treatment, unhindered by solemn respect. This may not be the most common technique, but I have no doubt

---

[104] In Freud's record books he mainly appears as "Fischer-Colbrie" and also as "Fischer-Col", "Fischer, C", and "Fischer". See Walder (2010), who has published the correspondence between Freud and Fischer-Colbrie, and the medical certificate cited below that Freud issued for Fischer-Colbrie.

[105] This is also assumed by Goldmann (1985, p. 271).

> that in your case I may permit myself to do this and that it will contribute to your liberation. (Quoted in Walder, 2010, p. 129)

This unusual arrangement was probably influenced by the patient's youth.

Rudolf Kriser

On 29 May 1918, Freud wrote to Abraham: "I am now having my portrait done by a patient who has been restored to art" (F/A, p. 378).[106] A few days later, on 2 June, we hear that the "drawing is finished, quite fine, and not very gratifying" (F/Fer 2, p. 285). The artist Rudolf Kriser (1885–?) came from Vienna and, as we can see in Freud's record book, had one-and-a-half hours daily for two weeks in July 1916. The analysis was not continued directly after the summer break but resumed in January 1917 for a further two years, by which time it comprised 472 hours and then was six hours per week except for a period of two weeks (20 May to 1 June 1918) during which there were no entries for "Kriser". It was exactly in this period that Freud wrote to Abraham and Ferenczi about sitting for a portrait with Kriser. That means that six months before the end of the treatment, Kriser was working on a drawing of Freud, a very unusual arrangement whose background and details we as yet know nothing about.

Georgina Weiss

We know even less about Georgina Weiss (1898–?), a younger sister of the Italian psychoanalyst Edoardo Weiss, who was also in analysis with Freud in 1918 (Roazen, 2005, p. 85).[107] We do not know why she approached Freud.[108] She appeared in the patient record book from

---

[106] See the complete correspondence between Freud and Abraham (F/A, p. 593, fn., German edition). The letters confirm that the record book entries of July 1916 refer to Kriser.

[107] According to information I received from the WSLA on 26 November 2006, she was born on 21 April 1898. Weiss was registered in Vienna from 5 November 1917 to 16 July 1918. The data in the archives, where her first name is spelled "Giorgina", show that she was born in Trieste and was studying music at that time.

[108] According to Roazen, Freud's analysis of Georgina Weiss was unsuccessful (2005, p. 85). Roazen further alleges that Freud considered Weiss to be a case of hysteria and later sent her to Helene Deutsch, who took her to Berlin when she herself went to have analysis with Abraham. He states that Weiss eventually developed schizophrenia.

2 January 1918 onwards and, unusually, with both her first *and* last names ("Georgina Weiss"). The treatment of the young woman lasted until the end of June (128 hours), and the number of hours per week varied frequently; usually it was five. Edoardo Weiss wrote that after the war Georgina returned to Trieste, which now belonged to Italy, which meant she was no longer able to travel to Vienna and had therefore not been able to continue the analysis after the summer break (F/W, p. 29).

Margarete Rie

Margarete Rie (1899–1986) was the daughter of Freud's friend Oskar Rie and the sister of Marianne Kris (née Rie), as well as a friend of Anna's. Later she became an actress and married Hermann Nunberg. Her analysis was mentioned in Young-Bruehl's biography of Anna Freud (1988, pp. 103–139). Thanks to Freud's record books, we now know the exact dates. "Rie" began her treatment in October 1918, almost always came six times a week, and stopped exactly at the end of the "season" in June 1919 (213 hours).[109] She began the analysis as a nineteen-year-old for reasons that we do not know.[110] Neither do we know how the analysis ended and what Freud's opinion of its duration and course was. In the 1920s, Margarete Rie received treatment a second time, this time with Franz Alexander in Berlin.[111]

Julius Hering

We know of Hering's analysis from the correspondence between Freud and Abraham (F/A, p. 438). In February 1921, Abraham inquired about a patient named "Julius Hering" who had been in analysis with Freud "at the end of 1919".[112] At that time, the patient had been suffering from a "psychosis", which had improved during Freud's treatment. On his way home, the patient had had a relapse, following which he remained hospitalised and, according to Abraham, suffered from a "fixated delusion of persecution" (ibid.). Freud confirmed the diagnosis, describing the

---

[109] Shortly after it had begun, the analysis was interrupted for ten days.

[110] In July 1919, after her analysis with Freud, Anna Freud wrote that Rie "had very little energy" and often had "a headache and palpitations" (F/AF, p. 155). After the analysis, Freud sent his regards via Anna a number of times.

[111] Interview by Robert Grayson with Marianne Kris, 25 July 1973; Abraham A. Brill Library, New York.

[112] We do not know the year of either Hering's birth or death.

patient as "a real persecution fanatic", and went on to write that the "first beginnings of an influence" broke down "when the money with which he should have paid me did not materialise" (F/A, p. 439, see also Appendix).

The name Hering (also Heryng) turned up in Freud's record books at the end of 1919, from 29 September through to 13 December, so one can assume that he is the man mentioned in the correspondence whose symptoms seem to have been psychotic. Hering underwent analysis regularly six times a week for a total of sixty-five hours. In view of Freud's comment, I assume that the analysis was prematurely terminated; it is not possible to say who initiated the termination.

Bieber

"Dr. Bieber", as Freud and Jones called him in their letters, was an American dentist who came to Freud via Jones (F/Jo, p. 360). He appeared for the first time ("Bieber") in Freud's record book on 6 December 1919 and suffered from a "genuine" delusional jealousy paranoia (ibid., p. 405).[113] As Freud had warned at the beginning, the therapy might be "long" (ibid., p. 360).

The patient received one hour per day; his wish for an additional hour was initially rejected (ibid., p. 361) but later occasionally fulfilled. In February 1920, after two months of analysis, Freud found that Bieber was doing very well, though "not yet cured to be sure" (ibid., p. 368). One month later, "Bieber is making a splendid analysis, I begin to like him [...] the core of him is sound" (ibid., p. 373). At the end of July (after 203 hours), Freud dismissed him before his summer break, which began later than usual that year, and was convinced that Bieber was cured.[114]

Back in New York, Bieber experienced a relapse, returned to Vienna in the autumn of 1920, and resumed his analysis on 29 October, now usually with two hours per day. Freud hoped for an improvement, provided the patient had "learned" from his relapse. The second section lasted until the end of January 1921 (F/Jo, p. 405) and comprised ninety hours until the end of December, and 134 hours if January 1921 is included.[115] After its completion Freud was satisfied that he had seen through the

---

[113] His first name and the years of his birth and death are not known.

[114] This information comes from an unpublished letter to Brill of 26 October 1920; my thanks to Ernst Falzeder for this source. The three sentences that follow are also based on this letter.

[115] When including January 1921 (for which there is no record book available) the second section could have lasted around 130 hours (90 + 40).

structure of a paranoid delusion, but was not sure "if the result *can* be a definite or a lasting one" (ibid., p. 405; italics in original).

So far, Bieber was the third patient who was diagnosed as psychotic. Within the group of "analysts", it was Anton von Freund who was suffering from an acute psychosis at the beginning of the first section of his analysis. From this one can conclude that Freud was less reluctant to treat psychoses than we had previously assumed. He was, as his remarks to Jones show, eager to understand and, if possible, to heal them (see Appendix).

George M. Young

George M. Young (1882–1959), who at that time was working in the foreign service, also came to Freud via Jones, with whom he had been in analysis a few years previously. We know his name, his biographical details, and about his analysis with Freud from the Freud-Jones correspondence (F/Jo, p. 394).

The reasons for his treatment mentioned by Jones and Freud include erythrophobia and sexual problems (ibid.). Young's analysis was discussed in several of Freud and Jones's letters (ibid., pp. 405, 409, 413).

According to Freud's record books, "Young" started his treatment in the middle of October 1920. Its frequency varied (between three and six hours per week) and was terminated by the patient the following January (ibid., p. 405). By the end of December 1920, a total of fifty-two-and-a-half hours had been entered.[116]

As Freud wrote, Young had to go to Innsbruck for professional reasons and so external circumstances were responsible for the discontinuation. Freud did not exclude that there might also have been inner reasons: "he halted where another man perhaps would have [...] hunted down the chance" (F/Jo, p. 405). A year after termination, Freud wrote to Jones that the "bit of treatment" had been of considerable help to Young (ibid., p. 468). The analysis had not been completed but the fact that Young had not approached him again was a clear indication that he was doing well (ibid.). It had, however, not been very nice of Young that now (1922) that he had become an "official and important personality" he no longer stayed in touch with Freud, "for I had been kind towards him and

[116] As there is no record book for January 1921, I have averaged the sessions of the previous month, so the analysis should have lasted about seventy-three hours.

resigned half of the fee, when he complained of his financial straits. Yet there is no matter for surprise or disappointment" (F/Jo, p. 405).

Freud did not insist that the treatment had been terminated prematurely, although he would surely have wanted to continue because he was fond of this patient (F/Jo, pp. 405, 409). His main priority was that the patient did not at that moment require analysis.

Duration of analyses and frequency of sessions—a comparison between "analysts" and "patients"

Table 4 contains the data relating to the analyses of the nineteen "patients": beginning and end of analysis, the number of hours for each section, the total number of hours, and the "actual" duration of the analysis, that is, the number of months during which there were entries in the record books. Freud's summer holidays and interruptions during treatment that lasted a week or more, as well as analysis-free periods between individual sections are not included in this column. "Mainly weekly frequency" refers to the number of hours per week that are the most common in the treatment. To find the frequency I used the record books entries as described above: I carefully examined each individual week in order to elucidate how the number of hours had come about.

I will now present the results of the *duration* of the analyses of "patients" and compare them with the duration of the analyses of "analysts". Then I will present the results on *frequency* and again compare the two groups.

Duration of analyses

As can be seen in the column "actual duration of analysis" (Table 4), the duration of the majority of the analyses, regardless of whether they were of "analysts" or "patients", was amazingly short. Some only lasted a few months or half a year; others were somewhat longer and very few went on for several years (von Dirsztay, Hirschfeld, and Pankejeff).

It does seem as if the "patient" analyses lasted longer than those of the "analysts" (Table 5) and as if Freud had only carried out very long analyses with "patients" (von Dirsztay, Hirschfeld, and Pankejeff), but not with "analysts". It is hard to say whether this can be generalised. We do know that at other times there were also analysts who were in

Table 4. Number of hours, frequency, and duration of Freud's analyses (therapeutic analyses) of nineteen "patients" (between 1910 and 1920).

Name	*Start and end of analysis*	*Hours for each section*	*Total hours*	*Weekly frequency*	*Duration in months*[1]
Elfriede Hirschfeld					
Section 1	11.10.1910 to 8.7.1911	392		9–12 hours	
Section 2	22.12.1911 to 25.1.1914	810	**1219**[2]	11½ hours	29
Section 3	29.6.1914 to 10.7.1914	17		9 hours	
Viktor v. Dirsztay					
Section 1	3.10.1910 to 8.7.1911	297		6, 8 and 12 hours	
Section 2	10.5.1913 to 31.12.1915	663	**1489**[2]	6–9 hours	55
Section 3	3.12.1917 to 3.3.1920	529		6 and 9 hours	
Sergej Pankejeff					
Section 1	3.10.1910 to 10.7.1914	1,067.5	**1165.5**[2]	6 hours and more	40
Section 2	11.11.1919 to 17.3.1920	98		6 hours	
Claire v. Wallentin-Metternich	4.11.1911 to 28.12.1911		**40**	6 hours and less	2
Tatjana Nacht	26.12.1911 to 29.6.1912		**151**	6 hours	6
Elma Pálos	8.1.1912 to 5.4.1912		**77**	6 hours	3
Loe Kann	16.6.1912 to 10.7.1914		**392**	6 hours	18½
Bruno Veneziani	4.10.1912 to 31.5.1913		**187**	6 hours and less	8
Lucy Hoesch-Ernst	30.10.1913 to 18.3.1914		**85**	6 hours and less	4½
Karl Mayreder	20.1.1915 to 27.3.1915		**41**	4 hours	2½

Aranka Schwarcz					
Section 1	4.10.1915 to 20.4.1916	183	**310**	6 hours	11½
Section 2	2.10.1917 to 2.3.1918	127		6 hours	
Rozsália v. Freund					
Section 1	1.11.1915 to 15.7.1916	399	**441**	Usually 12 hours	10
Section 2	2.11.1917 to 20.12.1917	42		6 hours	
Arthur Fischer-Colbrie					
Section 1	13.11.1915 to 6.7.1916	179	**319**	6 hours	14
Section 2	13.1.1919 to 12.7.1919	140		6 hours	
Rudolf Kriser	6.7.1916 to 15.7.1916	15	**472**	9 hours	19
	2.1.1917 to 31.12.1918	457		6 hours	
Georgina Weiss	2.1.1918 to 26.6.1918		**128**	3, 4, 5, and 6 hours	6
Margarete Rie	2.10.1918 to 30.6.1919		**213**	6 hours	9
Julius Hering	29.9.1919 to 13.12.1919		**65**	6 hours	2½
Bieber					
Section 1	6.12.1919 to 28.7.1920	203	**293**[3]	Usually 6 hours	10
Section 2	29.10.1920 to 31.12.1920	90		6–13 hours	
George M. Young	14.10.1920 to 31.12.1920		**52.5**[3]	6 hours and less	2½

[1]Duration without interruptions due to Freud's holidays and excluding time between sections.
[2]Excluding hours before October 1910.
[3]Excluding hours after December 1920.

Table 5. Duration of thirty-six of Freud's analyses: nineteen analyses of "patients" (therapeutic analyses) and seventeen analyses of "analysts", that is, men and women who were or became members of a psychoanalytic association (training analyses), measured in months (between 1910 and 1920).

Duration of analyses in months[1]	*Number of "patients" (therapeutic analyses)*	*Number of "analysts" (training analyses)*	*All analysands*
Up to 3 months	4	7	11
3 to 6 months	2	3	5
6 to 9 months	3	4	7
9 to 18 months	5	3	8
18 to 24 months	2	–	2
More than 24 months	3	–	3
Sum	19	17	36

[1]Excluding hours during Freud's vacation and excluding time between sections.

treatment with Freud for six, ten, and fifteen years; for example, Edith Jackson, Ruth Mack-Brunswick, or Dorothy Burlingham (Lynn, 2003; Lynn & Vaillant, 1998).

When looking at a possible connection between *domicile and length of analysis* it should be pointed out that in the group of "analysts" only Jekels (temporarily) and Deutsch were living in Vienna; in the group of "patients", only Wallentin-Metternich, Mayreder, Fischer-Colbrie, Kriser, and Rie were. As Table 4 shows, there is no difference in the length of the analysis. What first seems the most plausible explanation, namely that the analyses were so short because the analysands had to travel all the way to Vienna to see Freud and could not stay away from their families and their work clearly does not hold true.

Although Freud's analyses were often short, they nevertheless comprised many hours (Table 6), which, as mentioned before, was due to their high frequency. The upper limit of what medical insurance in present-day Germany cover is usually 240 hours. A comparison with Freud's "patients" shows the following: more than half (ten) completed their analysis within the 240-hour limit, six needed between 250 and 500 hours, and three required more than 1,000 hours. If "analysts" and "patients" are looked at together, it is quite similar: not quite half of the analyses

Table 6. Duration of thirty-six of Freud's analyses: nineteen analyses of "patients" (therapeutic analyses) and seventeen analyses of "analysts", that is, men and women who were or became members of a psychoanalytic association (training analyses), measured in number of hours (between 1910 and 1920).

Number of analysis sessions[1]	*Number of "patients" (therapeutic analyses)*	*Number of "analysts" (training analyses)*	*All analysands*
Up to 50 hours	2	5	7
50 to 100 hours	4	4	8
100 to 150 hours	1	3	4
150 to 200 hours	2	2	4
200 to 250 hours	1	2	3
250 to 300 hours	1	1	2
300 to 350 hours	2	–	2
350 to 400 hours	1	–	1
400 to 500 hours	2	–	2
500 to 1,000 hours	–	–	–
More than 1,000 hours	3	–	3
Sum	19	17	36

[1]Excluding hours before October 1910 and after December 1920.

(fifteen out of thirty-six) lasted for less than 100 hours; or, put differently, two-thirds (twenty-six out of thirty-six) were within the 240-hour limit, one third (ten out of thirty-six) required more. The majority of the thirty-six analyses were therefore *shorter* than our present-day treatments.

Another interesting result is the analysis in sections. It was not only with "analysts" that Freud would sometimes work in separate periods (van Emden, Ferenczi, Anton von Freund, and Révész) but also with "patients". Eight of the nineteen "patients" came to him more than once. For some, it would simply have been because they were only able to stay in Vienna for a limited period at a time. Others returned because of a renewed crisis in their lives. In these cases, as Freud once wrote, the first analysis "had not in fact brought to light all [...] pathological dispositions, and it was natural for the analysis to have been stopped when success was achieved" (1933a, p. 584). Again there were others as, for example, Hirschfeld and von Dirsztay, who were in a kind of continuous analysis that was interrupted by short treatment-free periods. These may have been the kinds of analysands Freud was referring to when he made the noteworthy observation:

> There are also severely handicapped people who are kept under analytic supervision all through their lives and are taken back into analysis from time to time. But these people would otherwise have been altogether incapable of existence and we must feel glad that they can be kept on their feet by this piecemeal and recurrent treatment. (1933a, p. 156)

Freud's analyses did not help all analysands, and sometimes only had a limited or temporary effect. Like the "analysts", some of the "patients" went to other analysts after Freud. In the group of "analysts" there were nine, among the "patients" at least eight: Rószi von Freund went to Ferenczi, Hirschfeld to Binswanger, Mayreder to Federn and Adler, Nacht to Abraham, Pálos to Ferenczi, Pankejeff to Mack-Brunswick, Rie to Alexander, Georgina Weiss to Deutsch, and Veneziani to Reitler, Tausk, Abraham, Groddeck, and Eduardo Weiss. Overall, at least seventeen of the thirty-six analysands had further treatment. For the "analysts", this could be ascribed to their search for training; however, in the group of "patients", it must be assumed that it was further therapy they were looking for.

When investigating Freud's contacts with the group of "analysts", I discovered that almost all of them took part in the meetings of the Vienna Psychoanalytic Society. This was very different in the group of "patients". Only Loe Kann was a guest of the society during the time of her analysis, and that was only on one evening.[117] None of the other "patients" ever took part in any of the meetings. That means that the mingling of analysis with private and professional life was limited to those women and men who were or became "analysts". Similarly, Freud gave none of the nineteen "patients" sessions during his vacation, whereas he did do so, albeit not very extensively, for his Dutch colleague Jan van Emden and the future analyst, Kata Lévy, Anton von Freund's sister (May, 2006b). The situation may have been similar with shared leisure time activities. Whereas Freud cultivated and sought out private

[117] The German edition of the *Minutes* has "Loe Kann" (Min 4, p. 248), the English edition "Loe (Lou?), Kaum, Krauss" (Min 4, p. 256).

contact with the "analysts", also during the period of their analyses, he seems to have behaved differently towards "patients". He apparently saw only Loe Kann and Rózsi von Freund outside the sessions. These were women whose husbands he regarded as colleagues and friends, supporters and allies in the "cause" of psychoanalysis.

Concluding comments on the duration of Freud's analyses of "analysts" and "patients"

The data and assessments that we have looked at here, to my mind, do not allow the conclusion that Freud was in principle against short analyses. He found some analyses that only lasted two or three months too short; in other cases, Freud was the one who terminated the treatment after a few months because he was, for example, satisfied with the result that had been achieved. Similarly, some analysands terminated the analysis themselves after a very short time because they believed they no longer needed it, and Freud was not inclined to make them stay against their wishes. He believed that the advantage of short, effective analyses was to "substantiate the medical importance of psychoanalysis" and they were also "of value in ministering to the therapist's self-esteem" (Freud, 1918b, p. 10). The disadvantage of short analyses was their lack of scientific value: "they only succeed so quickly because everything that was necessary for their accomplishment was already known" (ibid.).

The lack of scientifically rewarding insights in short analyses, however, did not stop Freud from carrying them out. He was equally pragmatic regarding existing time restrictions. He took people on as patients even if it was clear from the start that it could only be for a short time. In addition, I suspect that he sometimes did not let analyses reach their "natural" conclusion, but suggested the beginning of his summer vacation as a *possible* termination date. Why else would so many analyses have been concluded right before the summer break?

Sometimes the severity of a disorder made Freud wish for more time, which, however, could only rarely be realised. There were perhaps only one or two instances of "timeless" analyses not impinged upon by outer circumstances in the group of the nineteen "patients" discussed here. One example was Hirschfeld and Pankejeff's first section, when both patients were still financially well off and had no professional commitments or other reasons that prevented them from staying in Vienna for an extended time.

Freud saw the advantage of the "timeless" analysis of enabling changes that required a long period of preparation, as had been the case with Pankejeff. In addition, he believed that long analyses offered opportunities for scientific insights. Analyses, as he wrote, also took a very long time if we did not understand the disorder sufficiently. If one had a patient for a long period of treatment one ideally could expand one's knowledge and thereby "help substantially to reduce the length of the treatment in a subsequent case of equal severity, and [...] by submitting on a single occasion to the timelessness of the unconscious [the analyst] will be brought nearer to vanquishing it in the end" (Freud, 1918b, p. 10). That the gain in scientific insights did not immediately and automatically translate into therapeutic success was something Freud experienced several times in the years between 1910 and 1920—in particular in the analysis of Hirschfeld but also of Mayreder, Nacht, and Bieber. At the same time, he saw that there were analysands who needed long and sometimes lifelong analyses, so that there could be good therapeutic reasons for long analyses.

What about the assumption that between 1910 and 1920 Freud had "not yet" known that analyses took a long time and that it was not until the 1920s that he realised this? The available data does not confirm this; if anything, the opposite seems to have been the case. The long analysis of Hirschfeld began in 1908, and that of von Dirsztay in 1909 or 1910, and that of Pankejeff in 1910, all at the very beginning of the decade of our record books. Similarly, we can find very short analyses at the beginning of this ten-year period (Pálos, Wallentin-Metternich, Mayreder) and at its end (Hering, Young). Neither does this assumption correspond to what Freud wrote. In 1904, he had already expressed the opinion that analyses required "long periods, six months to three years" (Freud, 1904a, p. 254), less for milder cases, more when they were severe. Ten years later, his opinion had not changed much and he wrote, albeit somewhat opaquely, "psychoanalysis is always a matter of long periods, of half a year or whole years" (1913c, p. 129). Another twenty years later he wrote, "It is true that the treatment of a severe neurosis can easily extend over several years" (1933a, p. 156). Freud may have modified his opinion somewhat in the 1920s. In 1921, he told four colleagues—Pfister, Meng, Blumgart, Jelliffe—who wanted to be analysed by him, that he had changed his view of analyses of two or three months' duration because he now considered them too short and that at least four to six months were desirable.[118] We should note that he used the word "desirable" and not necessary.

Frequency of sessions

As Tables 4 and 7 show, the frequency at which Freud worked with analysands varied, not just with analysts and those planning to become analysts but also with "patients". For the group as a whole, in some cases the analyses were continuously held at the same weekly frequency (almost always six hours) but in a number of cases Freud changed the frequency during the analysis—sometimes several times. I will now present the typical frequency structures and include the assessment of the analyses of the "analysts". Table 7 shows the distribution of the frequencies.

Table 7. Weekly frequency of thirty-six of Freud's analyses (between 1910 and 1920).

Number of hours per week	*Number of "patients" (therapeutic analyses)*	*Number of "analysts" (training analyses)*	*All analysands*
6 hours	8	10	18
Alternately 6 hours and more	5	3	8
5 hours	–	1	1
4 hours	1	–	1
3 hours	–	2	2
Alternately 6 hours and less	–	1	1
Unclear patterns	5	–	5
Sum	19	17	36

[118] Freud to Meng on 20 October 1920 and 14 April 1921, and to Blumgart on 12 May 1921; with thanks to Ernst Falzeder. See also F/P, p. 81; Burnham & McGuire (1983, p. 207). In 1921, when Kardiner suggested coming to Vienna for six months, Freud responded that this was "a good term to achieve something both theoretically and personally" (Kardiner, 1977, p. 15). Some years later Freud said he did not think that four to five months was enough time to delve in "to the deepest layers of the unconscious and bring about permanent psychic change" (RB 4, p. 170). In the analyses he also wanted to search further for "something new" (ibid.). I understand the remark as an expression of Freud's desire for therapeutically useful and scientifically productive analysis.

The six-hour analysis

Eight (of the nineteen) patients had an hour every day from Monday to Saturday: Fischer-Colbrie, Hering, Kann, Kriser, Nacht, Pálos, Rie, and Schwarcz. Within the group of "analysts" ten (out of seventeen) had received treatment with six hours per week (May, 2006b).[119] That means that half of the analyses (eighteen out of thirty-six) were on a strict six-hour basis—the frequency that Freud said analyses should "as a rule" have (1913c, p. 127) and an intensity that is two or three times higher than the majority of present-day treatments (Schmid, 1988).

In order to give an idea of what such a six-hour analysis looked like in Freud's record books, I will describe the entries for Tatjana Nacht.

Nacht had her first hour on Tuesday 26 December 1911, Boxing Day (!). On this day Freud also saw a second patient, Hirschfeld. The odd appointment on a Sunday or a holiday turned up occasionally in the patient record books. In the same week Nacht came to Freud two more times, on Friday and Saturday, making it three hours that week. In the following week she had five hours because New Year's Day was a Monday. After that the entries were consistently six hours per week up to Easter. The Saturday before Easter Sunday in 1912 was part of Freud's long weekend so that Nacht had a total of five hours in that week. After Easter Freud started working in his practice again on Wednesday, and Nacht appeared on Thursday (11 April); perhaps she had spent the holidays with her husband in Berlin. That means that she only had three hours that week. Then the analysis resumed its usual pattern of six hours with the exception of the first week of May in which no hour is entered for her on 2 May. Freud took the Saturday before Pentecost off and the Monday was a holiday, so his consulting rooms remained closed: in these two weeks the patient again had only five hours. Subsequently, the analysis went back to its six-hour pace and was terminated on Saturday 29 June 1912. This means that Nacht had a strict six-hour analysis and according to the record book missed two of the hours of her six-month analysis (10 April and 2 May). Nonetheless, there were seven weeks when she in fact had less than

---

[119] These were: Stegmann, Oberholzer, Sokolnicka, Hollós, Dubovitz, Forsyth, Daly, Rickman, and Stern. I would also count Lévy in this group, because it was only at the beginning and due to external reasons that she had three and four hours per week.

six hours. This shows how important it is to know the details of the actual weeks and not to simply multiply the hours per week by the number of weeks.

Analysis with more than six hours

As became clear when examining the analyses of the "analysts", Freud worked with some analysands (three out of seventeen) for more than one hour a day: one-and-a-quarter, one-and-a-half, two, two-and-a-half, or even three hours. We can now see that this extremely high frequency was not limited to "analysts". Five "patients" also received more than one hour a day: Hirschfeld, von Dirsztay, Rózsi von Freund (first section), Pankejeff (first section), and Bieber (second section). One can distinguish two groups within the "six-plus analyses": in the first group the frequency only temporarily increased for a few days or weeks, while in the second group the basic frequency was always or over a long period of time more than six hours. Rózsi von Freund, for example, belonged to the second group: her first period of five months was twelve hours per week (6 × 2); similarly, Hirschfeld consistently received eleven-and-a-half hours per week (5 × 2 + 1 × 1½) for more than two years (January 1911–June 1913).[120]

The first section of Sergei Pankejeff's treatment can serve as an example of a temporary increase in the weekly number of hours.

In the first working year recorded in the patient record book (October 1910–July 1911), Pankejeff regularly had six hours per week; after the summer break in 1911, the analysis was resumed with the same frequency. In November, the weekly number of hours rose to nine, dropped to eight and six in the following weeks, then rose to 12. Between December 1911 and March 1912, Pankejeff again received six hours per

[120] After I had completed the original manuscript, I came across a letter from Freud to Pfister in which he responded to an inquiry that Pfister had made on behalf of a former patient, Elfriede Hirschfeld (F/P, p. 158, German edition, 2014). Freud wrote that it was out of the question that he could "devote two hours, that is, visit her in the hotel". Two strokes could therefore also mean that Freud visited the analysand at the hotel or sanatorium. Apart from Hirschfeld, this could have been the case for Anton von Freund and possibly for Bieber. In other cases—for example Ferenczi, van Emden, or Pankejeff, who also came for two hours daily—it can hardly have been because they were not so ailing that Freud had to call on them in a hotel or sanatorium. Nevertheless, the passage in Freud's letter to Pfister opens up a new and somewhat surprising way of explaining the six-plus analyses.

week. Then the weekly number of hours climbed first to nine, then 11, and around April 1912 was back to six hours. It seems that Pankejeff received these extra hours depending on when he needed them and when it was possible to do so; a consistent pattern is not visible. It was similar in the next year of treatment (1912–13). It began in October 1912 and was consistently six hours; by the end of February 1913, it had risen to a frequency of usually eight hours per week and stayed at this higher frequency until the summer break in 1913. After that, the treatment again began at six hours; by the middle of October, it had increased to eight and nine and occasionally ten hours per week, and it sustained this frequency until July 1914.[121]

The great flexibility in the weekly hours of this and other analyses is surprising. It does not conform to the idea of a fixed framework that we emphasise so much nowadays and that Freud did provide for other patients, as, for example, the strict six hours described above.[122]

To the best of my knowledge there is only one passage where Freud comments on the necessity of an analysis that exceeds six hours: "Occasionally, too, one comes across patients to whom one must give more than the average time of one hour a day, because the best part of an hour is gone before they begin to open up and to become communicative at all" (1913c, p. 127). These words apply to some of the analysands I have described but not to all of them. In some cases, external circumstances may have made Freud increase the frequency. Perhaps van Emden, for example, received twelve hours weekly during the first and fourth sections because he could not stay in Vienna very long. It could well be that Anton von Freund was needed in his factory in Budapest and therefore received between eight and fourteen hours per week. In Ferenczi's case, too, external circumstances may have been crucial in deciding on a very high frequency (between thirteen and nineteen-and-a-half hours per week).

External factors such as lack of money or time would not, however, have been the reason for patients who were wealthy and were not needed urgently somewhere else. This is true for the first period for Pankejeff while he was still well off, and it is also true for Rózsi von

---

[121] During the second period of his analysis, in 1919, the Wolf Man came six hours per week except for the last three weeks of the analysis when he received only three and two hours, probably to wean him off the treatment.

[122] How he organised the constant frequency changes in his practice is still unexplained.

Freund, von Dirsztay, and Hirschfeld. I suspect that Freud found these patients difficult but also interesting, rewarding, and likeable enough to undertake particularly intensive work with them. Of course, they needed to be able to afford it as well as to be willing to work this way. When he wrote the case history of Pankejeff, Freud commented (Freud, 1918b, p. 9) that some cases required a lot of time, partly because we have not understood the disorder sufficiently, partly because a long analysis was sometimes of therapeutic value. A long duration or a high number of hours per week may therefore also reflect Freud's spirit of inquiry and the intensity at which he worked to further his understanding of neuroses and psychoses. Analyses of similar density are no longer carried out nowadays, or at least they do not turn up in surveys (Schmid, 1988). Perhaps we have good clinical reasons to find such lengthy and close contact to be of dubious therapeutic value or we would find such intense work too taxing for the analyst. We may also not be fuelled by quite the same intense spirit of inquiry.

Three, four, and five hours

Among the "analysts" there were three (of seventeen) who regularly came to Freud for fewer than six hours per week (May, 2006b): Jekels, who at the beginning of the analysis had moved from Bistrai (Silesia) to Vienna, had five hours per week and usually did not come to Freud on Saturdays, so he may well have had an extended weekend. Helene Deutsch and Erzsébét Révész consistently came for three hours (usually Monday, Wednesday, Friday or Tuesday, Thursday, Saturday). As mentioned before, Freud may have considered them mild cases, the function of their analyses clearly was to train them, and that therefore "half" the usual frequency might have seemed sufficient.

In the group of "patients" there is only one case when Freud agreed on an analysis of constant low frequency: Karl Mayreder, who apart from the first week, always had four hours per week.

Unclear patterns

The frequency that Freud and the analysand had agreed on does not emerge in the courses of the remaining five analyses (Weiss, Hoesch-Ernst, Veneziani, Wallentin-Metternich, Young). The weekly number of hours never exceeds six and changes several times.

Georgina Weiss usually had five, sometimes three, four, or six hours without any connection of reduced hours to public holidays, for example. Lucy Hoesch-Ernst may have had a six-hour analysis and occasionally not appeared for a session. Her treatment began at the end of October 1913 with six hours, was interrupted in December, and for several weeks in January it was five or four hours. Since it was always a Saturday or Monday when a session did not take place, an extended weekend is a plausible explanation. After that, her treatment was resumed at six hours per week until it terminated in March 1914. The analysis of Bruno Veneziani is equally difficult to assess. The analysand quite often came only five times per week between October 1912 and Christmas. After Christmas, he returned to Freud a bit later than the other patients and missed four sessions in the period of his analysis, which ended in May 1913. The actress Claire Wallentin-Metternich came to Freud daily in the first three weeks, and after that less often. Perhaps her commitments at the theatre in Vienna did not allow her to come so frequently, or perhaps there were other reasons for the reduced number of weekly hours. It was only for a short period of two weeks that George Young's two-and-a-half-month analysis consisted of six hours. Otherwise Young had three, five, and five-and-a-half hours, and we have no indications what the reasons for the fluctuation might have been. Since he was employed at the British embassy in Vienna, his work may have prevented him from coming more often.

In all analyses of "analysts" the frequency agreed on with Freud becomes clear in the patient record books. René Spitz is an exception here but is explained in Freud's letter to Ferenczi in which he comments that the analysis had begun at six hours and was then reduced as "punishment". That is why I have allocated Spitz's case to the category "Six hours and less" in Table 7.

To summarise: the six-hour analysis was common in Freud's work; analyses comprising more than six weekly hours were not infrequent. The frequency sometimes changed several times during treatment. None of this corresponds to present-day approaches to analyses. We carry out our treatments with considerably lower density and (as I assume) a constant weekly frequency. The "high-frequency" analyses (four hours) in Germany would have been considered low frequency in Freud's time. If we set up the four-hour analysis as the norm, we cannot invoke Freud in our support.

The standard explanation for the six-hour analysis is that at the time the usual working week consisted of six days. The later reduction of weekly hours is usually attributed to the English weekend, the post-war introduction of the five-day working week and doctors' offices staying closed on Wednesdays in Germany: external conditions in society that would have affected the way in which psychoanalysis was carried out. As plausible as this may sound, not all facts bear this out, for example, the previously mentioned analyses at the Berlin institute in the 1920s mostly comprised three and four hours. In addition *none* of the analysands who lived and worked in Vienna—Helene Deutsch, Ludwig Jekels, Claire Wallentin-Metternich, George Young, and Karl Mayreder—had a regular *six-hour* analysis.

The intense sequence of hours and the days and weeks packed with activity may be best explained by how Freud worked. As in the 1890s when he searched for a theory of neuroses and psychoses with great intensity and for many years he carefully studied case after case, first creating, then discarding, reincorporating, abandoning and rewording countless hypotheses (May-Tolzmann, 1996). A similarly intense search may also underlie the analyses of six or more hours. Freud may have needed this arrangement for his work and have increased the frequency when he had the feeling he was close to a breakthrough—prying out the patient's "secret" or being able to see further into the depths of the disorder he was dealing with—and that by mustering all his energy he would achieve progress in his scientific inquiry and further enrich psychoanalytic theory. Dispersed contacts with patients once or twice a week would not have been sufficient to serve this intense spirit of inquiry. The analysis of six hours or more would not only be a reflection of societal and economic changes but also correlate to Freud's enormous hunger for knowledge.

Summary

In recent decades, many authors have pointed out that Freud worked differently from how we had thought. This led to a reading of Freud according to which he set up rules that he did not adhere to himself. This pattern of Freud criticism started with Lipton (1977, 1983) in the United States and with Cremerius (1984) in Germany; it was followed, among others, by Momigliano (1987), Lohser and Newton (1996), Lynn and Vaillant (1998), and Leitner (2001). I would like to suggest an alternative interpretation: Freud described what his experiences were—for example, that it is not helpful to have contact with analysands outside sessions, or that psychoses are not accessible to analysis. He, however, never "prohibited" personal contact or the analysis of psychoses but simply drew attention to the great difficulties that would ensue if one tried the one or the other. It was not Freud but the analysts following him who, it seems to me, have transformed Freud's recommendations and experiences into ironclad rules and prohibitions. This process of reinterpretation has gradually created the strictures, against which resistance has justifiably developed, a regimentation that, as my investigation has confirmed, is contradicted by Freud's own practice.

My impression throughout this investigation was that Freud's attitude to the duration of an analysis was undogmatic and liberal. He was realistic, pragmatic, *and* scientifically motivated and it is the combination of these traits that characterises his analytic work. He did whatever was possible and at the same time used his practice for scientific purposes. He mainly had a practice that included as many patients as conditions allowed and concentrated on the circumstances of the patient. It was within these bounds that he conducted his scientific inquiry, insofar as it was possible. The requirements of practice took precedence over science, and practice was guided by the internal and external circumstances of the analysand. The data on the duration of analyses are not to be considered as "guidelines", neither for Freud's time nor the present. They tell us neither how long analyses should last nor at what frequency they should take place. Instead they show the reality of a practice that was characterised by finding a compromise between what was doable and what was desirable.

* * *

Appendix

Analyses of psychotic patients

Some of the women and men presented above came to Freud to learn psychoanalysis; most of them, however, came because they sought help for a neurotic disorder. We know that Hirschfeld and Nacht suffered from severe, protracted, obsessional neuroses; Pankejeff is said to have had pronounced hypochondria, with paranoid and obsessional aspects. Fischer-Colbrie went to Freud because of neurotic symptoms (obsessional ideas, anxiety). Perversion played a central role in Veneziani's illness, erythrophobia in Young's. Kann may have suffered from sexual problems and was addicted to morphine; Veneziani was also said to be addicted. Only four patients had been diagnosed as psychotic when they came to Freud: Mayreder suffered from severe depression, Hering from delusional paranoia, and Bieber from delusional paranoid jealousy. In the case of von Freund, Ferenczi observed an "acute incipient psychosis", "hypochondriac-paranoid delusional phantasies, and hypomanic manifestations of excitation" (F/Fer 2, p. 265).

That Freud was willing to take on patients who had a diagnosis of psychosis contradicts the general idea that Freud did not or would not treat psychoses. I will now compile what we can say about how Freud dealt with psychoses in the time between 1910 and 1920, and I will limit the discussion to von Freund, Hering, and Bieber, disorders that are close to schizophrenic psychoses.

When Freud first saw Anton von Freund, he considered a diagnosis of depression but discarded it in favour of "postoperative hypochondria (anxiety hysteria with narcissistic content)" or "postoperative psychosis" (F/Fer 2, pp. 269, 272). After three weeks of treatment, he wrote, "The psychotic traits have receded to the extent that I can hope to begin a normal analysis with him in the next few days" (F/Fer 2, p. 269). The delusional ideas had "so to speak, withdrawn into a 'retirement home' and left the scene to the hysterical neurosis for which he is now doing a regular analysis" (ibid., p. 272). A few weeks later Freud reported that von Freund was still "free of delusion" (ibid., p. 275) and "is going through a proper analysis of neurosis which should take care of the accumulated material of his life" (ibid., p. 279). The analysis lasted until the end of June 1918 and was resumed for another few months in December of the same year. The delusions did not seem to have recurred before von Freund died in January 1920.

As becomes clear from the remarks above Freud seemed to have waited until the psychotic state had faded and then started the "proper" analysis. He treated the neurosis of the patient and not his psychosis, or in other words, he treated the patient analytically as long as he was neurotic but not when he was psychotic.[123]

The analysis of Julius Hering, which began in September 1919, shortly after the first period of von Freund's treatment, did not seem

[123] The patient received throughout the treatment one or two hours a day, whereas mentioned above, two may have indicated a visit to the hotel or sanatorium.

to have been satisfactory since Freud characterised him as a "bad" case in which therapeutic "influence" did not get very far (F/A, p. 439). As Abraham reported, the delusional paranoia had apparently resolved during the two months of treatment, but he subsequently relapsed and had to be hospitalised. Hering's analysis had a steady frequency of six hours per week; we do not know any details about its course.

As Hering was about to end his treatment, Freud had already accepted the next psychotic patient, Dr. Bieber from New York. His analysis was also six hours per week. Freud terminated it after eight months, believing that the patient had been healed. However Bieber had a relapse after his treatment was over. He returned to Vienna again and then received two hours of analysis daily. Before the second period began, Freud wrote to his colleague Brill in New York who apparently knew Bieber, "if he is cured I will be very proud as he may claim the diagnosis of paranoiac jealous delusion".[124]

Three months later, in January 1921, Freud discharged Bieber, and was now a little more sceptical about the extent of the therapeutic change: "To be sure I do not know if the result *can* be a definite or a lasting one" (F/Jo, p. 405). Although Freud was not sure whether a relapse would recur, he was very satisfied with his work: "The best work I ever did I could see through the structure of a true delusional Paranoia (Jealousy) down to the "hewn rock" and found some things I will relate at the Committee-meeting in Sept." (Ibid.)[125] As he had feared, the improvement was short-lived. In April 1923, Freud defended himself in a letter to Brill, writing that he was well aware that Bieber had not been cured, but "it is remarkable, so much could be done for him. Now the question is: is this all or can we do more for such a case of true Paranoia."[126] In this case, Freud seemed to have again distinguished between the psychosis where lasting change was highly unlikely and the improvement that analysis could nonetheless bring about.

---

[124] Freud to Brill on 26 December; thanks to Ernst Falzeder.
[125] Freud incorporated parts of his report to the committee into the paper, "Some Neurotic Mechanisms in Jealousy, Paranoia and Homosexuality", in the passages about paranoia (1922b, pp. 225–227). It is of interest that he described "neurotic" mechanisms of psychoses, that is, those aspects of psychosis that are psychically determined and can be approached by analysis.
[126] Freud to Brill on 25 April 1923; thanks to Ernst Falzeder.

We do not know if the 1910–1920 record books contained more patients with psychotic symptoms.[127] In his publications of this period, Freud refers to three women and men, whom, however, he saw only once or twice. In the *Lectures*, he mentions a woman with delusional jealousy who was still "fresh in my memory" in 1916, as well as a man with delusional paranoia (1916–1917, pp. 248–54, 425–26). A separate paper, "A Case of Paranoia Running Counter to the Psycho-Analytic Theory of the Disease" (1915f), is concerned with a woman who suffered from delusional paranoia. Freud wrote that he had seen her "some years ago" but only for two talks (ibid., pp. 263, 266).

In the 1920s Freud continued with the analysis of psychosis. Three long-lasting treatments of paranoid patients are known. A young American who was with Freud for five years (1925–1930) is mentioned in the correspondence with Ferenczi (F/Fer 3, p. 307; see also Lynn, 1993; Beam, 2001). Scofield Thayer, a friend of E. E. Cummings, also suffered from psychosis and was with Freud between 1921 and 1923 (Ozieblo, 2002; Sawyer-Laucanno, 2004). We know of a third psychotic patient whom Freud treated for three years (1925–1928) from a paper by Herbert Binswanger (1956).

In the years between 1910 and 1920, as well as in the years that followed, Freud had several patients with psychotic symptoms in analysis, cases where he had hoped to treat the psychotic aspects but did not succeed, yet still considered the analysis to have been therapeutically helpful and of scientific value. Judging from the comments on Bieber quoted above, one gets the impression that he may have been more interested in achieving a therapeutic effect than he showed.[128]

From the beginning, Freud was concerned with the question of whether a psychosis could be analysed and what its relation to neurosis was. Deliberations of this kind can be found in his writings of the 1890s,

---

[127] Brody (1970), who compiled all the cases Freud mentioned in the *Standard Edition*, found only one detailed description of a "major case" of psychosis between 1901 and 1938—the woman described above in the paper of 1915 (f). In addition, he found one briefly mentioned "minor case" between 1901 and 1912, and seven more "minor cases" between 1913 and 1924. Since Brody included manic-depressive cases in the category of psychosis, I cannot use his figures to compare results; and unfortunately, Brody provided us with the number of cases without saying where he had found them.

[128] I could well imagine that one might reach similar results regarding addiction: Freud took Loe Kann as a patient in spite of her addiction to morphine and tried very hard to help her cope with this problem. Although he did not succeed, he nevertheless considered the analysis to have been helpful.

in his letters to Fließ, in the *Minutes of the Vienna Psychoanalytic Society*, and above all, of course, in his letters to Jung, but also to Ferenczi and Abraham.[129] The years between 1905 and 1911 were practically dedicated to the "conquest" of psychiatry. Freud called the case of Schreber (1911c), which he wrote at the beginning of the decade of our record book, the "boldest thrust at +++psychiatry" (F/Ju, p. 380). He steadily continued his work on psychosis and its distinction from neurosis in this decade and presented his results in "On Narcissism" (1914c) and in several of his lectures (1916–1917, pp. 243–256, 422–430).

It is easy to miss Freud's great interest in the analysis of psychoses if one only focuses on the sceptical remarks he made over the years.[130] He sometimes assessed the possibility of analysing psychoses more optimistically, sometimes more pessimistically, and in the course of time and with increasing experience his assessments became more nuanced.[131] He repeatedly emphasised that cases of psychoses were not suitable for psychoanalytic treatment; they could not be "assailed" and did not develop any transference that was useful for analytic work. His comments were meant to counteract an overestimation of analysis as a method of cure. At the same time, he voiced the hope that the day would come when a therapy of psychoses could be considered and that even now, in spite of all the obstacles, "for the first time in the history of medicine—psychoanalysis has made it possible to get some insight into the origin and mechanism alike of the neuroses and psychoses" (1913j, p. 165). Psychoanalysis had succeeded in sometimes "casting an inquisitive glance over the top of the wall" (1916–1917, p. 423) and had seen the significance of denied homosexuality for paranoia and that of narcissistic identification for depression (ibid., pp. 423–428).

In 1920, he spoke of his great pride when he believed he had been able to help Bieber, and "seen through" his psychosis down to the "hewn rock".

One of Freud's most characteristic comments can be found in a lecture of October 1915. He posed the rhetorical question whether

---

[129] See, for example, Freud, 1894a; 1896b; 1985c, pp. 107–112, 167–168, 390; Min 1, pp. 59–61.

[130] See Freud, 1904a; 1905a; 1913j; 1916–1917; 1924f; 1925d; 1926f; 1933a; 1937c.

[131] One of the more optimistic assessments, for example, is: "Transference is often not so completely absent but that it can be used to a certain extent; and analysis has achieved undoubted successes with cyclical depressions, light paranoiac modifications, and partial schizophrenias" (1925d, p. 60).

psychoanalysis could cure a delusion, and answered it as follows: "No, Gentlemen, it cannot. It is as powerless (for the time being at least) against these ailments as any other form of therapy" (1916–1917, p. 255). What right do we then have to carry out such "fruitless" analyses? Freud's answer:

> We have a right, or rather a duty, to carry on our research without consideration of any immediate beneficial effect. In the end—we cannot tell where and when—every little fragment of knowledge will be transformed into power, and into therapeutic power as well. Even if psychoanalysis showed itself as unsuccessful in every other form of nervous and psychical disease as it does in delusions, it would still remain completely justified as an irreplaceable instrument of scientific research. It is true that in that case we should not be in a position to practice it. The human material on which we seek to learn, which lives, has its own will and needs its motives for cooperating in our work, would hold back from us. (ibid., p. 255)

Freud points to the essential difference between scientific inquiry and treatment. The idea of scientific inquiry is to lead to results that one day will benefit therapy but, according to Freud, we have not reached this stage yet. In addition, Freud views treatment as being something different from research. The analyst has to take the interests of the analysand into consideration, which differ from those of the scientist. Analysis, as Freud once said, is "not an impartial scientific investigation, but a therapeutic measure" (1909b, p. 104) that does not allow for unimpeded research. In a practical setting therapy takes precedence over research.

Even if Freud had often written that psychoses cannot be analysed, this does not mean that they "should not" be analysed. One does, however, have to be aware that one probably cannot change the tendency to psychotic reactions. This was, as far as I can see, Freud's position. He realistically recognised the limits of analytic therapy and emphasised them repeatedly. His main motive in nevertheless continuing to treat psychotic patients was the desire to gain new insight into the etiology of psychoses, hoping that this would one day bear therapeutic fruit. In this point, I again see no contradiction between what Freud said and what he did. It depends on how we read him.

Translated by Daniela Haller

SOURCES

Chapter 1

May[-Tolzmann], U. (1991). Zu den Anfängen des Narzissmus. Ellis—Näcke—Sadger—Freud [How the concept of narcissism came into being: from Ellis and Näcke to Sadger and Freud]. *Luzifer-Amor, Zeitschrift zur Geschichte der Psychoanalyse*, *4*(8): 50–88, 1991.

Chapter 2

May, U. (1997). Die Entdeckung der "bösen Mutter". Ein Beitrag Abrahams zur Theorie der Depression. *Luzifer-Amor. Zeitschrift zur Geschichte der Psychoanalyse*, *10*(20): 98–131.

Chapter 3

May, U. (2006a). Erbitterung und Nachdenklichkeit. Über Freuds Kommentar zu einem frühen Aufsatz von Karl Abraham. *Jahrbuch der Psychoanalyse*, *52*: 63–92.

Chapter 4

May, U. (2010b). Karl Abraham's revolution: from sensual sucking to the oral-aggressive wish of destruction. *Psychoanalytic Quarterly, 81*: 83–109, 2012.

Chapter 5

May, U. (2011a). Auf dem Weg zu Karl Abrahams "Versuch einer Entwicklungsgeschichte der Libido" (1924). Der Beitrag August Stärckes zur Theorie der Oralität. In: C. Diercks & S. Schlüter (Eds.), *Psycho-Sexualität. Grundlagen, infantile Sexualität, Libido, Todestrieb. Sigmund-Freud-Vorlesungen 2010* (pp. 131–153). Vienna: Mandelbaum.

Chapter 6

May, U. (2012). Zur Frühgeschichte der Analerotik. *Psyche, 66*: 213–246.

Chapter 7

May, U. (2015). Der Todestrieb im Kontext von Freuds Erkenntnisinteressen. In: *Freud bei der Arbeit*. Gießen: Psychosozial, 211–227.

Chapter 8

May, U. (2010a). Fourteen hundred hours of analysis with Freud: Viktor von Dirsztay. A biographical sketch. *Psychoanalysis and History 13*(1): 91–137, 2011.

Chapter 9

May, U. (2006b). Freuds Patientenkalender: Siebzehn Analytiker in Analyse bei Freud (1910–1920). *Luzifer-Amor. Zeitschrift für die Geschichte der Psychoanalyse, 19*(37): 43–97.

May, U. (2007). Neunzehn Patienten in Analyse bei Freud (1910–1920). Teil I. Zur Dauer von Freuds Analysen. *Psyche—Z Psychoanal, 61*(6): 590–625, and: Teil II. Zur Frequenz von Freuds Analysen und weitere Beobachtungen. *Psyche—Z Psychoanal, 61*(7): 686–709.

Archives consulted

Abraham A. Brill Library, New York Psychoanalytic Institute, New York.
Archiv der Österreichischen Nationalbibliothek, Wien.
Archiv der Wiener Stadt- und Landesbibliothek im Rathaus der Stadt Wien.
Archives of the Columbia University, New York.
Beinecke Rare Book and Manuscript Library, Wolff Archives, Yale University, New Haven.
Dokumentationsarchiv des österreichischen Widerstands.
Freud Museum, London.
Library of Congress, Sigmund Freud Papers, Washington.
Oskar-Kokoschka-Zentrum, Museum für Angewandte Kunst, Wien.
Sturm-Archiv der Staatsbibliothek Berlin.
Wiener Stadt- und Landesarchiv.

REFERENCES

The date given after the name of the author indicates the year of initial publication. If an edition other than the first has been cited, or a translation, the date of the pertinent edition or translation appears at the end of the notation.

SE = Standard Edition of the Complete Psychological Works of Sigmund Freud.

Abraham, H. C. (1974). Karl Abraham: An Unfinished Biography. *International Review of Psycho-Analysis, 1*: 17–72.

Abraham, K. (1907a). The experiencing of sexual traumas as a form of sexual activity. In: K. Abraham, *Selected Papers of Karl Abraham* (pp. 47–63). London: Grant A. Allan, 1927.

Abraham, K. (1907b). On the significance of sexual trauma in childhood for the symptomatology of dementia praecox. In: H. C. Abraham (Ed.), *Clinical Papers and Essays on Psycho-Analysis* (pp. 13–20). London: Grant A. Allan, 1955.

Abraham, K. (1908). The psycho-sexual differences between hysteria and dementia praecox. In: K. Abraham, *Selected Papers of Karl Abraham* (pp. 64–79). London: Grant A. Allan, 1927.

Abraham, K. (1909). Bericht über die österreichische und deutsche psychoanalytische Literatur bis zum Jahre 1909. *Jahrbuch für psychoanalytische und psychopathologische Forschungen, 1*(2): 575–594.

Abraham, K. (1911). Giovanni Segantini. A psycho-analytical study. In: H. C. Abraham (Ed.), *Clinical Papers and Essays on Psycho-Analysis* (pp. 210–261). London: Grant A. Allan, 1955.

Abraham, K. (1912a). Amenhotep IV. Psycho-analytical contribution towards the understanding of his personality and of the monotheistic cult of Aton. In: H. C. Abraham (Ed.), *Clinical Papers and Essays on Psycho-Analysis* (pp. 62–290). London: Grant A. Allan, 1955.

Abraham, K. (1912b). Notes on the psycho-analytical investigation and treatment of manic-depressive insanity and allied conditions. In: K. Abraham, *Selected Papers of Karl Abraham* (pp. 137–156). London: Grant A. Allan, 1927.

Abraham, K. (1913). Little Hilda: daydreams and a symptom in a seven-year-old girl. *International Review of Psycho-Analysis, 1*: 5–14, 1974.

Abraham, K. (1914). Spezielle Pathologie und Therapie der nervösen Zustände und der Geistesstörungen. In: *Bericht über die Fortschritte der Psychoanalyse in den Jahren 1909–1913* (pp. 343–363).

Abraham, K. (1916–1917). The first pregenital stage of the libido. In: K. Abraham, *Selected Papers of Karl Abraham* (pp. 248–279). London: Grant A. Allan, 1927.

Abraham, K. (1920). The narcissistic evaluation of excretory processes in dream and neurosis. In: K. Abraham, *Selected Papers of Karl Abraham* (pp. 318–322). London: Grant A. Allan, 1927.

Abraham, K. (1921). *Klinische Beiträge zur Psychoanalyse aus den Jahren 1907–1920*. Vienna: Internationaler Psychoanalytischer Verlag.

Abraham, K. (1923). Contributions to the theory of the anal character. In: K. Abraham, *Selected Papers of Karl Abraham* (pp. 370–392). London: Grant A. Allan, 1927.

Abraham, K. (1924). A short study of the development of the libido, viewed in the light of mental disorders. In: K. Abraham, *Selected Papers of Karl Abraham* (pp. 418–501). London: Grant A. Allan, 1927.

Abraham, K. (1925a). Epilogue [to "Giovanni Segantini"]. In: K. Abraham, *Clinical Papers and Essays on Psycho-Analysis* (pp. 258–261). London: Grant A. Allan, 1955.

Abraham, K. (1925b). The influence of oral erotism on character-formation. In: K. Abraham, *Selected Papers of Karl Abraham* (pp. 393–406). London: Grant A. Allan, 1927.

Abraham, K. (1925c). Preface to the second edition of "Giovanni Segantini". In: K. Abraham, *Clinical Papers and Essays on Psycho-Analysis* (p. 210). London: Grant A. Allan, 1955.

Abraham, K. (1927). *Selected Papers of Karl Abraham, M.D.* D. Bryan & A. Strachey (Trans.). International Psycho-Analytical Library, No. 13. London: Hogarth.

Abraham, K. (1955). *Clinical Papers and Essays on Psycho-Analysis*, with a preface by E. Jones. H. C. Abraham (Ed.), H. C. Abraham & D. R. Ellison (Trans.). International Psycho-Analytical Library, No. 49, London: Hogarth.

Abraham, K. (1971). *Psychoanalytische Studien: Volume 1* (1969) *& Volume 2* (1971). J. Cremerius (Ed.). Frankfurt: Fischer.

Adler, A. (1908). Der Aggressionstrieb im Leben und in der Neurose. *Fortschritte der Medizin, 19*: 577–584.

Alexander, F. (1922). The castration complex in the formation of character. *International Journal of Psycho-Analysis, 4*: 11–42, 1923.

Anderson, H. (1988). Einleitung. In: R. Mayreder (Ed.), *Tagebücher, 1873–1937* (pp. 10–40). Frankfurt: Insel.

Anderson, H. (1992). *Utopian Feminism: Women's Movements in Fin-de-Siècle Vienna*. New Haven, CT: Yale University Press.

Andreas-Salomé, L. (1916). "Anal" and "Sexual". *Imago, 4*: 249–273.

Andreas-Salomé, L. (1957). *The Freud Journal of Lou Andreas-Salomé*. St. A. Leavy (Trans.). New York: Basic, 1964.

Andreas-Salomé, L., & Freud, A. (2001). *"… als käm ich heim zu Vater und Schwester". Briefwechsel 1919–1937*. D. A. Rothe & I. Weber (Eds.) Göttingen: Wallstein.

Anon. (1914). = Reik, T. [& Zohn, H.] (1914). On the effect of unconscious death wishes. *Psychoanalytic Review, 65*: 38–67, 1978.

Anon. (1921a). Kleine Chronik. Todesfälle. *Neue Freie Presse*, 5 June, p. 9.

Anon. (1921b). Tagesneuigkeiten. Todesfälle. *Pester Lloyd*, Abendblatt, 6 June, p. 4.

Anon. (1924). Der Amtsschimmel gegen Psychoanalyse. *Wiener Sonn—und Montagszeitung*, 20 October, p. 4.

Anon. (1935a). Baron Dirsztay geht mit Gattin in den Tod. *Neues Wiener Journal*, 7 November, p. 1.

Anon. (1935b). Doppelselbstmord des Barons und der Baronin Viktor Dirsztay in Wien. *Pester Lloyd*, Abendblatt, 6 November, p. 5.

Anon. (1935c). Doppelselbstmord des Barons Dirsztay und Gattin. *Neue Freie Presse*, Abendblatt, 6 November, p. 1.

Anon. (1935d). Familientragödie eines Schriftstellers. *Das Kleine Blatt*, 7 November, p. 9.

Anon. (1935e). Tragisches Ende eines Freud-Jüngers. *Reichspost*, 7 November, p. 5.

Anon. (1935f). Tragödie des Ehepaares Dirsztay. *Wiener Zeitung*, 7 November, p. 9.

Appignanesi, L., & Forrester, J. (1993). *Freud's Women*. London: Virago.
Atwood, G. E., & Stolorow, R. D. (1993). *Faces in a Cloud. Intersubjectivity in Personality Theory*. Northvale, NJ: Aronson.
Avery, G. C. (Ed.) (2002). *Feinde in Scharen. Ein wahres Vergnügen dazusein. Karl Kraus—Herwarth Walden. Briefwechsel 1909–1921*. Göttingen: Wallstein.
Barron, J. et al. (1991). Sigmund Freud: The secrets of nature and the nature of secrets. *International Review of Psycho-Analysis, 18*: 143–163.
Beam, A. (2001). *Gracefully Insane: Life and Death Inside America's Premier Mental Hospital*. New York: Perseus.
Bergler, E. (1955). Ludwig Jekels 1867–1954. *International Journal of Psycho-analysis, 36*: 71–73.
Bericht über die Fortschritte der Psychoanalyse in den Jahren 1909–1913 (1914). *Jahrbuch für psychoanalytische und psychopathologische Forschung, 6*: 263–424.
Bericht über die Fortschritte der Psychoanalyse in den Jahren 1914–1919 (1921). Leipzig, Wien, Zürich: Internationaler Psychoanalytischer Verlag.
Bernfeld, S. (1962). On psychoanalytic training. *Psychoanalytic Quarterly, 31*: 453–482.
Bettelheim, A. (1920). *Marie von Ebner-Eschenbachs Wirken und Vermächtnis*. Leipzig: Quelle & Meyer.
Binswanger, H. (1956). Freuds Psychosentherapie. *Psyche, 10*: 357–366.
Bleuler, E., & Jung, C. G. (1908). Komplexe und Krankheitsursachen bei Dementia praecox. *Centralblatt für Nervenheilkunde und Psychiatrie, 31*: 220–227.
Blüher, H. (1914). Studien über den perversen Charakter (mit besonderer Berücksichtigung der Inversion). *Zentralblatt für Psychoanalyse und Psychotherapie, 4*: 10–27.
Bohleber, W. (2000). Die Entwicklung der Traumatheorie in der Psychoanalyse. *Psyche, 54*: 797–839.
Bohleber, W. (2007). Erinnerung, Trauma und kollektives Gedächtnis—Der Kampf um die Erinnerung in der Psychoanalyse. *Psyche, 61*: 293–321.
Bonomi, C. (1996). Mute correspondence. In: P. Mahony, C. Bonomi, & J. Stensson (Eds.), *Behind the Scenes. Freud in Correspondence* (pp. 155–201). Stockholm: Scandinavian University Press, 1997.
Brecht, K., Friedrich, V., Hermanns, L. M., Kaminer, I. J., & Juelich, D. H. (Eds.) (1985). *"Here life goes on in a most peculiar way …": Psychoanalysis Before and After 1933*. Ch. Trollope (Trans.). Hamburg: Kellner, 1992.
Brill, A. A. (1911). Ein Fall von periodischer Depression psychogenen Ursprungs. *Zentralblatt für Psychoanalyse, 1*: 158–164.
Brill, A. A. (1912–1913). Anal eroticism and character. *Journal of Abnormal Psychology, 7*: 196–203.

Broch, H. (1995). *Das Teesdorfer Tagebuch für Ea von Allesch*. P. M. Lützeler (Ed.). Frankfurt: Suhrkamp.

Brody, B. (1970). Freud's case-load. *Psychotherapy*, 7: 8–12.

Brome, V. (1982). *Ernest Jones. Freud's Alter Ego*. London: Butler & Tanner.

Burnham, J. C., & McGuire, W. (1983). *Jelliffe: American psychoanalyst and physician. His correspondence with Sigmund Freud and C. G. Jung*. Chicago: University of Chicago Press.

Canetti, E. (1974). Der neue Karl Kraus. In: K. Kraus, *Briefe an Sidonie Nádherný von Borutin 1913–1936, volume 2* (pp. 9–35). Göttingen: Wallstein, 2005.

Collins, B. (1997). *Leonardo, Psychoanalysis and Art History. A Critical Study of Psychobiographical Approaches to Leonardo da Vinci*. Evanston, IL: Northwestern University Press.

Couch, A. S. (1999). Therapeutic functions of the real relationship in psychoanalysis. *The Psychoanalytic Study of the Child, 54*: 130–168.

Cremerius, J. (1984). *Vom Handwerk des Psychoanalytikers. Das Werkzeug der psychoanalytischen Technik*. Stuttgart: Frommann-Holzboog.

Cremerius, J. (1997). Karl Abraham, Freuds Sündenbock und "Führer zur Wahrheitsforschung". *Luzifer–Amor. Zeitschrift zur Geschichte der Psychoanalyse, 10*(20): 64–80.

Czarnecki, B. G. (2004). *Ludwig Jekels (1867–1954) und die Anfänge der Psychoanalyse in Polen*. Dissertation. Tübingen.

Decke, B. (1997). Karl Abraham: Familie, Kindheit und Jugend in Bremen. *Luzifer–Amor, Zeitschrift zur Geschichte der Psychoanalyse, 10*(20): 7–63.

Deutsch, H. (1973). *Confrontation with Myself*. New York: Norton.

Dirsztay, F. v. (1919). *Zwischen Welten. Novelle*. Leipzig: Avalun.

Dirsztay, F. v. (1923). *Die Revolution der Parasiten*. Vienna: Atlantischer Verlag.

Dirsztay, F. v. (1924). *Kokotte Mann. Der Roman des erotischen Abenteurers*. Berlin: Altlantischer Verlag.

Dirsztay, F. v. (1930). *Der höhere Snobismus*. Essay. Vienna: Amalthea.

Dirsztay, V. v. (1909). *Streichquartett*. Budapest: Samuel Markus.

Dirsztay, V. v. (1911a). Pubertät. *Der Sturm, 69*: 551.

Dirsztay, V. v. (1911b). Wahrnehmungen. *Der Sturm, 78*: 623.

Dirsztay, V. v. (1911c). Unser Photo. Originalbericht der Neuen Freien Presse. *Der Sturm, 81*: 647; *82*: 656; *83*: 664; *84*: 672.

Dirsztay, V. v. (1917). *Lob des hohen Verstandes. Ein Umriss zur Morphologie des Menschen nebst Anmerkungen und einer Einführung*. Mit 6 Originallithographien und einer Titelvignette von O. Kokoschka. Leipzig: Wolff.

Dirsztay, V. v. (1923). *Der Unentrinnbare*. Mit Zeichnungen von Oskar Kokoschka. Munich: Wolff.

Diskussionen des Wiener psychoanalytischen Vereins (1910). Über den Selbstmord, insbesondere den Schüler-Selbstmord. Wiener Psychoanalytische Vereinigung (Ed.). Wiesbaden: Bergmann.

Drews, J. (1969). *Die Lyrik Albert Ehrensteins. Wandlungen in Thematik und Sprachstil von 1910 bis 1931. Ein Beitrag zur Expressionismus-Forschung.* Dissertation. Munich: University of Munich.

Dubsky, F. v. (1917). Erinnerungen an Maria v. Ebner-Eschenbach. *Neue Freie Presse*, 25 December, p. 16.

Dupont, J. (1994). Freud's analysis of Ferenczi as revealed by their correspondence. *International Journal of Psychoanalysis, 75*: 301–320.

Ebner-Eschenbach, M. v. (1890). *Hirzeprinzchen: ein Märchen.* Stuttgart: Union Deutsche Verlagsgesellschaft.

Ebner-Eschenbach, M. v., & Breuer, J. (1969). *Ein Briefwechsel, 1880–1916.* R. A. Kann (Ed.). Vienna: Bergland.

Ehrenstein, A. (1911). *Tubutsch.* Mit 12 Zeichnungen von Oskar Kokoschka. Vienna: Jahoda & Siegel.

Ehrenstein, A. (1915). Entwandlung. *Die weißen Blätter, 2*: 620–622.

Ehrenstein, A. (1987). *Werke, volume 1.* H. Mittelmann (Ed.). Munich: Boer.

Eisenberg, L. (1903). *Großes biographisches Lexikon der deutschen Bühne im XIX. Jahrhundert.* Leipzig: List.

Eissler, K. (1971). *Talent and Genius. The Fictitious Case of Tausk Contra Freud.* New York: Quadrangle.

Eissler, K. R. (2001). *Freud and the Seduction Theory. A Brief Love Affair.* Madison, CT: International Universities Press.

Eitingon, M. (1922). Bericht über die Berliner Psychoanalytische Poliklinik (März 1920—Juni 1922). *Internationale Zeitschrift für Psychoanalyse, 8*: 506–520.

Ellis, H. (1898a). Autoerotism: a psychological study. *Alienist & Neurologist, 19*: 260–299.

Ellis, H. (1898b). Hysteria in relation to the sexual emotions. *Alienist & Neurologist, 19*: 599–615.

Ellis, H. (1899). *The Evolution of Modesty, the Phenomena of Sexual Periodicity, Autoerotism.* Philadelphia: Davis.

Ellis, H. (1908). Review of "Jahrbuch für sexuelle Zwischenstufen". *Journal of Mental Sciences, 54*: 753–755.

Ellis, H. (1927). The conception of narcissism. *Psychoanalytic Review, 14*: 129–153.

Ellis, H. (1940). *My life: The autobiography of Havelock Ellis.* London: Heinemann.

Ellis, H., & Symonds, J. A. (1896). *Sexual Inversion.* London: Wilson and Macmillan, 1897.

Esman, A. (2001). Italo Svevo and the first psychoanalytic novel. *International Journal of Psychoanalysis, 82*: 1225–1233.

Etchegoyen, R. H. (1994). Presidential Message. *Bulletin of the International Psychoanalytic Association, 75*: 176–178.

Fallend, K. (1988). *Wilhelm Reich in Wien. Psychoanalyse und Politik*. Vienna: Geyer-Edition.

Fallend, K. (1995). *Sonderlinge, Träumer, Sensitive. Psychoanalyse auf dem Weg zur Institution und Profession. Protokolle der Wiener Psychoanalytischen Vereinigung und biographische Studien*. Vienna: Jugend & Volk.

Falzeder, E. (1994). My grand-patient, my chief tormentor: a hitherto unnoticed case of Freud's and the consequences. *Psychoanalytic Quarterly, 63*: 297–331.

Falzeder, E. (1996). Dreaming of Freud: Ferenczi, Freud and an analysis without end. *International Forum of Psychoanalysis, 5*: 265–270.

Falzeder, E. (2000). Profession—psychoanalyst: a historical view. *Psychoanalysis and History, 2*: 37–60.

Falzeder, E. (2002). Preface. In: E. Falzeder (Ed.), *The Complete Correspondence of Sigmund Freud and Karl Abraham 1907–1925* (pp. IX–XVII). London: Karnac.

Falzeder, E. (2004). Beruf: Psychoanalytiker. Über die Anfänge eines Berufsstandes (revised version of "Profession—psychoanalyst"). *Jahrbuch der Psychoanalyse, 49*: 139–168.

Federn, P. (1913–1914). Beiträge zur Analyse des Sadismus und Masochismus. *Internationale Zeitschrift für Psychoanalyse, 1*: 28–49; 2: 105–130.

Fenichel, O. (1925). *Introjection and the castration complex*. In: H. Fenichel & D. Rapaport (Eds.) *Collected Papers of Otto Fenichel, volume 1* (pp. 39–70). New York: Norton, 1953.

Fenichel, O. (1945). *The Psychoanalytic Theory of Neurosis*. New York: Norton.

Ferenczi, S. (1908). Das manisch-depressive Irresein in subjektiver Beleuchtung. *Zentralblatt für Psychoanalyse, 1*: 74–75.

Ferenczi, S. (1909). Introjection and transference. In: S. Ferenczi, *First Contributions to Psycho-Analysis* (pp. 35–93). London: Hogarth, 1952.

Ferenczi, S. (1911). On the part played by homosexuality in pathogenesis of paranoia. In: S. Ferenczi, *First Contributions to Psycho-Analysis* (pp. 154–187). London: Hogarth, 1952.

Ferenczi, S. (1911–12). Reizung der analen erogenen Zone als auslösende Ursache der Paranoia. In: *Bausteine zur Psychoanalyse, volume 2* (pp. 281–286). Vienna: Facultas, 1984.

Ferenczi, S. (1913). Stages in the development of the sense of reality. In: S. Ferenczi, *First Contributions to Psycho-Analysis* (pp. 213–239). London: Hogarth, 1952.

Ferenczi, S. (1914a). Beitrag zum Verständnis der Psychoneurosen des Rückbildungsalters [Contribution to the psychoneuroses of later life]. In: *Bausteine zur Psychoanalyse, volume 3* (pp. 180–188). Vienna: Facultas, 1984.

Ferenczi, S. (1914b). The nosoloy of male homosexuality (homo-erotism). In: S. Ferenczi, *First Contributions to Psycho-Analysis* (pp. 296–318). London: Hogarth, 1952.
Ferenczi, S. (1914c). The ontogenesis of the interest in money. In: S. Ferenczi, *First Contributions to Psycho-Analysis* (pp. 319–331). London: Hogarth, 1952.
Ferenczi, S. (1916). *First Contributions to Psycho-Analysis*. London: Hogarth, 1952.
Ferenczi, S. (1916–1917). Two types of war neuroses. In: S. Ferenczi, *Further Contributions to the Theory and Technique of Psycho-Analysis* (pp. 124–141). New York: Boni and Liveright, 1927.
Ferenczi, S. (1924). Thalassa: A Theory of Genitality. Albany, NY: *Psychoanalytic Quarterly*, 1938.
Ferenczi, S. (1927). *Further Contributions to the Theory and Technique of Psycho-Analysis*. J. I. Suttie (Trans.). New York: Boni and Liveright.
Ferenczi, S. (1933). Confusion of tongues between adults and the child. *International Journal of Psycho-Analysis, 30*: 225–230, 1949.
Fichtner, G. (1994). Die ärztliche Schweigepflicht, der Analytiker und der Historiker. Eine notwendige Stellungnahme zur Edition des Freud/Ferenczi-Briefwechsels. *Psyche, 48*: 738–745.
Forsyth, D. (1922). *The Technique of Psychoanalysis*. London: Kegan Paul.
Frank, C. L. (1999). *Melanie Kleins erste Kinderanalysen*. Stuttgart: Frommann-Holzboog.
Frankiel, R. (1991). A note on Freud's inattention to the negative oedipal in Little Hans. *International Review of Psycho-Analysis, 18*: 181–184.
Freud, A. (1969). Dr Herman Nunberg: an appreciation. *International Journal of Psychoanalysis, 50*: 135–138.
Freud, S. (1892–1893). A Case of Successful Treatment by Hypnotism. *S. E., 1*: 117. London: Hogarth.
Freud, S. (1894a). The Neuro-Psychoses of Defence. *S. E., 3*: 43. London: Hogarth.
Freud, S. (1895d). *Studies on Hysteria. S. E., 2*. London: Hogarth.
Freud, S. (1896b). Further Remarks on the Neuro-Psychoses of Defence. *S. E., 3*: 159. London: Hogarth.
Freud, S. (1900a). *The Interpretation of Dreams. S. E., 4–5*. London: Hogarth.
Freud, S. (1901b). *The Psychopathology of Everyday Life. S. E., 6*. London: Hogarth.
Freud, S. (1904a). Freud's Psycho-Analytic Procedure. *S. E., 7*: 249. London: Hogarth.
Freud, S. (1905a). On Psychotherapy. *S. E., 7*: 257. London: Hogarth.
Freud, S. (1905d). *Three Essays on the Theory of Sexuality. S. E., 7*: 125. London: Hogarth.

Freud, S. (1905e). Fragment of an Analysis of a Case of Hysteria. *S. E., 7*: 3. London: Hogarth.
Freud, S. (1906a). My Views on the Part played by Sexuality in the Aetiology of the Neuroses. *S. E., 7*: 271. London: Hogarth.
Freud, S. (1908a). Hysterical Phantasies and their Relation to Bisexuality. *S. E., 9*: 157. London: Hogarth.
Freud, S. (1908b). Character and Anal Erotism. *S. E., 9*: 169. London: Hogarth.
Freud, S. (1908c). On the Sexual Theories of Children. *S. E., 9*: 207. London: Hogarth.
Freud, S. (1908d). "Civilized" Sexual Morality and Modern Nervous Illness. *S. E., 9*: 179. London: Hogarth.
Freud, S. (1909b). Analysis of a Phobia in a Five-Year-Old Boy. *S. E., 10*: 3. London: Hogarth.
Freud, S. (1909d). Notes upon a Case of Obsessional Neurosis. *S. E., 10*: 155. London: Hogarth.
Freud, S. (1910a). Five Lectures on Psycho-Analysis. *S. E., 11*: 3. London: Hogarth.
Freud, S. (1910c). *Leonardo Da Vinci and a Memory of His Childhood. S. E., 11*: 59. London: Hogarth.
Freud, S. (1910d). The Future Prospects of Psycho-Analytic Therapy. *S. E., 11*: 141. London: Hogarth.
Freud, S. (1910g). Contributions to a Discussion on Suicide. *S. E., 11*: 231. London: Hogarth.
Freud, S. (1910h). A Special Type of Choice of Object made by Men. *S. E., 11*: 165. London: Hogarth.
Freud, S. (1910–1911a). Mehr Kinder. *Der Sturm, 1*: 444.
Freud, S. (1911b). Formulations on the Two Principles of Mental Functioning. *S. E., 12*: 215. London: Hogarth.
Freud, S. (1911c). Psycho-Analytic Notes on an Autobiographical Account of a Case of Paranoia (Dementia Paranoides). *S. E., 12*: 3. London: Hogarth.
Freud, S. (1912d). On the Universal Tendency to Debasement in the Sphere of Love. *S. E., 11*: 179. London: Hogarth.
Freud, S. (1912e). Recommendations to Physicians Practising Psycho-Analysis. *S. E., 12*: 111. London: Hogarth.
Freud, S. (1912–1913). *Totem and Taboo. S. E., 13*: 1. London: Hogarth.
Freud, S. (1913c). On Beginning the Treatment (Further Recommendations on the Technique of Psychoanalysis I). *S. E., 12*: 123. London: Hogarth.
Freud, S. (1913d). The Occurrence in Dreams of Material from Fairy Tales. *S. E., 12*: 281. London: Hogarth.

Freud, S. (1913f). The Theme of the Three Caskets. *S. E., 12*: 291. London: Hogarth.
Freud, S. (1913g). Two Lies told by Children. *S. E., 12*: 305. London: Hogarth.
Freud, S. (1913i). The Disposition to Obsessional Neurosis. *S. E., 12*: 313. London: Hogarth.
Freud, S. (1913j). The Claims of Psycho-Analysis to Scientific Interest. *S. E., 13*: 165. London: Hogarth.
Freud, S. (1914c). On Narcissism: an Introduction. *S. E., 14*: 69. London: Hogarth.
Freud, S. (1914d). On the History of the Psycho-Analytic Movement. *S. E., 14*: 3. London: Hogarth.
Freud, S. (1914g). Remembering, Repeating and Working-Through (Further Recommendations on the Technique of Psycho-Analysis II). *S. E., 12*: 147. London: Hogarth.
Freud, S. (1915b). Thoughts for the Times on War and Death. *S. E., 14*: 275. London: Hogarth.
Freud, S. (1915c). Instincts and their Vicissitudes. *S. E., 14*: 111. London: Hogarth.
Freud, S. (1915f). A case of Paranoia Running Counter to the Psycho-Analytic Theory of the Disease. *S. E., 14*: 263. London: Hogarth.
Freud, S. (1916–1917). *Introductory Lectures on Psycho-Analysis. S. E., 15–16.* London: Hogarth.
Freud, S. (1917c). On Transformations of Instinct as Exemplified in Anal Erotism. *S. E., 17*: 127. London: Hogarth.
Freud, S. (1917e). Mourning and Melancholia. *S. E., 14*: 239. London: Hogarth.
Freud, S. (1918b). From the History of an Infantile Neurosis. *S. E., 17*: 3. London: Hogarth.
Freud, S. (1919d). Introduction to *Psycho-Analysis and the War Neuroses. S. E., 17*: 207. London: Hogarth.
Freud, S. (1919e). A Child is being Beaten. *S. E., 17*: 177. London: Hogarth.
Freud, S. (1919h). The "Uncanny". *S. E., 17*: 219. London: Hogarth.
Freud, S. (1920a). The Psychogenesis of a Case of Female Homosexuality. *S. E., 18*: 147. London: Hogarth.
Freud, S. (1920c). Dr. Anton von Freund. *S. E., 18*: 267. London: Hogarth.
Freud, S. (1920g). *Beyond the Pleasure Principle. S. E., 18*: 7. London: Hogarth.
Freud, S. (1921c). *Group Psychology and the Analysis of the Ego. S. E., 18*: 69–143. London: Hogarth.
Freud, S. (1921d). Award of Prizes. *S. E., 17*: 269. London: Hogarth.

Freud, S. (1922b). Some Neurotic Mechanisms in Jealousy, Paranoia And Homosexuality. *S. E., 18*: 223. London: Hogarth.

Freud, S. (1923b). *The Ego and the Id. S. E., 19*: 3. London: Hogarth.

Freud, S. (1923e). The Infantile Genital Organisation. *S. E., 19*: 141. London: Hogarth.

Freud, S. (1924c). The Economic Problem of Masochism. *S. E., 19*: 157. London: Hogarth.

Freud, S. (1924d). The Dissolution of the Oedipus Complex. *S. E., 19*: 173. London: Hogarth.

Freud, S. (1924f). A Short Account of Psycho-Analysis. *S. E., 19*: 191. London: Hogarth.

Freud, S. (1924g). Extracts from a Letter to Wittels. *S. E., 19*: 286. London: Hogarth.

Freud, S. (1925d). *An Autobiographical Study. S. E., 20*: 3. London: Hogarth.

Freud, S. (1926d). *Inhibitions, Symptoms and Anxiety. S. E., 20*: 77. London: Hogarth.

Freud, S. (1926f). Psycho-Analysis: Freudian School. *S. E., 20*: 261. London: Hogarth.

Freud, S. (1926i). Dr. Reik and the Problem of Quackery. *S. E., 21*: 247. London: Hogarth.

Freud, S. (1930a). *Civilization and Its Discontents. S. E., 21*: 59. London: Hogarth.

Freud, S. (1931b). Female sexuality. *S. E., 21*: 223. London: Hogarth.

Freud, S. (1933a). *New Introductory Lectures on Psycho-Analysis. S. E., 22*: 3. London: Hogarth.

Freud, S. (1933c). Sándor Ferenczi. *S. E., 22*: 227. London: Hogarth.

Freud, S. (1937c). Analysis Terminable and Interminable. *S. E., 23*: 211. London: Hogarth.

Freud, S. (1940a). *An Outline of Psycho-Analysis. S. E., 23*: 141. London: Hogarth.

Freud, S. (1941d). Psycho-Analysis and Telepathy. *S. E., 18*: 177. London: Hogarth.

Freud, S. (1950a). *The Origins of Psycho-Analysis. S. E., 1*: 175. London: Hogarth.

Freud, S. (1955a). Original Record of the Case of Obsessional Neurosis (the "Rat Man"). *S. E., 10*: 259. London: Hogarth.

Freud, S. (1969–1979). *Sigmund Freud. Studienausgabe.* A. Mitscherlich, A. Richards, & J. Strachey (Eds.). Frankfurt: Fischer.

Freud, S. (1985a). *A Phylogenetic Phantasy: Overview of the Transference Neuroses.* I. Grubrich-Simitis (Ed.), A. Hoffer & P. T. Hoffer (Trans). Cambridge, MA: Harvard University Press, 1987.

Freud, S. (1985c). *The Complete Letters of Sigmund Freud to Wilhelm Fliess 1887–1904*. J. M. Masson (Ed.). Cambridge, MA: Harvard University Press. = F/Fl.

Freud, S. (1996). Schriften über Kokain. A. Hirschmüller (Ed.). Frankfurt: Fischer.

Freud, S. (2010). *"Unterdeß halten wir zusammen …". Briefe an die Kinder*. M. Schröter (Ed.). Berlin: Aufbau.

Freud, S. (2011). Autoreferat von "Ein Beitrag zum Problem der Neurosenwahl". *Luzifer–Amor, Zeitschrift zur Geschichte der Psychoanalyse, 24*(47): 46–47.

Freud, S. (2012). Briefe an Kata und Lajos Lévy (1918–1926). T. Aichhorn & M. Schröter (Eds.). *Luzifer–Amor, Zeitschrift zur Geschichte der Psychoanalyse, 25*(50): 7–61. = F/L.

Freud, S., & Abraham, K. (1965). *A Psycho-Analytic Dialogue: The Letters of Sigmund Freud and Karl Abraham 1907–1926*. H. C. Abraham & E. Freud (Eds.). London: Hogarth.

Freud, S., & Abraham, K. (2002). *The Complete Correspondence of Sigmund Freud and Karl Abraham, 1907–1925*. E. Falzeder (Ed.), C. Schwarzacher (Trans.). London: Karnac. = F/A.

Freud, S., & Abraham, K. (2009). *Briefwechsel 1907–1925*. Vollständige Ausgabe. E. Falzeder & L. M. Hermanns (Eds.). Vienna: Turia + Kant.

Freud, S., & Bernays, M. (2005). *Briefwechsel 1882–1938*. A. Hirschmüller (Ed.). Tübingen: Diskord.

Freud, S., & Binswanger, L. (1992). *The Freud-Binswanger Correspondence 1908–1938*. G. Fichtner (Ed.), A. J. Pomerans & T. Roberts (Trans.). New York: Other, 2003. = F/Bi.

Freud, S., & Bleuler, E. (2012). *"Ich bin zuversichtlich, wir erobern bald die Psychiatrie." Briefwechsel 1904–1937*. M. Schröter (Ed.). Basel: Schwabe. = F/Bl.

Freud, S., & Eitingon, M. (2004). *Briefwechsel 1906–1939*. M. Schröter (Ed.) Tübingen: Diskord. = F/E.

Freud, S., & Freud, A. (2006). *Briefwechsel 1904–1938*. I. Meyer-Palmedo (Ed.). Frankfurt: Fischer. [*Correspondence, 1904–1938. Sigmund Freud and Anna Freud*. I. Meyer-Palmedo (Ed.), N. Somers (Trans.). Cambridge: Polity, 2014] = F/AF.

Freud, S., & Ferenczi, S. (1993). *The Correspondence of Sigmund Freud and Sándor Ferenczi. Vol. 1: 1908–1914*. E. Brabant, E. Falzeder, & P. Giampieri-Deutsch (Ed.), P. T. Hoffer (Trans.). Cambridge, MA: Harvard University Press. = F/Fer 1.

Freud, S., & Ferenczi, S. (1996). *The Correspondence of Sigmund Freud and Sándor Ferenczi. Vol. 2: 1914–1919*. E. Falzeder & E. Brabant (Eds.). Cambridge, MA: Harvard University Press. = F/Fer 2.

Freud, S., & Ferenczi, S. (2000). *The Correspondence of Sigmund Freud and Sándor Ferenczi. Vol. 3: 1920–1933*. E. Falzeder & E. Brabant (Eds.), P. T. Hoffer (Trans.). Cambridge, MA: Harvard University Press. = F/Fer 3.

Freud, S., & Groddeck, G. (1974). *The Meaning of Illness: Selected Psychoanalytic Writings by Georg Groddeck, Including His Correspondence with Sigmund Freud*. New York: International Universities Press, 1977. = F/G.

Freud, S., & Groddeck, G. (2008). *Briefwechsel*. M. Giefer (Ed.). Frankfurt: Stroemfeld.

Freud, S., & Jones, E. (1993). *The Complete Correspondence of Sigmund Freud and Ernest Jones 1908–1939*. R. A. Paskauskas (Ed.). Cambridge, MA: Harvard University Press. = F/Jo.

Freud, S., & Jung, C. G. (1974). *The Freud/Jung Letters: The Correspondence between Sigmund Freud and C. G. Jung*. W. McGuire (Ed.). Cambridge, MA: Harvard University Press. = F/Ju.

Freud, S., & Pfister, O. (1963). *Psychoanalysis and Faith. The letters of Sigmund Freud and Oskar Pfister*. H. Meng & E. L. Freud (Eds.), E. Mosbacher (Trans.). New York: Basic. = F/P.

Freud, S., & Pfister, O. (2014). *Briefwechsel 1909–1939*. I. Noth (Ed.). Zürich: Theologischer.

Freud, S., & Weiss, E. (1970). *Sigmund Freud as a Consultant: Recollections of a Pioneer in Psychoanalysis*. M. Grotjahn (Ed.). New York: Intercontinental Medical Book Corporation. = F/W.

Früh, F. (2006). Anfang und Ursprung. Zur Genese der infantilen Sexualität. *Kinderanalyse, 24*: 244–261.

Früh, F. (2010). "… sonst bekommen wir ja Lumpen und nicht Neurotiker." Zu Karl Abrahams Rezeption der Freud'schen Sexualtheorie. *Luzifer–Amor, Zeitschrift zur Geschichte der Psychoanalyse, 23*(46): 44–57.

Gardiner, M. (1971) (Ed.). *The Wolf-Man by the Wolf-Man, with The Case of the Wolf-Man by Sigmund Freud*. New York: Basic.

Gay, P. (1988). *Freud: A Life for Our Time*. New York: Norton.

Gill, M. M. (1976). Metapsychology is not psychology. In: M. Gill & P. Holzman (Eds.), *Psychology versus Metapsychology* (pp. 71–105). New York: International Universities Press.

Gill, M. M. (1982). *Analysis of Transference. Theory and technique*. New York: International Universities Press.

Glover, E. (1924). The significance of the mouth in psycho-analysis. *British Journal of Medical Psychology, 4*: 134–155.

Glover, E. (1925). Notes on oral character formation. *International Journal of Psychoanalysis, 6*: 131–154.

Glover, E. (1932). On the aetiology of drug-addiction. *International Journal of Psychoanalysis, 13*: 298–328.

Glover, E. (1933). Review of M. Klein, "The Psycho-Analysis of Children". *International Journal of Psychoanalysis, 14*: 119–129.

Glover, J. (1922). Summary of "The psycho-pathology of suicide". *Bulletin of the International Psycho-Analytical Society, 3*: 507–508.

Göbel, W. (1977). *Der Kurt Wolff Verlag 1913–1930. Expressionismus als verlegerische Aufgabe*. Frankfurt: Buchhändler-Vereinigung.

Goldmann, S. (1985). Sigmund Freuds Briefe an seine Patientin Anna v. Vest. *Jahrbuch der Psychoanalyse, 17*: 269–337.

Good, M. (1995). Karl Abraham, Sigmund Freud, and the fate of the seduction theory. *Journal of the American Psychoanalytic Association, 43*: 1137–1167.

Graf -Nold, A. (1988). *Der Fall Hermine Hug—Hellmuth. Eine Geschichte der frühen Kinder-Psychoanalyse*. Munich: Internationale Psychoanalyse.

Grinstein, A. (1956–1975). *The Index of Psychoanalytic Writings*. New York: International Universities Press.

Gröger, H. (1990). Sigmund Freud an Paul Näcke. Erstveröffentlichung zweier Freud-Briefe. *Luzifer–Amor, Zeitschrift zur Geschichte der Psychoanalyse, 6*: 144–163.

Gross, O. (1907). *Das Freud'sche Ideogenitätsmoment und seine Bedeutung im manisch-depressiven Irresein Kraepelin's*. Leipzig: Vogel.

Grosskurth, P. (1980). *Havelock Ellis. A Biography*. New York: Knopf.

Grosskurth, P. (1986). *Melanie Klein, Her World and Her Work*. New York: Knopf.

Grubrich-Simitis, I. (1987). Trauma or drive—drive and trauma—a reading of Sigmund Freud's phylogenetic phantasy of 1915. *Psychoanalytic Study of the Child, 43*: 3–32, 1988.

Grubrich-Simitis, I. (1991). Freud's study of Moses as a daydream. In: I. Grubrich-Simitis (Ed.), *Early Freud and Late Freud: Reading Anew "Studies on Hysteria" and "Moses and Monotheism"* (pp. 53–106). P. Slotkin (Trans.). London: Routledge, 1997.

Grubrich-Simitis, I. (1993). *Back to Freud's Texts: Making Silent Documents Speak*. P. Slotkin (Trans.). New Haven, CT: Yale University Press, 1996.

Gulyás, P. (1943). *Magyar írók. Élete és munkái, volume 5*. Budapest: Magyar Könyvtárosok és Levéltárosok Egyesülete.

Gulyás, P. (1992). *Magyar írók. Élete és munkái, volume 11*. Budapest: Argumentum Kiadó.

Habermas, J. (1968). Knowledge and Human Interests. London: Polity, 1987.

Handlbauer, B. (1990). *Die Adler-Freud-Kontroverse*. Frankfurt: Fischer.

Handler, A. (1983). *Dori: The Life and Times of Theodor Herzl in Budapest (1860–1878)*. Tuscaloosa, AL: University of Alabama Press.

Hardin, H. T. (1987). On the vicissitudes of Freud's early mothering. *Psychoanalytic Quarterly, 56*: 628–644.

Hardin, H. T. (1988). On the vicissitudes of Freud's early mothering. *Psychoanalytic Quarterly, 57*: 72–86, 209–223.

Harmat, P. (1986). *Freud, Ferenczi und die ungarische Psychoanalyse*. Tübingen: Diskord, 1988.

Hattingberg, H. von (1914). Analerotik, Angstlust und Eigensinn. *Internationale Zeitschrift fürPsychoanalyse, 2*: 244–258.

Heck, V. A. (1930). *Autographen. Eigenhändige Briefe und Dokumente berühmter Persönlichkeiten*. Catalogue no. 51. Vienna: Heck.

Herzl, Th. (1985). *Zionistisches Tagebuch 1899–1904*. A. Bein, H. Greive, M. Schaerf, & J. H. Schoeps (Eds.). Berlin: Ullstein.

Herzl, Th. (1993). *Briefe und Tagebücher. Volume 6: Ende August 1900–Ende Dezember 1902*. B. Schäfer (Ed.). Berlin: Ullstein.

Hinshelwood, R. D. (1989). *A Dictionary of Kleinian Thought*. London: Free Association.

Hirschfeld, M. (1914). *The Homosexuality of Men and Women*. M. A. Lombardi-Nash (Trans.). Amherst, NY: Prometheus, 2000.

Hirschmüller, A. (1996). Einleitung zu: *S. Freud, Schriften über Kokain* (pp. 9–39). Frankfurt: Fischer.

Hitschmann, E. (1911). *Freud's Theories of the Neuroses*. C. R. Payne (Trans.). New York: Journal of Nervous and Mental Disease Publishing Company, 1913.

Hitschmann, E. (1913a). Gesteigertes Triebleben und Zwangsneurose bei einem Kinde. *Internationale Zeitschrift für Psychoanalyse, 1*: 61–68.

Hitschmann, E. (1913b). Paranoia, Homosexualität und Analerotik. *Internationale Zeitschrift für Psychoanalyse, 1*: 251–254.

Hitschmann, E. (1914). Trieblehre. In: Bericht über die Fortschritte der Psychoanalyse in den Jahren 1909–1913. *Jahrbuch für psychoanalytische und psychopathologische Forschung, 6*: 283–295.

Hoesch, L. (1906). *Anthropologisch-psychologische Untersuchungen an Züricher Schulkindern*. Leipzig: Nemnich.

Hoffer, A. (1996). Introduction. In: E. Falzeder & E. Brabant (Eds.), *The Correspondence of Sigmund Freud and Sándor Ferenczi. Volume 2: 1914–1919*. Cambridge, MA: Harvard University Press.

Holt, R. R. (1965). A review of some of Freud's biological assumptions and their influence on his theories. In: N. S. Greenfield & W. C. Lewis (Eds.), *Psychoanalysis and Current Biological Thought* (pp. 93–124). Madison: University of Wisconsin Press.

Holt, R. R. (1967). Beyond vitalism and mechanism: Freud's concept of psychic energy. In: J. H. Masserman (Ed.), *Science and Psychoanalysis* (pp. 1–41). New York: Grune & Stratton.

Holt, R. R. (1992). Freud's parental identifications as a source of some contradictions within psychoanalysis. In: T. Gelfand & J. Kerr (Eds.), *Freud and the History of Psychoanalysis* (pp. 1–28). Hillsdale, NJ: Analytic.

Huppke, A., & Schröter, M. (2011). IPV–Sekretär und Mäzen–Freuds Patient, Vermögensverwalter und Freund: Die Briefe Anton v. Freunds an Sigmund Freud (1916–1919). *Luzifer–Amor, Zeitschrift zur Geschichte der Psychoanalyse, 24*(48): 53–98.

Hurwitz, E. (1979). *Otto Gross. Paradies-Sucher zwischen Freud und Jung.* Zurich: Suhrkamp.

J. R. (1950). Claud Dangar Daly, Lt.-Col. (Ret.), 1884–1950. *International Journal of Psychoanalysis, 31*: 290–291.

Jacobson, E. (1930). Beitrag zur asozialen Charakterbildung. *InternationaleZeitschrift für Psychoanalyse, 16*: 210–235.

Jaeger, L. (2000). Das Auge, die Sonne und die Sonntagsneurosen. Ein verkannter Getreuer auf Wegen fern von Sigmund Freud: Der Psychoanalytiker Karl Abraham und die bildende Kunst. Frankfurter Allgemeine Zeitung, 2 March, p. 56.

Jekels, L. (1913a). Eine Symptomhandlung. *Internationale Zeitschrift für Psychoanalyse, 1*: 260–262.

Jekels, L. (1913b). Einige Bemerkungen zur Trieblehre. *Internationale Zeitschrift für Psychoanalyse, 1*: 439–443.

Jones, E. (1909). Psycho-analytic notes on a case of hypomania. *American Journal of Insanity, 66*: 203–218.

Jones, E. (1911). Offener Brief. *Zentralblatt für Psychoanalyse, 1*: 610.

Jones, E. (1912–13). Einige Fälle von Zwangsneurose. *Jahrbuch für psychoanalytische und psychopathologische Forschungen, 4*: 563–606; 5: 55–116. [Abridged version: Analytic study of a case of obsessional neurosis. In: E. Jones, *Papers on Psycho-Analysis* (2nd edn) (pp. 515–539), 1918.]

Jones, E. (1913). Hass und Analerotik in der Zwangsneurose. *InternationaleZeitschrift für Psychoanalyse, 1*: 425–430. [Abridged version: Hate and anal eroticism. In: E. Jones, *Papers on Psycho-Analysis* (2nd edn) (pp. 540–548), 1918.]

Jones, E. (1914). Die Empfängnis der Jungfrau Maria durch das Ohr. *Jahrbuch für psychoanalytische und psychopathologische Forschungen, 6*: 135–204. [Revised version: The Madonna's conception through the ear: a contribution to the relation between aesthetics and religion. In: E. Jones, *Essays in Applied Psycho-Analysis* (pp. 261–359), 1923.]

Jones, E. (1915). Krieg und Sublimation. *Internationale Rundschau, 1*: 497–506.

Jones, E. (1918a). Anal-erotic character traits. In: E. Jones, *Papers on Psycho-Analysis* (2nd edn) (pp. 413–437), 1948.

Jones, E. (1918b). *Papers on Psycho-Analysis* (2nd edn). London: Baillière, Tindall & Cox.

Jones, E. (1920). Recent advances in psycho-analysis. *International Journal of Psycho-Analysis, 1*: 161–185.

Jones, E. (1923a). Cold, disease and birth. In: E. Jones, *Papers on Psycho-Analysis* (5th edn) (pp. 320–324). London: Balliere, Tindall & Cox, 1948.

Jones, E. (1923b). *Essays in Applied Psycho-Analysis*. London: International Psycho-Analytical Press.

Jones, E. (1926a). Introductory memoir. In: K. Abraham, *Selected Papers of Karl Abraham* (pp. 9–41), 1927.

Jones, E. (1926b). Bibliography of scientific publications. In: K. Abraham, *Selected Papers of Karl Abraham* (pp. 503–510), 1927.

Jones, E. (1953, 1955, 1957). *Sigmund Freud: Life and Work (3 volumes)*. London: Hogarth.

Jones, E. (1959). *Free Associations. Memories of a Psychoanalyst*. New York: Basic.

Jung, C. G. (1907). *The Psychology of Dementia Praecox*. A. A. Brill & F. W. Peterson (Trans.). New York: Nervous and Mental Disease Monograph Series no. 3; 1909.

Jung, C. G. (1909). The significance of the father in the destiny of the individual. *Collected Works, 4*.

Jung, C. G. (1911–12). Symbols of transformation. *Collected Works, 5*.

Jung, C. G. (1913–15). The theory of psychoanalysis. *Psychoanalytic Review, 1*(1): 1–40, 1913; *1*(2): 153–177, 1914; *1*(3): 260–284, 1914; *1*(4): 415–430, 1914; *2*(1): 29–51, 1915.

Jung, C. G. (1970–1979). *The Collected Works of C. G. Jung*. H. Read, M. Fordham, G. Adler, & W. McGuire (Eds.), R. F. C. Hull (Trans). Princeton, NJ: Princeton University Press.

Jung, C. G., & Riklin, F. (Eds.) (1913). Vereinsberichte. *Korrespondenzblatt der Internationalen Psychoanalytischen Vereinigung. Internationale Zeitschrift für Psychoanalyse, 1*: 617–636.

Kardiner, A. (1977). *My Analysis with Freud. Reminiscences*. New York: Norton.

Kempelen, B. (1910). *Magyar Nemesi Almanach: az 1867–1909. Ben Magyar nemességre, bárói, grófi, és herczegi méltóságra emelt családok*. Budapest: Paria.

Kerr, J. (1993). *A most dangerous method. Freud, Jung and Sabina Spielrein*. New York: Alfred A. Knopf.

King, P., & Steiner, R. (Eds.) (1991). *The Freud/Klein-Controversies 1941–1945*. London: Tavistock.

Klein, M. (1928). Early stages of the oedipus conflict. *International Journal of Psychoanalysis, 9*: 167–180.

Klein, M. (1929a). Infantile anxiety-situations reflected in a work of art and in the creative impulse. *International Journal of Psychoanalysis, 10*: 436–443.

Klein, M. (1929b). Personification in the play of children. *International Journal of Psychoanalysis, 10*: 193–204.
Klein, M. (1930). The importance of symbol-formation in the development of the ego. *International Journal of Psychoanalysis, 11*: 24–39.
Klein, M. (1932). *The Psycho-Analysis of Children*. A. Strachey (Trans.). London: Hogarth.
Klein, M. (1935). A contribution to the psychogenesis of manic-depressive states. *International Journal of Psychoanalysis, 16*: 145–714.
Klein, M. (1940). Mourning and its relation to manic-depressive states. *International Journal of Psychoanalysis, 21*: 125–153.
Kohut, H. (1984). *How Does Analysis Cure?* A. Goldberg (Ed.). Chicago: University of Chicago Press.
Kokoschka, O. (1910–1911). Mörder Hoffnung der Frauen. *Der Sturm, 1*(20): 155.
Kokoschka, O. (1917). *Der brennende Dornbusch*. Schauspiel. Leipzig: Wolff, 1911.
Kokoschka, O. (1971). *Mein Leben*. Munich: Bruckmann.
Kokoschka, O. (1984). *Briefe, 1905–1919 (volume 1)*. Düsseldorf: Claassen.
Korrespondenzblatt der Internationalen Psychoanalytischen Vereinigung (1912). *Zentralblatt für Psychoanalyse* 2: 475–480, 545–550. = Korr.
Korrespondenzblatt der Internationalen Psychoanalytischen Vereinigung (1913). *Internationale Zeitschrift für Psychoanalyse, 1*: 617–636.
Korrespondenzblatt der Internationalen Psychoanalytischen Vereinigung (1919). *Internationale Zeitschrift für Psychoanalyse, 5*: 52–59.
Korrespondenzblatt der Internationalen Psychoanalytischen Vereinigung (1920). *Internationale Zeitschrift für Psychoanalyse, 6*: 99–112.
Korrespondenzblatt der Internationalen Psychoanalytischen Vereinigung (1921). *Internationale Zeitschrift für Psychoanalyse, 7*: 391–400.
Korrespondenzblatt der Internationalen Psychoanalytischen Vereinigung (1922). *Internationale Zeitschrift für Psychoanalyse, 8*: 391–394.
Korrespondenzblatt der Internationalen Psychoanalytischen Vereinigung (1923). *Internationale Zeitschrift für Psychoanalyse, 9*: 240–255.
Korrespondenzblatt der Internationalen Psychoanalytischen Vereinigung (1925). *Internationale Zeitschrift für Psychoanalyse, 11*: 501–528.
Krafft-Ebing, R. von (1886). *Psychopathia sexualis, eine klinisch-forensische Studie*. Stuttgart: Enke.
Kraus, K. (1912). Notizen. *Die Fackel*, 21 June, p. 53.
Kraus, K. (1915a). Nachts. *Die Fackel*, 5 October, pp. 94–168.
Kraus, K. (1915b). Eeextraausgabeee! *Die Fackel*, 10 December, pp. 1–10.
Kraus, K. (1915c). Elegie auf den Tod eines Lautes. *Die Fackel*, 10 December, pp. 107–110.
Kraus, K. (1916a). *Worte in Versen I*. Leipzig: Verlag der Schriften von Karl Kraus.

Kraus, K. (1916b). Die Sonne von Gibeon. *Die Fackel*, 5 May, pp. 58–64.
Kraus, K. (1924). Die Zauberlehrlinge. *Die Fackel*, December, p. 148.
Kraus, K. (1926). Störungen im Fremdenverkehr. *Die Fackel*, October, p. 36.
Kraus, K. (1931). Ich bin berühmt. *Die Fackel*, March, pp. 48–54.
Krause, R. (2012). Psychodynamische Aspekte der Gedächtnisfunktion. *Forum der Psychoanalyse, 28*: 11–25.
Kuhn, P. (2000). A scandal in Salzburg. Or Freud's surreptitious role in the 1908 Abraham-Jung dispute. *International Journal of Psychoanalysis, 81*: 705–731.
Laforgue, R. (1926). Über Skotomisation in der Schizophrenie. *Internationale Zeitschrift für Psychoanalyse, 12*: 451–456.
Landauer, K. (1914). Spontanheilung einer Katatonie. *Internationale Zeitschrift für Psychoanalyse, 2*: 441–459.
Laplanche, J., & Pontalis, J.-B. (1967). *The Language of Psycho-Analysis*. D. Nicholson-Smith (Trans.). London: Hogarth, 1973.
Leitner, M. (2001). *Ein gut gehütetes Geheimnis. Die Geschichte der psychoanalytischen Behandlungs-Technik von den Anfängen in Wien bis zur Gründung der Berliner Poliklinink im Jahr 1920*. Gießen: Psychosozial.
Lensing, L. (1986). "Freud and the child woman" or "The Kraus affair"? A textual "reconstruction" of Fritz Wittels's psychoanalytic autobiography. *German Quarterly, 69*: 322–332.
Lensing, L. (1989). "Geistige Väter" & "Das Kindweib": Sigmund Freud, Karl Kraus und Irma Karczewska in der Autobiographie von Fritz Wittels. *Forum, 36*(430/1): 62–71.
Lévy, K. (1990). Dernières vacances des Freud avant le fin du monde. *Le Coq-Héron, 117*: 39–44. In: S. Freud, Briefe an Kata und Lajos Lévy. *Luzifer–Amor, Zeitschrift zur Geschichte der Psychoanalyse, 25*(50), 52–60, 2012.
Lévy, L. (1957). Istvan Hollós. 19 April 1872—2 February 1957. *International Journal of Psychoanalysis, 38*: 280–281.
Lipton, S. D. (1977). The advantages of Freud's technique as shown in his analysis of the Rat Man. *International Journal of Psychoanalysis, 58*: 255–273.
Lipton, S. D. (1983). A critique of so-called standard psychoanalytic technique. *Contemporary Psychoanalysis, 19*: 35–45.
Löwenfeld, L. (1914). *Sexualleben und Nervenleiden nebst einem Anhang über Prophylaxe und Behandlung der sexuellen Neurasthenie* (5th edn). Munich: Bergmann.
Lohser, B., & Newton, P. M. (1996). *Unorthodox Freud: The View From the Couch*. New York: Guilford.
Lowenfeld, H. (1941). Psychic trauma and productive experience in the artist. *Psychoanalytic Quarterly, 10*: 116–130.

Lützeler, P. M. (1995). Afterword. In P. M. Lützeler (Ed.), *Das Teesdorfer Tagebuch* (pp. 171–222). Frankfurt: Suhrkamp.

Lützeler, P. M. (2000). *Die Entropie des Menschen. Studien zum Werk Hermann Brochs.* Würzburg: Königshausen & Neumann.

Lynn, D. J. (1993). Freud's analysis of A. B., a psychotic man, 1925–1930. *Journal of the American Academy of Psychoanalysis, 21*: 63–78.

Lynn, D. J. (2003). Freud's psychoanalysis of Edith Banfield Jackson, 1930–1936. *Journal of the American Academy of Psychoanalysis, 31*: 609–625.

Lynn, D. J., & Vaillant, G. E. (1998). Anonymity, neutrality, and confidentiality in the actual methods of Sigmund Freud. A review of 43 cases, 1907–1939. *American Journal of Psychiatry, 155*(2): 163–171.

Mack-Brunswick, R. (1928). A supplement to Freud's "From the history of an infantile neurosis". In: M. Gardiner (Ed.), *The Wolf-Man by the Wolf-Man* (pp. 286–331), 1971.

Maddox, B. (2006). *Freud's Wizard. The Enigma of Ernest Jones.* London: Murray.

Mächtlinger, V. (1997). Karl Abraham und Giovanni Segantini. Ein psychoanalytischer Versuch. *Luzifer–Amor. Zeitschrift zur Geschichte der Psychoanalyse, 10*(20): 81–97.

Maeder, A. (1910). Psychoanalyse bei einer melancholischen Depression. *Zentralblatt für Nervenheilkunde und Psychiatrie, 33*: 50–57.

Maeder, A. (1911). Referat von E. Jones: "Psycho-analytic notes on a case of hypomania". *Zentralblatt für Psychoanalyse, 1*: 344.

Mahler-Werfel, A. (1960). *Mein Leben.* Frankfurt: Fischer.

Mahony, P. (1986). *Freud and the Rat Man.* New Haven, CT: Yale University Press.

Marcinowski, J. (1912). Kurze Bemerkungen. In: "Offener Sprechsaal". *Zentralblatt für Psychoanalyse, 2*: 541–542.

Masson, J. M. (1984). *The Assault on Truth. Freud's Suppression of the Seduction Theory.* New York: Farrar, Straus & Giroux.

May[-Tolzmann], U. (1990). Ich- und Narzißmustheorie zwischen 1914 und 1922 im Spiegel der Internationalen Zeitschrift für ärztliche Psychoanalyse. *Psyche, 44*: 689–723.

May[-Tolzmann], U. (1991). Zu den Anfängen des Narzissmus. Ellis—Näcke—Sadger—Freud [How the concept of narcissism came into being: from Ellis and Näcke to Sadger and Freud]. *Luzifer-Amor, Zeitschrift zur Geschichte der Psychoanalyse*, 4(8): 50–88, 1991.

May[-Tolzmann], U. (1996). *Freuds frühe klinische Theorie (1894–1896).* Wiederentdeckung und Rekonstruktion. Tübingen: Diskord.

May[-Tolzmann], U. (1997). Abraham's discovery of the "bad mother": a contribution to the history of the theory of depression. *International Journal of Psychoanalysis, 82*: 283–305, 2001.

May, U. (2006a). Erbitterung und Nachdenklichkeit. Über Freuds Kommentar zu einem frühen Aufsatz von Karl Abraham (1907). *Jahrbuch der Psychoanalyse, 52*: 63–92 [From anger to reflection: remarks on Freud's commentary on an early paper by Karl Abraham (1907)].

May, U. (2006b). Freud's patient calendars: 17 analysts in analysis with Freud (1910–1920). *Psychoanalysis and History, 9*(2): 153–200, 2007.

May, U. (2007). Nineteen patients in analysis with Freud (1910–1920). *American Imago, 65*: 41–105, 2008.

May, U. (2008). Psychoanalyse in Berlin. 1920–1936. *Jahrbuch der Psychoanalyse, 57*: 13–39.

May, U. (2009a). Freud arbeitete anders. Bemerkungen zum Analysentagebuch von Anna G. In: A. Koellreuter (Ed.), *"Wie benimmt sich der Prof. Freud eigentlich?" Ein neu entdecktes Tagebuch von 1921, historisch und analytisch kommentiert* (pp. 155–174). Gießen: Psychosozial.

May, U. (2009b). Freud, Empfängnisverhütung, Sexualreform und Expressionismus. Zur frühen Rezeption des Psychoanalyse in Berlin (bis 1914). *Jahrbuch für Psychoanalyse, 58*: 37–80.

May, U. (2010a). Fourteen hundred hours of analysis with Freud: Viktor von Dirsztay. A biographical sketch. *Psychoanalysis and History 13*(1): 91–137, 2011.

May, U. (2010b). Karl Abraham's revolution: from sensual sucking to the oral-aggressive wish of destruction. *Psychoanalytic Quarterly, 81*: 83–109, 2012.

May, U. (2011a). Auf dem Weg zu Karl Abrahams "Versuch einer Entwicklungsgeschichte der Libido" (1924). Der Beitrag August Stärckes zur Theorie der Oralität [Towards Karl Abraham's "A short study of the development of the libido": August Stärcke's contribution to the theory of orality]. In: C. Diercks & S. Schlüter (Eds.), *Psycho-Sexualität. Grundlagen, infantile Sexualität, Libido, Todestrieb. Sigmund-Freud-Vorlesungen 2010* (pp. 131–153). Vienna: Mandelbaum.

May, U. (2011b). Ein ungarischer Baron in Analyse bei Freud. In: A. Berger, F. Henningsen, L. M. Hermanns, & J. C. Togay (Eds.), *Der psychoanalytische Aufbruch Budapest–Berlin 1918–1920* (pp. 25–33). Frankfurt: Brandes & Apsel.

May, U. (2011c). Freuds Autoreferat von "Ein Beitrag zum Problem der Neurosenwahl" (1913). Erstpublikation des Textes und Kommentar. *Luzifer–Amor, Zeitschrift zur Geschichte der Psychoanalyse, 24*(47): 46–54.

May, U. (2012). Zur Frühgeschichte der Analerotik [On the early history of anal erotism (1905–1924)]. *Psyche, 66*: 213–246.

May, U. (2013). The third step in drive theory: on the genesis of "Beyond the Pleasure Principle". *Psychoanalysis and History, 17*: 205–272, 2015.

Mayreder, R. (1906). Rezension von S. Freud: "Drei Abhandlungen zur Sexualtheorie". *Wiener Klinische Rundschau, 20*: 189–190.

Mayreder, R. (1988). *Tagebücher, 1873–1937*. H. Anderson (Ed.). Frankfurt: Insel.

McLaughlin, F. (1980). Report of the 31st International Psycho-Analytical Congress. *Bulletin of the International Psychoanalytical Association, 61*: 93–134.

Mészáros, J. (1998). The tragic success of European psychoanalysis. *International Forum of Psychoanalysis, 7*(4): 207–214.

Meyer-Palmedo, I., & Fichtner, G. (1999). *Freud-Bibliographie mit Werkkonkordanz* (2nd edn.). Frankfurt: Fischer.

Meylan, J.-P. (2004). *Die Internationale Rundschau—La Revue des Nations—The International Review, Zurich (1915–1918)*. Zurich: Zentralbibliothek. http:/homepage.mac.com/j. p.meylan/Resources/ IntRundschau04.pdf (access: 20.11.2006).

Molnar, M. (Ed.) (1992). *The Diary of Sigmund Freud: 1929–1939*. London: Hogarth.

Momigliano, L. N. (1987). A spell in Vienna, but was Freud a Freudian? An investigation into Freud's technique between 1920 and 1938, based on the published testimony of former analysands. *International Review of Psycho-Analysis, 14*: 373–389.

Mühlleitner, E. (1992). *Biographisches Lexikon der Psychoanalyse. Die Mitglieder der Psychologischen Mittwoch-Gesellschaft und der Wiener Psychoanalytischen Vereinigung 1902–1938*. Tübingen: Diskord.

Mühlleitner, E., & Reichmayr, J. (1997). Die Freudianer in Wien. Die Psychologische Mittwoch-Gesellschaft und die Wiener Psychoanalytische Vereinigung 1902–1938. *Psyche, 51*: 1051–1103.

Müller, T., & Hermanns, L. M. (2001). Margarete Stegmann—Psychoanalytikerin, Reichstagsabgeordnete und Frauenrechtlerin. *Luzifer–Amor, Zeitschrift zur Geschichte der Psychoanalyse, 14*(27): 36–59.

Näcke, P. (1899a). Die sexuellen Perversitäten in der Irrenanstalt. *Psychiatrische en neurologische Bladen, 3*: 122–149.

Näcke, P. (1899b). Kritisches zum Kapitel der normalen und pathologischen Sexualität. *Archiv für Psychiatrie und Nervenkrankheiten, 32*(2): 356–386.

Natter, T. G. (Ed.) (2002). *Oskar Kokoschka. Das modeme Bildnis 1909 bis 1914*. Cologne: Dumont.

Neiser, E. M. J. (1978). *Max Eitingon. Leben und Werk*. Unpublished dissertation. Mainz university.

Nunberg, H. (1969). *Memoirs. Recollections, Ideas, Reflections*. New York: Psychoanalytic Research and Development Fund.

Nunberg, H., & Federn, E. (Eds.) (1962). *Minutes of the Vienna Psychoanalytic Society,* Volume 1: 1906–1908. M. Nunberg (Trans.). New York: International University Press. = Min 1.

Nunberg, H., & Federn, E. (Eds.) (1967). *Minutes of the Vienna Psychoanalytic Society,* Volume 2: 1908–1910. M. Nunberg (Trans.). New York: International University Press. = Min 2.

Nunberg, H., & Federn, E. (Eds.) (1974). *Minutes of the Vienna Psychoanalytic Society,* Vol. 3: 1910–1911. M. Nunberg (Trans.). New York: International University Press. = Min 3.

Nunberg, H., & Federn, E. (Eds.) (1975). *Minutes of the Vienna Psychoanalytic Society,* Vol. 4: 1912–1915. M. Nunberg (Trans.). New York: International University Press. = Min. 4.

Nunberg, H., & Federn, E. (Eds.). (1976–1981). *Protokolle der Wiener Psychoanalytischen Vereinigung, Volumes I–IV.* Frankfurt: Fischer.

Ophuijsen, J. van (1920). On the origin of the feeling of persecution. *International Journal of Psychoanalysis, 1*: 235–239.

Ophuijsen, J. van (1925). Summary of "Some observations on the origin of sadism". *Internationale Zeitschrift für Psychoanalyse, 11*: 509.

Ophuijsen, J. van (1929). The sexual aim of sadism as manifested in acts of violence. *International Journal of Psychoanalysis, 10*: 139–144.

Ozieblo, B. (2002). Alyse Gregory, Scofield Thayer, and the Dial Twentieth Century Literature. *Twentieth-Century Literature, 48*: 487–507.

Pankejeff, S. (1971). The memoirs of the Wolf-man. In: M. Gardiner (Ed.), *The Wolf-Man by the Wolf-Man* (pp. 3–152). New York: Basic.

Payne, S. M. (1952). Dr. John Rickman. *International Journal of Psychoanalysis, 33*: 54–60.

Petersdorff, C. von (1997). Der frühe Tod des Giovanni Segantini und des Karl Abraham. *Luzifer–Amor, Zeitschrift zur Geschichte der Psychoanalyse, 10*(20): 132–150.

Petot, J.-M. (1990–1991). *Melanie Klein.* New York: International University Press.

Petzet, W. (1973). *Theater. Die Münchner Kammerspiele 1911–1972.* Munich: Desch.

Planta, V. von (2010). "Analysiere nie wieder einen jungen Menschen wie mich …". Emil Oberholzer und Mira Oberholzer-Gincburg, ein russisch-schweizerisches Analytikerpaar in der ersten Hälfte des 20. Jahrhunderts. *Luzifer–Amor, Zeitschrift zur Geschichte der Psychoanalyse, 23*(45): 70–104.

Plaut, E. S. (2007). *The Plaut Family: Tracing the Legacy.* Bergenfield, NJ: Avotaynu.

Pollak, T. (2001). Ist die psychoanalytische Identität bedroht? Zur aktuellen berufspolitischen Situation der Psychoanalyse in der Bundesrepublik. *Psyche, 55*: 835–863.

Praetorius, N. (1910). Die Bibliographie der Homosexualität aus den Jahren 1908 und 1909: I. Sadger, Zur Ätiologie der konträren Sexualempfindung. *Vierteljahresberichte des Wissenschaftlich-Humanitären Komitees, 1*: 209–214.

Praetorius, N. (1911). Die Bibliographie der Homosexualität aus den Jahren 1908 und 1909: I. Sadger, Heinrich von Kleist. *Vierteljahresberichte des Wissenschaftlich-Humanitären Komitees, 2*: 429–438.

Quinsac, A.-P. (1982). *Giovanni Segantini. Catalogo generale, Volume 2*. Milan: Electa.

Quinsac, A.-P. (1985). *Segantini. Trent'anni di vita artistica europea nei carteggi inediti dell'artista e dei suoi mecenati*. Oggiano-Locci: Vattane Ed.

Raabe, P. (1972). *Index Expressionismus. Bibliographie der Beiträge in den Zeitschriften und Jahrbüchern des literarischen Expressionismus 1910–1925*. Nendeln: Kraus-Thomsen.

Radó, S. (1923). Eine Traumanalyse. *Internationale Zeitschrift für Psychoanalyse, 9*: 368–383.

Radó, S. (1927). The problem of melancholia. *International Journal of Psychoanalysis, 9*: 420–438, 1928.

Rank, O. (1910). Ein Traum, der sich selbst deutet. *Jahrbuch für psychoanalytische und psychopathologische Forschungen, 2*: 465–540.

Rank, O. (1911a). Bericht über die I. private Psychoanalytische Vereinigung in Salzburg am 27 April 1908. *Zentralblatt für Psychoanalyse, 1*: 125–129.

Rank, O. (1911b). Ein Beitrag zum Narzissismus. *Jahrbuch für psychoanalytische und psychopathologische Forschungen, 3*: 401–426.

Rank, O. (1914). *The Double*. Chapel Hill, NC: UNC Press, 1971.

Rank, O. (1924). *The Trauma of Birth*. New York: Harper & Row, 1929.

Rank, O. (1925). The genesis of genitality. *Psychoanalytic Review, 13*: 29–144, 1926.

Rapaport, D. (1951). *Organization and Pathology of Thought. Selected Sources*. New York: Columbia University Press.

Rapaport, D. (1967). *The Collected Papers of David Rapaport*. M. M. Gill (Ed.). New York: Basic.

Rapaport, D., & Gill, M. M. (1959). The points of view and assumptions of metapsychology. In: M. M. Gill (Ed.), *The Collected Papers of David Rapaport* (pp. 795–811), 1967.

Reik, T. (1915). Einige Bemerkungen zur Lehre vom Widerstande. *Internationale Zeitschrift für Psychoanalyse, 3*: 12–24.

Reik, T. (1923). *Der eigene und der fremde Gott. Zur Psychoanalyse der religiösen Entwicklung*. Frankfurt: Suhrkamp, 1972.

Reik, T. (1939). The characteristics of masochism. *American Imago, 1*: 26–59.

Reik, T. (1940). *Masochism in Modern Man*. New York: Farrar, Straus, 1941.

Reik, T. (1953). *The Haunting Melody: Psychoanalytic Experiences in Life and Music*. New York: Farrar, Straus & Young.

Reik, T. (1956). *The Search Within: The Inner Experiences of a Psychoanalyst*. New York: Farrar, Straus & Cuhady.

Reik, T. (1976). *Dreißig Jahre mit Sigmund Freud*. Munich: Kindler.

Reik, T., & Zohn, H. (1978). On the effect of unconscious death wishes. *Psychoanalytic Review, 65*: 38–67.

Roazen, P. (1985). *Helene Deutsch: A Psychoanalyst's Life*. New York: Anchor/ Doubleday.

Roazen, P. (1995). *How Freud Worked: First-Hand Accounts of Patients*. New Jersey, NJ: Jason Aronson.

Roazen, P. (2002). The problem of silence: training analyses. *International Forum of Psychoanalysis, 11*(1): 73–77.

Roazen, P. (2005). *Edoardo Weiss. The House that Freud Built*. New Brunswick: Transaction.

Róheim, G. (1923a). Heiliges Geld in Melanesien. *Internationale Zeitschrift für Psychoanalyse, 9*: 384–401.

Róheim, G. (1923b). Nach dem Tode des Urvaters. *Imago, 9*: 83–121.

Rohleder, H. (1907). Der Automonosexualismus; eine bisher noch unbeachtete Form des menschlichen Geschlechtstriebes. *Berliner Klinik, 19*(225). Berlin: Fischer's Medizinische Buchhandlung.

Rosenberg, C. (1962). The place of George M. Beard in nineteenth-century psychiatry. *Bulletin of the History of Medicine, 36*: 245–259.

Rothe, H.-J. (1991). Einleitung. In: K. Landauer, *Theorie der Affekte und andere Schriften zur Ich-Organisation* (pp. 7–23). Frankfurt: Fischer.

Rotmann, M. (1988). Der Einfluß von Häufigkeit und Dauer der Sitzungen auf die Entwicklung eines kurativen psychoanalytischen Prozesses. *Bulletin of the European Psychoanalytic Federation, 31*: 151–164.

Rühle, G. (2007). *Theater in Deutschland 1887–1945. Seine Ereignisse—seine Menschen*. Frankfurt: Fischer.

Sadger, I. (1897). Das Wunder vom denkenden Eiweiß. *Deutsche Revue, 2*: 93–110.

Sadger, I. (1905a). Ein genialer Trunkenbold. *Allgemeine Zeitung. Beilagen, 176*: 217–220; *177*: 228–231.

Sadger, I. (1905b). Ibsens Bedeutung für das deutsche Drama. *Hamburger Nachrichten, Beilagen, 8*: 2–3; *9*: 3–4; *10*: 3–4; *11*: 2–3.

Sadger, I. (1905c). Zur Psychologie des Geschmacks. *Das Wissen für Alle, 5*: 418–419, 433– 436.

Sadger, I. (1907). Die Bedeutung der psychoanalytischen Methode nach Freud. *Centralblatt für Nervenheilkunde und Psychiatrie, 30*(18): 41–52.

Sadger, I. (1908a). Fragment der Psychoanalyse eines Homosexuellen. *Jahrbuch für sexuelle Zwischenstufen, 9*: 339–424.

Sadger, I. (1908b). Ist die konträre Sexualempfindung heilbar? *Zeitschrift für Sexualwissenschaft, 12*: 712–720.

Sadger, I. (1908c). Konrad Ferdinand Meyer. Eine pathographisch-psychologische Studie. *Grenzfragen des Nerven- und Seelenlebens, 59*. Wiesbaden: Bergmann.

Sadger, I. (1908d). Psychiatrisch—Neurologisches in psychoanalitischer Beleuchtung. *Zentralblatt für das Gesamtgebiet der Medizin und ihrer Hilfswissenschaften, 4*(7–8): 45–47, 53–57.

Sadger, I. (1909a). *Aus dem Liebensleben Nicolaus Lenaus*. Schriften zur angewandten Seelenkunde, Heft 6. Leipzig: Deuticke.

Sadger, I. (1909b). Ein Fall von Pseudoepilepsia hysterica psychoanalytisch erklärt. *Wiener Klinische Rundschau, 23*: 212–214, 226–228, 242–244, 259–262.

Sadger, I. (1909c). Zur Ätiologie der konträren Sexualempfindung. *Medizinische Klinik, 5*(2): 53–56.

Sadger, I. (1909d). Zur Wertung der Hypnose. *Therapeutische Rundschau, 3*(45): 705–707.

Sadger, I. (1910a). Analerotik und Analcharakter. *Die Heilkunde, 2*: 43–46.

Sadger, I. (1910b). *Belastung und Entartung. Ein Beitrag zur Lehre vom kranken Genie*. Leipzig: Edmund Demme.

Sadger, I. (1910c). Die Transvestiten. *Die Umschau, 14*(50): 999–1000.

Sadger, I. (1910d). Ein Fall von multipler Perversion mit hysterischen Absenzen. *Jahrbuch für psychoanalytische und psychopathologische Forschungen, 2*: 59–133.

Sadger, I. (1910e). *Heinrich von Kleist. Eine pathographisch—psychologische Studie*. Grenzfragen des Nerven—und Seelenlebens, Heft 70. Wiesbaden: Bergmann.

Sadger, I. (1910f). Krankhaftes im Seelenleben der Kinder. *Wissenschaftliche Rundschau, 5*: 103–106.

Sadger, I. (1910g). Über Urethralerotik. *Jahrbuch für psychoanalytische und psychopathologische Forschungen, 2*: 409–450.

Sadger, I. (1910h). Zum Verständnis der Hypnose und des hysterischen Delirs. *Zentralblatt für Psychoanalyse, 1*: 98–102.

Sadger, I. (1911a). Ist das Asthma bronchiale eine Sexualneurose? *Zentralblatt für Psychoanalyse, 1*: 200–213.

Sadger, I. (1911b). Zur Psychologie des einzigen und des Lieblingskindes. *Fortschritte der Medizin, 29*: 601–605.

Sadger, I. (1912). Über sexualsymbolische Verwertung des Kopfschmerzes. *Zentralblatt für Psychoanalyse, 2*: 190–197.

Sadger, I. (1913a). Über den sado-masochistischen Komplex. *Jahrbuch für psychoanalytische und psychopathologische Forschungen, 5*: 157–232.

Sadger, I. (1913b). Über Gesäßerotik. *Internationale Zeitschrift für Psychoanalyse, 1*: 351–358.

Sadger, I. (1914a). Sexuelle Perversionen. In: *Bericht über die Fortschritte der Psychoanalyse in den Jahren 1909–1913. Jahrbuch für psychoanalytische und psychopathologische Forschungen, 6*: 296–313.

Sadger, I. (1914b). Rezension von Magnus Hirschfeld: Die Homosexualität des Mannes und des Weibes. *Internationale Zeitschrift für ärztliche Psychoanalyse, 2*: 392–396.

Sadger, I. (1915). *Neue Forschungen zur Homosexualität*. Berliner Klinik, 27. Jahrgang, Heft 315. Berlin: Fischer's Medizinische Buchhandlung.

Sadger, I. (1921). *Die Lehre von den Geschlechtsverirrungen (Psychopathia sexualis) auf psychoanalytischer Grundlage*. Leipzig: Deuticke.

Sawyer-Lauçanno, C. (2004). *E. E. Cummings. A biography*. Naperville, IL: Sourcebooks.

Scharff, D. E., & Birtles, E. F. (1997). From instinct to self: the evolution and implications of W. R. D. Fairbairn's theory of object relations. *International Journal of Psychoanalysis, 78*: 1085–1103.

Schmid, R. (1988). *Psychoanalytische Tätigkeit in der Bundesrepublik Deutschland. Ergebnisse einer empirischen Studie*. Cologne: Masch.

Schmidbauer, W. (1992). Freud, Leonardo, Michelangelo. *Luzifer–Amor, Zeitschrift zur Geschichte der Psychoanalyse, 5*(10): 84–124.

Schmidt, W., & Dalbajewa, B. (1996). *Kokoschka und Dresden. Katalog zur Ausstellung*. Leipzig: Seemann.

Schnitzler, A. (1983). *Tagebuch 1913–1916*. Kommission für literarische Gebrauchsformen der österreichischen Akademie der Wissenschaften (Ed.). Vienna: Verlag der Österreichischen Akademie der Wissenschaften.

Schnitzler, A. (1993). *Tagebuch 1920–1922*. Kommission für literarische Gebrauchsformen der österreichischen Akademie der Wissenschaften (Ed.). Vienna: Verlag der Österreichischen Akademie der Wissenschaften.

Schnitzler, A. (1995). *Tagebuch 1923–1926*. Kommission für literarische Gebrauchsformen der österreichischen Akademie der Wissenschaften (Ed.). Vienna: Verlag der Österreichischen Akademie der Wissenschaften.

Schnitzler, A. (1997). *Tagebuch 1927–1930*. Kommission für literarische Gebrauchsformen der österreichischen Akademie der Wissenschaften (Ed.). Vienna: Verlag der Österreichischen Akademie der Wissenschaften.

Scholz, A. (2003). Ärzte und Patienten in Dresdner Naturheilsanatorien. *Medizinbibliothek-Information, 7*: 13–19.

Scholz, A. (2004). Künstler als Patienten in Dresdner Naturheilsanatorien um 1900. *Health Academy, 1*: 345–353.

Schröter, M. (1988). Freud und Fließ im wissenschaftlichen Gespräch. Das Neurasthenieprojekt von 1893. *Jahrbuch der Psychoanalyse, 22*: 141–83.

Schröter, M. (1995). Sollen Patientennamen in den Korrespondenzen Freuds verschlüsselt werden? Zehn Thesen zur Diskussion. *Psyche, 49*: 805–809.

Schröter, M. (2002). Fließ vs. Weininger, Swoboda und Freud. Der Plagiatsstreit von 1906 im Licht der Dokumente. *Psyche, 56*: 338–368.

Schröter, M. (2002). Max Eitingon and the struggle to establish an international standard for psychoanalytic training (1925–1929). *International Journal of Psychoanalysis, 83*: 875–893.

Schröter, M. (2010). Freuds Briefe an Emil und Mira Oberholzer (1912–1936). Edition mit Zwischentexten. *Luzifer–Amor, Zeitschrift zur Geschichte der Psychoanalyse, 23*(46): 104–133.

Schur, M. (1972). *Freud: Living and Dying*. New York: International Universities Press.

Schweiger, W. J. (1983). *Der junge Kokoschka. Leben und Werk, 1904–1914*. Vienna: Brandstätter.

Schweiger, W. J. (1986). *Oskar Kokoschka—Der Sturm. Die Berliner Jahre 1910–1916. Eine Dokumentation*. Vienna: Brandstätter.

Segantini, B. (1909). *Giovanni Segantinis Schriften und Briefe*. Zurich: Rascher, 1935.

Servaes, F. (1907). *Giovanni Segantini. Sein Leben und sein Werk*. Leipzig: Klinkhardt & Biermann.

Severit, F. (1999). *Ea von Allesch: Wenn aus Frauen Menschen werden. Eine Biographie*. Wiesbaden: Deutscher Universitäts-Verlag.

Shamdasani, S. (2002). Psychoanalysis Inc. *Semiotic Review of Books, 13*: 6–11.

Shengold, L. (1972). A parapraxis of Freud's in relation to Karl Abraham. *American Imago, 29*: 123–159.

Sherman, M. H. (1978). Reik, Schnitzler, Freud, and "the murderer": the limits of insight in psychoanalysis. *Psychoanalytic Review, 65*: 68–94.

Simmel, E. (1933). Author's summary of "Praegenitalprimat und intestinale Stufe der Libidoorganisation". *Korrespondenzblatt der Internationalen Psychoanalytischen Vereinigung, Internationale Zeitschrift für Psychoanalyse, 19*: 245–246.

Socarides, Ch. W. (1968). *The Overt Homosexual*. New York: Grune & Stratton.

Soussloff, C. M. (2006). *The Subject in Art*. Durham, NC: Duke University Press.

Spanjaard, J. (1955). August Stärcke (1880–1954). *International Journal of Psychoanalysis, 36*: 396–398.

Spielmann, H. (2003). *Oskar Kokoschka. Leben und Werk*. Cologne: Dumont.
Spielrein, S. (1912). Destruction as a cause of coming into being. *Journal of analytical psychology, 39*: 155–186, 1974.
Spillius, E. Bott (1988). *Melanie Klein Today. Developments in Theory and Practice*. London: Routledge.
Spitz, R. (1965). Interview, unpublished. New York: Archives of Columbia University.
Sprengel, P., & Streim, G. (1998). *Berliner und Wiener Moderne. Vermittlungen und Abgrenzungen in Literatur, Theater, Publizistik*. Vienna: Böhlau.
Stärcke, A. (1919). The reversal of the libido-sign in delusions of persecution. *International Journal of Psychoanalysis, 1*: 231–234, 1920.
Stärcke, A. (1921a). The castration complex. *International Journal of Psychoanalysis, 2*: 179–201.
Stärcke, A. (1921b). Psycho-analysis and psychiatry. *International Journal of Psychoanalysis, 2*: 361–415.
Steele, B. F. (1975). René A. Spitz, M.D. 1887–1974. *Psychoanalytic Quarterly, 44*: 3–4.
Stekel, W. (1908). Conditions of nervous anxiety and their treatment. London: Routledge, 1923.
Stekel, W. (1909). Dichtung und Neurose. Bausteine zur Psychologie des Künstlers und des Kunstwerkes. *Grenzfragen des Nerven- und Seelenlebens, 65*. Wiesbaden: Bergmann.
Sterba, R. (1982). *Reminiscences of a Viennese psychoanalyst*. Detroit: Wayne State University Press.
Stern, A. (1922). Some personal psychoanalytical experiences with Prof. Freud. *New York State Journal of Medicine, 22*: 21–25.
Strachey, J. (1955a). Editor's note to "Aus der Geschichte einer infantilen Neurose". *S. E., 17*: 3–6. London: Hogarth.
Strachey, J. (1955b). Editor's note to "Ein Kind wird geschlagen". *S. E., 17*: 177–178. London: Hogarth.
Strachey, J. (1957a). Editor's note to "Eine Kindheitserinnerung des Leonardo da Vinci". *S. E., 11*: 59–62. London: Hogarth.
Strachey, J. (1957b). Editor's note to "Trauer und Melancholie". *S. E., 14*: 239–242. London: Hogarth.
Stroeken, H. (2009). Johan van Ophuijsen, Padang/Indonesien 1882—New York 1950. *Luzifer–Amor, Zeitschrift zur Geschichte der Psychoanalyse, 22*(44): 7–44.
Sulloway, F. (1979). *Freud, Biologist of the Mind*. New York: Basic.
Sutherland, J. D. (1989). *Fairbairn's Journey into the Interior*. London: Free Association.

Tausk, V. (1916). Diagnostic considerations concerning the symptomatology of the so-called war neuroses. *Psychoanalytic Quarterly, 38*: 382–404, 1969.

Taylor, D. (1996). Über einige Aspekte von Melanie Kleins Einfluss auf die British Psycho-Analytical Society. *Luzifer–Amor, Zeitschrift zur Geschichte der Psychoanalyse, 9*(17): 113–123.

Timms, E. (1990). Kokoschka's pictographs: a contextual reading. *Word and Image, 6*: 4–17.

Timms, E. (1986). *Karl Kraus: Apocalyptic Satirist*. New Haven, CT: Yale University Press.

Tögel, C. (2006). Sigmund Freuds Praxis. Visiten und Ordination—Psychoanalysen—Einnahmen. *Psyche, 60*: 860–880.

Toulmin, S. (1978). Psychoanalysis, physics, and the mind-body problem. With discussions by P. Ricoeur and D. R. Swanson. *Annual of Psychoanalysis, 6*: 315–351.

Urban, B. (1975). Vier unveröffentlichte Briefe Arthur Schnitzlers an den Psychoanalytiker Theodor Reik. *Modern Austrian Literature, 8*: 236–247.

Veszy-Wagner, L. (Ed.) (1968a). Sigmund Freud, Gesamtregister. *Gesammelte Werke, 18*. Frankfurt: Fischer.

Veszy-Wagner, L. (1968b). Introduction to Sigmund Freud, Gesamtregister. *Gesammelte Werke, 18* (pp. VIII–XXXVI). Frankfurt: Fischer.

Walden, H. (1911). Der Sumpf von Berlin. "Spezialbericht": Café Größenwahn. In: J. Schutte & P. Sprengel (Eds.), *Die Berliner Moderne* (pp. 662–670). Stuttgart: Reclam, 1987.

Walder, C. (2010). "Ich will nicht ewig im Käfig meines Ichs eingesperrt sein …" Mutmaßungen zur Beziehung zwischen Sigmund Freud und seinem jugendlichen Patienten Arthur Fischer-Colbrie (1895–1968), mit einem Anhang: Freuds Briefe an A. Fischer-Colbrie. M. Schröter (Ed.). *Luzifer–Amor, Zeitschrift zur Geschichte der Psychoanalyse, 23*(45): 105–137.

Werfel, F. (1929). *Barbara oder die Frömmigkeit*. Berlin: Zsolnay.

Wettley, A., & Leibbrand, W. (1959). *Von der "Psychopathia sexualis" zur Sexualwissenschaft*. Stuttgart: Enke.

Will, H. (2003). *Was ist klassische Psychoanalyse? Ursprünge, Kritik, Zukunft*. Munich: Kohlhammer.

Wilsey, J. (2002). *H. Jones: The Life and Death of an Unusual Hero*. London: Random.

Wingler, H. M., & Welz, F. (1975). *Oskar Kokoschka. Das druckgraphische Werk*. Salzburg: Welz.

Winkler, J., & Erling, K. (1995). *Oskar Kokoschka. Die Gemälde 1909–1929*. Salzburg: Welz.

Wittels, F. (1910). *Ezechiel, der Zugereiste*. Berlin: Fleischel.

Wittels, F. (1924). *Sigmund Freud: His Personality, His Teaching and His School*. London: Eden & Cedar Paul.

Wittenberger, G., & Tögel, C. (Eds.) (1999–2006). *Die Rundbriefe des "Geheimen Komitees"* (*Volume 1, 1913–1920; Volume 2, 1921; Volume 3, 1922; Volume 4, 1923–1927*). Tübingen: Diskord. = RB.

Wolff, K. (1966). *Briefwechsel eines Verlegers 1911–1963*. B. Zeller & E. Otten (Eds.). Frankfurt: Scheffler.

Young-Bruehl, E. (1988). *Anna Freud: A Biography*. New York: Summit.

Zetzel, E. (1966). An obsessional neurotic: Freud's Rat Man. In: E. Zetzel, *The Capacity for Emotional Growth* (pp. 216–228). Madison, CT: International University Press, 1970.

INDEX

Note: Because of the frequency of its occurrence throughout the book, page referencing of Freud's name is omitted.

For Product Safety Concerns and Information please contact our EU
representative GPSR@taylorandfrancis.com
Taylor & Francis Verlag GmbH, Kaufingerstraße 24, 80331 München, Germany

www.ingramcontent.com/pod-product-compliance
Ingram Content Group UK Ltd.
Pitfield, Milton Keynes, MK11 3LW, UK
UKHW022114190926
475702UK00013B/1446
9781782205012